The Housing Divide

The Housing Divide

How Generations of Immigrants Fare in New York's Housing Market

Emily Rosenbaum and
Samantha Friedman

NEW YORK UNIVERSITY PRESS
New York and London

NEW YORK UNIVERSITY PRESS
New York and London
www.nyupress.org

Library of Congress Cataloging-in-Publication Data
Rosenbaum, Emily.
The housing divide : how generations of immigrants fare in New
York's housing market / Emily Rosenbaum and Samantha Friedman.
p. cm.
Includes bibliographical references and index.
ISBN-13: 978-0-8147-7590-5 (cloth : alk. paper)
ISBN-10: 0-8147-7590-X (cloth : alk. paper)
1. Immigrants—Housing—New York (State)—New York.
2. Assimilation (Sociology)—New York (State)--New York.
3. Social stratification—New York (State)—New York.
4. Discrimination in housing—New York (State)—New York.
5. Blacks—New York (State)—New York—Social conditions.
I. Friedman, Samantha R. II. Title.
HD7288.72.U52N77   2006
304.8'7471—dc22   2006026229

New York University Press books are printed on acid-free paper,
and their binding materials are chosen for strength and durability.

Manufactured in the United States of America

10 9 8 7 6 5 4 3 2 1

Contents

Acknowledgments

No book is written in a vacuum. There are many people we need to thank for their help and support throughout the process of writing this one, including the many who read drafts or listened to presentations and provided us with valuable comments. Among these are Doug Massey, Richard Alba, John Logan, Charles Hirschman, Michael Schill, and the participants at the "Color Lines" Conference held at Harvard University during the late summer of 2003.

We also wish to thank the Fannie Mae Foundation for financial support during the early stages of the research, and Pat Simmons for his unwavering support throughout the project. In addition, thanks must go to the Fordham University Faculty Fellowship Program for the year's leave during which much of the writing took place, and to our editorial team at NYU Press, Ilene Kalish and Salwa Jabado, for all their help and guidance in producing the final draft.

The members of our families deserve special recognition for their support during what is unarguably a difficult period of time. First are our spouses, Matt Morey and Recai Yucel, who directly bore the brunt of the ups and (especially) the downs inherent to the process, and our parents—Robert and Theodora Rosenbaum, and Robert and Roberta Friedman—for their support. Special thanks must go to Robert Rosenbaum for reading and editing two drafts of each chapter. Finally, we would like to dedicate the book to our kids, Ela Yucel and Tom and Claire Morey, and extend special thanks to Tom and Claire for postponing their birth until the final draft was submitted.

Introduction

New York City has always been a city of immigrants. During the great waves of European immigration in the nineteenth and early twentieth centuries, substantial numbers of new arrivals to the United States made New York their home. As a result, New York had larger shares of the foreign-born among its population than did any other city in the country.[1] In 1860, almost half (47 percent) of Manhattan's population had been born abroad, and this figure did not dip permanently below 40 percent until 1930.[2] For the city as a whole, fully 40 percent of the population was foreign-born in 1900, two years after the five counties (New York, Bronx, Kings, Queens, and Richmond) were consolidated to create Greater New York City.

The attraction of New York was particularly strong for certain immigrant groups that disproportionately chose to settle there over other possible destinations in the country. The lure that attracted large waves of immigrants in the past retains its strength today, ensuring that the city continues to be one of the most popular destinations for immigrants to the United States. Indeed, the more than 231,000 immigrants who arrived in the city in 1995–96 represented more than 14 percent of immigrants coming to the nation as a whole.[3] In 2000, more than one-third (35.9 percent) of the city's population had been born abroad.[4]

As in the past, New York City is a particularly popular destination for certain groups of immigrants. However, unlike the past, the immigrants who currently come to New York are not dominated by a few groups such as the Italians and Russian Jews at the turn of the century, and the Irish and Germans before them. Instead, the current waves of newcomers have numerous origins, coming from a wide range of Asian, Latin American, Caribbean, African, and European countries. Not only does this diversity of origin make New York a true mosaic of languages and cultures, but New York's most recently settled residents have also greatly diversified the city's population racially and ethnically. While the

1

city's population was just under two-thirds non-Hispanic white in 1970, when the latest wave of immigration began to swell, by 2000 the proportion of non-Hispanic whites had fallen by almost half, to 35 percent, and Latinos constituted a slightly larger share of the population (27 percent) than African Americans (24.5 percent).

To what degree are new immigrants welcomed by the city? The reception provided by New Yorkers, politicians, and scholars varies widely. Many people recognize the benefits that high levels of immigration provide to the city.[5] Among these benefits is the hard work that immigrants perform in a variety of occupations that are unattractive to the city's native-born workers (and thus might go unfilled were it not for immigrants) but that contribute to the vitality of the city's economy. Equally important, immigrants are recognized as making vital contributions toward stabilizing and reinvigorating many of the city's older neighborhoods. The post-1965 wave of immigration coincided with a period of severe population loss in New York; not only were whites leaving the city but so were native-born blacks and Puerto Ricans. Without the in-movement of immigrants, with their purchasing power and their capital investments in the housing stock and commercial establishments, many of New York's older neighborhoods would be largely depleted of population and in advanced physical and economic decline.[6] Although this conclusion is largely speculative, severe deterioration of neighborhoods is familiar in such cities as Philadelphia, Detroit, and St. Louis, which have been steadily losing population since 1970 without compensatory influxes of new immigrants.[7] Some cities, like Pittsburgh, are eagerly recruiting immigrants to stabilize their populations.[8]

In contrast to this eager welcome are some less-than-favorable feelings toward immigrants. In many communities that have received large inflows of immigrants, longtime residents have felt uncomfortable or ambivalent about the visible changes in the complexions of their neighborhoods and the shifts in goods and services offered by local establishments, and have resented what they perceive as a "loss of control of and identity with what they once considered to be 'their' community."[9] Indicative of the discord between new immigrants and longtime residents is the controversy over language usage on store signs. Many longtime residents of Flushing, Queens, and other neighborhoods feel excluded from stores advertising only in a foreign language, and thus feel unwelcome in what was once their own neighborhood.[10] Other negative reactions involve anger over some of the consequences of rapid growth, such as traffic, overcrowding, noise, and rising residential and commercial rents, which are often attributed not simply to immigrants but to "illegals" in particular.[11]

Some long-term residents are thus susceptible to the arguments of anti-immigration groups, such as ProjectUSA. These groups claim that immigration is responsible for a number of problems that detract from the quality of life for the native-born and imposes undue financial burdens on immigrant-receiving communities.[12] Anti-immigration feeling, moreover, has probably grown stronger in the wake of the attack on the World Trade Center on September 11, 2001.[13] (Ironically, ProjectUSA is based in Brooklyn as well as in Queens, the most diverse county in the nation and the borough with the largest concentration of the foreign-born.) Yet, in general, even in the neighborhoods most profoundly affected by immigration, there has not been the kind of violence and outright hostility aimed at newcomers that has occurred elsewhere, including communities on Long Island.[14]

A fear that many Americans (and at least some New Yorkers) have about today's new arrivals is that, by virtue of their origins in the developing world (rather than in societies and economies like those of the United States), the immigrants arriving today will be unequipped for assimilation into U.S. society and for full participation in the economy and, thus, will become a drain rather than a boost to the economy and society. Still others fear that many new immigrants will actually *refuse* to assimilate socially and economically and that their real motivation for coming to the United States is in fact to receive social-welfare benefits rather than to work.[15] Equally, if not more, prevalent is the discomfort many people may feel with the racial and ethnic diversity of today's arrivals, its inevitable effect on the racial and ethnic composition of the U.S. population, and its potential effect on racial/ethnic relations and alliances.

These negative reactions to immigrants are not new but, instead, have clear historical parallels to anti-immigrant attitudes held by many Americans in the late nineteenth and early twentieth centuries.[16] Although past fears have proved to have been largely unfounded, analyses are only beginning for the contemporary wave of immigrants.

This book contributes to this growing literature by asking some very basic questions. First, to what extent are fears about new immigrants rooted in truth? Or more simply, to what degree does social-scientific evidence support fears that immigrants, as a group, are unable, or unwilling, to assimilate into, participate in, or become incorporated within American society? To answer these questions we use New York City as a case study to examine generational patterns of housing-market outcomes, paying particular attention to the role that race plays in the allocation of housing opportunities to both foreign- and native-born households and to the way race may act to *block* the path to full incorporation.

Why housing? Housing is one of the best indicators of a population's living standard, when the standard is measured by the level of economic investment in infrastructure and the quality of amenities available. For example, few would argue that the eradication over time of housing units lacking access to piped water indicates an important advance in the living standards of the American population. However, as we discuss in greater detail in chapter 1, access to housing and neighborhoods is one of the most fundamental mechanisms promoting the broader process of stratification in U.S. society.[17] On the one hand, the extent to which different groups live together is a potent indicator of their social and economic similarities, whereas the extent to which they live apart reveals the social distance separating them. Indeed, it is in the neighborhood where people form primary, intimate relationships with others. Neighboring children and schoolmates form the "pool" from which young children choose their playmates and from which adolescents choose their first dating partners. For adults, neighbors often substitute for kin as more and more households live at distances from their immediate and extended families. Yet for all these examples of the kinds of intimate attachments people may form with their neighbors, the key is that people are more likely to live among and form these attachments with people who are similar to themselves. Thus, spatial outcomes are sociologically meaningful—yet also measurable—results of the general processes of social and economic mobility.

Indeed, for immigrants (and ethnic groups more generally), the story of social and economic mobility is intricately interwoven with residential mobility to better housing and neighborhoods, a process termed *spatial assimilation*.[18] The historical record documents that as each immigrant group gains a stronger foothold in the nation's social and economic structures, its members start moving to new neighborhoods that are often not only physically separate from the ethnic ghetto but also socially separate.[19] In the course of this move, they leave the crowded and deteriorated conditions typical of the immigrant ghetto for newer and less-crowded accommodations in higher-quality areas, which tend to be dominated by members of the majority group. As the upwardly mobile of the ethnic group leave the immigrant ghetto, they are replaced by members of new immigrant groups, who, needing inexpensive places to live near their best options for employment, inherit the aging and deteriorating housing stock. This general story underlies the replacement of the Irish and Germans by the Italians and Russian Jews in the city's immigrant ghettos, such as the Lower East Side, at the end of the nineteenth and the start of the twentieth centuries. The process of spatial assimilation experienced by individual group members creates the conditions necessary for the process of ethnic residential succession at the neighborhood level; yet both these processes point to the same conclusion: housing outcomes are key indicators of the assimilation process. Thus, an examination of the extent to which housing and neighborhood outcomes shift across generations in the current context constitutes a direct test of the ability of today's immigrants to assimilate socially and economically.

Although the spatial assimilation process describes the experiences of earlier waves of European immigrants, it is less well suited to describe the residential experiences of later arrivals to the city, namely Southern-born blacks and Puerto Ricans. The social, economic, and housing experiences of these groups were complicated by racial prejudice among individuals and community groups; racial discrimination by realtors, landlords, and financial institutions; and local and federal policies and programs that created a dual housing market—with one portion devoted to whites and the other to blacks and dark-skinned Latinos—that continues today to fortify the high levels of racial segregation that characterize New York City's neighborhoods.[20] As a result, African Americans and Puerto Ricans encountered far greater and more permanent obstacles than did European immigrants in their efforts to achieve higher socioeconomic and housing status.

The intervention of these structural constraints has given rise to an alternative theory of locational attainment, namely, *place stratification theory.*[21] As we describe more fully in chapter 1, this theory deviates from spatial assimilation theory largely by emphasizing the role of structural constraints in limiting the housing choices of those groups most at risk of experiencing discrimination, that is, blacks and Latinos.

Examining how race/ethnicity influences the locational attainment process will provide insight into the extent to which certain immigrant groups are *permitted* to assimilate residentially.[22]

While housing and neighborhood conditions can clearly serve as outcomes of the process of socioeconomic mobility, they can also be considered as important inputs to the same process. Owning a home is the most significant form of wealth accumulation for the majority of U.S. households. As an asset that can be transferred to the next generation or that can help underwrite other large expenses like college tuition, homeownership plays a significant role in the perpetuation of inequalities across class and racial lines.[23] In addition, a growing amount of research points to the importance of neighborhood-based resources in predicting a host of social and economic outcomes, especially for, but not limited to, children and youths.[24]

The role that neighborhoods can play in determining the current and future well-being of families and children takes on greater significance in light of the demonstrated link between residential segregation and neighborhood quality.[25] The quality and quantity of the kinds of place-based resources that can help residents achieve social and economic success are not available in equal amounts or equal quality in all areas. Instead, potentially beneficial resources are more likely to be found in more affluent and predominantly white neighborhoods than in poorer and predominantly black neighborhoods.[26] Thus, where you live plays a significant role in determining your life chances, and who you are (as indicated most significantly by race/ethnicity and, as we show, less so by class) determines quite strongly where you live. By increasing the chance that blacks and Hispanics reside in less salubrious housing and neighborhoods than do comparable whites, the persistence of structural barriers to housing choice may also raise the risk that the members of these groups experience a pattern of downward socioeconomic mobility across generations, one hypothesis proposed by *segmented assimilation theory*.[27]

Segmented assimilation theory, more generally, argues that race/ethnicity influences the path of incorporation taken by immigrant groups, by determining the "segment" of U.S. society into which immigrants are to be integrated. For immigrants who are phenotypically black, incorporation means becoming part of black America, not simply America per se,[28] and thus encountering the same kinds of structural impediments to advancement that native-born blacks experience.[29] This prospect is clearly recognized by Afro-Caribbean immigrants, who see retaining their ethnic identity as a way of avoiding a loss of status.[30] Retaining an ethnic accent and other markers of ethnicity affords Afro-Caribbeans better treatment by whites and thus opens doors to a variety of opportunities that are not available to native-born blacks.[31] Yet as these immigrants' descendants lose the cues that telegraph their ethnic identity to others, they are increasingly perceived and treated as part of the black American population, "with all of its associated disadvantages."[32] As a result, segmented assimilation theory implies that for certain groups of immigrants, specifically those who are phenotypically black, discrimination should increase and opportunities should diminish as generation rises. Thus, our examination of how race/ethnicity shapes generational differences in housing and neighborhood outcomes provides insight into the question of how race may differentially shape the life chances and incorporation of various groups of immigrants, as well as insight into the potential for the perpetuation of racial and ethnic inequality or for its eventual demise.[33]

We use a unique data set created specifically for this project, one that consists of observations of individual households and housing units from the 1999 panel of the New York City Housing and Vacancy Survey (HVS) and a variety of characteristics about the neighborhoods in which they live. One of the key features of this data set, in addition to its ability to describe in depth the neighborhoods in which individual households reside, is that the HVS contains data not only on the birthplace of householders but also the birthplaces of householders' mothers and fathers (i.e., their parentage). The latter data item was last included in the decennial census—the most frequently used data source for studies such as this—in 1970. As a result, we can identify more than two generational groups and thus conduct a more direct and thorough test of generational patterns of change than other researchers in the field have been able to do.[34]

Our findings tell a very clear story about the continuing relevance of assimilation as a process generating generational change, yet they also tell a disturbing story about the continuing significance of black race as a determinant of households' access to opportunity. That is, we find considerable evidence supporting the basic tenets of the spatial assimilation model, in that for all groups, higher levels of income and education and lower levels of need are related to higher levels of homeownership, better-quality housing, and residence in neighborhoods possessing a variety of resources that can lead to social and economic success. However, households of African heritage and dark-skinned Latinos, whether native-born or belonging to any of the immigrant generations we examine, occupy housing and neighborhoods of far lower quality than do white households of comparable socioeconomic status. Thus, as the place stratification theory suggests, our results demonstrate unequivocally that black race continues to determine where households live above and beyond the influence of socioeconomic status and thus remains a salient predictor of households' access to a range of resources that have been shown to be important in influencing social and economic mobility within and across generations.

While these findings point unmistakably to the persistence of institutional forces, such as housing-market discrimination, that undergird racial/ethnic inequalities, our most significant finding is that these forces appear to create very different opportunities for immigrants to become incorporated into American society. That is, we find, *among black households only,* that housing and particularly neighborhood conditions deteriorate in quality as generation rises, a finding that supports the more pessimistic hypotheses of segmented assimilation theory. The finding of a clear pattern of downward mobility underscores the unique position of blacks in American society, by suggesting that, in their pursuit of incorporation, immigrants of visible black race encounter obstacles that are sufficiently impermeable to ensure that they and their descendants will be relegated to the lower tiers of the social order. Thus, instead of doubting immigrants' willingness to assimilate, Americans need to recognize that there remain powerful forces that *prevent* certain groups of immigrants from achieving social and economic success and need to work to eliminate them once and for all.[35]

The significance of our findings raises the question of whether the story we tell is uniquely about New York City or one that can be generalized to other locations and the housing market as a whole. On the one hand, we are confident that our findings with respect to the lower quality of blacks' versus whites' housing and neighborhood conditions is not unique to New York; despite our omission of the suburban counties that compose the rest of the New York region and the reigning notion that suburbanization is a key phase in the spatial assimilation of racial/ethnic and immigrant groups,[36] research has demonstrated convincingly that this pattern of spatial inequalities is similar in cities and in suburbs and holds in a range of different metropolitan areas and regions of the country.[37] In addition, Clark (2003) has demonstrated that although entry to the middle class (measured by both income and homeownership) occurs at lower rates for most nonblack immigrants in the New York region, the patterns evident for New York replicate those for other large immigrant-receiving metros. Yet we recognize that by virtue of not including observations of suburban households we are at risk of misstating the "true" degree of difference between the housing and neighborhood outcomes of immigrant and native-born households and between those of differing races and ethnicities.

The extent to which our results pertaining to the unique pattern of generational decline in housing and neighborhood conditions for blacks would be generalizable to areas outside New York is somewhat less predictable. That is, there are not many other places in the United States that currently receive large inflows of black immigrants, let alone areas with a long history of black immigration. While the racial/ethnic diversity of New York's newest arrivals, the city's role as a historical destination for a variety of immigrants (including black Caribbean immigrants), and the racial/ethnic diversity of its native-born population clearly make New York an ideal case for our study, there are other features of the city that cause it to be unique and thus perhaps unrepresentative of the rest of the country. For example, the level of segregation between blacks and whites, both for the metropolitan area and the city, remains very high. The Index of Dissimilarity (D), the most popular measure of segregation, describes the extent to which two groups are evenly distributed across space (e.g., a city or metro area). The value of D ranges between 0 and 100 and indicates the percent of one of the two groups that would have to move for the two distributions to achieve parity. The value of D for the New York metro area in 2000 stood at 81.8,[38] slightly lower than the city's value at 83.9,[39] meaning that more than eight in ten blacks (or whites) in New York would have to move to balance out the disparity in distribution. Using the widely accepted rule of thumb that any D value in excess of 60 is high, it is clear that blacks and whites in New York live in distinctly different neighborhoods (which parallels our own findings of distinctly different levels of neighborhood-based resources). Equally important, these levels have barely changed since 1980, while the level of black-white segregation has declined in most other areas in the nation. Thus, it is likely that the factors that contribute to the persistence of these high levels of residential separation (among which is housing-market discrimination) make the prospects for incorporation among black immigrants bleaker in New York than in areas where black-white segregation levels are lower or have been declining.

However, when we look at other metros that also receive large numbers of black immigrants, for example, Washington, D.C., and Miami, we again find very high levels of segregation (the 2000 value of D for Washington is 62.7, and that for Miami is 72.4),[40] suggesting that the barriers to black immigrants' housing-market incorporation are not limited to New York. Furthermore, the housing and neighborhood conditions experienced by foreign-born blacks in metropolitan areas throughout the nation are consistently superior in quality to those of native-born blacks of comparable socioeconomic status, regardless of whether they own or rent and whether they live in suburbs or central cities.[41] By eliminating the role of socioeconomic status, such findings provide additional evidence for the notion that our findings of generational decline among blacks in New York may pertain to other locations. In other words, if we were able to repeat our analyses using data for the nation as a whole, we feel confident that the pattern of generational decline we find among blacks in New York City would be repeated.

Organization of the Book

In chapter 1 of this book, we develop the theoretical frameworks that guide our analysis. The discussion opens with the significance of housing and of spatial patterns as key social and economic indicators. The discussion moves on to residential mobility theory to elaborate on the process by which households come to live where they live and then turns to assimilation, spatial assimilation, and place stratification theories to specify how race/ethnicity and nativity status influence the mobility process. To close out the chapter, we identify and discuss the hypotheses we test in later chapters.

In chapters 2 and 3 we place the study in its historical context by discussing the history of immigration, race/ethnicity, and housing in New York City. The story that we tell in chapter 2 of the settlement patterns of the European immigrants who arrived in New York after the mid-nineteenth century provides the empirical data underlying the theoretical perspectives on spatial assimilation. In the course of the discussion on immigrants and their housing situations, we also pay attention to the rise of the tenement reform movement, which had as its main goal the alleviation of the housing problems of immigrants as a way to mitigate the city's growing social and economic problems. By discussing the arrival and settlement patterns of Southern blacks and Puerto Ricans (who began arriving shortly before the twentieth century) and the numerous barriers to spatial assimilation encountered by nonwhites, we highlight the historical events and processes that have given rise to place stratification theory. Chapter 3 concludes the story by providing a discussion of immigration trends and housing policy since 1970, with special attention paid to the patterns of settlement and their correlates among four of the city's largest immigrant groups: Dominicans, Soviet Jews, Chinese, and Caribbean blacks.

Chapters 4 and 5 present, respectively, the results of our analyses focusing on immigrant-status housing inequalities and on differences in the neighborhood conditions experienced by immigrant and native-born households. For each set of analyses, we examine models that include households of all races and ethnicities, and we incorporate variables controlling for immigrant status and generation—foreign-born, 1.5 generation (i.e., born abroad but arrived as a child), second generation (i.e., parents born abroad, householder native-born), and native-born—to test the fundamental tenets of the spatial assimilation theory. Although we find much support for the idea that each succeeding generation achieves increasingly better housing and neighborhood characteristics, our analyses reveal a persistent racial and ethnic difference in housing outcomes, with black and Latino households—regardless of nativity and generation status—more likely to live in lower-quality housing and disadvantaged neighborhoods than are whites (again, regardless of nativity). These results indicate that the spatial assimilation theory does not adequately explain the occurrence of housing and neighborhood inequalities for African Americans and Latinos and point to the persistence of racial discrimination in the housing market, a finding that strongly supports the basic tenets of the place stratification theory. Because the influence of racial discrimination may impede the affected groups' abilities to become fully incorporated within American society, in chapter 5 we estimate models for each racial/ethnic group to determine if, in fact, the patterns of housing and neighborhood outcomes worsen, rather than improve, over the generations for those groups most affected by discrimination—that is, blacks and Latinos—thereby evaluating the argument proposed by segmented assimilation theory. We find substantial support for this argument in the results pertaining to blacks in that we uncover a consistent pattern of *declining* housing and neighborhood conditions as generation increases.

Chapter 6 summarizes our findings and addresses their policy implications. Although the patterns we uncover throughout our study are consistent with the notion that housing-market discrimination stands as the root cause, our data do not allow us to definitively make this argument. Indeed, part of the explanation for our findings may reflect the influence that preferences have in driving housing choices. That is, although a household may not prefer per se to live in a lower-quality neighborhood, its preference for not being a minority pioneer in a predominantly or all-white neighborhood may overwhelm its preference for higher-quality place-based resources; as a result, such a household may opt for a diverse neighborhood of somewhat lower quality. Thus, our policy implications reflect the complexity of the presumed causes. We argue that fair-housing laws should be strengthened, but clearly this will not be the cure-all for the kinds of inequalities our study reveals. Added to the strengthening of fair-housing laws should be parallel efforts to enhance the resources available in New York's neighborhoods and to eliminate the inequalities that differentially expose certain groups to restricted opportunities for social and economic advancement.

1

Movin' on Up
Understanding Locational Attainment

Throughout U.S. history, there has been concern about the ability and willingness of new immigrants to become incorporated into "mainstream" American society. In the nineteenth and early twentieth centuries, observers worried that the newcomers, whether they hailed from Ireland, Italy, Russia, or some other foreign country, were either too handicapped by what was perceived as their inferior abilities to contribute to, or participate in, American society, or that they were merely too different and thus would never be able to assimilate. In the twentieth century, the descendants of those immigrant groups initially believed to be inassimilable achieved what was thought unachievable; over the course of time and generations, members of these groups acquired higher levels of education, got increasingly better jobs, earned ever rising incomes, moved to the suburbs, and became essentially indistinguishable from other *white* Americans.[1] Now, many descendants of these earlier waves of immigrants look with pride on the courage displayed by their ancestors to come to a new country to make a better life for themselves and their families, while arguing that the current waves of immigrants are unfit to make it in America and in fact are the cause of many of society's problems.[2]

What few of these individuals may recognize is that it may, in fact, be the *structure* of American society that limits the opportunities for incorporation for many of today's immigrants, rather than their own lack of motivation or the seemingly inferior attributes they arrive with.[3] Given the persistence of racial stratification in American society, and the range of inequalities this system creates, many of today's immigrants—who are no longer predominantly white—may encounter more impediments to their incorporation into American society than did the earlier waves of European immigrants. Although many earlier groups encountered prejudice and discrimination, because they were racially white in a legal sense and actively distanced themselves from African Americans through such means as occupational and residential segregation,[4] their perceived race progressively "whitened."[5] As a result, prejudicial attitudes and discriminatory actions diminished over time, until they all but entirely disappeared, clearing the way for complete integration into American society.

The same cannot be said of the experiences of nonwhites, particularly African Americans. One has only to refer to the history of residential segregation to see this. The white ethnic neighborhoods of the nineteenth and early twentieth centuries served as *temporary* spatial arrangements for new immigrants to the city, but the black ghetto—formed out of prejudice and discrimination—has proved far more permanent, especially in those cities, like New York, that have served as major destinations for the Southern blacks who began moving north at the end of the nineteenth century. The early white ethnic enclaves, relatively small and ethnically heterogeneous, never housed the majority of any one ethnic group. In contrast, in many cities, black areas are geographically extensive, racially homogeneous, and home to the majority of the area's African Americans.[6] Given the continuing salience of racial stratification in American society, some new immigrants may find their prospects for full incorporation limited and thus may not achieve the kind of continuous upward mobility associated with the experiences of the earlier waves of European immigrants.[7]

In this chapter we describe the theoretical approaches that guide our study. Our analyses in later chapters tell a story of the relative successes and failures that different groups, defined by their generational status and their race/ethnicity, have experienced in locating themselves in the residential hierarchy. We begin this chapter with context, by discussing the importance of housing and neighborhoods for socioeconomic mobility, and then examine the factors that have created and maintained high levels of residential segregation by race. We then show how these factors—including housing-market discrimination—have weakened the use of housing status as a marker for socioeconomic success among blacks and nonwhite Latinos, while enhancing the role of housing as a force promoting racial/ethnic inequality.

The process of acquiring housing is essentially one of moving, and so we then turn to a discussion of the theoretical frameworks surrounding the question of how households come to live where they live. We begin with traditional residential mobility theory to provide a foundation for the three theoretical models—spatial assimilation, place stratification, and segmented assimilation—that frame our analyses. The spatial assimilation model draws directly from traditional models of residential mobility by focusing on individual-level attainments, like education and income, as the primary determinants of residential mobility and its outcomes. As such, it parallels arguments that attribute patterns of racial residential segregation to group differences in economic status.[8] Place stratification theory is also explicitly a model of residential mobility, but it recognizes the persistence of structural barriers and their effects on minorities' housing choices, integrating these macrolevel factors into more traditional conceptualizations that see spatial assimilation as purely an individual-level process. These two models provide the framework for studies of racial/ethnic and immigrant-status residential outcomes, a body of literature to which our study contributes.

Our study differs from others in the area by using segmented assimilation theory to explain generational patterns in residential attainments. This model is not typically applied to residential mobility processes but instead has been largely used to explain generational patterns of adolescent behaviors and achievements that diverge from the standard "straight-line" upward progression often associated with general assimilation theory. However, the link between residential mobility and variation in generational patterns of adaptation is not completely absent; one of the factors argued to cause some groups of immigrant and second-generation youths—particularly those of African and Hispanic ancestry—to exhibit adverse patterns of adaptation is the persistence of housing-market discrimination, which concentrates these youths in disadvantaged inner-city neighborhoods lacking the kinds of resources (such as well-performing schools, numerous job opportunities and role models of economic activity, and safe and healthy environments) that help to ensure social and economic success in adulthood.[9] Furthermore, the theory argues that in such areas, immigrant and second-generation youths are exposed to, and often adopt, adversarial attitudes and behaviors that help to derail their educational and occupational success.[10] As a result, the potential for segmented assimilation derives from the same forces identified by place stratification theory, forging a key bond between the theoretical perspectives.

The differential concentration of certain immigrant groups in disadvantaged neighborhoods may help to account for racial/ethnic variation in adjustment among members of the second generation. Yet the element of segmented assimilation theory that speaks more clearly and forcibly to the potential for longer-range generational patterns of decline is its argument that for groups whose incorporation fates lie among disadvantaged native-born minorities, the link between becoming American and upward mobility is broken. Instead, becoming American entails a significant risk of downward mobility.[11] Underlying this risk is the preferential treatment from whites that foreign-born blacks receive relative to native-born blacks,[12] affording them wider access to jobs and housing. As markers of ethnicity and nativity status—such as accents and other obvious cues—weaken and eventually disappear over generations, structural barriers to housing opportunities strengthen, progressively restricting the choices of higher-generation households to less-adequate housing and less-advantaged neighborhood environments. Thus, for immigrants of African ancestry, incorporation within black America entails increasing experience with structural constraints on their housing choices, resulting in a steady pattern of generational decline in housing and neighborhood conditions.

The Social and Economic Significance of Residential Location

We begin by delineating the fundamental role played by housing in determining the social and economic well-being of families in the United States. The term "housing" in this sense encompasses not only the physical attributes of individual dwelling units, such as their size, structural adequacy, and overall level of maintenance, but their locational attributes as well.[13] Dwelling units are physically, and thus permanently, situated in neighborhoods. By virtue of living in a particular dwelling unit, a family or a household has access to, and can take advantage of, the full range of potentially beneficial resources that are spatially situated in the neighborhood. By the same token, families and households are also exposed to any undesirable conditions that may prevail in the area.[14] Thus, when we consider how families and households are housed, we must examine not only the attributes of the dwelling units in which they live but also the character of the surrounding area—the resources and disamenities physically situated in the neighborhood. Such neighborhood characteristics may include social factors (such as the neighborhood's socioeconomic status, crime level, school quality, and access to employment opportunities) as well as physical features, including the presence of boarded-up and abandoned buildings, vacant and trash-strewn lots, and the presence/absence and quality of local services and commercial establishments.

The social and economic significance of the housing status of families and households can be viewed through two lenses. Through the first lens, a family's housing status can be viewed as an *outcome* of the process of socioeconomic mobility; the kind of housing a family occupies is the most visible outward sign of that family's position in the social and economic hierarchy.[15] This function of housing is widely understood. Not only is owning a home an integral part of the "American dream,"[16] but people also consider their homes to be indicators of how well they have done socially and economically. Indeed, practically all Americans recognize the hierarchy of housing types and neighborhoods and know that this housing hierarchy largely parallels the social-class hierarchy. That is, it is clear to most observers that a family living in a large single-family home on a spacious lot in a leafy and well-appointed suburb occupies a higher position in the social-class hierarchy than does a family living in a cramped apartment in a dilapidated tenement in a deteriorating inner-city neighborhood. Moreover, if the inner-city family moves to a house in a higher-quality suburban neighborhood, most observers would immediately understand that this move likely resulted from an improvement in the family's socioeconomic status. Thus, *locational attainment,*[17] or the process of translating social and economic attributes into residence in housing units and neighborhoods that are of equivalent status, is a fundamental component of the broader process of socioeconomic mobility in the United States.

The second lens through which the social and economic significance of housing is viewed sees housing as an *input* to the socioeconomic mobility process. That is, not only does housing reflect a family's or a household's current position in society, but it also influences if, and how far, individuals can move up the ladder. This power of housing is reflected in both the short- and long-term economic benefits of owned housing. In the short term, households who own their homes may have stable housing costs and can deduct the interest paid on their mortgages from their taxes. These types of short-term benefits may provide homeowners with more disposable income, some of which they may save, invest, or spend on activities or goods that can enhance their own market skills or the future skills of their children (i.e., private schools and/or extracurricular activities such as summer camps, dance classes, and music lessons). In the long term, an owned home acts as an important financial asset that can be bequeathed to children or that can be borrowed against for some other large expenditure, such as college tuition. Thus, owned housing can be a key tool in enhancing a family's current social-class standing or in promoting the upward socioeconomic mobility of the next and succeeding generations.[18]

In addition to these wealth-generating functions of owned housing, there is also evidence of a link between housing quality and physical and mental health.[19] In the case of children, beyond the widely known link between exposure to lead paint and lowered cognitive development, researchers have identified a relationship between receiving housing subsidies and improved nutritional status in clinical samples of low-income children.[20] Given the links between children's nutritional status, health, and development, such evidence suggests that providing housing assistance to poor families may help to improve children's chances for success. Housing quality has also been linked to asthma, a leading cause of absence from school and work.[21] In addition, there is some evidence that homeownership is linked to improved cognitive skills and reduced behavioral problems in children,[22] although the positive influence of homeownership may be limited to low-income children.[23]

There is also a growing amount of evidence concerning the role of neighborhood conditions in influencing individuals' life chances. Neighborhoods vary greatly in the type and amount of resources they contain. Some are well stocked with resources that may enhance the chance for social and economic success, such as high-quality schools and numerous job opportunities. Others, however, contain disamenities, such as high crime rates and widespread poverty, that have the potential to derail their residents' attempts to finish school, get good jobs, and achieve other forms of upward mobility. In particular, residence in highly disadvantaged neighborhoods has been shown to be associated with lowered cognitive development for children and with teenagers' fertility, delinquency, and high-school dropout.[24] In addition, low neighborhood quality can adversely affect residents' physical and mental health,[25] which in turn can diminish residents' economic productivity. One hypothesized mechanism linking neighborhood quality to both health and cognitive outcomes involves the way in which the body reacts to stress. In short, when confronted by a stressful situation, the body releases a number of hormones that enhance the chance of surviving or overcoming the immediate, short-term threat. Chronic exposure to stress—as can occur by living in a violent neighborhood or in one characterized by a high degree of disorder—can overload the system with these hormones, which in turn is linked to a number of adverse consequences (e.g., an increased risk of hypertension and inflammatory disorders, and reduced cognitive functioning).[26] The evidence accumulated thus far on the linkage between neighborhood quality and a range of outcomes indicates quite strongly that where one lives can significantly affect where one ends up in life.[27]

Thus, housing is simultaneously a reflection of socioeconomic status as well as a determinant of future life chances. In particular, the place-based resources to which people have regular and easy access can promote or impede their potential to achieve upward mobility. The role that neighborhood conditions play in determining people's life chances takes on added significance in light of the connection between the degree of segregation and the quality of neighborhood resources. It is widely recognized that the kinds of place-based resources that can enhance the chance of social and economic success are not evenly distributed across space, but are more plentiful and of higher quality in more-affluent and predominantly white neighborhoods than in poorer and racially/ethnically mixed or segregated neighborhoods.[28] Furthermore, these spatial inequalities are intricately interwoven with the practices and policies that have created and maintained patterns of racial/ethnic segregation[29] and that continue to constrain the housing choices of members of certain groups, particularly African Americans and Latinos, to residences in underresourced areas. In so doing, the forces maintaining segregation ensure that the members of these groups are disproportionately exposed to potentially deleterious conditions and thereby help to maintain patterns of racial/ethnic inequality. Thus, while it is clear that where you live can influence how far in life you may be able to go, what sometimes gets overlooked is that who you are can influence quite strongly where you live. In short, any discussion of housing and neighborhoods must focus on the role of segregation in influencing not only where households live but also the quality of those environments.

Racial/Ethnic Segregation and the Geography of Opportunity

African Americans are more highly segregated from whites than are either Hispanics or Asians.[30] Black segregation levels have been declining slowly since about 1970, but they remain in the range of values considered high, especially in those cities that were the primary destinations of Southern black migrants. For example, the Census Bureau constructed a time series of segregation indices for metropolitan areas from 1980 to 2000 and found that, for New York, the index of dissimilarity between non-Hispanic whites and non-Hispanic blacks remained unchanged over the period at 82, out of a possible score of 100.[31] What this value means is that 82 percent of either whites or blacks would have to change locations in the metropolitan area to achieve an even distribution by race.[32] To place this value into further perspective, researchers use a value of 60 or more on the index of dissimilarity to denote a high level of segregation; thus, the level of segregation in New York is closer to perfect segregation (where blacks and whites would share no neighborhoods, indicated by a value of 100 on the index of dissimilarity) than to the lower bound of the "high" range. Furthermore, in 2000, the level of black-white segregation in the New York area ranked third among the fifty metros examined by researchers at the Lewis Mumford Center at SUNY-Albany, and New York was the only metro area that did not exhibit any decline at all in black-white segregation between 1980 and 2000.[33]

Three explanations have been advanced to explain the persistence of high levels of black-white segregation.[34] The first suggests that racial segregation persists because of differences in the economic status of whites and blacks. As this explanation goes, because the average black household commands fewer socioeconomic resources (such as income and education) than does the typical white household, black households on average cannot afford to live in the same kinds of neighborhoods that white households can afford to occupy.[35] There is, however, little evidence to support this argument. In particular, the level of black-white segregation does not vary much across levels of socioeconomic status and in fact remains in the extreme range in all categories of education, income, or occupational status.[36] If the "economic differences" argument were to explain high levels of black segregation, these levels would disappear or decline precipitously when the spatial patterns of African

Americans and whites of the same socioeconomic status are compared. Although Richard Alba and his colleagues have shown that middle-class and affluent blacks live in more affluent and whiter neighborhoods than do poorer blacks, their neighborhoods remain less well-off and more racially segregated than those occupied by socioeconomically similar whites.[37]

The second explanation for continuing high levels of racial segregation focuses on the varying preferences held by blacks and whites for neighborhoods of different racial compositions. The general form of this argument places the blame on an assumed preference among African Americans to live with "their own kind,"[38] yet the wealth of survey evidence shows that blacks are most likely to prefer neighborhoods in which blacks and whites are approximately evenly represented. In contrast, white respondents report discomfort in and a desire to leave neighborhoods with even a few black residents.[39] Similar patterns appear to hold in New York City. A 1987 *New York Times* poll revealed that almost three-fourths of black respondents would prefer a neighborhood where whites and blacks are about evenly represented, compared to just over one-third of white respondents.[40] Thus, the kinds of neighborhoods preferred by blacks contain a higher degree of diversity than the average white can tolerate, suggesting that varying preferences do, in fact, contribute toward maintaining the spatial distance separating whites and blacks. However, instead of benign preferences for living among similar neighbors, the evidence shows that it is intolerance for black neighbors that is more firmly at the root of continued patterns of segregation.[41]

The third explanation focuses on the intersection of whites' preferences for not living among minority, and especially black, neighbors and structural factors, such as discrimination in the housing market on the part of realtors and mortgage lenders (among others) against blacks. Proponents of this perspective argue that residential segregation is built on whites' prejudices against and stereotypes about minorities. Because of these prejudices and stereotypes, whites avoid living among minorities and encourage institutional actors, such as real-estate agents and others in the housing market, to engage in discriminatory behavior with the end goal being the separation of whites from blacks.[42] This perspective is strongly supported by historical and contemporary evidence. Indeed, research has unequivocally demonstrated that the segregation of African Americans has its roots in deliberate actions on the part of a wide range of actors, including the federal government, financial institutions (such as mortgage lenders), individual housing-market actors (real-estate agents, landlords), and neighbors.[43] The cumulative result of these actions is a dual housing market that has historically confined African Americans' housing choices to neighborhoods that are more ethnically diverse, less prosperous, and of lower quality than those available to whites.[44] In other words, not only do whites and African Americans by and large live in separate communities, but those to which African Americans have access also have, on average, fewer of the resources that facilitate social and economic success. Thus, for African Americans, the link between socioeconomic status and housing status has not been as strong as it has been for whites; as a group, African Americans are less able than whites to "cash in" their hard-earned gains in income, education, and occupational status for homes in better neighborhoods. This weaker link between socioeconomic status and housing means that middle-class black neighborhoods are often contiguous with low-income black neighborhoods, causing their residents to be exposed to the same neighborhood problems endured by their poorer neighbors.[45] Because racial segregation, and the dual housing market that undergirds it, has historically been *imposed* on African Americans, it limits their access to many of the amenities conducive to upward mobility and thus helps to maintain racial inequality.

In contrast to the experience of African Americans, levels of Hispanic and Asian segregation from whites are more moderate than levels of black segregation. In the New York metropolitan area in 2000, the level of Hispanic-white segregation stood at 67, and the level of Asian-white segregation stood at 51.[46] Most observers argue that the contemporary segregation of Asians and, to a lesser degree, Hispanics stems largely from voluntary reasons associated with immigration. Of particular importance here is "chain migration," or the process whereby new arrivals go where earlier arrivals—friends, family members, or other coethnics—have already settled, thereby forming an ethnic or immigrant enclave. This kind of voluntary or choice-based segregation may prove beneficial for both the individual and the group. For example, the individual may derive emotional and economic benefits by choosing to remain within the ethnic community to maintain cultural or linguistic ties or to take advantage of services or opportunities produced only within the ethnic economy. Similarly, the immigrant enclave provides an environment that eases the process of transition for newly arrived immigrants by being supportive of their cultural identity while they gradually adapt to the attitudes, behaviors, and institutions of the host society. Clustered enclaves of sufficient scale may also give rise to group benefits like indigenous economic resources, community organizations sensitive to local needs, and political strength expressed in the form of elected representatives.

The importance of voluntary factors in producing lower levels of Asian and Hispanic than black segregation from whites is also illustrated in the greater declines in segregation levels associated with increases in socioeconomic status for the two former groups. In each case, the decline in segregation associated with a rise in education is steeper for Asians and Hispanics than for blacks. Such differences suggest that more-affluent Asians and Hispanics are more successful than comparable African Americans in gaining access to the neighborhoods where similarly affluent whites reside,[47] an advantage empirically documented by a number of studies.[48]

At least part of this difference between blacks, Hispanics, and Asians lies in the fact that levels of segregation from whites are not fully determined by the actions or preferences of the minority group alone but are also determined by the willingness of whites to co-reside with minority-group members. Research on the residential preferences of whites suggests that Asians and Hispanics enjoy greater access to white neighborhoods than do African Americans by virtue of being preferred as potential neighbors. In particular, whites are least averse to sharing their neighborhoods with Asians among all minority groups and are less averse to living near Hispanics than near blacks.[49] These varying preferences on the part of whites point to a racial hierarchy of access to white neighborhoods, such that Asians have the broadest access to white neighborhoods and African Americans have the most limited access, with the access of Hispanics falling in between. These differentials clearly contribute to the varying levels of Asian, Hispanic, and black segregation from whites.[50]

The main exception to the general rules concerning the causes of Hispanic segregation relates to the experiences of Puerto Ricans and non-white Hispanics more generally. These groups typically exhibit spatial patterns similar to those of African Americans, namely, high levels of segregation from non-Hispanic whites.[51] In addition, the finding that nonwhite Hispanics are also segregated from white Hispanics provides further evidence suggesting that the root causes of nonwhite Hispanics' spatial patterns lie in the same kind of housing-market barriers experienced by African Americans.[52] Many observers have voiced concern that the influx of immigrants of black racial heritage (e.g., Afro-Caribbeans and Dominicans) may mean that these new arrivals will also encounter involuntary constraints on their housing choices, resulting in their concentration in low-quality neighborhoods offering few avenues for advancement. Mary Waters's research on West Indian immigrants in New York City demonstrates that this concern is well founded. Among the West Indian immigrants she interviewed, most were appalled by the poverty, crime, and physical deterioration plaguing the mostly black neighborhoods they found themselves living in by virtue of moving in with the friends and relatives already in New York City.[53] Moreover, research has shown that Hispanics who report themselves to be of black race reside in neighborhoods that are less affluent and have a higher concentration of African Americans than those in which white Hispanics live.[54] Such findings unequivocally underscore the penalty associated with having black skin.[55]

Thus, while housing is at once a reflection and a determinant of the social and economic well-being of families and households in the United States, these functions clearly vary for different racial and ethnic groups by virtue of the stratification system that offers greater opportunities to some groups and constrains the choices of others. The implications of this system of inequality for the locational attainment of members of different groups emerges more clearly when we consider how the persistence of housing-market barriers—the expression of the dual housing market—differentially influences how households of different race/ethnicity and immigrant generation search for housing. To this end we now shift attention to the theoretical models that describe the residential mobility process.

Residential Mobility

Traditional models of residential mobility have conceptualized the process of moving from one residence to another as consisting of two stages: the decision to move and the choice of where to move. The separation of these two stages is useful, especially when examining how members of different racial and ethnic groups may come to occupy dwellings and neighborhoods of very different quality. That is, conceptually, the importance of race/ethnicity as a determinant of housing status may be greater in shaping households' choices of where to move than in shaping their decisions to move, since it is when households have direct contact with housing-market actors that their ascribed characteristics become salient determinants of their residential options.

The Decision to Move

Why do people move? In general, the decision to move has been viewed as a reaction to a perceived imbalance between what housing amenities the household needs or prefers (such as space) and the attributes provided by the current dwelling unit (e.g., the number and size of rooms). Moving is thus seen as a way to relieve the "stress" or "dissatisfaction" experienced by the household in this situation.[56] The imbalance or mismatch between household needs or preferences on the one hand and the current unit's attributes on the other may arise from changes in the family life cycle, changes in available resources or the costs associated with living in the current unit, or preferences for a certain lifestyle, as would be the case for upwardly mobile households. Once the household reaches the threshold of dissatisfaction, traditional models of residential mobility argue that the household begins to evaluate alternative units that are available for occupancy and that fall within its budget. The simplest version of such models posits that once the household locates an alternative unit that better suits its needs and budget, it will relocate to that unit. Should the household fail to find a better alternative, however, it may decide not to move. Traditional models of residential mobility, then, are largely guided by assumptions implicit in a "rational choice" framework.

The needs and preferences that influence the decision to move are typically associated with household life cycle and demographic characteristics, including household composition and the age and marital status of the householder. For example, of all age groups, young adults are most likely to move, as they experience important life-cycle changes— such as college attendance, marriage, or the start of a new career—that may require relocation to a new city or region. Childless couples may be more likely to change residence than are couples with children, since the former will have fewer ties to their current location, such as the bonds that children establish with neighborhood friends and schoolmates.[57] However, having a first or an additional child—and thus increasing the size of the family—may compel a household to move to acquire additional space. Finally, single parents and widowed or divorced persons may be more likely to move than are married couples because of economic problems or the disruption associated with the breakup of a marriage.[58]

Other household characteristics may also influence the decision to move. Such factors may include length of residence in the current dwelling unit, socioeconomic status, and tenure status (whether the household owns or rents its current dwelling). Longer residence in a dwelling unit is associated with a higher degree of attachment to and stronger bonds with neighbors and neighborhood institutions. By increasing the psychic costs of moving, longer residence in a given dwelling may depress the chance of moving; the psychic costs of breaking important bonds and leaving social networks may outweigh the costs associated with any other unmet housing needs. More-affluent households, when compared to poorer households, have a broader range of homes they can afford and are in a better economic position to purchase new homes; these advantages suggest that the higher the household's socioeconomic status, the greater the chance of moving.[59]

Owning a home is associated with a reduced chance of moving. Part of this relationship may be due to the greater economic investments that owners (relative to renters) have made in their units. This relationship may also reflect the greater flexibility that owners have to alter their current units to match newly emergent needs or preferences, such as adding a room to accommodate a need for more space. Clearly, most renters do not have the same options in this regard and thus more often have to move to a different dwelling to satisfy an unmet need or preference. The greater latitude of owners to modify their housing units to suit their individual tastes also suggests that they may have deeper emotional or psychic attachments to their homes than do renters, which can also depress the motivation to move.[60]

It is clear, then, that traditional models of residential mobility have emphasized the role of household and housing-unit characteristics in determining the decision to move; they thus conceptualize the process as occurring only as a result of individual-level factors. In so doing, such models have paid less attention to the potential role of neighborhood amenities or of features of a larger geographic entity such as the city/ town or metropolitan area. Recent research has begun to fill this gap by examining "contextual" influences on the probability of moving. In this sense, the context referred to consists of the features of the neighbor-hood, city/town, or metropolitan area in which the household lives. This more-inclusive view of the determinants of residential mobility is consistent with the notion that the conditions in the surrounding areas are part of the "bundle" of housing characteristics that households evaluate.[61]

Researchers in this area have conceptualized contextual influences as consisting of both objective and subjective features of the area and as both "push" and "pull" influences on the decision to move. Objective characteristics consist of aggregate-level neighborhood features mea-sured by a data source independent of that providing the individual-level observations of movers and stayers, such as the decennial census. Examples include the racial/ethnic mix of the neighborhood, its social-class composition, and the proportion of owner-occupied dwellings. Other objective neighborhood characteristics might originate in admin-istrative data sources, including the rate of crime in the area and the percentage of students in the local school performing at or above grade level in math or English. In contrast, subjective features of neighbor-hoods typically consist of opinions or perceptions of the conditions pre-vailing in the neighborhood as expressed by the householder and would therefore derive from the same survey instrument that is collecting the information on residential mobility. Examples of subjective features may include the householder's perception of danger, of the quality of public services, and of the physical upkeep of the area.

Objective and subjective features of the area can act as both "push" and "pull" factors on the household's decision to move. An example of a push factor might be the case in which householders develop a nega-tive opinion about the area, which increases their dissatisfaction with their current situation and thus pushes them to seek residence in some other neighborhood perceived as being free of the particular problem. An example of a pull factor might be the case of a family with children living in an area with an underperforming school. Valuing their chil-dren's educational opportunities, the family hears of a vacant house in an area with a superior school and decides to move there to invest in their children's future. Another example of how contextual factors may act as pull factors is a high vacancy rate in a metropolitan area, which can encourage a high degree of residential mobility among metro resi-dents by providing an abundant supply of available dwelling units.[62]

However, the residential mobility process may not be as straightforward and rational as traditional theoretical approaches describe. On the one hand, there are often situations when individuals move without having ever planned to do so.[63] Such unplanned and hasty mobility has been shown to be especially prevalent among the urban poor and among African Americans, who are often the victims in the war over "exchange values."[64] These vulnerable groups are sometimes forced out of their homes because their neighborhoods become the sites for redevelopment and renewal. These same groups are at risk of moving without prior plans to move because they are unable to pay their rising rents and thus are evicted.[65]

However, there are also situations where, despite strong expectations for a move in the near future, households are unable to actuate the moves they expect to make. For example, Greg Duncan and Sandra Newman's study of mobility among families participating in the Panel Study of Income Dynamics (PSID) shows that over a three-year period, fewer than half of those who expected to move actually did so and that the likelihood of not moving was higher for the elderly, blacks, and poor and female-headed households.[66] Similarly, blacks have been shown to be significantly less able than whites to realize their plans for moving to a new home[67] and are far less likely than whites to move from urban, poor, and racially segregated areas to areas that are located in the suburbs, more affluent, and less diverse.[68] Nonpoor blacks are also no more likely than are poor blacks to escape poor neighborhoods, despite their higher levels of income.[69] When taken together, these findings suggest that blacks do not have access to the full range of housing and neighborhood options from which whites choose when searching for a new home. These apparent constraints on blacks' housing choices likely derive from the kinds of discriminatory actions that have been uncovered by housing-market audits and that help to perpetuate patterns of racial residential segregation.[70] By creating one pool of housing options for blacks and another for whites—the essence of the dual housing market—these actions interfere with blacks' choices of where to move, the second stage in the residential mobility process.

The Choice of Where to Move

Once a household has decided to move, what factors influence its choice of where to move? Traditional perspectives on residential mobility suggest that a household searches for available alternative housing units that feature a given set of attributes, evaluates their suitability, and ultimately selects that dwelling unit which best suits the household's needs, preferences, and budget. Thus, the same factors that precipitate a move in the first place—household needs or preferences, budgets, and housing characteristics—may play a primary role in determining the kinds of alternative housing units considered by a given household.

A household's needs, preferences, and purchasing power help to identify the *kinds* of units it considers, but the *actual pool* of units it identifies is shaped by other factors, including the household's awareness of and knowledge about available vacancies. This knowledge may depend on a number of factors, including the household's own familiarity with different neighborhoods; leads on available units provided by friends, family, and co-workers; and information from newspaper advertisements and formal contacts, such as real-estate agents. For example, a household that is familiar with a certain area will be aware of vacancies as they open and also whether it can afford to live there. Others with whom the household maintains close relationships—especially those who live in different neighborhoods—may be particularly good sources of information about available vacancies, since they will be familiar with the household's needs or preferences and budget constraints. Finally, real-estate agents and newspaper ads are primary sources of information on available housing in a variety of locations and in theory are available to anyone seeking them out.

Although this set of factors shaping the pool of units known to the household may appear to operate independently of race/ethnicity, it is instead quite likely that these characteristics directly influence the amount and content of information available to different households. There are a number of ways in which this can occur. For example, the extent to which members of different groups come into contact and establish intimate relationships by socializing at work or in other settings may influence the readiness with which they share information about available housing in their neighborhoods. However, because social networks are often bounded by race/ethnicity or by nativity status or by both, the amount of information transferred between groups in this way may be limited. Indeed, Maria Krysan finds racial differences in familiarity with the communities included in the interviews conducted for the Multi-City Survey of Urban Inequality (MCSUI), such that whites were less familiar than blacks with communities with a significant black population, and blacks were less familiar with certain suburban communities.[71] By paralleling patterns of segregation, these differences in community recognition could affect housing searches in ways that would ultimately strengthen patterns of segregation.

A second way that race/ethnicity could affect the information available to households is if vacancies in certain neighborhoods are selectively advertised in newspapers catering to specific audiences, discreetly advertised by word of mouth, or posted on signs seen only by persons already present in the neighborhood. Through this kind of selective advertising, some vacancies are made known to certain audiences while others are not. Should these forms of information transferral be conducted in a foreign language, then the targeted audience is even more circumscribed. Thus, the boundaries of social networks and social groups may retain information on housing opportunities within the group, preventing out-group members from learning of them.

Another, and perhaps more potent, way in which a household's race/ethnicity can influence its access to information on available housing is through the operation of housing-market discrimination. That is, landlords and real-estate agents may selectively provide or withhold information from a given household, directly limiting the number and type of vacancies made known to different households. Such methods of "selective recruitment"[72] have been described in case studies of various white ethnic neighborhoods in New York City.[73]

Although overt discrimination by real-estate actors was declared illegal by the 1968 Fair Housing Act, the wealth of housing-market-audit research has documented that covert forms of discrimination continue to flourish. In a housing-market audit, a pair of "testers," one white and one a minority-group member, approaches a real-estate agent about a specific unit, typically one that was advertised in a newspaper. The testers are provided with the same "cover story," namely, they assume the same set of socioeconomic and demographic characteristics. By equalizing their economic, social, and family characteristics, any differences in the treatment they receive from the realtor can be attributed to the characteristic on which they differ, that is, their race/ethnicity.

The vast literature on housing-market audits demonstrates that black and Hispanic home seekers receive less-adequate treatment than comparable white home seekers, including being told about and shown fewer vacancies, receiving less information about and help with financing options, and so on. Audit data from the 2000 Housing Discrimination Study (HDS) reveal that about one-fifth of black renters and home buyers in the nation encountered consistently adverse treatment, relative to that received by their white audit partners, as did 17 percent of Hispanic renters and 33 percent of Hispanic buyers.[74] Estimates produced for the New York metropolitan area are about equivalent for renters but are higher for black and Hispanic home buyers.[75] Although the overall estimates in the 2000 HDS suggest that the incidence of consistently adverse treatment of blacks and Hispanics has fallen since 1989, when the last HDS was fielded,[76] potential black owners appear to experience a higher incidence of steering away from predominantly white neighborhoods.[77] Perhaps more important, the overall findings from the 2000 HDS indicate that the housing searches of black and Hispanic households continue to be hampered by obstructive treatment on the part of realtors. Local investigators have found evidence of discrimination by brokers in New York City.[78]

One important consequence of such differences in the amount and type of information made available to different racial and ethnic groups is that the destinations chosen by relocating households will also differ by race/ethnicity, thereby perpetuating patterns of racial/ethnic segregation. This is particularly likely when steering occurs. A second consequence of these various constraints is that the optimal package of housing attributes *sought* by a given household may not be represented among the array of choices *known* to that household.[79]

A household that has not been able to find an alternative dwelling unit that is a better match to its needs or preferences than its current unit may, as a result, decide to postpone the move and stay in place. For example, blacks are far less likely than whites to undertake their expected moves, a differential attributed to the impact of structural constraints on blacks' housing choices.[80] Another possible decision for a household in this situation would be to settle for a new dwelling unit that represents a less-than-perfect match to its needs and preferences. In other words, a household may emerge from the search process "ill housed" because its housing choices were limited by external constraints operating in the housing market. A household in this situation may be ill housed in ways that have direct consequences for its immediate quality of life, as might happen if the household remains crowded as a result of the unavailability of more-spacious units. Equally, if not more, important, a household may emerge from the process ill housed in ways that have direct consequences for the long-term life chances of its members if, for example, the household is steered toward units located in crime-infested and otherwise underserved and underresourced neighborhoods. Thus, the interference of discriminatory treatment in the housing searches of minority home seekers clearly weakens the link between socioeconomic status and residential outcomes for these households.

The salience of race/ethnicity in structuring where households move has been demonstrated in analyses of "housing turnovers," or the process by which members of one racial/ethnic group move into units vacated by members of other groups. Studies focusing exclusively on whites and blacks have illustrated the social and physical distance that separates these groups in the relative rarity of racial housing exchange.[81] Using data on multiple racial/ethnic groups in New York City for the 1978–1987, 1991–1996, and 1991–1999 periods, Emily Rosenbaum and her colleagues[82] show that blacks are far less likely to replace whites than are Hispanics and Asians, even in the presence of a host of factors—including income and education—that theory suggests should influence destination choice. Moreover, the likelihood of different types of turnovers in New York City was significantly influenced by the racial/ethnic composition of the surrounding neighborhood in ways that suggest that these individual movements contribute to the persistence of segregation. For example, location in mixed and predominantly nonwhite areas increased the odds of white out-movement and of turnover to black and Hispanic, rather than white, occupancy, suggesting that these movements mutually reinforce one another to solidify the predominance of minorities in these areas. Similarly, location in predominantly white areas increased the odds that whites stayed in place, but it also increased the odds that other whites and Asians, but not blacks and Hispanics, moved in to replace those whites who did leave. Such results highlight the persistence of barriers disproportionately preventing black and Hispanic home seekers from acquiring homes in areas dominated by whites.[83]

In sum, there is a substantial amount of evidence indicating that black and Hispanic home seekers encounter structural barriers in their housing searches and that such constraints, as manifestations of the dual housing market more generally, contribute to racial/ethnic disparities in location and housing quality. But to what degree does immigrant status exacerbate or moderate the constraints on housing choices experienced by minority households?

Spatial Assimilation, Place Stratification, and the Potential for Segmented Assimilation

Assimilation theory has been the dominant model used by sociologists to explain the process of immigrant adaption in the United States. The classic or "canonical" model has its roots in the early twentieth-century writings of Robert Park and other members of the Chicago School of sociology, but it reflects the contributions of many other writers. Prominent among these was Milton Gordon, who, in his seminal work *Assimilation in American Life*, systematically disaggregated the broad assimilation process into seven distinct stages (cultural, structural, marital, identificational, attitude-receptional, behavior-receptional, and civic assimilation), thereby distinguishing between acculturation and those aspects of assimilation related more to social mobility and immigrants' access to the opportunity structure.[84]

Gordon's treatment, then, clarified that the process denoted by the term "assimilation" involves not only the gradual acquisition of the behaviors, habits, dress, and language of the host society (while simultaneously dropping those brought from the old country) but also upward social mobility and increasing access to the social and economic opportunities commanded by the "core" group (defined by Gordon as middle-class WASPs). Thus, assimilation is at once a story of different groups coming to share a common culture and language, as well as a story of how poor immigrants become socially and economically competitive in the American social system and progressively improve their social and economic standing. In essence, then, assimilation theory embodies the core ideology of the American dream.[85] However, unlike the American dream, which is ideally open to all,[86] the ultimate achievement of social and economic success is contingent on immigrants' becoming assimilated in a structural sense, which Gordon describes as being accepted into the social cliques maintained by the core group or engaging in primary relationships with members of the core. Once this happens, the other phases of assimilation occur in rapid succession, most notably attitude- and behavior-receptional, which describe the disappearance of any remaining vestiges of prejudice or discrimination against ethnic-group members.[87]

The classic version of this story is based on the experiences of the European immigrants arriving during the second half of the nineteenth century and the early years of the twentieth century, and it rests on several assumptions. Among these assumptions are the notion that the full process of assimilation is natural, that it is inevitable for most—if not all—ethnic groups, and that for its full completion, assimilation can take generations to occur.[88] This generational dynamic is fundamental to the notion of "straight-line assimilation," or the process by which each successive generation occupies a higher, or more advanced, stage of adjustment and a higher level of socioeconomic status.[89] This last assumption reveals the key notion in classical assimilation theory that "it raises an immigrant's social status to become American."[90]

Assimilation theory, therefore, describes the gradual acculturation and upward socioeconomic mobility of immigrant and ethnic groups over time and generations, with the ultimate outcome being the integration of the group into "mainstream" society. *Spatial assimilation theory* integrates these basic tenets of general assimilation theory with the observation that residential mobility follows from acculturation and socioeconomic mobility. As immigrant and ethnic groups gradually become integrated into mainstream society along the social and economic dimensions identified by assimilation theory, so too do they become integrated spatially, moving from a situation of physical distance from the core group to a situation of proximity to and even intermixture with that group. The spatial assimilation process, then, is the inverse of segregation.[91]

Spatial assimilation theory derives from the observation, rooted in the experiences of European immigrants in the nineteenth and early twentieth centuries, that immigrant or ethnic enclaves are located in older inner-city neighborhoods that have deteriorated over time as they have housed successive waves of new arrivals to the city. At an early stage of settlement in the city, new immigrants tend to be physically segregated from the native-born and to occupy low-quality, inexpensive housing located in rundown neighborhoods.[92] Such ethnic enclaves develop out of the processes that sustain migration streams, namely, social networks of family members, friends, and coethnics who share information about job and housing opportunities and provide assistance in the process of transition to life in the host society. Also important is the development and vitality of ethnic institutions and services, which help to strengthen ethnic identity and allow new arrivals to carry on daily life in their native tongues. Thus, collective processes help to build and sustain the ethnic neighborhood[93] and to foster the residential segregation of ethnic groups from the majority.

Working in opposition to these collective processes are the individual-level processes of acculturation and socioeconomic mobility. As ethnic-group members establish a stronger foothold in the mainstream economy—by acquiring higher levels of education, higher-status occupations, and higher incomes—they seek to translate these gains in socioeconomic status into residence in better locations.[94] These new neighborhoods are often more *socially* than *geographically* distant from the ethnic neighborhood. Moreover, just as the process of socioeconomic assimilation and mobility is theorized to occur over the generations, the accompanying process of residential mobility to better neighborhoods involves the same generational dynamic.

As a consequence of residential mobility following from socioeconomic mobility, these individual group members come into closer contact with members of the majority group—who are the dominant residents of the improved neighborhoods—and acquire the higher-quality housing and neighborhood conditions characteristic of higher-status neighborhoods. In so doing, upwardly mobile ethnic households ensure that the generational dynamic of additional assimilation will occur for their children. Moreover, as additional group members leave the ethnic neighborhood for improved residences elsewhere, the residential characteristics of the ethnic group and those of the majority group become increasingly similar, and the segregation between the groups declines.[95] An additional consequence of the dispersal of the ethnic group away from the ethnic neighborhood concerns the future composition of that area. That is, as vacancies open up, the units become available to other new arrivals to the city. Should these new arrivals belong to a different ethnic group, then the process of ethnic residential succession begins, with the eventual outcome that the old ethnic neighborhood acquires a new ethnic label.

The spatial assimilation model, then, relies on the tenets of traditional residential mobility theory to conceptualize the process of spatial mobility. Both models emphasize the role of individual-level attainments in spurring the decision to move (i.e., to leave the ethnic neighborhood) and the choice of where to move (in the case of spatial assimilation, the majority-dominated neighborhood that better matches the household's new position in the socioeconomic hierarchy). As a result, the spatial assimilation model suggests that, on the whole, immigrants should be disadvantaged, when compared to native-born households, in their housing and neighborhood characteristics. This relative disadvantage arises from the influence that immigrant status may have on the search for housing. In particular, knowledge of high-quality housing opportunities may be limited by a lack of familiarity with the broader housing market, particularly those neighborhoods that lie beyond the boundaries of the ethnic neighborhood. In addition, preferences for living among coethnics and near ethnic institutions may limit the housing searches of foreign-born households to inner-city ethnic neighborhoods, where the housing stock may be older and more deteriorated than that in other sections of the city. Finally, should they try to search for housing in the broader market, foreign-born households with distinct immigrant characteristics—such as limited English-language abilities—may encounter some form of discrimination by real-estate agents and landlords and thus may not learn of available high-quality housing opportunities.

However, while the spatial assimilation model would predict an overall disadvantage for foreign-born households on the basis of these kinds of limitations, it also predicts that these limitations will diminish over time and generation in the course of acculturation and social and economic mobility. Thus, the spatial assimilation theory posits two kinds of outcomes. First, that housing and neighborhood conditions enjoyed by the later generations of an ethnic group should be superior to those experienced by the newly arrived first generation. The second outcome posited by the spatial assimilation model parallels the argument that economic-status differences underlie patterns of segregation.[96] That is, when ethnic-group members are compared to native-born whites with the same levels of income and education and similar occupations, any observed housing and neighborhood disadvantages should disappear. In other words, socioeconomic status should mediate the effect of ethnicity as a predictor of residential outcomes.

The findings from numerous studies of a variety of residential outcomes among racial and ethnic groups have largely supported the main tenets of the spatial assimilation model. For example, residential outcomes, such as suburban location and the tract-level median income and proportion of whites, are found to be positively related to socioeconomic status for all groups and to acculturation-related variables such as years in the United States and English-language proficiency.[97]

Although spatial assimilation theory remains a useful tool to describe the locational attainment process among racial/ethnic groups in the United States, scholars agree that the model is less successful at describing the locational attainment process for certain groups, notably blacks, Puerto Ricans, and nonwhite Hispanics. The argument that socioeconomic status, and thus "free choice," should be the main predictor of residential outcomes is most clearly inadequate for African Americans, for whom levels of segregation from whites decline only modestly as socioeconomic status rises.[98] Furthermore, many studies of the locational attainment process among racial/ethnic groups have shown that even in the presence of statistical controls for the individual-level factors hypothesized to be at the root of group differences (e.g., income, education, life cycle), blacks, Puerto Ricans, and nonwhite Hispanics more generally still occupy lower-quality housing and neighborhoods than do comparable white households.[99] This weakness of the spatial assimilation model suggests that opportunities for converting social and economic achievements into improved residential circumstances are constrained by black race, precisely the outcome of housing-market discrimination discussed earlier. This conclusion is even more clearly arrived at when race (and in some cases ethnicity) is not conceived of as an individual-level attribute but as a macrolevel variable reflecting the operation of the racial hierarchy.[100] The significance of race is also evident in Gordon's argument that for full assimilation to occur, racial/ethnic groups must achieve full acceptance by the core group; the persistence of racial inequalities and tensions reveal that this has not occurred for those of black racial ancestry.

The importance of structural constraints in maintaining racial/ethnic inequality in residential outcomes has given rise to the second theoretical model, the *place stratification model*. This model begins with the recognition that individual-level factors are important predictors of residential outcomes, yet it expands this notion by incorporating the role of structural factors that interfere with the residential mobility process to more fully predict the housing and neighborhood outcomes experienced by blacks and nonwhite Hispanics and the persistent racial/ethnic inequalities in locational attributes. Specifically, the place stratification model recognizes the hierarchical ordering of places and social groups and maintains that minority groups' positions in the spatial hierarchy parallel their relative positions in society.[101] Households' access to the best positions in the hierarchy of place is not based purely on "free choice" (as spatial assimilation suggests) but is affected by the mechanisms that more-advantaged groups (such as whites) use to maintain social and spatial distance from their less-advantaged counterparts (e.g., minorities).[102] Among these mechanisms are discriminatory acts by individuals and financial institutions, including the adverse treatment of minority home seekers by realtors and landlords, the past use of racially restrictive covenants to prohibit minority in-movement, the opposition to minority in-movement staged by neighborhood associations, and the redlining of minority communities by financial institutions.[103] All these actions have helped to create and continue to maintain the dual housing market, which effectively constrains minority residential choices to areas that are more ethnically heterogeneous, less affluent, and of lower overall quality than those to which whites move.[104] Also included among the mechanisms that maintain the stratification of place are the actions of local governments, such as zoning decisions that prohibit the construction of multifamily housing or that maintain large lot sizes, as well as resistance to the placement of federally assisted housing within their jurisdictional boundaries. These kinds of actions operate to prevent the in-movement of low-income families and households.[105]

In conceptualizing spatial mobility, the place stratification model places emphasis on the varied ways that household race/ethnicity (when conceived of as a macrolevel variable)[106] can influence the housing-search process, specifically the choice of where to live. In particular, although recognizing that individual-level factors remain important predictors of locational outcomes, the place stratification model stresses that minority households encounter institutionalized obstacles in their housing searches that can limit their knowledge of the full range of available vacancies. These obstacles, such as the consistently adverse treatment of minority home seekers that was uncovered by the HDS,[107] end up channeling minority households away from predominantly white neighborhoods and those with abundant resources, thereby diluting their ability to translate their status improvements into residence in the kinds of housing and neighborhoods in which socioeconomically similar whites live. By emphasizing the importance of structural constraints on the housing choices of blacks and others of African ancestry, the place stratification model posits that even when individual-level characteristics relating to acculturation, socioeconomic status, and life-cycle stage are taken into account, significant disadvantages in spatial outcomes will remain—relative to native-born whites—for these groups.

The fact that black race remains a powerful predictor of location and access to place-based resources raises concerns about the opportunities for full integration faced by new immigrants who are phenotypically black. In fact, it is the persistence of racial stratification in general and its effect in concentrating certain new immigrants in disadvantaged inner-city neighborhoods that may give rise to the varied paths of incorporation posited by proponents of *segmented assimilation theory*.

Segmented assimilation theory arose out of criticisms that general assimilation theory would be inadequate to the task of describing the fate and experiences of the current wave of immigrants, who are more racially and socioeconomically diverse than were the "older" immigrants from Europe. One criticism focuses on the very different opportunity structures available to the older immigrants and to contemporary immigrants. In particular, the European immigrants arrived in industrializing cities with numerous job opportunities for those with few skills and little education. Although available jobs were generally low-paying and often unstable, workers could relocate and acquire new jobs relatively easily in the industrial economy. Opportunities to move up the occupational ladder also existed, especially for groups that had established particular occupational niches. Furthermore, the economic expansion that occurred after World War II also expanded opportunities for upward mobility, even for those with modest skills and education; of even greater importance, this period of expanding opportunities coincided with the coming of age of the second and third generations of earlier waves of European immigrants. In contrast, today's economy is shaped more like an hourglass, with many low-paying jobs requiring little education at the bottom, many high-paying job requiring advanced degrees at the top, and far fewer jobs in between. The dearth of middle-range jobs seriously impedes mobility upward from the lowest ranks.[108] These varying circumstances suggest that the generational dynamic described by the classical model may be historically specific to the period providing the observations that support the model.

Some scholars, however, argue that segmented assimilation theory's conceptualization of the consequences of economic restructuring for contemporary immigrants is incomplete, at best, and perhaps misguided, at worst.[109] For one, these critics argue that the theory overstresses the demand side of the economic-restructuring argument, while giving little, if any, attention to the rising supply of low-skilled labor resulting from immigration. This aspect of the theory also ignores the socioeconomic

diversity of contemporary immigrants and, especially, the sizable numbers of immigrant families that arrive with sufficient levels of human
capital to enable their direct entry into the middle class. The job prospects these "human capital" immigrants face are not limited to those at
the bottom of the job queue, and thus they are generally spared the
worst aftereffects of economic restructuring. Moreover, if their children
experience "second-generation decline,"[110] they will still likely remain
in positions of relative advantage.[111] A bifurcated job market is clearly a
problem for low-skilled immigrants, most notably Mexicans,[112] but
working-class immigrants are not the only group affected. Any risks
entailed by economic bifurcation are to be felt by all working-class families, regardless of their nativity status.[113]

A second criticism leveled at general assimilation theory is that, by
having been modeled on the experiences of immigrants who were largely white (or whose race would eventually "whiten") it may not be entirely applicable to the experiences of contemporary immigrants, many
of whom are not white in appearance. Segmented assimilation theory
argues that contemporary immigrants enter a society that is characterized not by one undiversified culture but by a variety of subcultures and
opportunity structures, organized largely by race and ethnicity.[114] As a
consequence, contemporary immigrants and their descendants may follow various paths of adaptation to life in the United States—as opposed
to the straight-line path associated with the experiences of the earlier
European immigrants—with the particular path depending on the segment of American society in which they are received.[115] For the second
generation, some of these paths lead to improvements in social and economic attainments relative to the attainments of the immigrant generation,[116] while others lead to losses or stasis. Race/ethnicity is one of the
key determinants that influence the direction of a particular group's
path, as it influences the segment of American society within which the
immigrant group is received.[117] Immigrants of African ancestry, then,
face the very real prospect of being incorporated not simply as Americans but as black Americans[118] and thus finding themselves near or at
the bottom of the racial hierarchy.[119] For such groups, it may be more
beneficial to retain a strong immigrant or ethnic identity and to remain
within the ethnic community for access to social networks and protection from the discrimination aimed at native minorities.[120] Thus, the
basic tenets of segmented assimilation suggest that for some immigrant

groups, the persistence of racial stratification means that the Americanization process no longer involves upward mobility, but instead may entail a significant degree of downward mobility.[121]

According to proponents of segmented assimilation theory, one of the key determinants of assimilation outcomes for members of the current second generation is the location in which immigrants settle. That is, the concentration of some immigrant groups in inner cities exposes their members to the "urban underclass," whose very existence and behaviors are the legacy of past discrimination and blocked opportunities.[122] In general, exposure to the underclass—especially when combined with constant exposure to prejudice and discrimination—increases the chance of adopting its "adversarial stance" to middle-class culture, which in turn has the potential of thwarting the upward progress of immigrant children. Implied here is that the prospects for success will vary depending on the social groups with whom immigrant children come into contact and thus on the neighborhood context in which immigrant children find themselves. Moreover, the immigrant groups at greatest risk of exposure to the underclass are those that share with native-born minorities the experience of discrimination on the basis of race/ethnicity, namely, those of African and Hispanic ancestry.[123] Thus, implicit within segmented assimilation theory is the notion that structural constraints on the housing choices of immigrant households of African and Hispanic ancestry may limit them to residence in disadvantaged neighborhoods and will thus operate to impede their children's chances for social and economic success.

The emphasis on exposure to the underclass and the adoption of its potentially harmful behaviors has elicited criticism. Some scholars argue that the focus on underclass culture exaggerates the size and significance of this segment of the urban population, ignoring the presence and potential influence of the many black and Latino families in impoverished urban neighborhoods who exhibit mainstream behaviors such as marriage, high-school graduation, and engagement in productive economic activity.[124] In addition, the focus on the underclass overlooks the influence of black middle-class culture, which "provides strategies for economic mobility in the context of discrimination and group disadvantage and [responses to] distinctive problems that usually accompany minority middle-class status."[125] Similarly, others point to the potential role of minority institutions and organizations in fostering the upward mobility and positive adaptation of nonwhite immigrants.[126] In short, assimilation into minority America does not have to inevitably lead to downward mobility.[127]

However, most if not all of those scholars who take segmented assimilation to task agree that some groups may in fact be vulnerable to the risk of downward mobility. This risk is strongly associated with the skills immigrants bring with them (i.e., whether they are labor migrants or human-capital migrants), the context of their reception in the United States, residence in disadvantaged inner-city neighborhoods, proximity to and identification with native minorities, insufficient or nonexistent ethnic niches, and dark complexions. More specifically, most agree that Afro-Caribbean and African immigrants, along with Puerto Ricans, Dominicans, and Mexicans, are most likely to encounter serious obstacles to their incorporation into American society. A number of studies suggest that these concerns are well-founded. For example, foreign-born Mexican women and island-born Puerto Rican women have superior birth outcomes (lower rates of infant mortality and low birth weight) relative to their U.S.- and mainland-born counterparts.[128] For island-born Puerto Rican women, the likelihood of infant mortality increases with time since arrival on the mainland, suggesting that the positive qualities that encourage infant survival among newcomers erode in the face of increasing exposure to life on the mainland.[129] In addition, living in a single-parent-headed household, and the associated risks of poverty, increase in prevalence across generations for certain groups of Latino children, notably Dominicans.[130] There is also evidence of significant deficits in high-school enrollment for island-born Puerto Rican and foreign-born Dominican and Mexican youths[131] and of downward mobility among Puerto Rican young adults in New York City.[132] In addition, Latino youths in South Florida and Southern California face significantly higher risks of academic failure and psychological distress than do other second-generation adolescents.[133] Finally, second-generation West Indian youths who have adopted an American or racial identity are at an elevated risk of experiencing educational and occupational failure.[134]

Although the accumulation of such findings suggests concern for the adjustment of second- and possibly later-generation Mexicans, Dominicans, Puerto Ricans, and some Afro-Caribbeans, other studies argue that "most pessimistic readings of second generation decline lack warrant."[135] Such studies indicate improved educational and occupational outcomes among second- versus first-generation young adults,[136] second-generation young adults versus their parents,[137] and second-generation young adults versus first-generation members of the age cohort likely to have contained their parents.[138] Notably, studies in this group also find that the progress achieved by the second generation varies across race/ethnicity, with Puerto Ricans, Dominicans, and Mexicans typically exhibiting the smallest intergenerational gains, whites and Asians the largest, and those of blacks and other Hispanics falling in between these extremes.

Studies of this sort also often find that although the second generation posts superior achievements relative to the first generation, its outcomes also tend to exceed those of the third generation.[139] This pattern has been most consistently documented for Mexicans, the "new" immigrant group with the longest history in the United States (and thus the most generational diversity).[140] The extraordinary accomplishments of the second generation have been interpreted as evidence of "immigrant optimism,"[141] or of the second generation's inheriting or responding to the optimism that their foreign-born parents hold with respect to the opportunities they see in the American educational and occupational system (relative to those in their home countries). However, declines in achievement by the third and later generations suggest that this optimism withers as immigrants' descendants confront the reality of structural constraints to opportunity.[142] Thus, the relative gains made by the second generation may not refute the hypothesis of generational decline proposed by segmented assimilation theory but instead may be a variant of the general pattern (just as the "bumpy line" pattern was to the "straight line" pattern of assimilation).

Thus, there is, to date, little consensus concerning generational patterns in outcomes but a general level of agreement that some groups appear to fare less well than others. What has hampered the development of this line of research is the varied approaches to testing segmented assimilation theory. Many studies have focused on racial/ethnic differences in the second generation;[143] others have examined generational patterns in pooled samples of adolescents[144] or young adults;[145] and while still others have focused on comparisons of two generations—immigrants and the native-born—within racial/ethnic groups.[146] Fundamental to segmented assimilation theory is the hypothesis that generational patterns over the long term (i.e., more than two generations) will diverge across race/ethnicity, spiraling downward for some groups, staying even for others, and improving for still others. Such a hypothesis requires a research design that compares more than two generations for separate racial/ethnic or national-origin groups.[147] Unfortunately, the data necessary for such tests are generally unavailable. Yet our unique data set enables us to perform exactly this kind of analysis, using housing and neighborhood conditions as the criteria measuring incorporation.[148]

Given the social and economic significance of housing as we demonstrated at the outset of this chapter, our use of these outcomes is consistent with the theory's emphasis on social and economic attainments.[149] Moreover, by focusing on outcomes that are partially a result of the kinds of attainments typically examined in studies of the adolescent and young-adult members of the second generation (i.e., educational attainment and employment), we refocus attention on the structural determinants of opportunity and move away from explanations that rely on the adoption of a pathological culture. That is, although some members of the second generation may have less success in the areas of education and employment as a result of adopting an oppositional stance to such behaviors, we incorporate education as a predictor of housing and neighborhood outcomes, thereby eliminating variation on this status attainment (and its presumed causes) as an explanation of patterns that vary across generations. Instead, the patterns we uncover better reflect the variation in opportunities afforded to different generational groups, rather than the tendency for some youths to reject specific paths to upward mobility.

To successfully apply segmented assimilation theory to residential attainments requires adapting it to conceptualize how the process of spatial mobility may vary for different generations of immigrant groups. One of the key aspects of segmented assimilation theory is its contention that immigrant groups that are phenotypcially black face the prospect of incorporation not into American society at large but specifically into black America,[150] and they thus find themselves at the bottom of society's racial hierarchy.[151] The prospect of this fate is not lost on Afro-Caribbean immigrants, the largest group of immigrants of African ancestry to be studied to date, who see becoming American in this way as entailing a significant loss of status as well as an increasing degree of exposure to interpersonal and institutional racism and the attendant restriction of opportunity.[152]

Many Afro-Caribbean immigrants recognize that they receive preferential treatment from whites, relative to the treatment received by

American-born blacks, and this better treatment affords them opportunities for jobs, promotions, and housing that are unavailable to American blacks.[153] The key to receiving such treatment, and thereby accessing better opportunities, lies in demarcating themselves from American
blacks.[154] Although active distancing from blacks was also a strategy
used by earlier waves of European immigrants (although it involved far
more enmity),[155] the dilemma faced by Afro-Caribbeans and other immigrants of African ancestry is that they must try to do so within a society that refuses to recognize the possibility of ethnic variation among
blacks as easily as it does for whites and that associates black skin with
a variety of negative traits and behaviors.[156] To differentiate themselves
from black Americans, many Afro-Caribbeans telegraph their ethnicity
through their retention and use of accents and the use of other obvious
cues of their foreign origins. Thus, for immigrants of African ancestry,
remaining tied to and closely identified with their ethnic origins engenders socioeconomic opportunities and benefits, turning the association
of Americanization with improved status on its head.[157]

However, although markers of ethnicity are easily available to members of the immigrant generation, their children and their children's children do not have the same kind of easy access to such indicators of ethnic origin.[158] Instead, the second and later generations must consciously
and overtly adopt ways to distinguish themselves as being of Caribbean
heritage, in order to gain access to the same kinds of opportunities that
came the foreign-born generation's way and to avoid the stronger forms
of discrimination experienced by American blacks. For example, Mary
Waters describes how a young woman carried a key chain emblazoned
with the flag of Guyana, the country from which her parents immigrated. By exhibiting it conspicuously, she was able to draw attention to
her ethnicity, instigate discussion of it, and thus gain access to opportunities that were more typically denied to those viewed as being "simply"
black.[159] Thus, as generation rises, the strength and viability of ethnic
markers weakens, a fundamental relationship articulated by both classical and segmented assimilation theories. Yet because of their black
race, as ethnic markers dissipate, descendants of Afro-Caribbean immigrants become increasingly indistinguishable from American blacks in
the eyes of whites and thus increasingly become exposed to structural
impediments to opportunity. With respect to housing, the persistence
of structural barriers results in a steady narrowing of housing options
as generation rises. Thus, the way that segmented assimilation theory

conceptualizes how the process of spatial mobility varies by generation is that, among racially stigmatized groups, the foreign-born generation should experience the fewest restrictions on their housing options, with each succeeding generation experiencing progressively greater limitations on their choices of where to live. As a result, we should see a steady pattern of declining housing and neighborhood outcomes as generation rises among blacks and black Hispanics.

Conclusion

In summary, spatial assimilation views spatial mobility as the outcome of free choice on the part of the individual, or the simple acquisition of residential location on the basis of socioeconomic attainments. As a result, spatial assimilation theory suggests that we will find that immigrant households will live in lower-quality housing and neighborhood environments and that their conditions should improve as generation rises. However, the theory also suggests that once we statistically account for the kinds of social, economic, and acculturation-related variables that are theorized to account for generational and racial/ethnic differences, these differences should disappear or diminish in size and strength.

In contrast, place stratification theory recognizes that institutional forms of discrimination interfere in the housing-search process for home seekers who are phenotypically black, differentially limiting the housing choices of these groups to options that are less desirable and of lower overall quality than those made available to white home seekers. Consequently, place stratification suggests different hypotheses. Specifically, this theory suggests that when households of similar socioeconomic status are compared, racial/ethnic differences in housing and neighborhood outcomes will persist, with blacks and Latinos (especially nonwhite Latinos) less likely than comparable whites and Asians to live in high-quality housing and neighborhoods.

The persistence of housing-market barriers gives rise to the potential for the kinds of varied patterns of incorporation suggested by segmented assimilation theory. Yet as we envision it, the perverse effect of racial stratification on the incorporation prospects of black immigrants suggests that for this group (and for black Latinos) housing-market barriers may be more permeable for foreign-born households, given their greater acceptability over black Americans in the eyes of society. As a result, in their pursuit of the American dream, immigrants of African ancestry must maintain and broadcast a decidedly un-American identity, since becoming identified as a black American entails being denied full access to all the trappings of success. Thus, housing and neighborhood conditions for blacks and black Latinos should deteriorate across the generations, while for other groups we should see a pattern of improving outcomes as generation rises, as predicted by spatial assimilation (and general assimilation) theory.

2

Immigration, Race/Ethnicity, and Housing in New York through 1970

Throughout the nation's history, New York City has always been a destination of choice for immigrants and migrants alike. During the nineteenth century, the city's phenomenal growth—both physically and economically—drew millions with its promise of a better life than that possible at home. In the early years of the century, when the city's neighborhoods were clustered at the most southern tip of Manhattan and undifferentiated as to their use, poor newcomers may have lived in smaller or dirtier residences than their bosses, but everyone lived in the same areas, nearby their places of work. As industrialization created new social and economic classes, building speculators began "cashing in" on the tastes of newly emergent middle- and upper-class families for larger and sturdier homes in neighborhoods far from the bustling and increasingly unhealthy lower wards by developing land for residential use farther uptown. These "pro-growth" actions of speculators were aided by the implementation of the "grid plan," which increased the marketability and profitability of the undeveloped portions of Manhattan. Meanwhile, landlords of buildings left behind by uptown-moving families carved up the space in their buildings to rent out to working-class individuals and families and often refused to add such new "urban amenities" as sewer connections, enabling them to maximize the profit-making potential of their investments. The cooperation of city officials, active speculators, and profit-seeking landlords represents an early example of the type of pro-growth coalition that is fundamental to the "urban growth machine,"[1] and it served to more clearly distinguish the housing and neighborhood amenities available to the different social classes.

For immigrants from Europe, the low-quality housing conditions they encountered upon arrival tended to be temporary and a function of their ability to pay for housing. As described by spatial assimilation theory, as time passed and immigrants and their descendants improved their socioeconomic standing, they were able to leave these conditions behind and move to better housing located in better neighborhoods. These new neighborhoods were sometimes in Manhattan, but were also increasingly in areas in Brooklyn, Queens, and the Bronx. Although the precise amount of time and the size of the quality gains may have varied across the European groups, by the mid-twentieth century they were all firmly integrated—socially, economically, and spatially—in American society.

The story for black immigrants and migrants and for Puerto Rican migrants, however, was different. Although the residential location of the members of the city's small black community in the early decades of the nineteenth century was determined largely by their lack of financial resources—as they were for all the city's residents—opportunities for spatial assimilation in the later years of the century were denied by hardening white attitudes toward integrated living and were obliterated by direct governmental intervention in housing during the early and mid-twentieth century. Whites began to flee neighborhoods where blacks—regardless of their socioeconomic status—began to arrive, creating large expanses where black residents rarely saw faces that were not also black. These areas grew denser as pro-growth forces determined that redevelopment for public use (as in the case of Penn Station) and "urban renewal" would displace poor, minority residents, leaving them few options other than to move deeper into the ghetto. As a result, black-white segregation rose precipitously from the turn of the century to 1970, and overcrowding (resulting at least partially from subdivision of existing housing units to meet rising demand for housing stemming from in-migration and constricted opportunities) and limited financing because of redlining caused both housing and neighborhood deterioration. The historical record of blacks' experiences in New York City underscores the extreme vulnerability of politically and economically weak neighborhoods and populations to the forces of the urban growth machine, and the events and processes that gave rise to the dual housing market, and that record thus serves as a paradigm for the development of place stratification theory.

In this chapter we describe the interrelated histories of immigration, race, and housing in New York, up until approximately 1970. The story we tell not only provides the historical backdrop for the analyses that follow but also animates the main propositions of spatial assimilation and place stratification theories. The choice of 1970 as an ending point is natural given that that year is largely recognized as the start of the contemporary era of immigration to the United States. This view derives from the passage in 1965 of the Hart-Celler Act, which repealed the national-origins quotas that had been in place since the 1920s. As a result, the origins of immigrants to the country and especially to New York shifted dramatically from those based primarily in European nations to a wide variety of nations in Latin America, Asia, and the Caribbean. Moreover, by 1970, the descendants of the European immigrants who arrived during the nineteenth and early twentieth centuries had become firmly incorporated within American society.

New York at the Start of the Nineteenth Century, 1790–1840

According to the first national decennial census in 1790, the city of New York (which consisted, at the time, only of the island of Manhattan) had a population of just over 33,000, the vast majority of whom (just over 89.5 percent) were white. Of the city's black population of just under 3,500, more than two-thirds were slaves.[2] Fifty years earlier, the city's black population had been smaller, but its share of the total population had been larger (21 percent in 1746 versus less than 12 percent in 1790). As the economy grew in the decade following the first census, the number of both slaves and free blacks rose dramatically. The slave population grew between 1790 and 1800 as the number of white households with slaves more than tripled.[3] The factors contributing to the growth in the free black population included in-migration from other areas within the United States as well as the arrival of (voluntary) immigrants from the West Indies, particularly Haiti.[4] By 1800, over half of the city's blacks were free. Over the next decade, the number of slaves declined, as the effects of the 1799 gradual-emancipation law began to take effect. By 1810, fully 84 percent of the city's blacks were free,[5] and by 1830 no slaves were present in the city.[6] However, as a percentage of the total population, the black population was declining, as white migrants, both native and foreign, arrived in large numbers.

The white population in 1790 comprised a mix of nationalities. The majority were of English background, but there was a sizable Dutch contingent, estimated at approximately one-sixth of the total white population.[7] The English population element aligned New York's ethnic composition with that of the nation more than at any other period in its history, but the Dutch element was a distinctive feature of the city, resulting from the city's founding by the Dutch West India Company. Other prominent white ethnic groups at this time included two that would dominate the immigration streams arriving during the first half of the nineteenth century: the Irish[8] and Germans. Members of both groups began arriving early in the eighteenth century.[9] The city's German population in 1790 may have been as high as 2,500 (about 7 percent of all whites); the Irish population may have numbered 5,000 (14 percent of all whites).[10]

At the start of the nineteenth century, the built-up portion of the city occupied about 1.5 square miles, extending as far north as Canal Street. Like "walking cities" elsewhere, a number of spatial features characterized New York, including a mixture of land-use functions. Apart from warehousing along the waterfront, no neighborhoods were devoted exclusively to either residential or commercial uses. Instead, artisans' shops, public buildings, homes, and taverns were interspersed throughout the city. High levels of congestion characterized New York and other walking cities. The density level in New York in 1800—40,326 persons per square mile—exceeds the current level, with the greatest crowding in 1800 occurring in the southeastern wards, particularly the Third Ward, by the East River.[11]

Another feature of New York's landscape that was common to other walking cities was the tendency for the "best" addresses—that is, those for the most respectable and fashionable families—to be located close to the town's center. Prior to the American Revolution, New York's wealthiest residents lived on lanes at the southeastern tip of the island in order to be near their shipping businesses. After the Revolution, such families were more likely to be found near Columbia College, along Chambers, Warren, and Murray Streets, west of Broadway, yet still within walking distance of their places of business. Some prosperous families also owned estates north of the settled portion of the city, to which they fled in the summer and in times of disease outbreaks.[12] Despite the identification and recognition of fashionable addresses, class segregation was not a key feature of the walking city, poor residents often living in closer proximity to the wealthy than is common today.

Housing during the period consisted largely of wooden structures, making fire a constant danger. Those who could afford to often lived in more substantially built houses made of brick or stone. Such "urban amenities" as plumbing and sewers would not be available until mid-century, making it necessary for households to fetch water from nearby wells and to rely for their sanitary needs within the house on bedpans and chamber pots, which were emptied into wooden privies located in the backyards. Because of the lack of municipal services—such as sanitation, police, fire protection, and especially clean water—the city was filthy, its streets cluttered with piles of household debris, the refuse of slaughterhouses, distilleries, and other businesses, as well as the waste of horses, pigs, and people.

The social and economic relations of the preindustrial economy located home and work within the same house, the labor required for both being provided by household members.[13] Households consisted not only of family members but also of apprentices, boarders, servants, and slaves. At the heart of this system was the institution of *proprietorship;* skilled craftsmen had to possess a physical structure—a house and adjoining yard—in which to conduct their trade.[14] During the last decade of the eighteenth century, the generations-old "household dependencies [that] had bound labor to property"[15] began to give way. New York's superb harbor and command over a strong and growing regional market, war in Europe, and the increasing dependence of the West Indian plantation economies on American goods spurred the city's economic growth to surpass Philadelphia as the nation's leading port. The supremacy of New York as a shipping center was further solidified with the opening of the Erie Canal in 1825, which made New York the entrepôt for vast new hinterlands. With the expansion of shipping came changes in the city's commercial life. Merchant capitalism expanded in scale and complexity, giving rise to a variety of new occupations and methods of commerce. Wholesale merchants emerged and the numbers of clerks and bookkeepers multiplied, while retail establishments began selling products that traditionally had been sold directly off of ships. Meanwhile, manufacturing began to rise in significance. Major industries included shipbuilding and sugar refining, but the bulk of manufacturing in the city involved small firms, such as printing, shoemaking, and tailoring establishments.

Economic growth was fueled by population growth. Between 1790 and 1820 the population of Manhattan more than tripled, growing from just over 33,000 to just over 123,000. The source of this growth was in-migration from rural areas within New York State, from New England, and from farther afield.[16] Before 1820 the heavy flows of immigrants dwarfed foreign immigration. After that date, however, immigration from Europe quickened. Rosenwaike notes that while "only 8,000 immigrants were reported to have arrived in the United States in the fiscal year ending September 30, 1820, the first year for which statistics were published by the Department of State . . . by 1860 some four million . . . had reached American shores."[17] He estimates that about 20 percent of the city's population was foreign-born in 1820; this proportion would rise and peak in 1855 at just over 51 percent.

Population growth was accompanied by the northward expansion of the city. In 1811, the city's northernmost boundary lay at approximately Houston Street. In that year, the city commissioners approved the "grid plan" to govern the city's growth. This called for twelve numbered avenues, each about 100 feet in width. The avenues were to run north from the edge of town and to be crossed every 200 feet at right angles by numbered streets approximately 50 or 60 feet in width. Every half mile or so the cross street would be wider, reaching approximately 100 feet in width. Each of the blocks formed by the intersections of avenues and streets would be further subdivided into lots of a standardized size, typically 25 feet wide by 100 feet deep. By creating lots that were easily located in reference to a numbered street and avenue, the grid plan greatly facilitated their development. In fact, increasing the land's marketability and development potential was the underlying rationale of the grid plan, and the plan marked the rise of the "urban growth machine"[18] in New York. Concomitantly, by about 1825 the northernmost boundary of the city's built-up portion had reached about Fourteenth Street, and as far north as Twenty-third Street fifteen years later.[19]

The movement uptown was not shared by all, but involved mainly those households that could afford to separate work from home, to build or buy new single-family houses, and to pay for the commute downtown on the emerging modes of public transportation.[20] Such households were no longer members of the landed gentry; economic growth and diversification after the Revolutionary War gave rise to a variety of new classes of New Yorkers, differentiated as much by their occupations as by their housing. For one, the "shift from shop to factory, from small to large scale manufacturing" clearly evident by the late 1820s gave rise to new classes of business owners and wealthy merchants who increasingly found the waterfront streets of the lower wards unsuitable for living.[21] Many factors contributed to this view, including the frequency of pestilential diseases (yellow fever, small pox, typhoid, and cholera), the rising pace of business and commerce, the proliferation of warehouses and artisanal workshops, and the growing numbers of impoverished immigrants. Households in this new affluent class sought to separate themselves from these problems of urban living by relocating to new single-family houses in new uncongested areas organized solely as residential.

By transforming the nature of master-worker relations and weakening the connection of labor to property, industrialization created a second new class of New Yorkers: tenants. This class, constrained in their choice of residences by the cost of commuting, remained in lower Manhattan within walking distance of their places of work. Finally, there emerged a new class of building speculators, who saw manifold opportunities for profit in the spectacular rise in Manhattan land values[22] and the need to house the growing population. In the 1830s, investments in speculative building rivaled investments in the more traditional areas of shipbuilding and other manufacturing.

The main focus of speculative builders was the commercial area in the lowest portion of the island. There, streets were widened and former residences were converted to commercial use or demolished and replaced by warehouses and other buildings serving the needs of the rapidly expanding mercantile and financial communities. Commercial building was especially rapid in the years after 1835, when a disastrous fire demolished over six hundred buildings, practically wiping out all the structures below Wall Street.

Yet speculative builders were also interested in residential construction uptown for the affluent classes seeking to distance themselves from the increasingly congested and commercial lower wards. As a result, areas that had once been remote were developed as residential areas and settled. In 1820, the "best" addresses were three-story brick row houses on the lower west side of Broadway, stretching from Bowling Green to Chambers Street, and on the side streets connecting Broadway with Greenwich Street to the west. From these locations, gentlemen could still walk to their places of business in the commercial and financial districts. Yet as commerce expanded northward along Broadway, and various nuisances infiltrated in from nearby poorer areas, this area began to lose its appeal as a genteel neighborhood. As a result, more and more well-to-do families began moving uptown in search of new areas more befitting their status.

The northward march of the city also overran areas that had been home to the city's poorest residents, including many of the city's African Americans. For example, a number of black settlements lay on the periphery of the city's settled areas, on both the east and the west sides, primarily along the water.[23] But as the city expanded northward, these black settlements had to move as well, typically continuing northward ahead of development.

The northward expansion and development of "elite" and "genteel" residential neighborhoods increased in the 1830s. One destination for the genteel was an area bounded by Hudson, Varick, Erickson, and Laight Streets; Bond Street and Bleecker Street were especially fashionable addresses. The single-family houses constructed in these new neighborhoods were substantially built three- or four-story brick structures, much more spacious than those the owners had left behind. Moreover, these houses were increasingly equipped with new "urban amenities" such as gas lighting (after 1823), Croton water (after 1842), and sewer connections (after 1849). The style and furnishing of these new houses were key to the creation, maintenance, and display of middle-class status and identity.[24]

Perhaps more important than the design and quality of these new residences as outward signs of enhanced status was the distance separating the middle and upper classes from the working and laboring classes. Indeed, concomitant with the rising levels of class differentiation during the industrial period was the expression of this differentiation across space,[25] with neighborhoods assuming not simply different patterns of land use (e.g., commercial versus residential) but also social meaning. The notion that the "right" address could solidify a family's class standing was increasingly recognized and adhered to. A neighborhood appropriate for genteel residence was to be "respectable"—that is, organized around private residential use—as well as "healthy." The health of a neighborhood, or more specifically the ability of the neighborhood to promote the health of family members, was a concept created and reinforced by the greater toll that epidemics always took in poorer neighborhoods.[26] Thus, a healthy and respectable neighborhood was by definition one located at a great distance from the wharves and the poorer residents of the city.

The houses that the more affluent left behind in the lower wards largely experienced one of three fates. One was conversion to commercial use, as indicated earlier. Land values in the lower wards were quite high, and property owners could profit more from its commercial rather than residential use.[27] As a consequence, the lower wards, particularly those below City Hall, became increasingly dominated by business and commercial use, while retaining only a small resident population. The fact that only two persons died in the great fire of 1835 vividly illustrates how the lower tip of the island had become basically devoid of residents.

The second fate experienced by the houses left behind by the uptown-moving wealthy was transformation into boarding houses, which increasingly served the housing needs of single male workers but were also occupied at times by working-class families. The third fate was subdivision into apartments, with the result that two, three, or even more in-moving households would replace the single out-moving household.[28] Subdivision was partly a response to the need for working-class housing, since housing construction—particularly the construction of working-class housing—could not keep pace with population growth. Although a few speculators built working-class housing, most concentrated their investments in the residential market for middle- and upper-class households. Subdivision was also a response to the landlords' recognition that the working class was essentially a captive market. Unable to afford housing outside the older lower wards, working-class households had no choice but to remain near their places of work. Among such working-class strongholds were Corlear's Hook, which was home to those who worked in shipping, and Five Points, where a variety of trades could be found, including breweries, tailoring, shoemaking, and printing.

Because of the age of these "barracks-style" structures, and the fact that many had been insubstantially constructed in the first place, the condition of housing in the lower wards was far worse than that in the more prosperous neighborhoods uptown. Exacerbating the structural problems was the overcrowding produced by extensive subdivision as well as by the need of working-class households to take in boarders and lodgers to help pay the rent. Although the actual range of housing conditions varied from decent (though crowded) to positively horrid, the worst of the slum conditions attracted the most attention at the time. Overcrowding, moreover, exacerbated what were already serious sanitation problems, as outdoor privies were overwhelmed by growing numbers of users. Regarding the conditions in Five Points, "a Health Department report noted that the commodes 'were in a most filthy and disgusting condition; in several places there were accumulations of stagnant fluid, full of all sorts of putrifying matter, the effluvia from which was intolerable.' "[29] Landlords had little incentive to make substantial improvements, such as connecting their properties to the Croton water supply and to the sewers, especially when it was clear that they could not pass on the cost of such improvements to their tenants in the form of higher rents. As landlords let their properties deteriorate, their tax assessments declined, netting them even greater profits. By minimizing costs (improvements and taxes) and maximizing revenues (rents), landlords and other housing-market actors reaped substantial profits.[30] For the working-class and laborer residents, however, housing conditions—the quality of the structure, presence of amenities, and crowding—were bad and destined to grow worse.

The group that experienced by far the worst of the city's housing was African Americans. Although New York was not a place where African Americans could live wherever they chose, the primary reason for their concentration in the city's poorest areas and lowest-quality housing was their poverty. Discrimination and prejudice generally restricted African Americans to the lowest-paying unskilled jobs, providing the typical black New Yorker with few means to pay for housing. Indeed, the importance of income as a predictor of blacks' residential choices is evidenced by the fact that the city did not have the kind of distinct racial ghettos that are familiar today. Instead, poor blacks lived interspersed with poor whites, often sharing the same blocks if not the same houses.[31]

In the early decades of the nineteenth century, a significant black settlement existed in Five Points. Named for the five-cornered intersection of Anthony, Orange, and Cross Streets, and located where today's Chinatown sits, Five Points was the city's first notorious slum, serving as home to some of the city's poorest residents. Like other poor areas, Five Points was ethnically diverse, housing poor immigrants from Ireland, Italy, and Germany, along with African Americans. By the 1830s, the black population of Five Points began to decline, as many African Americans relocated west and north into Greenwich Village, settling largely on Bleecker, Sullivan, Thompson, McDougal, and Carmine Streets. Two factors speeded the African American departure from Five Points. First, as immigration from Ireland increased after 1830, the scores of poor and destitute new arrivals began competing with

African-Americans for housing in Five Points; by 1860 the Five Points area was predominantly Irish.[32] Perhaps a more significant factor was the racial tension and violence in the area, most clearly illustrated in the 1834 anti-abolition race riot there. With the destruction of many blacks' homes and institutions and the wounding of several black area residents, "the riot left the Five Points African American community devastated, both physically and emotionally."[33] Afraid for their lives and their homes, many black Five Pointers abandoned the area, hoping for greater safety and peace uptown.

Thus, in the opening decades of the nineteenth century, the emergent industrial economy spawned a number of important interrelated social, economic, and spatial changes. Primary among these changes was the increasing class differentiation, by various forms of consumption but especially housing. Related to rising residential spatial segregation was the growing class stratification in housing type, density, and conditions, the upper classes residing in well-built single-family houses they owned, while the working class paid rent to occupy aging boarding houses and multiple-family dwellings in deteriorating condition. These class differences were partly the result of basic differences in the ability to pay for higher-quality housing, but another contributing factor was the filtering down, to those of lesser means, of the aging housing stock, whose deterioration was hastened by the crowding required by inadequate incomes and encouraged by profit-seeking landlords and landowners.

1840s–1880s

Between 1840 and 1880, the population of New York City more than tripled in size, growing from almost 313,000 to just over 1,200,000. While migrants from other states continued to arrive seeking opportunities in the expanding city, their contribution to the city's growth was dwarfed by the immigration from abroad. The arrival of hundreds of thousands of unskilled and semiskilled young adult immigrants dramatically transformed working-class life and culture.[34] As the working class became increasingly dominated by immigrants, growing class divisions began to overlap with growing nativity-status divisions. As a result, immigrants, because of their poverty and alien ways, became the objects of growing reform movements, especially in the realm of housing.

A second dramatic impact of immigration was its effect on the racial/

ethnic composition of the city's population. This impact of immigration is most clearly seen when we compare the changes in the white and black subpopulations between 1840 and 1880. Numbering 296,352 in 1840, the city's whites expanded fourfold over the period—a growth outpacing that for the city's population as a whole—reaching 1,185,843 at the time of the 1880 census. In contrast, the city's black population grew only 20 percent over the period, from 16,358 in 1840 to 19,663 in 1880. Rosenwaike argues that the growth of the city's black population had to derive from migration, given the very high mortality experienced by this group. The very different rates of growth between blacks and whites during the period resulted in a steep drop in the share of the city's population that consisted of blacks, from 5 to only 1.6 percent.[35] Similar population movements were occurring in neighboring Brooklyn, where blacks came to constitute only 2 percent of the population in 1860, after making up 27 percent sixty years earlier.[36]

Not only did the hundreds of thousands of immigrants arriving during the period overwhelm the city's black population numerically, but their general lack of skills and capital meant that they also competed directly with blacks for jobs and housing. In general, the greater numbers of white immigrants and stronger preferences for white than black workers fueled large-scale racial turnover in many of the unskilled occupations in which African Americans had previously concentrated (such as barbers and domestic workers), seriously diminishing blacks' employment opportunities and all but devastating the economic viability of the African American community.[37] In the realm of housing, because there were no large and contiguous racial ghettos during this period, the shared experience of poverty meant that white and black laborers basically lived in the same neighborhoods and sometimes shared the same tenements. Yet while white immigrants—particularly the Irish—lived interspersed among African Americans, racial tensions ran high, sometimes exploding in violence; the potential volatility of race relations was most clearly demonstrated by the 1863 Draft Riots.

Immigration and the City

Two great waves of immigration occurred during the nineteenth century. The first, starting in the 1830s and lasting until approximately the 1880s, originated largely from the countries of Western and Northern Europe. The largest immigrant groups during the period were the Irish and Germans, primarily "because they were the most numerous of those who experienced the profound economic and social changes in the first half of the nineteenth century."[38] The second wave, beginning around the 1880s and lasting into the first decades of the twentieth century, consisted of immigrants from Eastern and Southern Europe, chiefly Italians and Russians.

THE IRISH AND THE GERMANS

Between 1847 and 1860, over 1.1 million Irish and 979,575 Germans arrived at the Port of New York.[39] Both groups had been present in the city as early as the 1730s, but their relatively small communities were overwhelmed by the volume of newcomers who arrived after 1840. The relative predominance of the two groups among all immigrants arriving at the Port of New York varied over time, with the Irish constituting a much larger share of all immigrants until the 1850s. Although the number of Germans exceeded that of the Irish arriving in New York throughout most of the 1850s, at the close of the decade the Irish again achieved numerical dominance. How many of these arrivals at the Port of New York planned to stay in New York City is unknown. Data for 1855–60 on the intended state of destination among immigrants arriving in New York suggest that the proportion of all immigrants indicating a destination who intended to stay in New York State rose from slightly below 40 percent to just over half.[40] However, according to Richard Stott, in 1860 the city inspector estimated that only about 14 percent of immigrants intended to stay in New York City.[41] Others argue that a minority of immigrants arriving during the period chose to remain in New York City, while most continued on to the Midwest to acquire farmland. Even if only a small proportion of all newcomers decided to stay in New York City, the absolute numbers of immigrants were so large that a dramatic impact on population size and composition was inevitable.

The Irish and German immigrants who arrived during the period shared many things in common. For one, they were generally young and male.[42] Stott reports that 50 percent of the immigrants arriving in 1850 from the British Isles were between the ages of fifteen and thirty, and 57 percent arriving between 1855 and 1860 were male. Stanley Nadel finds a similarly disproportionate representation of young adults and men among the German-born in New York in the early years of the 1845–80 period.[43] Both Irish and German immigrants in general were motivated by economic considerations; when viewed in terms of "push" and "pull" factors, economic changes and agricultural disasters in Europe— most notably the potato famine in Ireland—during the period were clear factors compelling many Irish and Germans to leave their home- lands. These factors only compounded what was generally an abysmal standard of living among European peasants. On the "pull" side, the abundant opportunities for work in the growing economy of New York City, particularly after the opening of the Erie Canal, offered the chance for a better material standard of living. Outside the city, of course, were opportunities in the Midwest to own land, which drew many to the United States. However, conditions on both sides of the Atlantic were clearly important; the waves of migrants ebbed during recessions and the Civil War, but they rose again once the economy recovered or peace- time returned.

The Irish who arrived prior to 1820 were religiously diverse and largely from the northern portions of Ireland, whereas those arriving after that date were predominantly Catholic and peasants, often arriv- ing penniless and with at best only rudimentary skills. Once established in New York, the Irish predominated in those occupations requiring the fewest skills and paying the lowest wages. Indeed, in 1855 Irish immi- grants represented approximately 87 percent of the city's unskilled la- borers, and this occupational category was the largest one for Irish-born men. The Irish played a dominant role in building much of the city's infrastructure in the period, including docks, bridges, and railroad tracks, and they also worked on the docks, offloading cargo from ships. The Irish also worked in such service jobs as barbers, waiters, and do- mestics, often displacing African American workers.[44] As a consequence of the low skill level of the Irish, and their predominance in fairly unsta- ble jobs, the Irish in New York were in general quite poor, constituting the majority of those receiving various forms of relief, including resi- dence in the city's almshouse.[45]

One consequence of the poverty of the Irish was their concentration in very poor neighborhoods and in deteriorated housing. In 1820, the core of the Irish community was located in the Sixth Ward, around the Five Points slum. Because of the area's relative affordability, the Irish shared the neighborhood with other poor New Yorkers, notably African Americans, Italians, and the city's very small Chinese population. As a result, Five Points was notorious not only for its poverty and its role as a breeding ground for disease but also for the interracial liaisons that often occurred there. As the numbers of newcomers outpaced the capacity of the area to house them, the community spread east into the Fourth Ward, closer to the docks and shipyards that provided employment. Despite the concentration of Irish in these older lower wards, the Irish were in fact spread out throughout the city, as the need for unskilled labor in different areas—and particularly the need for household servants—brought many to areas far from the established ethnic community. For example, the Irish laborers working on the construction of the Croton High Bridge settled in Highbridge in the Bronx, and those who worked for the New York and Harlem Railroad settled in the villages growing alongside new stations, such as Melrose, Morrisania, and Tremont in the Bronx. Similarly, Irish laborers who built turnpikes and drained meadows in Queens settled in Astoria, and in Brooklyn, settlements emerged around the Navy Yard, in the village of Bedford, and in Red Hook. As a result, the level of segregation of the Irish from the non-Irish was quite low. Indeed, the average ward-level Irish–non-Irish indices of dissimilarity for the 1855–75 period was only 17, an extremely low level of residential segregation.[46]

In contrast to the Irish, the Germans arriving in New York were more likely to possess some skills and to be literate, having originated in regions from which artisans were disproportionately likely to emigrate. In addition, some German immigrants were able to arrive with some capital derived from the selling of their interests at home, whereas the Irish who arrived were largely without much, if any, money. The higher skill levels of German immigrants formed a formidable advantage, enabling them to assimilate more rapidly than the Irish—despite the serious handicap of a foreign language—and to achieve other forms of social and economic mobility. Indeed, while Irish men almost uniformly joined the ranks of the laboring classes and some Germans too experienced poverty, many other Germans were able to put their skills and capital to work, opening up small corner groceries, newsstands, bakeries, and butcher shops. Skilled German immigrants also specialized in breweries, piano making, cigar making, and printing.

The German neighborhood, Kleindeutschland, was already the largest residential concentration of the German-born in the city by 1820. Originally concentrated in the Tenth and Thirteenth Wards, when the great streams of newcomers began arriving in the 1840s, the neighborhood began expanding north, into the newer Eleventh and Seventeenth

Wards. Ultimately, Kleindeutschland was bounded by the Bowery on the west, the East River to the east, Division Street to the south, and Fourteenth Street to the north. Although identified as a German enclave, Kleindeutschland was—like other ethnic neighborhoods—ethnically heterogeneous, including among its residents Irish and English as well as native-born Americans. Moreover, the Germans themselves were quite heterogeneous, with immigrants from the various German states differing in language, culture, and religion. As a result, within Kleindeutschland itself were smaller communities of Bavarians, Prussians, and other German subgroups, as well as communities organized along the lines of religion. Yet when we consider the Germans as a whole and compare them to the Irish, the evidence shows the Germans to have been more residentially concentrated than the Irish, with an average ward-level German–non-German index of dissimilarity of 29 for 1855–75.[47] Although the Germans were more concentrated than the Irish, an index of dissimilarity of 29 still represents a very low level of segregation, at least when compared to current levels for certain groups, such as African Americans.

IMMIGRANTS' HOUSING CONDITIONS

For both groups, the variety in locations translated into varying housing conditions. The Irish who "lived in" as domestics may have experienced the best possible housing conditions, by virtue of working for more-affluent households in newer neighborhoods. Other immigrants occupied relatively decent housing, such as in the newer portions of Kleindeutschland, but the poorest of the newcomers, particularly the Irish, had few housing options and ended up living in shanties made of whatever materials they could find. Others who could afford to pay rent typically could not afford to pay much, and thus their lot tended to be the meanest of slum housing. As wealthier residents began relocating uptown to newer wards, the houses they left behind were converted to nonresidential use or were divided up for use as boarding houses or multiple-family dwellings. Those houses experiencing the last fate were the city's earliest tenements, dubbed "barracks" by later reformers, where families lived in small, dark, and poorly ventilated rooms. Other housing opportunities were found in rear tenements, shabbily built buildings located behind preexisting housing, accessible only through narrow alleyways. The walls of such buildings were often flush with those of neighboring buildings, or were hard by backyard privies, resulting in very little light or fresh air. Other newcomers with few means to live anywhere else ended up in basements, attics, sheds, and stables. Cellar dwellers paid some of the lowest rents and experienced some of the most miserable conditions, their quarters being dark, damp, and poorly ventilated. The population living in basements and cellars expanded dramatically as a consequence of the great waves of Irish and German immigration; just under 7,200 persons lived in basements and cellars in 1843, but before twenty years had passed more than 29,000 lived in such conditions.

The housing supply in the lower wards of Manhattan, already in short supply by the 1820s, was overwhelmed by the thousands of newcomers pouring in after 1840. The pressing need for working-class housing, combined with developments in the construction industry, offered substantial profits, which provided the impetus for building speculators to start focusing on the working-class market.[48] Indeed, it is in this period, the mid- to late 1840s, that those tenements built expressly to house multiple families began to appear in New York. In the lower wards, these new tenant houses tended to be built as rear houses or to replace other structures demolished because of fire, overuse, or old age. Yet, in the areas undergoing rapid development after 1845, between Fourteenth and Twenty-third Streets in the Fifteenth, Sixteenth, and Seventeenth Wards, tenements were the main form of residential construction. This was especially the case in the newer portions of Kleindeutschland (in the Seventeenth Ward), where the cumulative market power of residents helped to make tenement construction profitable. In general, most of the new tenements were stripped-down versions of the row houses developers had been producing uptown for middle- and upper-class households; developers realized that keeping such structures plain in ornamentation and devoid of all amenities (save, perhaps, for stoves), they could turn a profit within the working-class market.[49]

Profits were also maximized by making use of practically all the space available in the standard 25-by-100 foot lots created by the grid plan; tenements often covered more than 90 percent of the 100-foot depth of the lot and rose to five or six stories. The internal hallways were dark due to the absence of windows, and stairways were narrow, steep, and pitch dark. The apartments within were dubbed "railroad flats" since the rooms were lined up in a row like train cars. In such a situation, only the rooms at the front and rear of the building received light, yet frequently the presence of back buildings blocked the light from rear windows. Indeed,

> usually such a building contained a narrow hall opening from a street or court; on each floor, including the cellar, two suites of rooms opened into the hall. Front and rear rooms of the building contained windows, but the bedrooms and closets in the middle were dark. In most cases there was another tenement in the back yard, frequently altogether enclosed and accessible only through an alley. Alongside these buildings and in the yards were many little irregular frame structures, some in dilapidated condition, serving partly as sheds and partly as homes for the overflow of the tenements. Such haphazard combinations of front and rear buildings on the same lot created an intricate array of rear courts and alleys, notoriously dark, foul-smelling, and encumbered with accumulations of filth.[50]

Although the construction of new tenements helped to reduce the size of the cellar-dwelling population, this new housing form combined with the massive inflows of immigrants to produce ever-increasing neighborhood densities. Indeed, the average number of persons per acre in the seven wards below Canal Street rose from 94.5 in 1820 to 163.5 in 1850, while the corresponding average block densities rose from 157.5 to 272.5 persons in the same period.[51]

The new tenements initially provided somewhat better housing options for the poor and working class than did their alternatives, yet they soon proved to be less than adequate. Indeed, when sanitation officials and reformers inspected the relatively recently built tenements in the late 1840s and early 1850s, they noted that the generally inferior construction and "contracted scale" of the buildings caused noticeable deterioration in conditions. The intensive crowding that prevailed in tenement districts also magnified the dangers of fire and especially contagious disease. As a result, mortality rates in these areas began climbing rapidly. In the city as a whole, death rates had been rising steadily since about 1820, and in the late 1850s the mortality rate in New York exceeded that in all other large American cities.[52] Yet mortality was always higher in poorer neighborhoods, as the combination of poverty, little available clean water, crowding, and poor sanitary conditions provided the conditions necessary for the spread of endemic diseases like diarrhea and tuberculosis. Not coincidentally, it was also in the poorest wards where epidemic diseases, such as yellow fever, cholera, and ty-phoid/typhus, took their greatest toll.[53] In 1856, while one out of fifty-five persons in the city's most affluent ward died, one out of twenty-three persons died in the poorest ward.[54]

The Birth of Housing Policy: The Early Years of Tenement Reform, 1864–1879

By 1840 it had become common opinion that the conditions in ten-ant neighborhoods posed the primary threat to the city's general health, as well as to its morals. In his 1842 report, *The Sanitary Conditions of the Laboring Population,* the city inspector and physician John Griscom pointed specifically to the crowding and lack of ventilation of working-class dwellings as the primary causes of the city's bad health conditions, and he pointed to crowding in particular as the cause of what was seen as the moral degradation of the poor.

> Multiple families living in close quarters not only produced a vitiated atmosphere, but also "an indifference to the common decencies of life, and a disregard of the sacred obligations of moral propriety, which result in a depressing effect upon the physiological energies, and power-fully heighten the susceptibility to aggravate the type, and render more difficult the cure, of diseases among them." Not only did early death follow, but such conditions also sapped the capacity of individuals to take responsibility for their own lives and well-being of their families.[55]

Identifying the link between bad housing conditions and the city's overall well-being was one matter, but deciding precisely who was to blame and how to remedy the situation was another. In an era of lais-sez-faire capitalism, it was virtually impossible to view housing specula-tors and primary landlords as responsible for the prevailing conditions, especially when these housing-market actors formed a key political con-stituency needed to pass any form of housing-reform legislation. Indeed, "the urban real estate speculator resented community control over his domain. He, not the community, would determine the level of structural and sanitary standards. . . . In an age of liberal capitalism, the right of one kind of entrepreneur to pursue his economic destiny was the same as any other."[56] Instead, Griscom identified the sublandlord as the per-son responsible for the housing conditions of the poor, equating the sublandlord's pursuit of profit with extortion while arguing that the primary landlord's pursuit of profit was justified.

Perhaps recognizing the need to win over the business community in his effort to improve the housing conditions of the poor, Griscom couched his appeals for housing reform in terms of its potential effect on the city's economy and labor force. Stressing that inadequate housing produced a chronically ill labor force, he argued that unless regulations were instituted, taxpayers would ultimately bear the expense of diminished productivity and of the charity required to support those who would become paupers upon the premature death of the primary earner.

Griscom's proposed reforms had two basic emphases that would frame efforts at housing reform for the rest of the century. First, Griscom called for various forms of restrictive legislation, arguing that the legislature should require landlords to provide tenants with adequate space, fresh air, and light and should also ban the use of cellars. To alleviate overcrowding and its consequences, he called for a limit on the number of residents per building and for regulations that would hold landlords responsible for building maintenance. To ensure compliance, Griscom also called for the creation of a Board of Health staffed by medical experts to replace the politically corrupt health-warden system. Moreover, he proposed that inspectors from such a new Board of Health be given the authority to identify and close places judged unfit for human habitation.

The second emphasis of Griscom's proposals centered on the construction of model tenements that would feature building standards conducive to the improved health of their residents. Rather than blaming the rich for the deplorable housing conditions of the poor, Griscom appealed to benevolent capitalists to provide new and decent housing for a fair profit. "[B]uilt by the individual capitalist or company which voluntarily limited profits in favor of higher structural and sanitary conditions than those found in the ordinary speculative tenement . . . [m]odel tenements, sound investments rather than speculative adventures, might reap diminished profits but investors would be rewarded by the pleasure of having served the poor."[57]

In this effort Griscom was joined by the Association for the Improvement of the Condition of the Poor (AICP), which not only championed the idea of the model tenement but also sponsored one that was built in the area of Elizabeth and Mott Streets. With rents in its eighty-seven suites of apartments at $5.50 to $8.50 a month, it was expected to return a profit of 6 percent.[58] However, it proved to be a financial failure and was ultimately declared unfit for human habitation in the 1880s, ironically by its original sponsor, the AICP. Other efforts at building model tenements were also pursued in various parts of Manhattan and Brooklyn, but the prevalence of alternative investment opportunities yielding far higher profits meant that this housing-reform tactic would never achieve much success.[59]

Although Griscom's and the AICP's efforts to have housing-reform legislation enacted ultimately proved futile, subsequent events—including the economic crisis of 1857, riots in 1849 and 1857, and the draft riots of 1863—clarified in the minds of the elite the connection between poverty and squalor in tenement districts and social division, unrest, and instability. Pressure mounted for some form of government intervention in the tenement problem. In 1864 the Citizen's Association appointed a special subcommittee, the Council of Hygiene, to carry out a detailed survey of the city's housing and sanitary problems. The council's report identified 15,511 tenements (defined as structures with three or more families), housing a total population of 486,000.[60] When the 15,224 persons living in cellars are added to the population in tenements, the 501,224 tenement and cellar dwellers represented more than half of the city's total population.[61] In addition, the highest number of tenements and the largest tenement population were found in the Eleventh and Seventeenth Wards (2,049 and 1,890 tenements, and 64,254 and 63,766 residents, respectively), which formed the northern part of Kleindeutschland.

The Council of Hygiene's 1864 report formed the basis of the state's 1866 legislation that created minimum standards for housing construction in the city and the state's first comprehensive housing law, the Tenement House Act of 1867. The 1867 act focused largely on the structural aspects of housing, identifying proper room dimensions and ceiling heights, creating provisions for ventilation and light, and requiring a minimum of one water closet for every twenty residents. Previously, one water closet would serve the needs of a hundred residents. However, the legislation failed to limit the proportion of a lot that a tenement could cover, and it left many of its provisions couched in vague and unenforceable terms. As an example, although the law required the provision of fire escapes, "by leaving the approval of the form of egress up to the inspector, even an inconveniently located wooden ladder . . . satisfied the legal requirements."[62] However weak and vague its provisions, the 1867 law represented at least in principle the acceptance of the idea that the community had the right to limit the freedom of tenement builders and landlords and thus was a promise of things to come.

The Tenement House Act of 1879 was the next major piece of housing-reform legislation and revised a number of provisions of the 1867 act. In particular, the 1879 legislation required that every tenement bedroom have a window. This requirement ultimately gave rise to the "dumbbell tenement," which was to serve as the typical, if not the sole, type of working-class multiple dwelling to be built until 1901, when the next significant piece of housing-reform legislation was passed. Dumbbell tenements were not only built in lower Manhattan but all over the island and in the Bronx as well; twenty thousand were constructed in the two boroughs alone between 1880 and 1900, with nearly one-third of these built uptown in Yorkville and Harlem.[63] The proliferation of dumbbell tenements created the foundation for new working-class and immigrant neighborhoods outside the traditional receiving areas.

The dumbbell tenement was typically five or six stories high on a standard 25-by-100-foot lot and contained fourteen rooms to a floor, half on each side of the building. Flush toilets were located in the hallway of each floor, near the central stairway. The rooms in each apartment were arranged in a straight line just as they were in earlier tenements, with the front four on each side constituting one apartment and the rear three a separate apartment. Of the fourteen rooms on each floor, ten relied on a narrow air shaft, an indentation separating neighboring buildings but enclosed on all sides, for light and air. These narrow air shafts were typically only about 28 inches in width and quickly proved to be more hazardous than beneficial to the well-being of residents. In addition to conducting noise and odors between apartments, the air shaft was a fire hazard, often conveying flames from one story to the next.

Thus, during the period from the 1840s to around 1880, New York experienced a number of new developments. For one, the city received its first epic flow of immigrants, dominated by Irish and German peasants and laborers seeking a better material standard of living. The arrival of tens of thousands of new immigrants gave rise to new ethnic neighborhoods located largely in the lower wards of the island. Initially crowded in subdivided single-family houses, new arrivals lived in housing of far lower quality than that of the more affluent uptown, and the poorest competed with the city's blacks for housing and jobs. Shifts in the economy and the housing market gave rise to the development of the tenement, the first form of housing built expressly for residence by more than one family. Although the early tenements initially appeared to alleviate some of the worst aspects of working-class housing conditions, they soon proved to be just as inadequate. The dismal living conditions of the working class became linked in the minds of the elite with the city's misfortunes, including high mortality and morbidity and social unrest, and thus became a focus of housing reformers. As a result, the nation's first pieces of housing legislation were passed with the intent to rectify some aspects of the tenement-house problem. Although vaguely worded and lacking enforcement, the Tenement House Act of 1867 represented the right of the community to intervene in the affairs of housing speculators and landlords, potent economic actors, and to protect (at least in principle) the health and well-being of working-class and other poor residents. Toward the end of the period, the dumbbell tenement was introduced in an ill-fated effort to achieve improved building standards within the limitations of the 25-by-100-foot lot. The dumbbell tenement was to predominate among all forms of working-class housing up to the end of the nineteenth century and thus was built not only in Manhattan's lower wards but also in emerging tenement districts elsewhere on the island, as well as in the Bronx and Brooklyn.

1880s–1920s

In the forty years straddling the turn of the twentieth century, New York City experienced a number of significant events that would indelibly change the city's character, both in its population and its geography. The first such event was the consolidation of New York, Kings, Queens, Bronx, and Richmond counties into Greater New York City on January 1, 1898. On a single day, the city became the most extensive geographically and the most populous city in the nation.

A second event that powerfully shaped the city's character was demographic: a shift in the immigrant stream from Western and Northern Europe to Southern and Eastern Europe. As shown in figure 2.1, the Irish and the Germans continued to settle in the city, but the inflow of immigrants from these and other countries in Western and Northern Europe began to decline, as the social and economic conditions in these countries

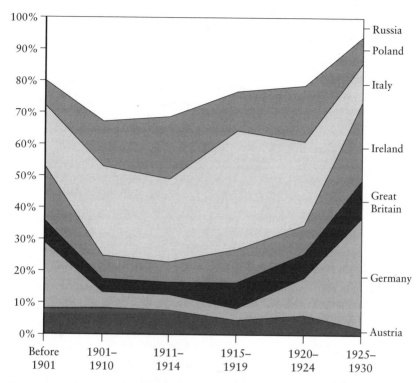

Fig. 2.1. Percentage of Foreign-Born Whites in 1930 Census, from Principal Countries of Birth, by Year of Arrival, New York Ciy. *Source*: Rosenwaike 1972: 94, table 37.

began to improve. In place of these "old" immigrants emerged increasing numbers of "new" immigrants originating from countries in Eastern and Southern Europe, notably Italy, Russia, Poland, Austria-Hungary, and Romania. What began as a trickle of immigrants from these countries in the 1870s and 1880s gained strength and became far more of a flood, especially around the turn of the twentieth century. The influx of Italians and Jews from Eastern Europe among the full range of immigrants from Eastern and Southern Europe would alter not only the city's ethnic composition but also the geographic organization of its ethnic communities, as new immigrants succeeded older immigrants in the city's ethnic communities. In addition, the rising numbers of newcomers led to a worsening of housing problems in the lower wards; "[a]s older residents retreated before the flood of newcomers, living quarters in lower Manhattan became progressively more unkempt and dangerous."[64]

A second demographic shift to occur during the 1880–1920 period was the tremendous surge in the city's black population. The 60,666 blacks counted in the 1900 census would have at least an additional 90,000 added to their ranks by 1920, with over 170,000 more counted in the 1930 census (for a total black population in that year of 327,706).[65] A large portion of this impressive growth was due to the arrival of blacks from the South. Blacks had been leaving the South since the end of the Civil War, with more than 80,000 leaving between 1870 and 1890, followed by over 100,000 each in the 1890s and 1900s and another half million during the "Great Migration" of 1910–20.[66] New York was a primary destination for many Southern migrants, especially those from Virginia and the Carolinas, and increasingly, as the years passed, those from Georgia and Florida. The substantial inflow of Southern-born blacks overcame the depressing effects of high mortality on the size of the black population, allowing the black share of the total population to edge up to approximately 4 percent in 1930.[67]

Another contributing factor to the growth in the black population during the period was the significant arrival of black immigrants. The 1900 census counted in the city 3,552 foreign-born blacks,[68] whose origins lay mostly in the West Indies. Most of these immigrant blacks were fairly new to the city, having arrived only during the previous decade. Philip Kasinitz notes rising numbers of Caribbean-born blacks arriving each year, from 412 in 1899, to 832 in 1902, to 2,174 in 1903 and 5,633 in 1907. The number of new arrivals then stabilized at between 5,000 and 8,000 per year, reaching a peak of 12,243 in 1924.[69] The foreign-born black community in New York City was the largest in the nation, with a total count of over 54,000 in 1930.[70] Data from the 1920 and 1930 censuses indicate that the percent of all foreign-born blacks living in the city rose from just over 41 percent to just under 56 percent, an increase resulting from the tendency of new arrivals to settle in New York. Moreover, the share of all foreign-born blacks who settled in New York City rose from less than 20 percent among those arriving before 1901 to just under 70 percent of those arriving in the decade preceding the 1930 census.[71]

Foreign-born blacks arriving in New York in the early decades of the twentieth century tended to settle among native-born blacks rather than form the kind of ethnic neighborhoods that European immigrants had.[72] The dramatic growth among all blacks in the period contributed to another event that changed the character of the city, namely, the emergence around 1910 of Harlem as the capital of black New York. As mentioned, prior to this time, blacks had lived interspersed among whites, although individual blocks or tenements may have been predominantly, if not all, black. Black neighborhoods, insofar as they existed at all, were typically only a block or two in length and thus had neither the size nor the density of the black neighborhoods that exist today in New York and other cities. Indeed, black areas of the era were neither predominantly black nor did they house the majority of the city's blacks. The relative integration of blacks in New York in the middle nineteenth century is reflected in the ward-level index of dissimilarity for 1860, which stood at 40.6,[73] a level of segregation that falls in the moderate range and is far lower than the city's level of 83.9 in 2000.[74] In the nineteenth century and earlier, income predominated over race as a determinant of residential location. Osofsky in his 1971 study, *Harlem: The Making of a Ghetto, Negro New York, 1890–1930*, argues that the dramatic growth in the black population beginning in the late nineteenth century may have been the most important factor accounting for the development of the city's first large contiguous racial ghetto; indeed, he argues that *some* neighborhood was destined to become home to the majority of the city's blacks and that it was simply the peculiar circumstances of the time that caused Harlem to assume this role.

Finally, this period witnessed the beginning of Puerto Rican migration to the city, as well as growth in the city's Chinese population and the ensuing solidification of Chinatown as a Chinese enclave. Although a few Puerto Ricans were found in the city as early as 1890, migration to the mainland began soon after the island of Puerto Rico was ceded to the United States at the end of the Spanish-American War in 1898.[75] Like European immigrants before them, the earliest of the Puerto Rican migrants settled near job opportunities, and thus new settlements arose in East Harlem, the Lower East Side, and near the Brooklyn Navy Yard.[76] A very small Chinese population was present in the city in the mid-nineteenth century, consisting largely of sailors and merchants who were active in trade between China and the United States.[77] Most of these individuals were in the city only temporarily, as most of the Chinese immigration to the United States during the period consisted of "sojourners," who were looking to make a fortune to bring back to their villages in the Canton (now Guangdong) region.[78] The Chinese were concentrated in the Five Points slum, and the community began to grow after 1880 when Chinese laborers, escaping the increasingly virulent and violent anti-Chinese sentiment on the West Coast, began arriving in large numbers. The area became known as Chinatown, and it became a refuge for its residents from the hostilities and discrimination of the majority-white society.[79] The anger, frustration, and political activism of the white working class, with whom Chinese laborers had competed for work in the West, culminated in the Chinese Exclusion Act of 1882, the first piece of immigration legislation to ban a group based on its nationality. The 1882 act and other related legislation passed through the early 1890s prevented any further Chinese immigration to the United States, which also meant that the Chinese who were in the country could not have their families come and join them. As a result, the sex ratio among Chinese was grossly imbalanced, and Chinatowns throughout the United States remained "bachelor" societies.

The Chinese Exclusion Act of 1882 was one of a series of legislative moves made during the late nineteenth and early twentieth centuries to meet increasing demands for immigration restriction. During the period, nativist sentiments were growing throughout the country, and were becoming increasingly racist in nature. Specifically, nativists used the work of eugenicists to argue that certain groups of immigrants—particularly those of Asian origin and those from the nations of Southern and Eastern Europe—were inferior to persons of Western and Northern European stock and would never assimilate into American society. Ultimately, such fears gave rise to a series of quota-based laws in the 1920s, culminating in the National Origins Quota system, which was put into effect in 1929.[80] This system limited the total number of immigrants to 150,000 per year, and each European country received visas in proportion to that country's representation among all whites counted in the 1920 census. It thus assured that the number of new arrivals from Southern and Eastern Europe would be far below what it had been prior to World War I, as well as below the numbers to arrive from Western and Northern Europe.[81] Because the quota-based system dramatically limited immigration from the countries that had been sending large numbers to New York City during the previous three decades, they had a significant effect not only on the size of the inflows but also on the longevity of the city's ethnic neighborhoods. Because of the upward mobility experienced by the city's white ethnics during this period, the continuing inflow of coethnics was vital to maintaining ethnic institutions and cultures. The restrictive new legislation caused many of the city's white ethnic working-class neighborhoods to begin to disintegrate.[82]

From North and West to South and East: Changes in the City's Newest Arrivals from Europe

By the 1880s, a significant number of German immigrants and their descendants had entered the middle class, so many that some scholars have identified the middle class in that year as being "largely German" in ethnic composition.[83] Along with rising class status came geographic dispersion out of Kleindeutschland. Upwardly mobile Germans established settlements in Yorkville (located between Seventy-second and 100th Streets, east of Lexington Avenue), which by World War I would become identified as the center of the city's German community. Others with means moved to Central Harlem, occupying new town houses built especially for middle-class residents, while still others moved to Brooklyn, particularly Williamsburg, and to Astoria in Queens. As a result of this dispersion out of Kleindeutschland, first- and second-generation Germans were fairly well integrated with native whites of native parentage in 1920; the tract-level index of dissimilarity for the two groups was 28 in that year.[84]

The Irish, who were poorer than the Germans to begin with, took longer to achieve a solid footing in the middle class, with the "lace curtain" Irish appearing only toward the end of the century. Up until World War I, most Irish in the city remained solidly working class, occupying not only the traditional downtown wards but also other working-class areas in Chelsea and particularly Hell's Kitchen, the area bounded by Fifty-seventh Street on the north and Thirty-fourth Street on the south and running west from Ninth to Twelfth Avenue. By about 1890, however, many of Irish parentage had entered the middle class as entrepreneurs, lower-level managerial and clerical workers, and municipal employees courtesy of the group's affiliation with Tammany Hall, and they began moving uptown to newer communities on both the west and east sides of Manhattan. In addition, the availability of better housing in Washington Heights and Inwood in northern Manhattan attracted many Irish households, and new Irish settlements also developed in Long Island City, Woodside, Sunnyside, and Rockaway Beach in Queens. As was the case with the Germans, by 1920 first- and second-generation Irish were not very segregated from native whites of native parentage; the tract-level index of dissimilarity between the groups was 29.[85]

While improvements in their economic means pulled many Germans and Irish out of the old ethnic neighborhoods to newer areas (a process described by the spatial assimilation model), a significant push factor was the crowding of thousands of new immigrants into already heavily congested tenement districts in the lower wards. Like the Irish and Germans before them, the Italians and Jews of the "new" immigration arrived with few means and had to settle in older areas where rents were the least expensive and where they could easily find and walk to work. The combination of growing residential opportunities outside lower Manhattan (a result of expanding transportation lines) and the large inflows of poor newcomers produced large-scale ethnic neighborhood turnover, largely from Irish to Italian predominance and from German to Jewish predominance.

The size of the new immigration was quite large. Between 1880 and 1910, approximately 1.4 million Eastern European Jews arrived in New York, with the result that Jews constituted fully one-fourth of the city's population in 1910.[86] Similarly, the number of foreign-born Italians in Manhattan and Brooklyn more than doubled between 1880 and 1890 (rising from 23,411 to 49,514), and the respective number for the consolidated Greater New York region doubled yet again between 1900 and 1910 (rising from 145,433 to 340,770).[87] One consequence of such large inflows of new immigrants was a substantial reordering of the city's ethnic groups. Persons of Russian and Italian parentage were the fourth- and fifth-largest groups among whites in New York in 1900, but by 1930 they had moved up to the second and third ranks, respectively.[88] A second consequence was simple population growth; between 1900 and 1910, the white population of the city grew by about 1.3 million (while the entire population of the city grew by 1.33 million). The year 1910 was also the year in which the percentage of foreign-born residents in the city peaked, at 40.8 percent.[89]

THE ITALIANS AND THE JEWS

Prior to the start of the large inflows in the last decades of the nineteenth century, a small colony of Italians existed in the Five Points area, especially around Mulberry Bend. The population of just under 1,500 foreign-born Italians in 1860 originated largely from the north of Italy and represented a variety of occupations, including rag pickers, musicians, and artists. Most, however, worked at unskilled jobs or on the nearby wharves.

After 1860, economic conditions in Italy deteriorated, prompting thousands to leave. As a result, the once small colony in New York began to grow, reaching some 12,000 by the 1880 census. With competition for housing already intense in the congested Sixth Ward, the colony began spreading into the adjacent Fourteenth Ward, which soon became identified as "Little Italy." Although the general area was identified with Italians, it was not composed exclusively of Italians but housed other ethnicities as well. Moreover, within the Italian settlement, clusters formed of compatriots from specific towns and regions.

The Italians arriving in the city after 1880 were largely illiterate peasants and laborers originating from agricultural regions of Southern Italy and Sicily. Men dominated among Italian immigrants, as did the young. In fact, 80 percent of Italian immigrants arriving between 1880 and 1910 were male, and 83 percent were between the ages of fourteen and forty-four. Especially in the early years, the dominant goal of Italian immigrants was to make enough money to return home and purchase land. Indeed, the temporary nature of the Italian migration is illustrated by the finding that for every hundred Italians arriving during the 1892–96 period, forty-three would return home, and seventy-three would return home for every hundred arriving during the 1907–11 period.[90] However, what began as a temporary, male-dominated migration eventually evolved into a family-oriented flow, as married men returned home to bring their wives and children back, and unmarried men returned home to find spouses with whom they could establish families in America. In any case, the primary motivation for immigration among Italians was economic, either to achieve an improved economic position back in Italy or to secure a better life in New York than was possible at home.

Arriving with few if any skills, like the Irish before them, Italians after 1880 took their place at the bottom of the occupation ladder. In 1900, more than 60 percent of Italian men were in unskilled and semi-skilled occupations.[91] Many worked in the construction trades, building much of the infrastructure required for the continued growth of the city. Italian laborers played a prominent role in building the subway system in the first decade of the twentieth century, digging tunnels and laying tracks. Italian laborers also paved streets and built bridges and reservoirs. As more factories were built in the city, many Italian men took jobs in manufacturing.

After 1900, many Italians began moving uptown and to the Bronx and Brooklyn, largely following the Irish but also following geographically determined job opportunities. That is, as was the case with the Irish, to a very large degree Italian residential location was determined by place of work. Those who worked on the subway system settled near the expanding lines, and those who built bridges or reservoirs settled nearby those sites. A notable community developed in East Harlem stretching from about 106th to 116th Streets running east from Third Avenue to the East River. Originally settled in the 1870s as a shanty town of Italian laborers brought uptown to act as strikebreakers, East Harlem quickly became a primary destination of Italian immigrants seeking work on the expanding transit lines and in housing construction throughout Harlem.[92] Yet no matter where they settled, because of their low earnings and limited disposable income, the housing that Italians occupied was of poor quality. Those replacing the out-moving Irish inherited aging and rundown tenements that lacked most amenities and whose deterioration had been hastened by years of overuse through overcrowding. But even among those immigrants acquiring fairly new housing, such as those moving to East Harlem, the quality of housing remained poor, largely because the new tenements they could afford were built specifically for the working class, using substandard materials and methods and following the dumbbell design that facilitated overcrowding and ill health. By World War I, Italians and their descendants had begun to enter the middle class and to move to improved housing in better areas, including the Bronx, which was viewed by some as the "ultimate in geographic attainment."[93] However, because of the recency of their arrival in New York, first- and second-generation Italians were fairly segregated from native whites of native parentage in 1920, as revealed by the value of 63 on the index of dissimilarity.[94] The Italians leaving East Harlem were increasingly replaced by newly arriving Puerto Rican migrants, igniting the process of neighborhood transition.

In contrast to the Italian migration, the Jewish migration was more of a family migration. Far more women, children, and elderly were counted among the Jews than was the case for any other European immigrant groups; between 1899 and 1910, 43 percent of all Eastern European Jewish immigrants were women, compared to 22 percent among southern Italians, and fully 25 percent of Jewish immigrants were younger than fourteen, compared to 12 percent among all immigrants.[95] Jewish immigrants were also far more likely than the Italians to be literate and to possess skills, as well as to have had some experience living in towns and urban areas, especially those arriving after 1900. Moreover, the Jewish migration was far more likely to be permanent; during the 1908–10 period, while overall thirty-two immigrants left America for every hundred who arrived, the comparable number of returnees among Jews was eight.[96] The Jews coming to America not only were seeking a better life in an economic sense but were also fleeing widespread persecution in their homelands, especially those emigrating from Russia. In essence, for many Jews from Eastern Europe, there really was no place to return to.

In the early years of the Eastern European Jewish migration, newcomers clustered in and around Kleindeutschland. Indeed, as upwardly mobile Germans began leaving Kleindeutschland, Eastern European Jews replaced them, resulting in the lower portions of the area (the Tenth and Thirteenth Wards), along with the Eleventh Ward, gaining greater fame as the Jewish Lower East Side than they had as Kleindeutschland. The geographic concentration of Jewish immigrants in the early years of the migration was quite high, with the Lower East Side containing fully 75 percent of the city's Jews in 1892.[97] As a result, densities in the area, particularly the Tenth Ward, rose precipitously, from 432.2 persons per acre in 1880 to 701.9 persons per acre in 1894. In fact, in 1894, the Tenth Ward had the highest density of all Manhattan's wards, followed by its neighbors the Eleventh Ward (446.9 persons per acre) and the Thirteenth Ward (543.7 persons per acre).[98] Thus, the Jewish Lower East Side as a whole had the worst population congestion problems of all areas in the city, including areas of Italian settlement. A contributing factor to the higher densities in Jewish than Italian areas in lower Manhattan was the fact that the Jewish wards had been the locus of high levels of tenement construction; in the Tenth Ward alone, the number of tenements had more than doubled in the final two decades of the nineteenth century.[99] In addition, Jewish districts tended to house light industry, with tenements serving as both residence and sweatshop. In contrast, the Italian areas of lower Manhattan housed warehouses and some factories, which occupied space without adding residents.

Although Jewish housing conditions can be said to have been worse than Italian housing conditions when population density is considered, when the conditions of the actual units is considered, it appears that the Italians lived in lower-quality units. Thomas Kessner cites a report written by investigators of the Immigrant Commission which studied 472 Russian Jewish ghetto apartments and 419 southern Italian dwellings. The investigators rated 34 percent of the Jewish dwellings as being in "good" condition, 57 percent as being in "fair" condition, and only 9 percent as deserving a rating of "poor." In contrast, among the apartments occupied by Italians, only 17 percent were rated as "good," 49 percent as "fair," and fully 34 percent as "poor." The variation in rated quality correlated with differences in rents, given that the Jewish households were paying an average of about three dollars more a month in rent while also occupying larger apartments on average (3.55 rooms versus 3.12 rooms for the Italians).[100]

The predominance of the Lower East Side as the focus of Jewish life in the city was already on the wane before the nineteenth century drew to a close. As early as 1890 a considerable movement out of the area to other parts of Manhattan and to Brooklyn was already under way. One factor influencing this dispersion was rising status among many Jewish immigrants, enabling them to afford better accommodations in less-congested areas. Yet, for New York's Jews, residential dispersion was also a function of the reduced capacity of the Lower East Side to accommodate the thousands who kept arriving. As a result of the creation of parks, the widening of streets, and the construction of the Williamsburg and Manhattan bridges (1903 and 1909, respectively), tens of thousands of housing units were demolished, forcing many area residents to find new homes and other new immigrants to make their initial settlement somewhere outside the Lower East Side.

By the 1890s, a number of new Jewish settlements had been established, and by 1920 the focus of Jewish life had shifted fully from the Lower East Side to areas in upper Manhattan, the Bronx, and Brooklyn. In Brooklyn, Jews moved to Williamsburg, where German and other Central European Jews had established neighborhoods decades earlier. So many working-class Jews settled in Brownsville that by the start of World War II the area contained the largest concentration of Jews in the United States.[101] Initially Brownsville was a somewhat rural area in western Brooklyn, but the production of tenements grew along with the rise in land values, so that by 1910, 96 percent of new buildings constructed there were tenements.[102] Most of the Jews living in Brownsville were involved in the garment trades, as a result of the relocation of numerous menswear manufacturers to the area from the Lower East Side. The popularity of Brownsville as a place of residence skyrocketed; by the early 1890s, 4,000 lived in and around the Brownsville area, but by 1905 the Jewish population had swelled to around 50,000, and to about 200,000 by 1925.[103] More-affluent and religiously observant Jews moving to Brooklyn tended to choose Borough Park, which featured single- and two-family homes, a suburban lifestyle, and numerous Jewish religious facilities.[104] Despite the dispersion to other areas, first- and second-generation Russians were very unevenly distributed relative to native-born whites of native parentage; the index of dissimilarity for these groups stood at 71 in 1920.[105]

Within Manhattan, many prosperous Jews followed the Germans to Yorkville, and according to Jeffery Gurock in his 1979 study, *When Harlem was Jewish, 1870–1980,* by 1900 many Jews of varying status had found their way to Harlem, mainly between Ninety-seventh and 142nd Streets. The Upper West Side was another favored destination for upper-class Jews, who lived in the area's luxury apartment buildings built after World War I. By 1910, Harlem was home to tens of thousands of Jews, many living among the earlier-arriving German residents in the better town houses located on streets between Seventh and Lenox Avenues, while other, less-prosperous Jews crowded into the tenements between Lenox and Fifth Avenues. Still others moved to the Bronx, again to a variety of neighborhoods according to their class. In the east Bronx, the working-class tenements provided housing that was not much different or of better quality than the housing left behind in the Lower East Side, but middle-class settlements emerged in other Bronx neighborhoods, notably the Grand Concourse, where Jews lived in spacious apartments located in art-deco-style buildings.[106]

IMMIGRANT HOUSING CONDITIONS

Although available reports suggest that Italian housing conditions were worse than those experienced by Jews, in general the state of working-class housing in the city remained quite poor. At the turn of the twentieth century, many people remained consigned to cellars, while thousands of others resided in the 2,379 rear houses still standing.[107] In 1900, approximately 69 percent of the population of the five boroughs lived in tenements. Only one-third of the tenements in the city had running water, and the vast majority of people living on the Lower East Side continued to rely on backyard privies even as hallway toilets became standard amenities elsewhere. Similarly, in 1893 only 2 percent of Italian families living on Centre Street had a toilet on their floor.[108] And as late as 1903, approximately 15 percent of Lower East Side tenements were still without fire escapes, resulting in a disproportionate concentration of the city's fire-related mortality in the area.[109]

THE TENEMENT HOUSE ACT OF 1901

The compromised living conditions in the city's tenements, and particularly those in lower Manhattan, compelled a number of reformers—notably Jacob Riis, Lawrence Veiller, and Lillian Wald—to investigate and document conditions and to indict the inadequacies of the dumbbell design. The most well known, in a popular sense, of these efforts is undoubtedly Riis's 1890 work, *How the Other Half Lives*. The work of reformers ultimately secured legislation that led to improved conditions as well as improved building designs, namely, the Tenement House Law of 1901. The 1901 act required several improvements to be made in preexisting or "old-law" tenements, including the provision of fire escapes accessible to each family, as well as a toilet and running water for each family. The act also created the Tenement House Department, which had the power to pressure landlords of old-law buildings to comply with the new standards.[110]

With regard to improving design, the minimum size requirements for side courts and rear yards for new buildings (12 feet), along with other requirements, made it uneconomical to build on the traditional 25-foot lots. As a result, the act ended the construction of dumbbell tenements and limited tenement construction to lots of up to twice the traditional width. Consequently, the 1901 law led to the construction of tenements that were far more solid than previous designs and that featured such amenities as light, air, and plumbing. The extension of subway lines into such developing neighborhoods as Washington Heights in upper Manhattan, Brownsville in Brooklyn, and Morrisania in the Bronx led to the placement of improved "new-law" tenements in these areas. Thus the first- and second-generation working-class Jews and Italians moving to newer neighborhoods after 1901 still moved to tenements, but to tenements that offered a far higher standard of living than their predecessors enjoyed.

A Different Migration Stream: The Arrival of Southern Blacks and the Emergence of Harlem

The economic condition of the black population in New York in the late nineteenth century was less favorable than it had been earlier in the century. While still relegated to the most menial positions, blacks had been displaced from many unskilled occupations by the enormous waves of immigrants—particularly the Irish—arriving after 1830.[111] Although a small black elite had emerged during the nineteenth century, the typical African American in the city occupied a position in the socioeconomic hierarchy that was near, if not at, the bottom. As a result, blacks tended to occupy the meanest housing in the city, whose unsanitary and overcrowded conditions contributed greatly to the extreme levels of mortality that kept the population from growing.[112]

Until about 1880, a primary black settlement existed in Greenwich Village. But faced with increasing competition from the newly arrived Italian immigrants looking to settle in the emerging Little Italy in the area, many blacks began moving north, into a broad area that today encompasses much of midtown Manhattan. Specifically, many blacks moved into the area known as San Juan Hill, which was bounded by Sixty-fourth Street to the north, Sixtieth Street to the south, Tenth Avenue to the east, and Eleventh Avenue to the west, as well as the notorious Tenderloin, which ran south of San Juan Hill down to the twenties. Although the city lacked the kind of large and contiguous racial ghetto that is familiar today, this large area housed many of the city's blacks as late as 1890 and 1900, when the population began to expand with the arrival of Southern migrants as well as West Indian immigrants. Encountering limited housing options as well as limited finances in most cases, these new arrivals to the city tended also to settle in San Juan Hill and the Tenderloin, replacing out-moving white households.

At the turn of the century, Harlem was predominantly white, serving as home to middle- and upper-class Jews and Germans, as well as older immigrants from Britain and Ireland and native-born Americans. Italians had formed a community in East Harlem where tenements dominated the housing stock, and the general Harlem area also housed a handful of blacks, many of whom worked as domestics in the homes of the area's more-affluent residents. With the arrival of the elevated train lines in 1878–81, the area underwent a huge building boom, which netted many speculators good profits on the increasingly valuable land, while builders constructed solid brownstones and fashionable apartment buildings, whose rents were affordable only by the wealthy. A second wave of land and housing speculation occurred in the late 1890s in anticipation of the completion of the Lenox Avenue subway. This second wave of speculation focused on the area between 110th Street (on Central Park North) and 125th Street, west of Lenox Avenue, where profits were made on tenements and apartment houses that appealed to Eastern European Jews leaving the Lower East Side. In addition, starting around 1900, speculators constructed numerous luxury apartment buildings along Seventh and Lenox Avenues in the 130s and 140s. However, this spurt of construction occurred too far in anticipation of the subway's completion date and entailed buildings whose asking rents were too far in excess of what the general population could afford. As a result, the housing market in Harlem collapsed in 1904–5; numerous new apartments remained vacant, builders and landlords became increasingly desperate for tenants, and banks foreclosed on mortgages.

The bust in Harlem's housing market coincided with an era of spectacular growth in the city's black population. The population of 60,666, blacks as enumerated in the 1900 census, expanded dramatically as large waves of migrants from the Southern states and smaller, though still substantial, waves of immigrants from the Caribbean arrived in the city. These inflows combined to swell the black population to almost 328,000 in 1930. Before the turn of century, most new black arrivals in the city had settled in preexisting black communities, replacing out-moving whites and inheriting their aging and deteriorating housing units. The demand for housing in these rundown sections was so great that they soon became even more congested than before, and rents higher than those paid by comparable whites added affordability problems to the problems of insufficient sanitation and physical deterioration already experienced by the city's blacks. The demand for housing in the area, already acute from population growth, was worsened by commercial development, which eliminated buildings from the residential stock and replaced them with structures devoted purely to commercial uses. Most notable here was the construction of Pennsylvania Station, covering two blocks at Thirty-third Street between Seventh and Eighth Avenues, which began in 1902 and ended in 1911. With increasing numbers of blacks arriving in the city, and decreasing housing opportunities in these traditional yet rundown areas of settlement, the forces of supply and demand determined that some other neighborhood in the city would have to become the locus of the black community. As circumstances would have it, the glut of apartments in Harlem made this area the most likely candidate.

But circumstances alone do not fully explain the transition of Harlem into the capital of black New York. Indeed, the cumulative actions of individuals and institutions helped to focus blacks' housing options onto the limited geographic area of Harlem, given the more general context of rising racial tensions in the early years of the twentieth century. Although New York had never been a place where blacks had been accepted as equal to whites, as blacks' numbers grew after 1890, whites' more permissive racial attitudes deteriorated, and the color line in the city grew more rigid. For example, there were many churches throughout the city that had allowed blacks to attend services, but as the number of black communicants grew beyond the tolerance level of white communicants, many churches either established racially separate services or requested that their black members leave the congregation and set up their own. Blacks also encountered increasing resistance to their use of a variety of public services and accommodations (e.g., streetcars, restaurants, etc.) and were almost completely barred from membership in unions, which continued their relegation to the most menial jobs. More significantly, racial tensions also sporadically erupted into violence, including a race riot in August 1900 in the Tenderloin. Thus, as the number of blacks in the city grew, whites became increasingly uncomfortable with blacks' rising presence and began to institute formal methods to achieve physical and social distance, methods that were not necessary when blacks constituted a negligible fraction of the city's population.

The transition of Harlem from a middle- and upper-class white neighborhood to an all-black area thus occurred within the context of increasing racial intolerance and antagonism. In Harlem, landlords, realtors, and other housing-market actors used the increasing antipathy among whites toward blacks to their advantage. Indeed,

[t]he individuals and companies caught in Harlem's rapidly deflated real estate market were threatened with ruin. Rather than face "financial destruction" some landlords and corporations opened their houses to Negroes and collected the traditionally high rents that colored people paid. Others used the threat of renting to Negroes to frighten neighbors into buying their property at higher than market prices. Shrewder

operators (. . . referr[ed] to [today] . . . as "blockbusters") hoped to take advantage of the unusual situation by [renting to blacks to push down the prices of adjoining buildings].[113]

Not all such housing-market actors, however, were white. Philip Payton Jr. was an African American who "was keenly aware of the housing needs of New York City's growing black population" and who recognized the "unusual money-making opportunit[y]" that the glut of vacant apartments in Harlem represented. "Payton . . . lease[d] Harlem apartment houses from . . . white owners and assure[d] them a regular annual income. He, in turn, would rent these homes to Negroes and make a profit by charging rents ten percent above the then deflated market price."[114] The use by landlords of whites' antipathy toward living among blacks as a tool is evident by Payton's "first break" as a black tenement manager, which came when a white landlord sought Payton's services to rent out his apartments to other blacks and manage the property to "get even" over a dispute with a fellow white landlord in Harlem.[115] Opportunities followed for Payton to assume the management of other properties, and he ultimately cofounded the Afro-American Realty Company and played a prominent role in opening Harlem's housing market to African Americans.

Black tenants, tired of the rundown and congested conditions elsewhere in the city, largely welcomed the chance to move to higher-quality housing in a fashionable neighborhood and began moving to Harlem in large numbers. Among the first arrivals were black businessmen and their families who had made substantial profits selling their businesses and houses downtown to commercial interests. Indeed, by 1910, most of the prominent blacks in the city had already moved to Harlem. The elite of Manhattan's blacks were soon followed by others, representing more of a cross-section of the black population. By 1920, the "midbelly of Harlem" was predominantly black, and the area was home to the vast majority of the city's blacks as well as to almost every established black church.[116] By 1930, blacks had moved as far south as Central Park North and east into East Harlem, rapidly replacing the out-moving first- and second-generation Jews and Italians who had moved in only a few decades earlier. The increasing concentration of the city's blacks into one large contiguous and predominantly black area is illustrated in rising isolation indices. In 1890, the typical black New Yorker lived in a ward that was only 3.6 percent black. By 1910, the isolation index had risen modestly to 6.7, but after that date it rose precipitously. Indeed, the isolation index more than tripled between 1910 and 1920, and then doubled again by 1930, when just over 40 percent of the average black citizen's neighbors were also black.[117] The transition from white to black in Harlem was thus fairly quick, occurring within the space of a couple of decades. This transition was not simply a function of strong black demand for housing, and especially for housing of better quality than that available in other areas of black settlement, but also of diminishing white interest in moving to and staying in the area. That is, although whites continued to move to Harlem in the first decades of the twentieth century, they became increasingly anxious about living in proximity to such a large black community; the inflow of whites to the area, then, ultimately disappeared. In addition, although at first white residents, land owners, and landlords organized to resist the large-scale in-movement of blacks to the area by agreeing to restrictive covenants and organizing block-specific committees and associations, their resistance ultimately failed, and white residents left the area with increasing speed. Between 1920 and 1930, the broader Harlem area lost 118,792 white residents while gaining 87,417 blacks,[118] and some tracts shifted from having only a token representation—2 percent or less of blacks in 1920—to having less than 1 percent of their populations composed of whites only ten years later.[119]

Yet the out-movement of whites from Harlem was not unique to the area. During the 1920s all of Manhattan experienced a net loss of whites as first- and second-generation white ethnics left the borough to seek newer and better housing being built in developing areas in the outer boroughs of the Bronx, Brooklyn, and Queens as well as in the suburbs. The strong economy during the 1920s translated into a huge construction boom; housing went up in areas of eastern and southern Brooklyn, in portions of the Bronx, and throughout Queens where once-vacant lots were increasingly connected to Manhattan by expanding transit lines or made more accessible by the increasingly popular automobile.[120] In these areas, residential development was more similar to that in the suburbs, with low-density housing types such as one- and two-family homes and "garden apartments."[121] As a result, the mostly white population of Queens more than doubled between 1920 and 1930 (growing from 469,042 to 1,073,129), while Manhattan lost almost 500,000 whites, for a total net loss of 400,000 persons during the decade.[122]

Although Harlem initially offered the city's blacks the opportunity to occupy high-quality accommodations for the first time in the city's history, during the 1920s the desirability of Harlem and its housing stock diminished. "Largely within the space of a single decade Harlem was transformed from a potentially ideal community to a neighborhood with manifold social and economic problems called 'deplorable,' 'unspeakable,' 'incredible.' "[123] Osofsky argues that the emergence of Harlem as a slum is related to a number of interwoven factors. For example, because the dramatic growth in the black population was limited to a fairly narrow geographic area, the forces of supply and demand forced the typically higher rents charged to blacks even higher; between 1919 and 1927 alone, rents in Harlem doubled. When combined with the low income of the typical black New Yorker, high rents required that residents take in lodgers to help meet each month's rent. The increasing congestion taxed the aging housing stock and local services, and conditions were exacerbated by the rural migrants' lack of familiarity with the ways of urban life. Moreover, the majority of tenements in Harlem were built prior to 1900 and thus featured all the disamenities that the Tenement House Act of 1901 sought to remedy. In addition, this portion of the housing stock had been built insubstantially in the first place (given that it had been speculatively built for working-class tenants) and had already undergone a significant degree of wear courtesy of the now-departed white ethnics. Many of the large apartments and homes that had been designed and built to house larger middle- and upper-class white families and their servants did not suit the needs of the area's new residents, many of whom were young and single. Thus, these structures were often subdivided and transformed into boarding houses for Southern migrants desperate for a place to live, even an overpriced one. Finally, landlords were increasingly unwilling to maintain their properties and allowed them to deteriorate. "[H]alls were left dark and dirty, broken pipes were permitted to rot, steam heat was cut off as heating apparatus wore out, dumb-waiters broke down and were boarded up, homes became vermin-infested."[124] In many ways, the deterioration in Harlem is reminiscent of the deterioration that had occurred in earlier working-class neighborhoods. The main difference, though, is that the color line would prohibit blacks from leaving Harlem for newer and better areas, as described by the place stratification model. "The Negro ghetto remained and expanded and other ethnic ghettos disintegrated. The economic and residential mobility permitted white people in the city was, and would continue to be, largely denied Negroes."[125]

The Early Puerto Rican Migration

The turnover that occurred in Harlem was not, however, a strictly racial one. Indeed, it is during this period that another of the city's important ethnic groups first appeared in significant numbers, namely, Puerto Ricans. The Puerto Rican migration to the mainland began soon after the island of Puerto Rico was ceded to the United States from Spain at the close of the Spanish-American War in 1898. But the size of the migration began to grow dramatically during World War I, as immigration from Europe ebbed and job opportunities beckoned, and again in the 1920s, as restrictive immigration legislation essentially halted the inflows of Europeans, opening up opportunities for other groups to take on the unskilled and semiskilled positions earlier waves of immigrants had occupied. As citizens of the United States, Puerto Ricans could do so easily. The lure of jobs in New York was complemented by a "push" off the island of Puerto Rico in the form of very high unemployment.[126] As a result, the number of Puerto Ricans in the city rose eightfold during the 1920–40 period, from just over 7,000 to more than 60,000, and the strong tendency for Puerto Ricans to settle in New York rather than elsewhere strengthened as the share of the nation's Puerto Ricans living in the city during this period rose from 62 to 88 percent.[127]

Like the waves of immigrants to the city that came before them, the Puerto Ricans initially sought housing near potential job opportunities. Although the earliest Puerto Rican migrants tended to possess skills, increasingly those who made the move were qualified more for the city's unskilled and semiskilled jobs than for higher-status and higher-paying positions. As a result, new settlements initially arose among the working-class neighborhoods of earlier European immigrants, notably in East Harlem, the Lower East Side, and near the Brooklyn Navy Yard. In East Harlem, newly arriving Puerto Ricans initially settled among the area's Italian residents, increasingly coming to replace them as the Italians joined the large-scale white ethnic out-movement from Manhattan to the outer boroughs and the suburbs in the 1920s. The East Harlem community would become the most significant "colonia" in the city, El Barrio. Similarly, as upwardly mobile white ethnics left the Lower East Side, Puerto Ricans moved into some of the vacant units they left behind. As a result of being the city's newest migrant group and following in the footsteps of earlier immigrants by taking over the well-worn immigrant neighborhoods, Puerto Ricans inherited some of the city's oldest and worst housing. However, Puerto Ricans' access to housing was likely also affected by race, as almost 12 percent of island-born Puerto Ricans in New York in the 1900 census, and over 13 percent in the 1940 census, were recorded as being nonwhite.[128] Indeed, the potential influence of the same structural constraints that limited blacks' housing choices is revealed by the finding that, over time, the spatial patterns of Puerto Ricans in the city were far more similar to those of blacks than to those of whites.[129] In 1960, Puerto Ricans would be almost as segregated from native whites of native parentage as were blacks (indices of dissimilarity of 79 and 84, respectively), while the segregation of all-white ethnic groups from native whites in 1970 was typically at least 25 points lower.[130]

Thus, the forty-year period straddling the turn of the twentieth century witnessed a number of significant events that would forever alter the character of the city's population and its neighborhoods. For one, the shift in origins among the city's European immigrants at the start of the period diversified the city's white population and ignited a process of neighborhood transition. As a result, Eastern European Jews largely inherited the housing abandoned by upwardly mobile Germans, while Italians replaced the Irish in tenement districts throughout the city. The city's population became even further diversified by the arrival of tens of thousands of black migrants from the South, black immigrants from the West Indies, Puerto Ricans, and Chinese.

However, the neighborhood dynamics involving these groups differed greatly from those involving their white ethnic predecessors. Most significantly, the growth in the number of black residents in the city pushed the black share of the population up for the first time in decades and pushed it well beyond the tolerance of most whites in the city. As a result, the color line grew more rigid, tensions mounted, violence erupted, and new mechanisms to ensure social and physical separation between the races were implemented. Such changes in the city's race relations were most evident in the transition of Harlem from a virtually all-white area to a predominantly black area within the span of twenty years or so. The creation of a large, contiguous black neighborhood was unique in the city's history and was mirrored in the creation of ghettos in other large cities,[131] as well as in Brooklyn in the following decade.[132]

In addition, the creation of Harlem and other ghettos signaled that the opportunities for mobility afforded to urban white ethnics were not similarly available to urban blacks and marked the birth of the high levels of racial residential segregation that continue to plague many large cities, including New York.[133]

1930s–1960s

The population dynamics from 1930 to 1970 differed greatly from those in the periods immediately before and after. The restrictive immigration legislation passed in the 1920s and the stock market crash and ensuing Great Depression greatly reduced the levels of immigration to the United States, and to New York in particular. In fact, during the Depression, more Caribbean immigrants—immigrants relatively unaffected by national-origins quotas—*left* New York to return home than arrived in New York.[134] Similarly, the tide of Puerto Rican migration that had risen during the 1920s also ebbed, as hard times in New York meant few or no job opportunities for newcomers.

Immigration resumed after World War II as a result of more liberalized legislation, such as the Displaced Persons Act of 1948, the War Brides Act of 1946, and the repeal of the Chinese Exclusion Act in 1943. Yet the new immigrants in the immediate postwar period came in numbers far smaller than those observed before the 1920s, and from somewhat different origins. The Displaced Persons Act permitted the immigration of European refugees, and the War Brides Act and especially the repeal of the Chinese Exclusion Act enabled the entry of Asians, although in very modest numbers.[135] In addition to Asians and Europeans, Colombians, Haitians, and Dominicans began arriving in the postwar period to take advantage of the city's rising prosperity and its burgeoning opportunities.[136]

In 1952 Congress passed the McCarran-Walter Act, which maintained the national-origin quotas established in the 1920s but assigned very small quotas to Asian countries. In addition, the McCarran-Walter Act restricted immigration from the Caribbean, which previously had been uncontrolled along with all immigration from countries in the Western Hemisphere. Immigration to the city remained modest through 1965, when the national-origins quotas were repealed. As a result, the percentage of foreign-born residents in the city dropped over the period, reaching 18 percent in 1970, a level far lower than the peak of almost 41 percent in 1910.[137]

Instead of immigrants coming from abroad, Southern-born blacks continued to come in large numbers during the Depression, choosing the limited job opportunities in the city over the more dire economic conditions prevailing in the South.[138] Black migration from the South continued in response to the growing number of employment opportunities both during and after the war. In addition, Puerto Rican migration again picked up during the 1940s; 61,463 persons of Puerto Rican birth were counted in the 1940 census, 187,586 and 429,710 counted in the next two censuses. Thus, in the course of two decades, the number of Puerto Ricans who had been born on the island but now called New York City their home rose by almost 600 percent.[139] During the 1960s, the in-migration of both blacks and Puerto Ricans declined; among Puerto Ricans, the decline resulted in levels of migration below those observed in the 1940s.[140]

The Southern-born blacks and Puerto Ricans arriving in the postwar period encountered an economy that was less hospitable to unskilled and uneducated newcomers than in earlier decades. The kinds of jobs that earlier immigrants had taken and that had provided an engine for upward mobility were beginning to disappear, as New York began the transition from industrial city to postindustrial city.[141] Consequently, many blacks and Puerto Ricans found themselves mired at the bottom of the city's economic structure with little chance of escape.

As the number of blacks and Puerto Ricans in the city grew, the number of whites declined, both absolutely and relatively. Table 2.1 illustrates the magnitude of these changes. In general, the data show that relative growth in the black population far outpaced that among whites and that for the city's total population in every period. The contrast is greatest during the 1950s, when the total population and the city's white population both *shrank* in size. The continued loss registered among whites in the following decade was compensated for by growth among nonwhites, resulting in a positive—though marginal—gain for the entire population. The observed declines in the city's white population would have been larger if immigration had not brought more than a million Southern and Eastern Europeans to the city between 1946 and 1970.[142] The loss in the city's white population occurred as part of the rapid suburbanization of whites that was occurring throughout the country, continuing the trend begun in the 1920s. The postwar develop-

TABLE 2.1
Absolute and Relative Change in New York City's Population
by Decade and by Race, 1930–1970

	Population at start of period	Absolute change during the period	Relative change during the period	Percentage of total population at end of period
Total population				
1930–1940	6,930,446	524,549	7.57%	
1940–1950	7,454,995	436,962	5.86%	
1950–1960	7,891,957	−109,973	−1.39%	
1960–1970	7,781,984	112,878	1.45%	
Whites				
1930–1940	6,589,377	388,124	10.81%	93.59
1940–1950	6,977,501	138,940	2.00%	90.17
1950–1960	7,116,441	−475,729	−6.69%	85.33
1960–1970	6,640,662	−591,821	−8.91%	76.62
Blacks				
1930–1940	327,706	130,738	39.89%	6.15
1940–1950	458,444	289,164	63.08%	9.47
1950–1960	747,608	340,323	45.52%	13.98
1960–1970	1,087,931	580,184	53.33%	21.13

Source: Rosenwaike 1972:133, table 64.

ment of the suburbs and the generous home financing provided by governmental programs during the period provided urban whites with a more attractive option than to defend their neighborhoods against in-moving blacks and Puerto Ricans; in the postwar period far more whites chose flight over fight.[143] As a consequence of these population shifts, the percentage of the total population consisting of blacks grew from 6.15 percent in 1940 to 21.13 percent in 1970, while the percentage of whites steadily declined.

These population dynamics interacted with developments in housing policy to dramatically alter the geography of race and ethnicity in the city. During the Depression, housing construction virtually stopped. The lack of new housing combined with tremendous losses in the city's low-cost housing stock[144] to create a serious shortage of housing for both middle- and low-income families. The housing shortage worsened when the servicemen returned after World War II. As a consequence of severe shortages and escalating rents, the system of rent control was implemented in 1943; in New York, this system (although modified tremendously over time) remains in effect.[145]

Newcomers to the city, largely black and Latino, thus faced a very tight housing market and racial attitudes that prevented their access to housing in many of the city's neighborhoods. Puerto Ricans arriving in the postwar period settled in the established communities of El Barrio and the Lower East Side, as well as in Hell's Kitchen and parts of the West Side (including West Harlem) in Manhattan,[146] replacing the white ethnics who had resumed their flight from the city. Other Puerto Rican communities emerged in Brooklyn and in the South Bronx, largely in formerly white working-class areas.[147] Blacks, meanwhile, were increasingly moving to Brooklyn; although Manhattan had historically been home to the majority of the city's blacks, Brooklyn emerged during the period as the borough with the largest black population. Between 1920 and 1930, the black population in Brooklyn more than doubled, increasing from 31,912 to 68,921. Growth during the following decade was less dramatic but still substantial at 56 percent.

Many of the new black Brooklynites, especially during the 1920s, replaced white households who were leaving the older areas in the northern portion of the borough for new housing and neighborhoods along the southern perimeter of the borough. The relocation of whites from northern to southern Brooklyn was partly motivated by desire for a more suburban lifestyle and partly manipulated by discriminatory lending practices of local financial institutions. The investments made by local financial institutions to enable the development of southern and eastern Brooklyn were mirrored by a parallel withdrawal of capital from the aging neighborhoods in the northern portion of the borough. As a result, a number of neighborhoods in the north that had once been home to affluent residents, including Fort Greene and Bedford-Stuyvesant, began to show clear signs of decay. Facing the prospect of the value of their homes declining, many whites in these neighborhoods chose to relocate to the newer areas in southern and eastern Brooklyn. The impact of these uneven lending patterns was so strong that "by 1936 it was irrational for middle-class white residents to remain in northern Brooklyn."[148] Frequently, the departing white residents sold their homes at a loss to local realtors or investors who then rented the properties to blacks, whose desperation for shelter was high. Moreover, landlords could offset whatever decline in property values they were experiencing by charging the higher rents typically imposed on blacks. Thus, as a result of the actions of local financial institutions and local housing-market actors, the process of large-scale racial change in Brooklyn and the creation of the Bedford-Stuyvesant ghetto was under way.[149]

Yet the geography of Brooklyn was not sharply divided by race until the federal government "armed banks, insurance companies, and developers with public money and public authority" to impose racial segregation on the borough's residents.[150] Indeed, the individual and collective acts of prejudice and discrimination that had been so crucial in the creation of Harlem and other early ghettos continued to act as potent forces facilitating neighborhood transition during the Depression and the postwar period. What distinguished this later period was the direct involvement of the federal government in creating and maintaining urban black ghettos.[151] This occurred through the implementation of the "two-tiered" housing policy during the Roosevelt administration that continued to shape the federal government's approach to housing for decades to come.[152] Although the primary intent of all of the housing-related programs initiated during the New Deal was to put people back to work, they singly and cumulatively had profound effects on patterns of residential segregation and on racial/ethnic inequalities in housing access and consumption.

The Two Tiers of National Housing Policy: Reinforcing Racial Segregation

The first tier of housing policy consisted of programs designed to strengthen the private housing market by infusing it with federal capital to subsidize mortgages and construction costs. Among these programs was the Home Owner's Loan Corporation (HOLC), which was created in 1933. HOLC provided funding to prevent the default and foreclosure of mortgages and to enable former owners to reacquire the homes they had already lost through foreclosure. In addition, HOLC introduced the long-term self-amortizing mortgage featuring uniform payments throughout the life of the loan. But perhaps the most significant and long-lived legacy of HOLC was that it transformed the prejudices against racial/ethnic and low-income groups and against aging housing and neighborhoods that were already prevalent in the lending industry into an appraisal system that systematically undervalued ethnically mixed, densely populated, and physically aging neighborhoods. By ensuring that such neighborhoods received low ratings, HOLC starved them of badly needed capital, ensuring their eventual decline and thus their turnover to black occupancy.

The appraisal system rated areas in four categories, lettered A to D; few funds, if any, were made available to neighborhoods receiving the lowest rating, D. Areas receiving a D rating were color-coded red on HOLC maps, giving rise to the phrase "redlining." Many scholars argue that the adverse impact of HOLC on cities nationwide was less in its lending patterns than in its influence on later federal programs and private lending institutions,[153] but Craig Wilder argues that much of the responsibility for the increasing segregation of blacks in northern and central Brooklyn can be attributed to the actions of HOLC.

Indeed, Wilder argues that HOLC acted in collusion with developers to ensure the success of private developments in the southern and eastern portions of the borough, while ignoring the potential needs and demands of individual buyers and sellers. Using the detailed justifications provided by HOLC underwriters for the ratings assigned to each of the thirty-six areas delineated in the borough, Wilder demonstrates the arbitrariness of particular ratings, as well as the apparent influence that private interests had in ensuring that a given area received a particular rating. Perhaps even more significantly, Wilder also demonstrates the emphasis placed on ethnicity, religion, national origin, and especially race in arriving at the two lowest ratings. Indeed, "the simplest rule for determining a 'hazardous' community [i.e., one that received a D rating] was any with at least 5 percent black residency."[154] As a result, most areas in northern Brooklyn received ratings of either C or D, while the newer areas in the south and east typically received ratings in the range of B. Bay Ridge in southern Brooklyn was the only neighborhood to receive the highest rating, which Wilder attributes to the heavy investments made in the area by private developers. Thus, "white north Brooklyn residents were forced to choose between holding on to devalued properties in declining areas or selling out and fleeing to the perimeter districts with government guaranteed mortgages. . . . Financially choked and hemorrhaging middle-class residents, north Brooklyn's decay was written into government policy."[155] As whites left the neighborhoods of northern Brooklyn, they were replaced by blacks desperate to find housing in the increasingly segregated New York City housing market.

While the actions of HOLC clearly propelled the process of racial transition in Brooklyn forward, the actions of the subsequent federal programs—the Loan Guarantee Program of the Federal Housing Administration (FHA) and the Home Loan Guarantee Program of the Veterans Administration (VA)—helped to solidify Brooklyn's ghetto. FHA originated in the National Housing Act of 1934 and was supplemented by the Serviceman's Readjustment Act of 1944, more commonly known as the G.I. Bill, which created the VA's program. Together the FHA and VA insured the long-term loans made by private lenders for both the construction and purchase of homes. Relying on the appraisal system developed by HOLC and its own practices and regulations that effectively eliminated most urban housing types from eligibility for funding, the vast majority of FHA loans went to suburban locations; the disparity between urban and suburban locations was starkest in New York, where the per capita amount of FHA loans made in neighboring suburban Nassau County between 1934 and 1960 was more than eleven times greater than the comparable per capita amount lent in Brooklyn and fully sixty times greater than the amount lent in the Bronx.[156] In addition, reflecting its concern with the presumed adverse effects on property values arising from racial mixing, the FHA all but required restrictive covenants prohibiting black occupancy as a prerequisite of funding. As a result, "by the late 1950s, many cities were locked into a spiral of decline that was directly encouraged and largely supported by federal policies. As poor blacks from the south entered cities in large numbers, middle-class whites fled to the suburbs to escape them and to insulate themselves from the social problems that accompanied the rising tide of the poor."[157] Under FHA and VA programs, New York and many other cities lost substantial numbers of white middle-class residents to neighboring suburbs. The vacancies they left behind were filled by blacks, and thus black ghettos throughout urban America expanded in geographic size and grew more densely populated. In Brooklyn, the boundaries of the Bedford-Stuyvesant ghetto expanded as whites fled neighboring communities—such as Brownsville, Bushwick, Crown Heights, and East New York—for newer, higher-quality, and government-subsidized housing in the suburbs.

The effects of ghetto expansion and consolidation are evident in changing indices of isolation. Whereas in 1930 the black ward-level isolation index of 41.8 indicated that the typical black New Yorker lived in an area where almost 42 percent of his or her neighbors were also black, in 1970 the tract-level index stood at 60.2.[158] Thus, by 1970 blacks in New York (along with blacks in most Northern cities) lived in neighborhoods where the majority of the people they saw and lived among were also black, ensuring that informal, casual social contact between the races would be very rare. Although it is possible that the pent-up demand for housing, growing tastes for suburban locations, and the capital accumulated by households during the war would have been sufficient to encourage the development of the suburbs, the additional capital made available by the federal government under these programs helped to make the postwar suburbanization process more rapid and complete.[159] And the discriminatory lending practices of FHA and VA, and later by private lending institutions, ensured that suburbanization would be available mainly only to whites, leaving blacks and other minorities increasingly behind in decaying urban neighborhoods. Thus, the cumulative effects of the programs in the first tier of federal housing policy were to drain cities of their middle-class white constituents and to solidify patterns of racial residential segregation across the metropolitan area by creating the geographic pattern that would come to be known as "chocolate cities, vanilla suburbs."[160]

The second, and lower, tier of federal housing policy to emerge during the New Deal used federal funds to build public-housing projects to house families unable to afford private-market housing. Even before the Depression began, it was clear that private housing entrepreneurs were uninterested in producing low-income housing, given the all-too-likely unfavorable returns on such an endeavor. While many policy makers still believed strongly in the traditional view that the government should only be in the business of enforcing housing regulations and thus should avoid direct involvement in construction and management of low-income housing, the desperate housing situation of the poor and working classes, along with the generalization of poverty and need that arrived with the Depression, spurred others to advocate direct government intervention.[161] However, unlike the policies within the first tier, which disproportionately benefited the white middle class and suburban areas, the second-tier housing policies were increasingly identified with minority families, severely underfunded, and subject to political wrangling at the national level and to corruption at the local level. In the end, these policies helped to solidify suburban-urban disparities in income and race, while also dramatically altering the geography of the inner city.

At the national level, government-sponsored housing production had its origins in the National Industrial Recovery Act of 1933, which had among its main purposes the increase of employment, the improvement of housing for the poor, and the elimination and rehabilitation of slum areas. The act authorized the Public Works Administration (PWA) to accomplish these goals. The housing division of the PWA assumed responsibility for projects begun under the aegis of Hoover-administration programs, including the Reconstruction Finance Corporation (RFC). Such programs granted "low-interest loans to limited-dividend housing corporations through state and municipal agencies" and "were intended primarily for middle-income families."[162] In New York City, the PWA completed three limited-dividend middle-income housing developments that had originated with the RFC: Knickerbocker Village on the Lower East Side (1933), Hillside Homes in the Bronx (1933), and Boulevard Gardens in Queens (1935). Although initially the emphasis of the PWA's program was to stimulate private development through federal loans, it became clear rather quickly that private enterprise alone would be unable to rebuild the slums (the PWA approved only seven of the five hundred applications it received), and thus the PWA housing division closed its limited-dividend program in mid-1934.[163]

In New York, the state legislature passed the Municipal Housing Authority Act in 1934, which allowed municipalities to form local authorities to develop housing projects financed with federal funds or by the sale of municipal bonds.[164] Mayor Fiorello H. La Guardia, who was passionate about housing and determined to establish and maintain a close relationship with Washington and to use available federal funds to rebuild the city, had already convinced Secretary of the Interior Harold Ickes to include slum clearance and low-cost public housing in the PWA's budget plans.[165] As a result of La Guardia's relationship with Ickes, the PWA promised a full quarter of its housing allocation—$25 million in all—to the development of low-cost housing in New York City in January 1934. All that was needed was a local administrative structure to build, manage, and own the housing; as a result, La Guardia signed city legislation soon after the passage of the 1934 state legislation, creating the New York City Housing Authority (NYCHA).[166] The first approved PWA public-housing project was to be built on a slum-clearance site in Williamsburg, Brooklyn, but shifting priorities within the PWA (including an increasing insistence on direct federal involvement in all phases of the project) delayed the delivery of the promised funds.[167]

In the meantime, La Guardia and NYCHA wanted to move forward on public-housing development and settled on a project to be located on the Lower East Side that would combine extensive rehabilitation of old-law tenements with new construction. The newly constructed buildings would follow the original exterior designs of the rehabilitated buildings, ensuring that the development would blend into the neighborhood. Completed in 1935, this project, symbolically named First Houses, was financed by the city and built with the use of relief workers from the Works Progress Administration (WPA). Located on Third Street and Avenue A, First Houses, like all the city's initial public-housing projects, provided housing conditions far superior to those they replaced, but at rents that were not affordable by the poor and unemployed; indeed, prospective tenants were screened on many factors, including citizenship, employment, possession of insurance and a bank account, family structure, and housekeeping habits. As a consequence, those who were admitted hardly represented a cross-section of the residents displaced by the project. As with all of NYCHA's early projects, the authority could be selective in choosing tenants; demand for public housing far outstripped the supply.[168]

The next two PWA projects to be built in the city were the Williamsburg Houses and the Harlem River Houses (both completed in 1937). Under the PWA's neighborhood-composition rule, public-housing projects were to reflect the area's racial composition; as a result, the Williamsburg Houses project was to be tenanted only by whites. Built on a slum-clearance site that had originally consisted of twelve separate blocks but had been reconfigured to be four "super blocks," the 1,622 units in twenty four-story buildings were available at rents comparable to those charged for the units they replaced but were of markedly better quality. But again prospective tenants were screened to keep out the least desirable but most in need, that is, the very poor and the unemployed.

The origins of the Harlem River Houses project lay partly in response to the riot that occurred in Harlem in March 1935 and partly in a desire and even need to divert the growing black demand for residence in the Williamsburg development.[169] Although it was clear that a project designated for black tenancy was necessary, it was equally clear that one could not be placed just anywhere. In addition to considerations of land cost and site size, race would have to be a "dominant factor in site selection." Indeed, site selection for public-housing projects would play a prominent role in consolidating and confining the growth of the black ghetto. In discussions surrounding the likely location for a black public-housing project,

The idea of a major project on vacant land in the isolated Hunt's Point section of the Bronx to rehouse black slum dwellers from Harlem was briefly put forward, but found to be unrealistic politically and economically. A site adjacent to the Harlem River, on the northeastern edge of developed Harlem, was an ideal solution; it was vacant and therefore cheaper to acquire than occupied land, and it lay between the existing ghetto and the Harlem River, thus "threatening" no neighboring white community.[170]

Race was as important a criterion in tenant selection as it was for site selection; all tenants chosen to move into the Harlem River Houses were black. Although the tenants selected to occupy units in the Harlem River Houses differed racially from tenants in other new NYCHA developments, they were similar in being better off socially and economically than many other residents in the surrounding neighborhood. The Harlem River Houses also resembled the Williamsburg Houses and First Houses in being low-rise walk-ups that also contained a number of project-wide amenities (such as social rooms, kindergartens and nurseries, and commercial establishments) that would make these low-rent projects far more similar to middle-class housing than to the housing options available for the same rents in the private market.[171] Perhaps of equal significance, these design considerations would set NYCHA's early projects apart from the tall towers devoid of commercial space that dominated public-housing designs after 1948.[172]

In 1937 Congress passed the Wagner-Steagall bill (or the Housing Act of 1937), which created the United States Housing Authority (USHA) to replace the PWA's housing division and thus "marked the first time the federal government accepted permanent responsibility for the construction of decent, low-cost homes."[173] Under the act, state and local housing authorities were empowered to administer federal programs by entering into contracts with USHA to plan and construct housing developments under the supervision of the federal agency. In addition, the act placed ceilings on rents and tenant incomes and stipulated that each unit built had to replace a slum unit demolished in the same locality.[174]

The linkage of the public-housing program to slum clearance in the 1937 legislation created a locational bias within the program, in that it ensured that public housing would be spatially concentrated in those cities with a sufficient number of physically inadequate housing units. The act contained other provisions that strengthened this locational bias, by extending it to fortify suburban-urban disparities in income and racial compositions. Specifically, by emphasizing local participation and discretion, the act allowed localities to decide for themselves whether to apply for public housing. Consequently, suburban localities that did not want to allow poor and minority residents within their boundaries could simply opt not to create a local authority nor to make an application for public housing (of course, the overall program would have benefited from the lower land costs on the periphery). Finally, because local authorities had the discretion to decide where to place public-housing projects, siting decisions more often than not catered to the interests and demands of the politically powerful elites who made up the membership of local authorities, rather than responding to the best interests of the prospective residents of the projects. As was the case in the siting decisions for the Harlem River Houses, public-housing projects were invariably placed in declining minority neighborhoods or in racially changing areas to either stem or divert the growth of the black ghetto.[175]

The locational biases of the 1937 legislation were reinforced in the Housing Act of 1949. Title I and Title III of the 1949 act helped to magnify the existing inequalities between suburban locations and the inner city and were used to remove entire neighborhoods within the city, indelibly altering the urban landscape. Title III of the 1949 act was the first time since 1938 that Congress authorized funding for new public-housing units, 810,000 to be built over six years (amounting to approximately 10 percent of the actual need).[176] It retained the requirement that for every new unit of public housing built one slum unit had to be demolished, and it maintained income and rent ceilings. Title I of the 1949 legislation instituted the urban-redevelopment program that, along with public housing, would be used by local officials and white elites to reshape the urban landscape and to reinforce patterns of racial segregation.

The 1949 legislation was welcomed by local officials and prominent white citizens who worried that the outflow of middle-class whites, the dramatic growth in the number of blacks and Latinos, and the spread of slum neighborhoods would sound the death knell for cities nationwide. The legislation, along with the 1954 Housing Act, "provided federal funds to local authorities to acquire slum properties, assemble them into large parcels, clear them of existing structures, and prepare them for 'redevelopment.' "[177] The legislation further required that residents displaced from areas undergoing renewal would be rehoused in decent and adequate housing at affordable rents. Given the general shortage of affordable housing in most cities, the required alternative housing simply did not exist in sufficient supply; families displaced by renewal, who were disproportionately poor and minority, ended up relocating themselves into whatever accommodations they could find in the segregated market. Frequently this meant moving to nearby neighborhoods or deeper into the ghetto. In New York, many landlords in neighborhoods adjacent to renewal sites responded to the rise in demand for housing in the same way that landlords in the city had always responded to increased demand for shelter: they subdivided existing apartments and crowded as many people into these small spaces as they could. The resulting increases in densities in these areas had the same deteriorating and destabilizing effects witnessed in the immigrant neighborhoods of the nineteenth and early twentieth centuries and in the black ghettos like Harlem in the early decades of the twentieth century: the housing stock decayed, local services were overwhelmed, and the neighborhoods declined. Exacerbating this situation was the fact that urban-renewal sites typically contained less residential construction than had existed prior to redevelopment, and the new residential units were often more expensive than previous residents could afford. Thus, rather than eliminating urban blight and slum conditions, urban renewal typically simply shifted the problems of the slums into other neighborhoods, which then quickly became slums themselves.[178] And because a disproportionate number of redevelopment sites consisted of minority neighborhoods, within the context of a racially segmented housing market, urban renewal had the effect of displacing poor blacks and Latinos into other minority neighborhoods, thereby further concentrating minorities spatially and reinforcing patterns of segregation.

Among the criticisms of urban renewal were the failure of local authorities to ensure that dislocated families were rehoused and the use of urban-renewal funds to develop "conspicuous profitable buildings, whether the areas were slums or not."[179] These criticisms were perhaps nowhere more valid than in New York, where the urban-renewal and public-housing programs were under the control of Robert Moses. In his quest to retain control over development in the city, Moses gave renewal sites to politically powerful elites and private developers who profited mightily at the expense of the populations eventually displaced from these sites and who would be beholden to Moses in the future when he proposed new projects and needed political support.

For example, as part of the redevelopment site at Lincoln Square, Moses gave a portion of the site to Fordham University, a Jesuit institution, to establish a satellite campus in Manhattan. This gift was a quid pro quo for the past and future political support of the powerful New York archdiocese.[180] With respect to the relocation of site residents, Moses callously identified the same public-housing projects for use in several renewal projects, knowing full well that the limited vacancies could hardly house the dispossessed from one site, let alone the refugees from several sites.[181]

With his power over housing, and his unfavorable view of minorities, Moses also helped to reinforce patterns of racial/ethnic residential segregation. Moses determined unilaterally where public housing would be sited, and rarely did he choose vacant land, preferring the elimination of slum housing above all else. Thus, projects were disproportionately built in poor neighborhoods and required the razing of tenements and the displacement of thousands of residents.[182] Although NYCHA dropped its neighborhood-composition rules after World War II, Moses made sure that public housing was built only in established minority neighborhoods or in racially mixed neighborhoods that he determined would be the most likely location for any future expansion of the ghetto. In so doing, Moses was able to divert the course of neighborhood change and decline into the areas he chose for this fate. These neighborhoods, including Brownsville in Brooklyn, were chosen for large public-housing sites "to relieve pressures from other neighborhoods fighting black incursion."[183] As a result, Moses was instrumental not only in determining the course and timing of racial transition but also in using public housing to build segregation directly into the city's landscape.

Under Moses's reign, it was not just public housing that was used to shore up patterns of racial segregation. Indeed, middle-class housing developments were also used to this end. Middle-class housing was a serious concern to city officials as the flight of the middle class drained the city of needed tax revenues. Moses worked with insurance companies to enable these enterprises to construct middle-class housing that would be at least somewhat competitive with what suburban communities could offer. Metropolitan Life was particularly active in the development of middle-class housing, creating four projects during the 1940s: Parkchester in the Bronx and Stuyvesant Town, Peter Cooper Village, and Riverton in Manhattan. For the Stuyvesant Town development, Moses provided almost seventeen acres of land on the Lower East Side that the city cleared of existing housing and residents, as well as tax waivers for twenty-five years, making this private endeavor quite public in nature. This largesse drew criticism on its own, but what was completely unacceptable to many critics was the fact that the city was heavily subsidizing a project that was intended for whites only.[184] A great controversy over the whites-only policy ensued, which Moses in essence refused to acknowledge. At least partly in response to the charges of racism leveled at Metropolitan Life over the Stuyvesant Town controversy, the company embarked on Riverton, a smaller Stuyvesant Town–like development placed within the confines of Harlem. Although the controversy illustrates the direct use of housing policy and programs to reinforce racial residential segregation, it also led to the passage of a 1943 city law blocking discrimination in publicly assisted housing.[185]

Housing discrimination also affected the housing options of middle-class blacks who sought to leave established black neighborhoods like Harlem for neighborhoods more in line with their newly achieved social status. During the postwar period blacks achieved a significant degree of upward mobility, although less than that realized by white ethnics. Although most private businesses continued to refuse to hire blacks into the 1950s, the municipal government emerged during this period as perhaps the leading employer of blacks in the city. Historically, black employment by the city government had remained far lower than blacks' representation in the population, but a mixture of political pressure, commitment to equal opportunity in the public sector, and affirmative-action programs in the 1960s created unprecedented opportunities for blacks.[186] Many of the families that gained or solidified their middle-class status during the period behaved like their white counterparts: they decided to seek out new homes in neighborhoods that were reflective of their socioeconomic mobility. However, unlike their white counterparts, middle-class black home seekers found that their options were limited to areas that already had a black presence and that would undergo further racial transition in the future. Many middle-class black families thus sought out housing in the solidly middle-class neighborhoods of southeastern Queens, such as St. Albans, Laurelton, and Springfield Gardens. These areas contained single-family houses and thus exuded the kind of suburban atmosphere that blacks were prevented from enjoying outside the city limits. Blacks had resided in St. Albans since the 1940s, when prominent actors, musicians, and athletes (including Lena Horne, Count Basie, and others) left Harlem.[187] The influx of additional black homeowners and renters made the area less attractive to whites, who of course had suburban options available to them, with the result that by the early 1970s St. Albans was almost exclusively black. After 1970, the neighborhoods of southeastern Queens attracted West Indian immigrants, who helped to solidify the racial profile of the area.

Thus, during the period from 1930 to 1970, dramatic population changes combined with new government approaches to housing to reshape the city. Migration from the South and Puerto Rico brought thousands of brown and black newcomers to the city where housing—and especially low-cost housing—was in very short supply. Given the prevailing attitudes against interracial residential patterns, the inevitable overflow of African Americans from established black neighborhoods into adjacent neighborhoods would have sparked some degree of racial transition in the city. However, the pace and course of transition were abetted and even directed by new federal policies that enabled the white middle class to leave the city for the burgeoning suburbs and ensured that the neighborhoods they left behind would be starved for capital. Desperate for shelter and facing limited options elsewhere, blacks and Puerto Ricans moved into the older areas abandoned by whites, inheriting the aging and deteriorated housing. As a result, this tier of federal housing policies drained the city of its white middle-class residents while trapping blacks and Latinos in declining inner-city neighborhoods, thus heightening the suburban-urban disparities in race and income. Other federal policies worked to reinforce these disparities while also forcibly reshaping the city's landscape. Urban renewal was manipulated by city officials and white elites to remove entire minority neighborhoods that were encroaching on white neighborhoods and elite institutions, displacing the largely poor and minority residents of these sites into nearby areas or deeper into the ghetto. Public-housing projects built in existing ghettos or in racially changing areas not only helped to determine the pace and direction of neighborhood racial change but also used bricks and mortar to build the spatial separation of the races permanently into the urban landscape.

3

The New New Yorkers
Immigration from the 1970s to the Present

As the 1970s opened, non-Hispanic whites made up almost two-thirds of the city's population, non-Hispanic blacks almost one-fifth, Hispanics about 15 percent, and non-Hispanics of "other race" —the vast majority of whom were Chinese—constituted just under 2 percent.[1] Thirty years later, the majority of the city's population consisted no longer of whites but of minorities. According to Census 2000, only 35 percent of the city's population was made up of non-Hispanic whites, while blacks made up 24.5 percent, Hispanics 27 percent, and Asians almost 10 percent.[2] Not only did each large minority group grow in size, but by 2000 each had become extremely diverse; being Hispanic in New York was no longer equivalent to being Puerto Rican, and the Chinese were no longer the only visible Asian group. The driving force behind the racial/ethnic redistribution of the city's population after 1970 was immigration, which brought not only large numbers of newcomers to the city but also the most diverse—in their national origins and especially in their race/ethnicity—streams in the city's long history of immigration. Indeed, immigration was the main population dynamic leading to population growth over the period; without the large numbers of immigrants arriving in New York City, the net outflows of native-born whites, native-born blacks, and Puerto Ricans that had been occurring since 1970[3] would have caused the city to experience the same continuous declines in population suffered by those Northeastern and Midwestern cities that do not receive many immigrants, such as Detroit and Pittsburgh. In fact, a number of cities are now implementing policies and programs to recruit immigrants to offset long-term population loss.[4]

Because by 1970 there was relatively little vacant land within the boundaries of the city that was available for new development, the settlement of new immigrants had to occur within an essentially fixed housing stock and spatial structure; new entrants to the city had few options for housing other than to replace those households that were departing the city for other locations. Much of this turnover occurred in majority-white, essentially middle-class areas with fairly young and reasonably decent housing. An example is the Elmhurst-Corona area (Queens Community District 4), where the loss of 37,000 whites between 1960 and 1980 was more than counterbalanced by an increase of 50,000 Latin Americans and 20,000 Asians. The tremendous surge in the area's Latin American and Asian populations, consisting largely of immigrants, outpaced the addition of 11,000 blacks during the period, some of whom were also foreign-born.[5] Consequently, since 1970, the city has witnessed the transition of neighborhoods that had only recently been the strongholds of white ethnics into ethnic enclaves and multiethnic communities. The specific pattern of neighborhood succession that occurred, however, was influenced by race. Some neighborhoods transitioned from majority white to majority black during the thirty years after 1970, while others witnessed the replacement of white out-movers by new immigrants from Asia and/or Latin America. In some cases, these turnover patterns produced ethnic-group dominant enclaves, and in others they created highly diverse multiethnic structures. In Elmhurst-Corona, for example, the vast majority of Latin American and Asian in-movers settled in the portion of the area dominated by one- and two-family homes, while black in-movers disproportionately settled in the area's cluster of apartment buildings, resulting in ever-heightening levels of black spatial concentration within the larger community district.[6]

To a degree, these current succession processes appear to have much in common with the patterns of succession witnessed throughout New York's history, that is, the arrival of new immigrants who move into housing abandoned by those seeking new residences elsewhere. Yet an important distinction emerges. In this last era, the neighborhoods in which these transitions occurred were largely lower-middle- and middle-class areas, many of which contained single- and two-family houses that were in fairly good shape and would become available for sale. Thus, many of the new immigrant groups were inheriting fairly decent housing and neighborhoods that were far more stable and prosperous than those acquired by the immigrants of the nineteenth century or by the Southern-born blacks and Puerto Ricans of the mid-twentieth century.

Indeed, the traditional immigrant-entry neighborhoods—such as the Lower East Side and other tenement neighborhoods—were no longer able to accommodate newcomers, as large portions of their housing stocks had been replaced during urban renewal with public housing (to which immigrants have little or no access, only partly because of long waiting lists), and the previous waves of newcomers to those neighborhoods—Southern-born blacks and Puerto Ricans—had unfortunately discovered that the paths of mobility that had led earlier white ethnics out of the ghetto were blocked for them by discrimination. Without the kind of large-scale residential dispersion that earlier waves of white ethnics experienced, the traditional entry neighborhoods could not continue to serve as the first stage in the spatial assimilation process.[7] Thus, new entry neighborhoods emerged, many of a far higher quality than the traditional neighborhoods were in their heyday.

Shifts in Immigration Policy: The Doors Reopen

The resumption of immigration to the city was largely ignited by the passage of the Hart-Celler Act of 1965. The Hart-Celler Act eliminated the discriminatory national-origins quotas that had been in place since the 1920s, replacing them with numerical ceilings on the number of immigrants allowed to enter the country. The ceiling set for the countries of the Eastern Hemisphere was 170,000, with a per-country limit of 20,000 per year, and the ceiling set for Western Hemisphere countries was 120,000 legal admissions per year. A 1976 amendment established a per-country limit on Western Hemisphere countries of 20,000, but an amendment passed two years later replaced the hemispheric limits with a worldwide ceiling of 290,000. This worldwide ceiling was raised by the Immigration Act of 1990 to at least 675,000.[8]

In addition to substituting ceilings for national-origin quotas, Hart-Celler also instituted a system whereby visas would be issued on a first-come, first-served basis according to a preference system that prioritized family reunification and the entry of persons with needed occupational skills. Immediate family members (minor children, spouses, and parents) of U.S. citizens can enter in numbers not counted against the numerical ceiling of 226,000 visas under the family-sponsored preferences. The total number of visas that can be issued under the employment-based preferences is 140,000.[9] The Immigration Act of 1990 added another category of visas, namely, diversity visas. The U.S. Diversity Immigrant Visa Lottery Program was created to allocate visas to countries that had been adversely affected by the switch to an emphasis on family reunification. Typically, these countries included European countries whose large-scale inflows had ended decades earlier and whose current demand for visas exceeded the capacity of group members present in the United States who could sponsor family members. One such country was Ireland. Between 1992 and 1994, 40 percent of diversity visas were set aside for Ireland, but in 1995 the permanent diversity program went into effect, which mandated that the group of countries eligible for diversity visas would change annually depending on the pattern of preference visas.[10]

In 1986, Congress passed the Immigration Reform Control Act, more commonly known as IRCA. IRCA had its origins in increasing concerns about the growing numbers of undocumented aliens in the United States and their presumed adverse effect on the wages and employment opportunities available to native-born workers. IRCA comprised three fundamental provisions. The first allowed certain groups of undocumented aliens (i.e., those who could demonstrate continuous residence in the United States since 1982 and those who had been engaged in agricultural work for at least ninety days per year during 1983–85) to legalize their status. The second instituted sanctions on employers who knowingly hired undocumented workers, and the third related to increases in border patrols. A surprising consequence of IRCA for New York City was the finding that Mexicans—a small, if not invisible, immigrant group up to that point—constituted the second largest group (after Dominicans) to apply for legalization.

The growth in the number of immigrants to the country and to New York City in particular after the passage of Hart-Celler was dramatic. During the 1946–49 period, an average of 153,725 immigrants were legally admitted to the United States each year; for the 1995–96 period, 813,730 were legally admitted, representing a more than fivefold increase. The increase in New York was not as staggering but still impressive, 32,269 arriving on average each year between 1946 and 1949, versus 115,687 per year during 1995–96 (a more than threefold increase). Just as the growth of immigration to New York City did not keep the rapid pace exhibited by immigration to the country as a whole, the percentage of all immigrants legally admitted to the United States who chose New York City as their intended destination fell from 21 percent in 1946–49 to 14.2 percent for the later period.[11] Despite this modest decline, New York remains one of the predominant destinations for immigrants to the United States, along with such cities as Los Angeles and Miami.

In addition to helping to increase the size of the flows coming to the city and the nation, the Hart-Celler Act inaugurated a sharp shift in the origins of immigrants. No longer dominated by Europeans, the new flows of immigrants were far more likely to originate in the countries of Latin America and Asia. However, not all immigrant destinations in the country receive an identical profile of immigrants, and the immigrants who choose New York as their destination may have one of the most distinctive profiles. Compared to all immigrants to the nation, immigrants coming to New York City are less likely to come from Asia, Central America, and North America (a flow dominated by Mexicans) but more likely to come from the Caribbean, South America, and Europe.[12] Immigrants from Africa make up a small and equal proportion of all immigrants to the United States and to New York City; however, between 1990–1999 and 1995–96, the number and proportion of African immigrants to the city rose dramatically.[13] Thus, the patterns of immigration to the city have not only diversified the city's overall racial/ethnic profile but have also diversified each large racial/ethnic group by nativity status. No other city in the country can claim an equivalent degree of diversity.

Because the diversity of immigrants to New York City is so extreme, in the following pages we will focus on just a few groups culled from the "top twenty source countries" list published by the New York City Department of City Planning in their sequence of reports on immigration.[14] The groups chosen—Dominicans, Soviet Jews, Chinese, and the range of Caribbean immigrants—have stayed on the list continually since the early 1980s and represent each major racial/ethnic group. In the interests of brevity, our emphasis here will be on the similarities and dissimilarities with earlier waves of immigrants and on current settlement patterns and their correlates.

The New New Yorkers

The Dominicans

Immigrants from the Dominican Republic began arriving in the city during the postwar years, but in very small numbers. The small scale of the Dominican exodus was due mainly to severe restrictions on emigration imposed by the dictator Rafael Trujillo. After his assassination in 1961, the restrictions were lifted, and with the passage of Hart-Celler, Dominicans began leaving for the United States in far larger numbers, with most choosing to settle in New York.[15] And the increase in the size of the flows was impressive: almost 10,000 registered immigrants from the Dominican Republic arrived in New York City each year during 1972–79; this number rose to almost 14,500 during 1982–89 and to just over 22,000 during 1990–94.[16] The size of the Dominican influx made the Dominican Republic the top-ranked source country for new immigrants to the city. This changed during 1995–96, when the number arriving legally each year dipped to 19,600, making Dominicans the second-largest group of new arrivals after immigrants from the former Soviet Union.[17]

The earliest waves of Dominicans to the city were largely members of that nation's middle class, who were seeking to escape the repressive Trujillo regime. With the arrival of greater political stability and freedom in the Dominican Republic, economic motivations for emigration began to predominate. The relative dominance of the middle class among Dominicans continued into the 1970s, but after that decade the presence of workers with far fewer skills began to increase; these migrants were pushed by the limited economic opportunities in the Dominican Republic and pulled by the demand for low-wage labor in the United States. Although the overall socioeconomic status of this immigrant stream declined, the very poorest members of Dominican society continue to be vastly underrepresented among immigrants to the United States and New York.[18]

In New York, Dominicans have, like Puerto Ricans before them, concentrated in sectors of the economy, such as manufacturing and wholesale/retail trades, that have experienced a significant contraction and wage decline in the course of economic restructuring. These declining opportunities, when combined with the increasing supply of low-wage labor from other new immigrant groups, have contributed to the significant degree of economic disadvantage that is observed in this group. Indeed, Dominicans, on average, are one of the poorest groups in the city, with a median household income of $20,000 in 1998, compared to $35,000 for the city as a whole. Compounding the negative effects of declining economic opportunities is the low level of human capital exhibited by this group. While just over half (51.5 percent) of Dominican adults aged twenty-five and older in the city had at most a high school diploma in 1999, the comparable figure for all adults in the city was 75 percent.[19]

Upon arriving in the city, Dominicans tended to settle in some of the relatively low-cost areas already occupied by Puerto Ricans, enabling the newest arrivals to easily function in their daily lives without the use of English. However, this settlement pattern meant that Dominicans tended to inherit deteriorated and overwhelmingly renter-occupied housing and inferior neighborhood conditions. Such areas of initial settlement included the Lower East Side, parts of the West Side of Manhattan from Fifty-ninth Street up into Hamilton Heights, as well as the neighborhoods of Bushwick and Williamsburg in Brooklyn.[20] However, the neighborhood in New York that became the center of the Dominican community was Washington Heights/Inwood in upper Manhattan. More than 80 percent of immigrants settling in this neighborhood during the 1983–89 period were Dominican, and the area remains one of the dominant destinations in the city for new arrivals.[21] Consequently, in 1999, almost two-thirds (64.4 percent) of all Dominican households lived in the area, and almost half (45.3 percent) of the area's households reported being of Dominican origin.[22]

Over time, the Dominican community has expanded geographically. During the 1980s, a clear movement eastward began from Washington Heights/Inwood into the neighborhoods of the west Bronx (such as University Heights, Morris Heights, Highbridge, and Tremont). Expansion out from the early settlements in Williamsburg and Bushwick in Brooklyn also occurred throughout the past two decades. In addition, Dominicans also live in Queens, settling in multiethnic neighborhoods such as Jackson Heights, Elmhurst, Corona, and Flushing in the northeastern portion of the borough, where the majority of new Hispanic immigrants from Central and South America also tend to settle, along with many Asian immigrants.[23]

Although it appears that the Dominicans' incorporation into the lower rungs of the housing hierarchy parallels their incorporation into the lower tiers of the economy,[24] it is likely that the range of housing options available to Dominicans is not shaped only by choice (i.e., an affinity for areas where Spanish is spoken) or by ability to pay. Because Dominicans are most likely among all Latino groups in the city to report being of black race (27 percent versus 19 percent among all Hispanics in 1999),[25] it is likely that their housing choices have been and continue to be affected by the same kinds of constraints experienced by African Americans and Puerto Ricans (18 percent of whom report black race). Indeed, when foreign-born Dominican households are compared to a full range of other native- and foreign-born households of differing race/ethnicity, they exhibit, along with other groups of African and Latino ancestry, the least advantageous housing and neighborhood outcomes, even when a variety of factors—such as income, education, and household structure—are controlled.[26] The similarity in effects among groups of African and Latino ancestry strongly suggests the influence on households' housing choices of similar factors, among which may be various forms of discrimination. Moreover, Dominicans in the New York Primary Metropolitan Statistical Area (NY-PMSA) are even more segregated from non-Hispanic whites than are Puerto Ricans.[27]

The Soviet Jews

The modern outflow of Jews from the former Soviet Union began in the early 1970s, after the Soviet government lifted restrictions on emigration. Restrictions were again put into place in 1982, but relaxed in 1987 as part of Mikhail Gorbachev's policy of *glasnost*. These changes in Soviet emigration policy are reflected in the numbers of immigrants from the former Soviet Union arriving in New York: an annual average of 2,664 arrived during 1972–79; the figure dipped to 1,347 during 1982–89 but mushroomed to 13,260 in 1990–94 and to over 20,000 in 1995–96.[28] Indeed, as indicated above, by the latter period, former Soviets had overtaken Dominicans to rank as the largest single immigrant group arriving in New York City.

Like the waves of Eastern European Jews arriving at the turn of the twentieth century, Jews from the former Soviet Union were largely escaping a hostile atmosphere of anti-Semitism that limited their own and their children's economic futures, as well as their overall well-being. The problems and dangers faced by Jews in the Soviet Union outweighed by far the importance of more-general reasons to leave, including chronic food shortages and the many other difficulties associated with life in the Soviet Union. As a result, just like their Eastern European Jewish predecessors, Soviet Jews coming to the United States and to New York were coming to stay. There was no homeland to which they would dream of returning.[29]

Because Soviet Jews were fleeing persecution in their homeland, many—85 percent of all immigrants from the former Soviet Union during 1995–96[30]—qualified to enter the United States as refugees, a status that entitled them to a range of services and benefits including public assistance and housing subsidies. This status and the benefits that attend it distinguish Soviet Jews from other new immigrants in the city. In addition, unlike other immigrant groups, Soviet Jews benefit in the resettlement and incorporation processes by aid provided from long-established private Jewish agencies. These agencies include the Hebrew Immigrant Aid Society (HIAS), which was formed in 1909 through the merger of other agencies to facilitate the adjustment of the earlier waves of Eastern European Jewish immigrants, and the New York Association for New Americans (NYANA), which was formed in 1949 to assist Jewish refugees arriving after World War II.[31]

One key way in which these agencies have helped the modern Soviet Jewish immigrants is in the settlement process. They have helped newly arriving Soviet Jews to settle in many of the city's aging Eastern European Jewish neighborhoods, including Brighton Beach, Borough Park, Midwood, and Williamsburg in Brooklyn, Rego Park and Forest Hills in Queens, and Washington Heights in Manhattan,[32] enabling this group to inherit a housing stock that was in fairly good condition. These actions have helped to revive the Jewish character of these areas and offered Soviet Jews an opportunity to live among persons with whom they may share some cultural ties. However, by essentially steering these white immigrants into fading white neighborhoods, the agencies have effectively helped to reinforce patterns of racial segregation in the city. In fact, during the 1970s, many white residents in Canarise, in southern Brooklyn, when facing the spillover of African Americans and Caribbean blacks from neighborhoods in the northern portion of the borough, welcomed the new immigrants and even actively pursued their settlement to block the entry of blacks.[33] In 1995–96, the neighborhoods in the southern portion of Brooklyn (Gravesend, Homecrest, Bay Ridge, Bensonhurst, Sheepshead Bay, Brighton Beach, and Midwood) remained the major destinations of new arrivals from the former Soviet Union, while Rego Park, Forest Hills, and Kew Gardens in Queens also continued to receive substantial numbers of new immigrants from the former Soviet Union. Washington Heights in Manhattan and the neighborhoods of Parkchester/Van Ness, Kingsbridge, and Norwood/Williamsbridge also served as destinations for smaller numbers of new arrivals from the former Soviet Union.[34]

The Chinese

Before the 1940s, most Chinese immigrants in New York were from Canton, and thus Cantonese was the dominant—if not the sole—language spoken in Chinatown. Chinese immigrants arrived as sojourners, planning to make a sufficient amount of money to enable them to return home and buy land in their native villages. After World War II and with the liberalization of immigration laws, Chinese from other parts of China, Hong Kong, and Taiwan increasingly came to New York, among them speakers of other dialects, including Mandarin and Fukienese.[35]

After the passage of Hart-Celler, Chinese immigration increased in size and in diversity. During 1972–79, an average of 5,190 immigrants from mainland China, Taiwan, and Hong Kong came to New York City each year. The flows of Chinese swelled to almost 9,000 per year during 1982–89 and to just under 12,000 each year from 1990 to 1996. The size of the immigration from mainland China, Hong Kong, and Taiwan would be so large as to consistently rank China (as a single category) as the third-largest source country of immigrants to New York City over the period.[36] In addition, the surge of immigrants from China as well as of ethnic Chinese immigrants from elsewhere in Asia figured strongly in the more than fivefold growth in the city's Chinese population over thirty years (from just under 70,000 in 1970 to just over 360,000 in 2000)[37].

The recent flows of Chinese immigrants to the city come from a variety of origins, both rural and urban, in mainland China, Hong Kong, and Taiwan. From mainland China come both rural and urban migrants seeking greater economic and political freedom and opportunity. Rural migrants generally are poor, with little education and little or no English-language skills, and those from urban areas have better job skills but still lack the ability to speak English well. Chinese immigrants from Hong Kong are all urban in origin and have work experience, training, and skills that are easily transferred to the United States. Many left Hong Kong in anticipation of that country's return to mainland rule in 1997; these immigrants tend to be better off financially than those from the mainland, with many arriving with capital derived from the liquidation of their interests in Hong Kong. Immigrants from Taiwan also tend to be better off than those from the mainland, with many having received Western-style educations and thus possessing English-language skills as well as skills that are easily absorbed by the U.S. economy.[38]

Unlike the original Chinese immigrants who arrived in the nineteenth century, the current waves come as settlers rather than sojourners. The large size of the immigration from China quickly overwhelmed the ability of Chinatown to absorb all the newcomers. As a result, its boundaries overflowed and the area expanded to incorporate areas that had housed Jews and Puerto Ricans, as well as almost the entire area of Little Italy. In addition, new satellite Chinatowns began to emerge by the early 1980s, which were all accessible to Old Chinatown by subway. One important satellite community is in Flushing, Queens, a neighborhood that also receives a substantial number of Korean and Asian Indian immigrants. The Flushing satellite differs from Old Chinatown in being more affluent and culturally distinct, largely because of the predominance of the Taiwanese there. Mandarin is more often spoken in the Flushing enclave. In contrast, Old Chinatown, the heart of the ethnic economy, is disproportionately composed of a culturally diverse set of Chinese immigrants who tend to have recently arrived, possess very few skills, and generally lack the ability to speak English.[39] Flushing had been an overwhelmingly white neighborhood prior to the resumption of large-scale immigration after 1965, with a relatively well-maintained housing stock of single- and two-family houses. As a result, the Chinese who moved to Flushing inherited better-quality housing—much of which they would purchase—than did those who moved to Old Chinatown, with its older housing stock dominated by tenements and other rundown older rental housing.[40] In addition to Flushing, many Chinese also live in Elmhurst, Jackson Heights, and Corona in Queens, neighborhoods where significant numbers of immigrants from Korea, the Philippines, India, Ecuador, and Colombia also settle, as well as in Woodside, Forest Hills, and other communities in that borough.

A second satellite Chinatown emerged in Sunset Park, Brooklyn. Sunset Park is a multiethnic working-class community that attracts other new immigrants in substantial numbers, including Dominicans and Mexicans. In general, the satellite in Sunset Park has more in common with Old Chinatown than does the satellite in Flushing. In particular, the Chinese community in Sunset Park is more likely to be working class than of higher socioeconomic status and is dominated by rental rather than owner-occupied housing. As such, the satellite in Sunset Park can be considered more an extension of Old Chinatown than a completely new community like Flushing. However, the housing stock in Sunset Park is not as old as that in Chinatown, and like Flushing, it offers more opportunities for homeownership. As a result, Chinese residents of Sunset Park are more likely to own their own homes than are their compatriots in Old Chinatown. This is no small thing; for many Chinese, the true symbol of success is owning a home, rather than the kind of job or amount of money that one makes.[41] Other Brooklyn neighborhoods that also attract new Chinese immigrants include Bay Ridge, Borough Park, and Gravesend/Homecrest, the same neighborhoods where many new immigrants from the former Soviet Union also have settled.[42]

Caribbean Blacks

Caribbean immigration to New York City has a long history. The influx of foreign-born blacks from Caribbean countries had been sufficiently substantial at the turn of the twentieth century to have the foreign-born constitute 16.7 percent of all blacks in the city in 1930.[43] Immigration from the West Indies declined during the Depression and World War II. A postwar resurgence of immigration was curtailed by the McCarran-Walter Act, which prohibited the use of "home country" visas by colonial subjects. With the United States no longer an option for migrants wishing to leave the West Indies, the flows were redirected to Britain; this redirection was short-lived, however, as the British government imposed restrictions on colonial migration in 1962 and the Hart-Celler Act reopened the door to America in 1965. As in the past, about half of new Caribbean immigrants to the United States after 1965 chose to settle in New York City.[44]

Unlike the flows of Chinese and former Soviets, the flow of non-Hispanic Caribbean immigrants to the city stayed fairly stable in size over time. During 1972–79, an average of 16,522 immigrants arrived in the city each year from the non-Hispanic Caribbean, and the corresponding figures for 1982–89 and 1990–94 were 19,167 and 15,152. Evidence for 1995–96 suggests a decline in the total flow from the non-Hispanic Caribbean, as fewer newcomers from some of the largest individual groups—Jamaicans, Guyanese, and Trinidadians and Tobagoans—arrived each year than was the case during 1990–94. Despite these declines, these countries (along with Haiti) individually remain among the top-twenty source countries of immigrants to the city.[45]

The West Indian immigrants arriving in the early decades of the twentieth century did not form their own ethnic neighborhoods, but the same is not true today, when West Indian enclaves are evident within and near established African American areas. Instead of concentrating in Manhattan, as early West Indian migrants did, post-1965 Caribbeans have disproportionately chosen Brooklyn. The geographic core of the West Indian community to develop in the wake of Hart-Celler was in Crown Heights, in central Brooklyn. Gradually the community expanded into neighboring East Flatbush and then into Flatbush during the 1970s. In the following decade, new West Indian settlements were also visible in southeastern Queens, in such areas as Springfield Gardens, Laurelton, and Cambria Heights, as well as in the northeast Bronx in Wakefield and Williamsbridge. These areas continue to receive large numbers of new immigrants from the Caribbean.[46]

As was the case with many other immigrant groups, West Indians largely replaced ethnic whites departing those neighborhoods for other locations, typically outside the city. However, what made the resettlement process for West Indian immigrants distinctive from that experienced by most other new immigrant groups was that the neighborhoods into which the Caribbeans moved rapidly turned over, eventually coming to have black majorities. Two basic processes appear to have been at work. First, the neighborhoods to which Caribbean blacks moved, although majority white, were located near established majority-black areas. Proximity to majority-black neighborhoods has been shown to be a significant predictor of rapid growth in black population.[47] The second process at work in the rapid succession of these neighborhoods from majority-white to majority-black occupancy appears to be a long-standing reluctance among whites to live among blacks, particularly when the presence of blacks exceeds a threshold of comfort (typically above 20 percent or so).[48] As blacks enter a white neighborhood, some whites choose to leave; because the presence of blacks deters many white movers from moving in, most out-moving whites are replaced by blacks, which raises the black presence in the area beyond the tolerance level of some of the remaining white residents. As a result, more whites leave, only to be replaced by blacks. The process continues in a self-feeding manner until the area is predominantly—if not exclusively—black. Although a number of authors have argued that this traditional pattern of change is no longer the exclusive pattern of change in U.S. cities,[49] it is a process that seems to characterize neighborhood change in New York even to this day. As described above, this was the pattern serving to concentrate both foreign- and native-born blacks in one corner of the broader Elmhurst-Corona area during the 1960s and 1970s.[50] The same dynamic occurred in New York in the 1990s when Caribbean-born blacks began to move into Canarsie and Flatlands, an area in Brooklyn where a real estate agency was firebombed three times over the summer and early fall of 1991 for selling homes to blacks.[51] Describing the racial change in the area between 1990 and 2000, *New York Times* reporter Janny Scott writes,

> Mr. Palmer found his house in Brooklyn near the border of Flatlands and Canarsie. . . . There were just a handful of black families on the block back then. But within a few years, he recalled, most of the white people up and left. "I guess they see black people coming," Mr. Palmer said, chuckling. "And they run away from black people."[52]

The process Mr. Palmer described led to a very rapid turnover; whereas the area was less than 10 percent black in 1990, almost 60 percent of its residents in 2000 were black.[53] The emergence of Canarsie and Flatlands as Caribbean enclaves has also brought new arrivals to these areas. Indeed, these areas appear to receive growing numbers of new arrivals from the Caribbean, especially from Jamaica.[54]

The tendency for neighborhoods to shift rapidly from a majority-white occupancy to a majority-black occupancy following the entry of Caribbean-born blacks illustrates how race defines the life chances and residential opportunities of this immigrant group. Moreover, the rapid transition of these neighborhoods and the fact that they are situated near and even adjacent to established black neighborhoods indicates that the settlement process of foreign-born blacks is associated with the persistence of racial segregation and with the growth and consolidation of black areas in the city.[55] Indeed, when measured by the index of dissimilarity, the overall level of segregation between West Indians and non-Hispanic whites in 1990 was about equal to the high level between African Americans and non-Hispanics whites—83 and 84, respectively —each increasing by about one point since 1980. These same factors contribute to the far lower levels of segregation between West Indians and African Americans; the 1990 dissimilarity index for this pair of groups stood at 42, which was almost two points *lower* than the value for 1980.[56] Thus, whereas both African Americans and West Indians inhabit neighborhoods that are physically separate from those occupied by whites in New York, they appear to be increasingly likely to share the same neighborhoods.[57]

Although levels of segregation suggest that the housing and neighborhood characteristics of African Americans and West Indians should be indecipherable, available data suggest that West Indians (and the larger group of foreign-born blacks) actually experience an advantage, relative to African Americans, on these outcomes.[58] Specifically, homeownership is more prevalent among West Indians than African Americans. Part of this difference may be due to the economic advantage enjoyed by West Indian households, which tend to have more workers and therefore higher household incomes than comparable African American households. Another important factor in the greater prevalence of homeownership among West Indians is the cultural emphasis placed on owning a home, as described by scholars of the diaspora, novelists, as well as the immigrants themselves.[59] Indeed, as Mr. Palmer, the Jamaican immigrant, explains,

> A house to the Caribbean man is something very important. . . . He has to have a house, as opposed to an apartment. Whatever happens, the house comes first, so you can have a family and your friends can meet there. So when I came here, the desire also was to achieve this house, this houseness.[60]

These factors both enabled and motivated many West Indian households to seek out ownership opportunities in formerly white neighborhoods. Moreover, the tendency for West Indian households to occupy better-quality housing and neighborhoods than African Americans directly results from their relative concentration in formerly white middle-class neighborhoods that had stocks of owner-occupied homes. The concentration of owned homes in these areas helped to prevent the kind of deterioration that occurred in other predominantly rental areas like Brownsville and Harlem in the wake of racial transition.[61] However, although West Indians may have an advantage in their residential characteristics relative to African Americans, the marked disadvantage that is associated with black race all but ensures that their position relative to other immigrant and native-born groups will be less favorable.[62]

Thus, since 1970, a variety of new immigrant groups have made New York City their home. The outflows of native-born blacks, Puerto

Ricans, and especially native-born whites during the period helped to open vacancies into which new immigrants could settle. However, within the context of New York's segmented housing market, the locations in which specific groups settled tended to be determined by their race/ethnicity. At one extreme is the case of Caribbean blacks, whose in-movement to white neighborhoods fueled a process of neighborhood succession that adjoined these emerging Caribbean enclaves to neighboring black areas. As a result, not only have patterns of racial segregation been reinforced, but the geographic scope and density of black areas have grown.

At the other extreme is the case of Soviet Jews, whose settlement was assisted by rent subsidies received from the federal government and by private Jewish agencies that relocated many newcomers in aging Jewish neighborhoods. Of course, it is unlikely that these new immigrants, if left to negotiate the racially segmented market on their own, would have settled in more racially diverse areas. However, the intervention of these private agencies clearly represents a force that is wholly external to the "pure" operations of the housing market and that helps to reinforce the color line in housing.

Between these extremes lie the experiences of the myriad new Asian and Hispanic immigrants. Some, especially members of various Asian groups, have developed enclaves in relatively stable and well-preserved neighborhoods that had once housed a previous generation of new middle-class homeowners. Other groups, such as Dominicans, have not been as successful in their quest for incorporation into New York's economy and its housing market. Although it is difficult, if not impossible, to empirically disaggregate the portions of this outcome that are associated with pure choice, preferences, and low income from that which is associated with discrimination, the available research points to a potent role played by the persistence of discrimination that may limit Dominicans' housing choices to the least desirable neighborhoods and to lower-quality housing units overall.[63]

Housing Policy and Development

By 1974, government intervention at all levels had turned to providing rent subsidies instead of producing new housing, effectively eliminating new construction in the city. In the 1980s, construction picked up slightly, concentrated mainly in Manhattan in the form of luxury housing below Ninety-sixth Street. This growth spurt largely resulted from the phasing out of tax-abatement programs for private developers in Manhattan, but it also responded to the demand for luxury accommodations growing out of the Wall Street boom. The demand for luxury housing was also met by rapid growth in ownership possibilities, largely through new construction or the conversion of existing buildings to condominiums and cooperatives.

The concentration of financial investment in Manhattan south of Ninety-sixth Street stands in stark contrast to the widespread abandonment that had been destroying entire neighborhoods in upper Manhattan and, especially, in Brooklyn and the Bronx since the 1960s. The rate of abandonment reached its peak in the 1970s, when approximately 40,000 units were lost each year during 1970–78; after that, the rate of abandonment steadily dropped, reaching about 13,600 per year in the mid-1980s.[64] To put the consequences of abandonment in relative terms, housing losses in the Bronx and Brooklyn alone accounted for more than 80 percent of net housing losses *nationwide* during 1970–80.[65] Abandonment was such a powerful force that new construction in combination with other additions to the housing supply (i.e., conversions from nonresidential use) could not offset losses until the 1981–84 period, when 11,000 total units were added to the housing stock. Moreover, abandonment was concentrated in specific neighborhoods that had already experienced serious decline and that had been predominantly populated by blacks and Puerto Ricans. The result was the differential destruction of poor, already disenfranchised communities and the widespread displacement of minority households without the resources to secure new housing in an increasingly unaffordable and segregated market. Moreover, because abandonment was at its peak at a time when the city was nearly bankrupt, there were neither local nor federal moneys available to meet the increasingly desperate demand for affordable housing.

In response to the abandonment crisis, the City Council in 1976 enacted Local Law 45, which allowed the city to take ownership of tax-delinquent properties after one year rather than the previously defined three-year period of arrears. As a result, the number of tax-foreclosed, or *in rem,* buildings began to skyrocket; by 1986 the city owned over 100,000 units of *in rem* housing units, over half of which were occupied. The size of the *in rem* stock in that year made the city government the fourth-largest manager of low-income housing in the nation, sur-passed only by the public-housing authorities of New York, Puerto Rico, and Chicago.[66]

Following the economic recovery of the early 1980s, in 1986 the city began its "ten-year plan," in which it devoted over $5 billion to create some 150,000 new units of affordable housing. Some of these new units would derive from new construction, but the majority would derive from the rehabilitation of city-owned properties. The ten-year plan has created new homeownership opportunities and returned tens of thou-sands of rental units to the city's housing stock through a variety of pro-grams and partnerships with various local and national organizations, including the Local Initiatives Support Corporation (LISC), the Enter-prise Foundation, and the New York City Housing Partnership.[67] De-pending on the program, new units have been allocated to homeless, low-, middle-, and moderate-income families, and rents have been de-termined according to federal guidelines of affordability. Units intended for the non-homeless have been rented to families who were selected by a lottery and who were subsequently determined to be stable tenants, and units for the homeless have been filled by families already in the city's shelter system. Homeless units were first tenanted in 1986, and the first five hundred non-homeless units were tenanted in 1989; in that year, over 90 percent of new (non-homeless) tenants were black or Hispanic, and almost two-thirds had come from an overcrowded or doubled-up situation,[68] illustrating that city-sponsored production has helped to answer the housing needs of many disadvantaged households.

The ten-year plan has been widely praised for renewing many of New York's devastated neighborhoods,[69] even receiving the praise of former president Clinton during a visit to the South Bronx.[70] A small number of academic studies have tried to quantify the impact of the ten-year plan on surrounding neighborhoods. In general, production under the ten-year plan appears to be associated with positive "spillover" effects, such as rising sales prices for housing near ten-year-plan proj-ects.[71] In addition, there is some evidence that the program is associated with declining prevalence of vacant and boarded-up buildings,[72] a find-ing that may lead to further gains for affected neighborhoods given the association of vacant and boarded-up buildings with various forms of physical and social disorder and the salience of such structures in the minds of potential investors.[73] However, some evidence suggests that the plan is associated with increasing concentrations of poor, welfare-receiving, and single-parent households.[74] Although the extent and direction of the ten-year plan's overall effect on New York's housing and neighborhoods has yet to be definitively identified, what is clear is that the city has spent more of its own money on housing programs than all the other major cities in the nation *combined*.[75] The city continues to work with a variety of organizations to bring its remaining stock of *in rem* housing back into the general housing stock. The success of the ten-year plan has left the city with relatively few and far smaller parcels, and thus the current programs operate on a smaller scale. Rather than bringing entire neighborhoods back to life, the city's current programs focus largely on redeveloping individual buildings and lots to increase the availability of affordable housing.

Conclusion

The passage of the Hart-Celler Act reopened the nation's door. Immigrants, however, do not just settle randomly but instead concentrate in certain cities or metropolitan areas. The shift in key source regions from Europe to Asia and Latin America that characterizes this latest period propelled some U.S. cities (like Los Angeles) onto the list of key receiving areas, yet hundreds of thousands of immigrants continued to make New York their new home. Not only did this enable the city to retain its historic role as one of the premier destinations for newcomers to the country, but the influx of new immigrants also enabled the city to avoid the dramatic population losses suffered by other cities that did not attract immigrants.

The post-1965 immigrants encountered a housing market far different from the one greeting their predecessors who arrived in the nineteenth and early twentieth centuries. What would be likely receiving neighborhoods according to the spatial assimilation model, namely, lower-income and rundown areas, were largely unable to accommodate new arrivals. Many of these areas had undergone structural changes in their housing stocks during the period of urban renewal, including the replacement of tenements and other older buildings by public housing, which placed these areas out of the reach of newly arrived immigrants. The most recent in-movers to many of these areas, that is, black and Puerto Rican households, having found their prospects for residential mobility blocked by discrimination, were simply not leaving for better neighborhoods in the same way that earlier waves of immigrants had done, thereby constraining the potential for large-scale turnover. And finally, the widespread abandonment that afflicted many of these areas resulted in large swaths of uninhabitable housing pockmarked by rubble-strewn lots and the occasional inhabited—but seriously rundown—apartment building.

So instead of making their first homes in the least desirable portions of the city, many of the new immigrants were able to find accommodations in middle-class areas that had only recently been left behind by whites moving to the suburbs. As the ten-year plan began returning large numbers of units back to the housing market, these renovated units would also become available for immigrant home seekers. The in-movement of new immigrants to once solidly white, middle-class areas sparked a new round of neighborhood transition, but the precise path of transition was determined by the race of the in-movers and the proximity of the areas to black neighborhoods. The distaste among whites for integrated living with blacks practically ensured that in-movement by black Caribbeans would spark a wholesale transition to a black majority within a decade's time, especially if the area was deemed too close to an established black neighborhood. In contrast, whites' greater tolerance for having Latino and especially Asian neighbors led many neighborhoods to develop a truly multiethnic profile. Thus, the hardening of the color line that began early in the twentieth century would serve to narrow the range of opportunities available not only to native-born blacks and dark-skinned Latinos but also to new immigrants who shared the stigma of black racial ancestry.

4

Assimilation or Stratification?
Predicting Housing and Neighborhood Conditions for New York City Households

As each new group of European immigrants arrived in New York during the nineteenth and early twentieth centuries, they began the process of assimilation. Although some groups were initially greeted with disdain and were believed to be unfit for American society, the fact that they would eventually be recognized as white meant that the initial obstacles to social and economic improvements they encountered would diminish and eventually disappear altogether. Indeed, by 1970, the descendants of these early European immigrants were basically indistinguishable from one another and from other whites with a longer history of settlement in the city and the nation.

The experiences of the European immigrants illustrate the main tenets of assimilation and spatial assimilation theories, but the experiences of black and Latino immigrants and migrants tell a much different story. Rather than seeing increasing opportunities for better jobs, higher incomes, and better living conditions—as did their European counterparts—these groups witnessed growing *restrictions* on their choices, especially in the realm of housing. The source for these narrowing opportunities lay, to a significant degree, in hardening white attitudes and an increasingly impermeable color line that fed not just individuals' reactions to the arrival of blacks in formerly white neighborhoods but also public and private decisions regarding the redevelopment of, and availability of financing to, deteriorated neighborhoods. The unmistakable importance of structural barriers to minorities'—and especially blacks'—free choice underlies the growth of the dual housing market and illustrates the basic propositions of place stratification theory.

But to what degree do these theoretical approaches continue to describe the process of locational attainment? In this chapter we address this question, basing our evaluations on a series of statistical analyses. The story our analyses tell is a mixed one, partly optimistic in what it says about the overall assimilation process for immigrants, but decidedly pessimistic in what it says about the persistence of the color line in the urban housing market. The "good" news is that our analyses reveal continuing support for the overall process of spatial assimilation, in that households that have higher income and higher education, that own their homes, and that do not receive any government income assistance tend to live in higher-quality housing and neighborhoods than do households with fewer socioeconomic resources and those that rent or live in public housing. Of at least equal importance, there is a clear tendency for housing environments to improve as generation rises and time passes, indicating that contemporary immigrants are, by and large, like their predecessors and gradually becoming integrated into the fabric of American society. Indeed, the kind of structural integration that is reflected by residential assimilation is a key step toward other important forms of integration, including intermarriage.

Although our findings may help to quiet fears about the willingness and ability of today's immigrants to become integrated into American society, we also find substantial evidence that this form of structural integration is simply less available to black and Hispanic households than to those households that are white or Asian. Indeed, on every one of our nine measures of housing and neighborhood quality, black households live in decidedly worse conditions than do comparable white households, and often by a very large margin. A similarly bleak picture emerges for Hispanic households, particularly for Puerto Ricans and Dominicans, while the housing environments of whites and Asians do not consistently differ in quality (yet when they do, it is in whites' favor, but only marginally so).

That Hispanic and particularly black households reside in the lowest-quality housing and in neighborhoods with the fewest resources, even after we statistically take account of the variety of characteristics related to preferences and the ability to pay for high-quality environments, provides indisputable evidence for the continuing salience of stratification processes. However, we also find that stratification works to ensure that even the most affluent black and Hispanic households live in neighborhoods that are far lower in quality than those in which the poorest whites live. As such, our findings reveal fundamental racial/ethnic disparities in access to the kinds of place-based resources that can facilitate social and economic stability and set the next generation on its way to achieving more than their parents did. In short, the stark divisions in housing and neighborhood environments that separate whites and Asians from African Americans and Latinos signals the inevitable continuation of racial/ethnic inequality not just in housing but in all aspects of social and economic life.

Our Approach

Before we proceed to our analyses, a few words are needed regarding the analytical approach we take. We examine a total of nine outcomes (all of which are described in detail in appendix A): three housing conditions (homeownership, crowding, and the presence of three or more maintenance deficiencies) and six neighborhood conditions (percentage that is white, rates of crime and teenage fertility, the percentage of the population receiving public assistance, the percentage of students underperforming in math, and the percentage of housing units that are either one- or two-family homes, all measured for subareas). The housing conditions we examine are important as indicators of socioeconomic status and the creation of wealth (homeownership), as widely accepted indicators of housing status (crowding and undermaintenance), and as indicators of conditions that can adversely affect the health of residents (undermaintenance),[1] and thereby their educational attainment and economic productivity. The neighborhood conditions we examine are standard in studies of locational attainment (percentage that is white), reflect the kinds of behaviors that can derail an individual's chances for future social and economic success and thwart the potential for upward mobility across generations (rates of crime and teenage fertility, underperforming schools, and percentage receiving public assistance), and approximate suburban environments within the city's boundaries (percentage of units that are one- or two-family homes). Thus, by selecting these nine outcomes, we cover a broader range of outcomes than other studies have examined and include outcomes with important theoretical and practical implications.

Our analytical approach involves using both descriptive and multivariate statistical techniques; with respect to the latter, we estimate regression models predicting each of the nine outcomes.[2] The "locational attainment" models we employ are conceptualized in the same manner as the "status attainment" model.[3] The status attainment model uses the characteristics of individuals to predict their placement in the occupational structure; the locational attainment model follows the same strategy to predict households' placement in the hierarchy of place. In short, both models reveal how individual-level characteristics are converted into access to larger social groupings, such as occupations or communities, that form the stratification system within society.

We conceptualize each model as reflecting a *process* culminating in the particular residential outcome, although our models use variables measured at a single point in time.[4] The predictors we use include those that are common to both spatial assimilation theory and place stratification theory,[5] as they originally derive from traditional residential mobility theory (i.e., the householder's generational status, year of arrival, age, and education; household composition, income, and receipt of public assistance).[6] In addition, we include variables whose influence is disputed by the two theories (household race/ethnicity), as well as variables that speak to the relevance of one or the other theory (the subarea percentage of recent immigrants for spatial assimilation theory and the subarea percentage of blacks for place stratification theory).[7] We gather evidence pointing to the relevance of each process—the spatial assimilation process or the process of stratification—from the effects of key variables. The clearest example comes from the influence of household race/ethnicity, the source of disagreement between the two theories. Our findings that white and Asian households often live in similar residential environments once we account for how the two groups differ in socioeconomic status, generation, time since arrival, and life-cycle stage implies that the general process of spatial assimilation characterizes the Asian experience. In contrast, persistent housing and neighborhood disadvantages for black and Latino households, relative to statistically comparable white households, indicate that members of these groups encounter barriers in their housing searches that block the spatial assimilation process. As such, these findings underscore the continuing relevance of stratification as the main process channeling racial/ethnic groups to neighborhoods that differ not only in distance from one another but also in the amount and quality of the resources needed to achieve social and economic success.

The Case for the Spatial Assimilation Process

Our evaluation of the continuing relevance of spatial assimilation as a process generating immigrant adaptation in American society relies on the most important of the range of factors described in the theory, namely, measures of acculturation and socioeconomic status. We begin with the variable of prime interest, generational status.

Table 4.1 presents generational patterns in the housing and neighborhood conditions we examine. We note here that for some outcomes (homeownership, subarea percentage that is white, and percentage of

TABLE 4.1
Housing and Neighborhood Characteristics of Households by Nativity and Generation in New York City, 1999 (Percent)

	Generation[a]			
Characteristic	First	1.5	Second	Third-plus
Housing Characteristics				
Owner	26.10**	26.83**	39.56**	34.75
Crowded	16.15**	15.08**	5.62**	3.84
Three or more deficiencies	13.92	16.83**	11.79	12.81
Neighborhood Characteristics				
Crime rate[b] (per 1,000 residents)	8.13*	8.41	7.36**	8.35
Percentage of households receiving public assistance[c]	8.25*	9.53**	7.24**	7.90
Percentage of students at or below grade level in math[d]	47.71**	50.36**	44.21**	46.23
Percentage white[e]	33.85**	30.82**	43.77**	41.07
Teenage fertility rate[f] (per 1,000 residents)	3.94	4.32**	3.58**	4.00
Percentage one- to two-family housing units[g]	30.23	29.62	31.86**	29.37
N	3,979	1,373	2,243	4,450

** p < 0.01; * p < 0.05; † p < 0.10—indicates difference between the group and the third-plus generation is significant.

[a] A householder in the (1) first generation is foreign-born and his/her parents are foreign-born, and he/she entered the United States over age eighteen; (2) 1.5 generation is foreign-born and his/her parents are foreign-born, and he/she entered the United States at age eighteen or younger; (3) second generation is native-born and at least one of his/her parents is foreign-born; and (4) native-born generation is native-born and his/her parents are both native-born.

[b] Crime refers specifically to crimes against persons (i.e., murder, rape, robbery, assault); measured for 1999.

[c] Public-assistance receipt includes individuals on AFDC (which includes those receiving Aid to Dependent Children, ADC unemployed fathers, and predetermined ADC recipients) and those receiving Home Relief; measured for 1999.

[d] Refers to eighth-graders; measured for 1998–1999.

[e] Measured for 2000.

[f] Average annual number of births to women aged twelve to seventeen for 1997–1999.

[g] Measured for 2000.

one- and two-family homes), rising values indicate improvements in quality, and for the others (crime and teen-fertility rates, percentage on public assistance, percentage of underperforming students) declining values denote improving conditions. The data indicate that at this simple and purely descriptive level of analysis, housing and neighborhood quality tend to improve as generation rises, as spatial assimilation theory describes. For example, crowding consistently falls (i.e., improves) as generation rises, and for five other outcomes (homeownership, percentage of the area's population receiving public assistance, percentage of underperforming students, percentage that is white, and the teenage fertility rate) conditions also improve but only until the second generation, when they shift direction and fall to lower levels by the third-plus generation.

Why should the third-plus generation, the group that should be the most advantaged in housing and neighborhood conditions, live in lower-quality conditions on these dimensions than the second generation? One possibility is that the members of the third-plus generation who reside in New York City may be different from those we would study if we had data for the entire metropolitan area. That is, the third-plus generation living in New York City may have been shaped by selective mobility patterns into and out of the city and thus may currently be described by features that would influence the group to live in lower-, rather than higher-, quality housing units and neighborhoods. For example, the most affluent members of the third-plus generation may have disproportionately left the city to seek homeownership and other residential opportunities in the surrounding suburbs, a process we saw for many of the white ethnic groups throughout the recent history of the city. Indeed, suburbanization has traditionally been regarded as a key stage in the spatial assimilation process.[8] As a result, the members of the third-plus generation remaining in the city would be less well-off on measures of socioeconomic status than the second generation, which, in turn, would be reflected in the relatively lower-quality housing conditions indicated in table 4.1.

An alternative to this scenario relies on New York's attraction to young people from all over who are seeking careers in business, the professions, or the arts. Should inflows of young migrants be large enough to distort the characteristics of the third-plus generation, then we would expect this group to be not only relatively young but also single and childless. According to traditional residential mobility theory, these characteristics would increase the tendency to rent rather than own and would be related to residence in less-desirable areas.

Thus, to understand the source of the third-plus generation's relative disadvantage in housing and neighborhood conditions, we need to look at the characteristics of each generational group, shown in table 4.2. The data here are not consistent with the idea that the third-plus generation residing in the city is disproportionately composed of households without the means to live in the suburbs. Instead, there is a strong tendency for all measures of socioeconomic status to improve as generation rises, as we would expect from assimilation theory more generally. Moreover, nearly all the differences between the third-plus and other generational groups are statistically significant. As for the second

TABLE 4.2
Characteristics of Households by Nativity and Generation, 1999 (Percent)

Characteristic	Generation[a]			
	First	*1.5*	*Second*	*Third-plus*
Race/Ethnicity				
White, non-Hispanic	28.24**	21.83**	60.68**	57.31
Black, non-Hispanic	18.58**	15.76**	8.08**	38.84
Hispanic	34.95**	53.69**	28.18**	3.49
Asian	18.24**	8.72**	3.06**	0.37
Household Characteristics				
Age (mean)	50.10**	41.93**	52.06**	47.08
Single-person-headed household	48.45**	59.62**	64.29	66.13
Presence of				
Children under eighteen	24.13**	30.96**	22.34	21.36
Others in the household beyond the nuclear family	39.48**	39.25**	24.84**	28.22
Education				
Less than high school	33.11**	29.61**	16.74**	13.89
High school diploma	26.08	27.74†	31.05**	25.16
College or more	40.81**	42.65**	52.21**	60.94
Total household income (median)	27,500	30,300	30,500	40,000
Receiving public assistance	19.99**	19.66**	14.95	13.96
Neighborhood Characteristics				
Mean percentage				
Recent immigrants	15.06**	14.46**	11.79**	10.63
Black	22.52**	23.81*	17.71**	25.74
N	3,979	1,373	2,243	4,450

** p < 0.01; * p < 0.05; † p < 0.10—indicates difference between the group and the third-plus generation is significant.

[a] A householder in the (1) first generation is foreign-born and his/her parents are foreign-born, and he/she entered the United States over age eighteen; (2) 1.5 generation is foreign-born and his/her parents are foreign-born, and he/she entered the United States at age eighteen or younger; (3) second generation is native-born and at least one of his/her parents is foreign-born; and (4) native-born generation is native-born and his/her parents are both native-born.

argument—namely, that the third-plus generation has been shaped by selective inflows of young migrants—this also is not well supported by the data; relative to the second generation, the third-plus generation is significantly younger, but it is also as likely to consist of couple-headed households and to have children co-residing in the household. Although the difference in age could contribute to the dip observed in housing and neighborhood conditions after the second generation, it is probably not the sole, or even a main, cause of this pattern.

Instead, other characteristics of the third-plus generation stand out more sharply as potential causes of this pattern, particularly those involving race. As shown in table 4.2, not only does the third-plus generation have a far larger proportion of blacks than does the second generation, but the neighborhoods in which it lives also contain larger proportions of black residents than do the second generation's neighborhoods. Blacks in the city have long encountered various forms of housing-market discrimination, and evidence suggests that such barriers continue to constrain blacks' housing choices.[9] Moreover, the disinvestment experienced by racially mixed and predominantly minority neighborhoods in the city and elsewhere has contributed to the relative lack of resources and lower quality that still characterize these communities today. Thus, as would be predicted by the place stratification model, it is likely that these two features of the third-plus generation contribute to the downward shift in housing and neighborhood quality after the second generation.

The fact that the four generational groups tend to differ on the variables identified as key influences on residential location indicates that we must take these characteristics into account before we can clearly see how housing and neighborhood conditions are related to generation. We do so by estimating our regression models for the entire sample of households and then using these results to simulate, or predict, the levels of housing and neighborhood conditions (e.g., the percentage of households that own their homes or the percentage that is white in the surrounding subarea) for each of the four generational groups.[10] Once again, spatial assimilation theory suggests that the changes we see in housing and neighborhood conditions across generational groups should be largely the result of the higher-order generations possessing more of the socioeconomic and acculturation-related resources that enable households to reside in high-quality locations. Thus, because our regression models equalize the generational groups on the basis of these characteristics, if the theory is a valid tool to explain households' residential outcomes, we should see predicted values that either do not differ across generations or that continue to reflect improving conditions as generation rises.

The predicted values of all nine outcomes for each generational group are shown in table 4.3. Like the information in the descriptive tables (4.1 and 4.2), the values in table 4.3 speak to the continuing prominence of spatial assimilation processes, in that some outcomes continue to improve as generation rises, while for others, the improvements we saw earlier either diminish or disappear altogether. For example, household crowding continues to improve with each increment in generational status, falling from just over 4 percent of first-generation households to a low of 1.58 percent among households in the third-plus generation. Furthermore, when we separate the foreign-born generations (the first and 1.5 generations) according to time of arrival, we see that crowding tends to decline the longer households have lived in the United States. These findings suggest that there is something salient about membership in an immigrant generation—such as proximity to and participation in the networks that drive immigration—that predisposes foreign-born and newly arrived households toward overcrowding, even those who can afford to buy larger housing units. For example, households in the immigrant generations and those that have only recently arrived may be hosting friends and family members who have followed them to a new life in New York City. Yet by the third-plus generation, the strength of these ties has greatly weakened, freeing households from any further obligations and thus resulting in relatively low levels of crowding.

The patterns for homeownership also indicate that assimilation forces continue to integrate immigrants into the housing market, but in a way that reflects the unique features of New York City. That is, the predicted values for homeownership tend to rise until the second generation, then they reverse, falling again to lower levels for the third-plus generation. Although the depressed levels of homeownership for the third-plus generation are not entirely consistent with the generational dynamic described by spatial assimilation theory, the pattern with respect to time since arrival is: recently arrived members of the first generation are about half as likely to be homeowners relative to first-generation households that arrived before 1980, and a similar pattern of difference emerges for 1.5-generation households. In effect, for immigrant households, entering the owned market—a key aspect of the

TABLE 4.3
Prediction of Housing and Neighborhood Characteristics: Assessing the Effects of Generation

Predictor	Housing characteristics			Neighborhood characteristics					
	Own	Crowded	3+ defs.	Percentage white	Crime rate	Teen fertility rate	Percentage using public assistance	Percentage under-performing in math	Percentage one- and two-family homes
Generation									
first	23.08***	4.12***	9.10	35.84*	7.73	3.73*	6.41	46.78***	28.13***
1.5	34.87***	3.25***	9.39	35.11**	7.72	3.77	6.67	47.11*	28.73***
second	31.24*	2.56***	9.99	36.60	7.60	3.75†	6.50	47.04**	28.79***
third-plus	28.47	1.58	9.37	37.06	7.62	3.82	6.56	47.89	26.54
first, arrived 1980 and later	16.15***	4.67***	9.17	35.44**	7.76†	3.72**	6.47	46.85***	29.00***
first, arrived before 1980	34.32***	2.94***	8.92	36.45	7.68	3.76	6.30†	46.66***	26.85
1.5, arrived 1980 and later	24.52	3.58***	8.64	33.61***	7.79	3.80	6.46	47.25	30.32***
1.5, arrived before 1980	38.23***	3.29***	9.86	35.80†	7.68	3.76	6.77	47.05*	28.05*
second	32.11**	2.67***	10.00	36.70	7.59	3.75†	6.50	47.03**	28.69***
third-plus	28.26	1.65	9.36	37.07	7.63	3.82	6.56	47.89	26.61

Note: Predicted values are based on means shown in Appendix Table B.1. Significance is shown only for those categories achieving statistical significance, and reference categories are shown in italics.
*** p < 0.001; ** p < 0.01; * p < 0.05; † p < 0.10.
Source: 1999 HVS and *Infoshare*, authors' calculations.

"American dream"[11]—happens only over time, presumably after immigrants acquire the acculturation-related resources that enable them to navigate the process of purchasing a home.

However, the fact that some members of the immigrant generations should be *more* likely to own their homes than members of the third-plus generation reflects a combination of circumstances, unique to New York, that push some generations toward, and others away from, home-ownership. One such circumstance may be a particularly high premium placed on homeownership by immigrants. For example, scholars studying Jamaican immigrants[12] and Chinese immigrants[13] have described how many in these groups see homeownership as a paramount goal because it is the clearest symbol of success in their new country. Such a strong preference for homeownership and the drive it engenders may combine with the acculturation-related changes associated with the passage of time to create a potent force that disproportionately raises the tendency to own among the immigrant generations. Counterbalancing this drive for homeownership among the immigrant generations, the third-plus generation has experienced a range of other housing options with substantial economic incentives, such as residence in public housing or in rent-controlled and rent-stabilized units, that may have *reduced* the appeal of owning a home, in the city and elsewhere. These kinds of housing options, and the economic incentives they entail, are not as available to immigrants as they are to longer-term residents of the city; the waiting list for public housing is often longer than the length of time many immigrants have been in the United States,[14] and upon vacancy, rent-controlled units either become completely decontrolled (meaning that their rents rise to market levels) or become rent stabilized (but at market-rate rents). In short, the economic benefits of rent control and rent stabilization only accrue over time if the tenant stays in his or her apartment, which increases the incentive to remain in place and to forgo other housing options like ownership. These alternatives may have reduced the appeal and indeed the chance of owning among the third-plus generation that remained in the city.

In addition to crowding and homeownership, the generational patterns in the subarea percent of the population receiving welfare and the subarea percentage white are also consistent with the operation of assimilative processes, by continuing to show generational patterns of improvement (percentage that is white) or by losing this pattern of improvement when other factors are taken into account (percentage on

TABLE 4.4
Prediction of Housing and Neighborhood Characteristics: Assessing the Effects of Socioeconomic Status

Predictor	Housing characteristics			Neighborhood characteristics					
	Own	Crowded	3+ defs.	Percentage white	Crime rate	Teen fertility rate	Percentage using public assistance	Percentage underperforming in math	Percentage one- and two-family homes
Socioeconomic status									
Education									
less than high school	18.83***	3.68***	11.12**	33.11***	8.01***	4.01***	7.27***	49.04***	27.85†
high school diploma	27.21***	2.67***	8.54	34.32***	7.44***	3.82***	6.73***	48.04***	29.70***
some college or more	*33.53*	*1.98*	*8.99*	*38.19*	*7.49*	*3.67*	*6.12*	*46.39*	*27.14*
Income									
$25,000	24.13***	2.52	9.28	35.59***	7.71***	3.81***	6.57***	47.63***	28.00
$75,000	28.40***	2.47	9.31	36.04***	7.67***	3.78***	6.53***	47.41***	27.98
$100,000	31.10***	2.44	9.32	36.30***	7.65***	3.77***	6.46***	47.29***	27.98
Receives public assistance									
Yes	11.37***	4.20**	12.44***	32.90***	8.10***	4.04***	7.51***	49.03***	26.78***
No	*32.84*	*2.22*	*8.76*	*36.63*	*7.59*	*3.74*	*6.34*	*47.11*	*28.23*
Housing-market sector									
owned		*1.26*	*3.69*	*35.85*	*7.54*	*3.66*	*6.12*	*47.02*	*32.16*
rental (not public housing)	14.07***	3.39***	14.07***	35.58	7.73***	3.84***	6.69***	47.78***	26.28***
public housing	13.53***	3.23***	13.53***	39.23***	7.80*	3.88***	7.03***	46.63	24.49***

Note: Predicted values based on coefficients from model including generation * year of arrival interactions, and means shown in Appendix Table B.1. For income, significance is shown for all predicted values. For categorical variables, significance is shown only for those categories achieving statistical significance and reference categories are shown in italics.

*** p < 0.001; ** p < 0.01; * p < 0.05; † p < 0.10.

Source: 1999 HVS and *Infoshare*, authors' calculations.

public assistance). In addition, the subarea percentage that is white also tends to rise as first- and 1.5-generation households have spent more time in the United States, highlighting again the strength of assimilation processes. In contrast, for two other outcomes—the percentage of underperforming students and the teenage fertility rate—conditions tend to *deteriorate* as generation rises, once we account for the range of factors that influence where households live. This pattern is more distinct for underperforming students and occurs regardless of immigrants' time of arrival. Although this overall reversal in pattern indicates that immigrant households have access to better-performing schools than do households in the third-plus generation, a factor that might *accelerate* the processes of upward mobility and assimilation, the differences in the predicted values are quite small (with just about one percentage point separating the first and third-plus generations), despite their significance from a statistical standpoint. Joining the group of outcomes with generational patterns of declining quality is the percentage of one- and two-family homes in the surrounding subarea, an outcome that exhibited little noticeable change across generations in table 4.2. Yet again, despite the statistical significance of the differences between the third-plus and earlier generations, the measured predicted values differ only minimally.

Thus, a plurality of outcomes tends to show generational patterns that conform to the dynamic described by spatial assimilation theory. Yet a far clearer story of the importance of the assimilation process is told by how the measures of socioeconomic status influence the levels of all nine outcomes (Table 4.4).[15] This next set of predicted values demonstrates unequivocally that households that are more educated, earn more, do not receive public assistance, and own their homes[16] live in far better residential situations than do less-educated, poorer, and renter households. A few simple examples amply suffice. For one, while just under 12.5 percent of households receiving public assistance live in severely undermaintained units, the figure drops to under 9 percent for households that do not rely on any form of government income assistance, a decline of more than 25 percent. Similarly, households whose heads have less than a high school education live in areas with higher crime and teenage-fertility rates, more widespread welfare use, and relatively fewer white neighbors and neighboring students who perform at grade level in math than do households with the most highly educated heads. Finally, living in public housing or other rental housing is associated with higher levels of crowding, lower levels of unit quality, and higher levels of neighborhood crime, teenage fertility, and public-assistance use than is living in a unit that one owns. Unexpectedly, given the history of site-selection practices that differentially placed large public-housing projects in low-income and at least racially mixed neighborhoods, residence in public housing is associated with a higher percentage of whites in the surrounding subarea than is living in an owned unit. This counterintuitive result may reflect a number of unique features of the analysis, such as the relatively large size of subareas and particularly the tendency for many homeowner neighborhoods in the city to be largely black, a result of the historical inability of blacks to gain access to owned homes in the suburbs.

An additional and final test of the power of the assimilation process comes from examining how the three housing conditions differ for households living in subareas that vary according to the presence of recent immigrants among their residents.[17] Using the percentage of recent immigrants as a predictor of housing conditions is consistent with two basic tenets of the spatial assimilation model: first, as generation rises, households are less likely to live in ethnic neighborhoods or those with high concentrations of immigrants; and second, immigrant areas tend to be older and more rundown than other parts of the city. This latter proposition suggests that immigrant areas may offer some of the least desirable housing opportunities to their residents; as a result, if an immigrant household restricts its housing search to such areas, it is at risk of acquiring low-quality housing and neighborhood amenities.

The influence of the percentage of recent immigrants is shown in table 4.5. The values used in predicting homeownership, crowding, and maintenance quality reflect actual subarea conditions experienced by households in New York City in 1999. These values are no recent immigrants (the lowest level of recently arrived immigrants is 2 percent), 10 percent (which is slightly below the 11 percent experienced by the median household), and 40 percent (the highest level of concentration of recently arrived immigrants at the subarea level is just over 35 percent). The predicted values show that as the concentration of recent immigrants in the subarea rises, so does housing quality. For example, while about 43.5 percent of households living in subareas with no recent immigrants are predicted to be homeowners, the value falls to less than 11 percent of households living in subareas where about a third of their neighbors were born abroad, a drop of almost 75 percent. Simi-

TABLE 4.5
Prediction of Housing Characteristics: Assessing the Effects of Subarea Percentage of Recently Arrived Immigrants

Percentage of recent immigrants in subarea	Housing characteristic		
	Own	Crowded	3+ defs.
0	43.51***	1.99**	7.03***
10	31.14***	2.36**	8.76***
35	10.67***	3.60**	14.86***

Note: Predicted values based on coefficients from model including generation * year of arrival interactions, and means shown in Appendix Table B.1. Significance is shown for all predicted values.
*** p < 0.001; ** p < 0.01; * p < 0.05; † p < 0.10.
Source: 1999 HVS and *Infoshare*, authors' calculations.

larly, the chance of living in a badly maintained housing unit is about twice as high for households living in subareas with many recent immigrants than in subareas where no recent immigrants are found, and the likelihood of crowding also rises with the concentration of recent immigrants. Thus, the influence of this variable provides extremely strong support for the notion, expressed in spatial assimilation theory, that immigrant neighborhoods tend to offer housing opportunities of far lower quality than do those areas where fewer immigrants reside.

The Continuing Significance of Place Stratification

Although the results of our analyses strongly indicate that reports (and fears) of assimilation's demise have been premature, we find just as much—if not more—evidence of the persistent power of place stratification in determining where certain minority households live. The evidence underlying this statement derives from a series of tests. The first uses the same strategy we just used to evaluate the relevance of spatial assimilation, but here we focus on household race/ethnicity (the variable on which the two models disagree) and how the percentage that is black in the surrounding subarea (a variable with specific implications for place stratification theory) influences housing conditions.

Using the percentage that is black in the neighborhood as a predictor of housing conditions is essential to testing place stratification theory's argument that structural housing-market barriers limit the housing choices of racially stigmatized groups. It follows that the chance that

TABLE 4.6
Prediction of Housing and Neighborhood Characteristics: Assessing the Effects of Subarea Percentage of Blacks and Householder Race/Ethnicity

Predictor	Housing characteristics			Neighborhood characteristics					
	Own	Crowded	3+ defs.	Percentage white	Crime rate	Teen fertility rate	Percentage using public assistance	Percentage under-performing in math	Percentage one- and two-family homes
Percentage of blacks in subarea									
0	27.03†	2.37	8.05***						
10	27.49†	2.42	8.57***						
40	28.89†	2.55	10.35***						
90	31.32†	2.78	14.03***						
Race/ethnicity of householder									
white	34.35	2.05	7.17	49.89	6.30	3.07	4.67	40.82	29.95
black	29.51**	3.15***	13.33***	17.08***	9.98***	4.76***	9.28***	55.84***	27.29***
Puerto Rican	15.93***	1.81	11.15***	25.77***	8.58***	4.47***	8.47***	53.41***	24.63***
Dominican	12.95***	2.49	11.28***	21.51***	8.47***	4.79***	9.46***	56.25***	19.47***
Central/South American	18.22***	3.23**	10.07*	31.98***	7.59***	3.79***	5.84***	49.42***	27.96***
Other Hispanic	19.13***	5.00***	8.28	32.62***	7.73***	3.83*	6.53***	49.95***	28.51***
Asian	35.94	3.19***	8.85	43.11***	6.69***	3.20*	4.54	42.59***	30.69

Note: Predicted values based on coefficients from model including generation * year of arrival interactions, and means shown in Appendix Table B.1. For percentage black in subarea, significance is shown for all predicted values. For householder race/ethnicity, significance is shown only for those categories achieving statistical significance, and reference category is shown in italics.
*** p < 0.001; ** p < 0.01; * p < 0.05; † p < 0.10.
Source: 1999 HVS and *Infoshare,* authors' calculations.

members of these groups will occupy high-quality or owned housing will be a function of the availability of such opportunities in the areas that are open to them. One corollary of racial residential segregation is that social and physical resources are not distributed evenly over space, but are more plentiful and of higher quality in predominantly white than in mixed or predominantly nonwhite areas. The uneven distribution of high-quality housing and neighborhood amenities has its roots in the investment and mortgage-lending behaviors of public and private lenders that helped to destabilize New York's racially mixed and predominantly nonwhite communities, while subsidizing the postwar white exodus to the suburbs. Such differentials in quality were exacerbated in New York during the 1970s when harsh economic conditions resulted in widespread neglect and abandonment by landlords of tens of thousands of housing units in low-income, predominantly black and Puerto Rican neighborhoods in Manhattan, Brooklyn, and the Bronx. Thus, using the percentage that is black to predict housing conditions takes into account the uneven distribution of high-quality conditions that favors areas with few or no black residents and the fact that many blacks and nonwhite Hispanics find that their access to such areas remains quite limited.

As we did with the subarea percentage of recent immigrants, we chose values for this variable to reflect actual subarea conditions experienced by households. These values are no blacks (the lowest percentage of blacks in subareas is 0.5 percent), 10 percent (which is just below the 11.5 percent experienced by the median household), 40 percent (which is just above the level experienced by households at the third quartile, 38.9 percent), and 90 percent (the highest level of black concentration in subareas is 88 percent). We predict that the chance of living in undermaintained housing units rises precipitously as the concentration of blacks rises, suggesting that physically deteriorated housing units are in greater supply in the city's predominantly black neighborhoods than in those where whites dominate (table 4.6). That is, whereas about 8 percent of households in subareas with no black residents live in severely undermaintained housing, the corresponding figure for households living in subareas where almost all their neighbors are black is 14 percent, an increase of 43 percent.

In contrast to the effects on the likelihood of living in badly maintained housing units, the subarea percentage that is black does not affect crowding, but the chance of homeownership tends, somewhat unexpectedly, to *rise* along with the percentage that is black. Although contrary to the general expectations of place stratification theory, this finding makes sense in the New York City context: since blacks were historically denied access to homeownership opportunities in the sub-urbs surrounding New York, their homeownership preferences had to be met by owning within the city. As a result, middle-class homeown-ing black neighborhoods have long existed in the city, as many middle-class and more affluent blacks, including celebrities, began moving from Harlem to homeowner neighborhoods in southeastern Queens in the first half of the twentieth century. These areas, including the neighbor-hoods of St. Albans and Cambria Heights, remain largely black mid-dle-class enclaves characterized by fairly high levels of homeownership and suburban features, including housing stocks composed primarily of single-family homes. In addition, in more recent decades, immigrant and native-born blacks have purchased homes throughout portions of Brooklyn, often setting off a process of rapid white-to-black transition. This has most recently occurred in the southeastern portion of the bor-ough, as once stalwart white ethnic homeowner neighborhoods in Ca-narsie and Flatlands have experienced rapid racial transition following the in-movement of blacks seeking to purchase homes.[18] Thus, not only do black homeowner neighborhoods have a long history in New York City, but the persistence of rapid racial turnover in such neighborhoods has helped to solidify this aspect of the city's racial and housing geogra-phy and thus contributes to the unexpected finding that the chance of homeownership rises as blacks constitute a larger portion of the sub-area's population.

Perhaps the most incontrovertible evidence of the continuing salience of the place stratification process comes from the influence of household race/ethnicity, since the role of this variable is the main source of dis-agreement between the two theories. The predicted values indisputably demonstrate that when we eliminate differences between the groups in socioeconomic status, generation, time since arrival, and all the other factors we examine, blacks and Latinos live in far worse conditions than do whites on basically *all* the outcomes, and Asians live in more disadvantaged conditions on only five outcomes (table 4.6). Moreover, the Asian-white differences tend to be fairly small, whereas large gaps separate the predicted values for whites, on the one hand, and those for blacks and Latinos, on the other. This is most easily seen when we ex-press the predicted values for each minority group as a ratio of the com-

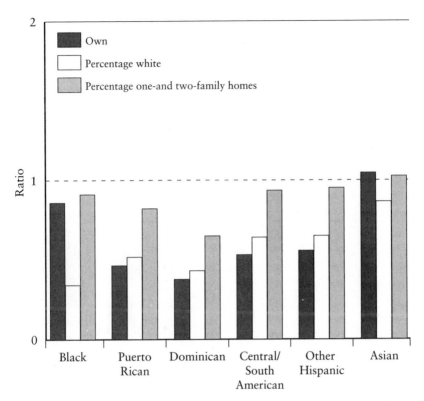

Fig. 4.1. Predicted values of ownership, percentage white, and percentage one- and two-family homes for minority households, relative to white households

parable value for white households, as shown in figures 4.1 (for outcomes where *higher* values reflect better quality) and 4.2 (for outcomes where *lower* values reflect better quality). In figure 4.1, we see that the predicted values for Asian households approach or even exceed the predicted values for white households (i.e., with ratio values hovering around a value of 1.0), but those for black and Latino households consistently fall below, and often very far below. In particular, the predicted percentage of whites in the neighborhoods where blacks, Puerto Ricans, and Dominicans live is between one-third and one-half the predicted value for whites. The highest predicted level of homeownership among Latino groups is exhibited by other Hispanics, but the homeownership rate is only a bit more than half the level for whites. Dominicans, meanwhile, have the lowest relative level of homeownership (less than 40

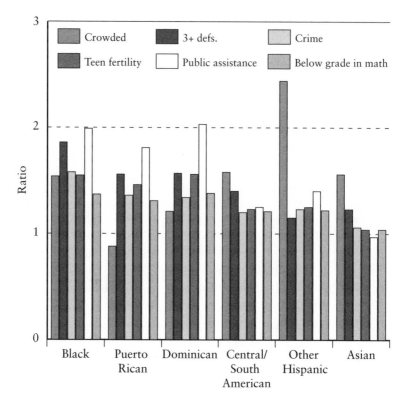

Fig. 4.2. Predicted values of crowding, 3+ deficiencies, crime rate, teen fertility rate, public assistance, and underperforming schools, for minority households relative to white households

percent the level of whites). In contrast, because of the history of discrimination that blacks in New York have faced, and this group's resulting high level of ownership within the city limits, blacks' levels of homeownership and residence in suburban-like neighborhoods approach the levels for comparable whites but remain statistically lower (and lower than those for Asians also).

Figure 4.2 tells a very similar story. Again, the ratio values for Asians are uniformly closer to 1.0, indicating that Asians live in housing environments that are more similar to those whites live in (the main exception here is crowding). In contrast, black and Latino households tend to live in far less desirable circumstances, with the highest relative levels of disadvantage apparent, once again, for blacks, Puerto Ricans, and

Dominicans. For example, these groups live in subareas where the predicted level of welfare use approaches or exceeds *twice* the level in the neighborhoods where comparable whites live, and the crime levels in blacks,' Puerto Ricans,' and Dominicans' subareas are between 34 and 58 percent higher. Similarly, these groups are between 56 and 86 percent more likely than whites to live in severely undermaintained housing units, and they live in areas where the teenage fertility rate is about 50 percent higher. Although other Hispanic households are more than twice as likely as white households to be crowded, everything else being equal, the predicted levels of the various outcomes for other Hispanics and for Central/South Americans do not deviate as greatly from the predicted values for whites, although they typically indicate lower overall quality.

Another, and related, test of the power of stratification processes is to see if black and nonblack Hispanic households live in different kinds of residential circumstances. Place stratification theory argues that they should, with black Hispanics living in lower-quality housing and neighborhoods, since their dark skin would incite discriminatory behavior on the part of housing-market actors. To evaluate whether race influences where Hispanics live, we follow a strategy similar to that used above, but we use the results of a regression model estimated for Hispanics only, which contains a variable that differentiates black from nonblack Hispanics.[19] In addition, we predict only the neighborhood outcomes (largely for simplicity's sake), and do so for "affluent" Hispanic households only. We define "affluent" households as those that own their homes, do not receive any public assistance, earn $100,000, and have at least some college education.[20] We limit our attention to this highly advantaged segment of the Hispanic household population as a conservative test of stratification. That is, whereas place stratification theory argues that race should matter regardless of socioeconomic status, spatial assimilation theory suggests that race differences should disappear among the most affluent households.[21]

Even among the most privileged members of the Hispanic household population in New York City, race clearly matters (table 4.7). Black Hispanic households of the highest socioeconomic status live in areas with fewer whites, more crime and welfare use, more teens with babies, more failing students, and more-urban environments than do nonblack Hispanic households. Moreover, the differences in neighborhood quality that arise from differences in race are highly statistically significant

TABLE 4.7
*Predicting Neighborhood Conditions for Nonblack and Black "Affluent"
Hispanic Households: Assessing the Effect of Stratification*

Neighborhood condition	Nonblack	Black
Percentage white	35.75	31.55***
Crime rate	7.58	7.99***
Teen fertility rate	3.51	3.99***
Percentage on public assistance	4.40	5.51***
Percentage of students underperforming in math	48.31	49.89***
Percentage of housing units that are one- and two-family homes	31.08	28.57***

Note: All households are native-born, Central/South American, headed by a forty-five-year-old, couple headed, with no children under eighteen present and no other adults present. "Affluent" households own their homes, do not receive public assistance, earn $100,000, and have at least some college. Predictions are based on results of a regression model estimated for Hispanics only, using the interaction of generation * year of arrival.
*** $p < 0.001$; ** $p < 0.01$; * $p < 0.05$; † $p < 0.10$.
Source: 1999 HVS and *Infoshare*, authors' calculations.

($p < 0.001$). Thus, not only does race/ethnicity stratify the housing and neighborhood outcomes available to all households, but race serves to separate Hispanic households, ensuring that those with African ancestry are exposed to less desirable circumstances and have access to fewer high-quality resources than those available in the neighborhoods where nonblack Hispanics live.

Although the previous tests provide straightforward evidence of the existence of stratification processes, we can conduct two additional (and final) tests to evaluate the importance of place stratification as the process by which some households come to live in better neighborhoods while others are relegated to neighborhoods lacking many of the resources necessary to advance in the postindustrial economy. Both tests evaluate the relative success each group has in "cashing" their socioeconomic characteristics into residence in better neighborhoods; thus, they rely on separate regression models estimated for each racial/ethnic group. Unfortunately, because the number of Asian households in the survey cannot support such an analysis, we limit our focus here to comparing whites, blacks, and Latinos.[22]

The basic tenets of the place stratification perspective suggest that the persistence of housing-market barriers means that the "cost" that different groups have to pay (in their educational credentials or their income levels) to gain entry to high-quality neighborhoods will vary. For example, barriers to housing choice may mean that some groups are less able than whites to efficiently translate their socioeconomic credentials into high-status residential outcomes; in other words, a household belonging to the adversely affected group would gain fewer units of high quality (i.e., less exposure to crime, high teen fertility, and underperforming schools) per dollar (or year of education) than would a similar white household. As a result, such households would have to pay *more* (again, in their socioeconomic credentials) than comparable whites do for the same "bundle" of housing and neighborhood amenities. In statistical terms, this would mean that the regression coefficients for education and income for such a group would be smaller than the same coefficients for whites.

On the other hand, members of minority groups may actually receive *more* units of desirable housing and neighborhood resources for each year of education or for each dollar of income. Because the rate at which they may exchange their socioeconomic credentials into higher-quality environments would, in this scenario, exceed that of whites, they might be able to "catch up" to whites at the high end of the socioeconomic spectrum and live in fundamentally similar kinds of housing and neighborhoods. This is precisely the scenario described by spatial assimilation theory.[23]

However, even if members of a group were able to achieve "more bang for their buck" (relative to whites) when seeking to exchange their socioeconomic credentials for high-quality neighborhood resources, the starting point (in housing and neighborhood quality) for the group may be *so much lower* that even the most affluent members of the group would end up living in neighborhoods of far lower quality than the least advantaged whites. This outcome reflects the essence of place stratification: regardless of socioeconomic achievements, the penalty for being black or Latino is so extreme that even very high income or advanced degrees will not be enough to level the playing field and allow blacks and Latinos to access desirable housing and neighborhood resources to the same degree as whites do. This case describes a "stronger" version of place stratification:[24] not only will high levels of socioeconomic status fail to erase group differences in residential circumstances, but the neighborhoods of the best-positioned minority households will still fail to "stack up" against those of the poorest whites.

Previous research has conducted similar tests and has generally found that blacks are less able than whites to translate education and income into better residential outcomes, whereas Hispanics tend to acquire more high-quality neighborhood resources per year of education or per

TABLE 4.8

Direction of Significant Differences in the Effect of Education and Income on Neighborhood Conditions: Assessing the Effect of Stratification

Measure of household SES/ Neighborhood condition	Blacks vs. whites	Hispanics vs. whites	Hispanics vs. blacks
Education			
Percentage white	−		+
Crime rate		+	
Teen fertility rate	+	+	+
Percentage receiving public assistance		+	+
Percentage of underperforming students		+	+
Percentage of one- and two-family homes	−	−	
Income			
Percentage white	−		+
Crime rate			
Teen fertility rate	+	+	
Percentage receiving public assistance	+	+	
Percentage of underperforming students			
Percentage one- and two-family homes	−	−	

Note: Direction is shown *only* for those differences in coefficients that were statistically significant at at least the $p < .01$ level. A negative sign indicates that the coefficient for the first group is significantly smaller than that for the second, and a positive sign indicates that the first group has a significantly larger coefficient.

Source: 1999 HVS and *Infoshare,* authors' calculations.

dollar of income relative to whites.[25] Hispanics also receive a higher return on their socioeconomic credentials than do blacks.[26] Moreover, previous evidence indicates that even the most affluent blacks do not live in neighborhoods comparable in quality to those in which the least-advantaged whites live, whereas the Hispanic-white differential in neighborhood quality reverses for households of moderate socioeconomic status and disappears among the affluent.[27]

Our findings, limited to neighborhood conditions for simplicity's sake, both replicate and diverge from these previous findings. As shown in table 4.8, Hispanic households in New York are able to convert their years of education at a higher rate than do white households when seeking to live in neighborhoods with lower rates of crime, teen fertility, and public-assistance use and with relatively fewer failing students, and they also get more neighborhood quality for each dollar of income in terms of teen fertility and concentrated welfare use. However, Hispanics have to pay more than whites when trying to live in neighborhoods with housing stocks dominated by one- and two-family homes. Blacks, on the other hand, are far more likely to experience difficulties (relative to whites) when trying to exchange their socioeconomic attributes for residence in well-appointed areas. Specifically, although blacks get a higher return per year of education and per dollar of income in lower teen fertility rates (and in lower rates of public-assistance use by neighbors), they get a far *lower* return on their socioeconomic attributes when seeking residence in subareas with higher percentages of whites and housing stocks that resemble suburban landscapes. Finally, the rate at which Hispanics can convert their socioeconomic achievements into residence in higher-quality neighborhoods exceeds that for blacks on four of the six outcomes for education and on percentage of whites for income.

Thus, this test tells us quite a bit about the stratification processes allocating different neighborhood environments to blacks, Hispanics, and whites. Generally speaking, blacks are stymied in their attempts to convert their socioeconomic gains and are thus forced to pay a higher cost than do either whites or Hispanics to live in high-quality neighborhoods. The lower returns that blacks receive for their education and income are clear consequences of stratification processes that limit their housing options. However, the final test draws an even starker picture of the import of these differences. Table 4.9 presents predicted levels of neighborhood outcomes for three types of households—"poor," "moderate," and "affluent"—according to race/ethnicity. Each household composite reflects a realistic combination of socioeconomic attributes; because of the strategy we used in calculating predicted values,[28] all the variation in predicted neighborhood conditions reflects the effect of socioeconomic status and the starting point for each group (inherent to the intercept of each regression model).

The predicted values shown in table 4.9 illustrate the strength of stratification processes in determining neighborhood conditions in New York City. Although Hispanics generally receive a larger return for each year of education and dollar of income, because they start out at far lower levels of neighborhood quality than do whites, even the most affluent Hispanic households live in neighborhoods that are less white, are more dangerous, contain more teens with babies, and have less successful schools than those in which the poorest whites live (intercepts for all group-specific models are available in appendix C, tables C.2–C.10). In contrast, the rate of public-assistance use prevailing in the neighborhoods where the richest Hispanics live is only marginally better (lower) than that characterizing the neighborhoods housing the poorest

TABLE 4.9

Predicting Neighborhood Conditions for Poor, Average, and Affluent
Households, by Race/Ethnicity: Assessing the Effect of Stratification

Neighborhood condition/	Household race/ethnicity		
Level of household SES	Whites	Blacks	Hispanics
Percentage white			
Poor	51.31	12.38	27.83
Average	56.65	14.13	30.35
Affluent	58.96	17.33	35.75
Crime rate			
Poor	6.13	11.37	9.48
Average	5.64	10.85	8.26
Affluent	5.44	10.48	7.58
Teen fertility rate			
Poor	2.83	5.71	4.52
Average	2.81	5.35	4.11
Affluent	2.81	4.82	3.51
Percentage on public assistance			
Poor	4.83	12.93	9.12
Average	4.20	11.49	6.74
Affluent	3.75	9.19	4.40
Percentage of students underperforming in math			
Poor	38.92	60.10	53.35
Average	38.05	59.31	52.06
Affluent	37.53	57.48	48.31
Percentage of housing units that are one- and two-family homes			
Poor	35.79	23.17	24.29
Average	33.43	25.72	26.95
Affluent	29.75	36.32	31.08

Note: All households are native born, headed by a forty-five-year-old, couple headed, with no children under eighteen present and no other adults present. "Poor" households have the following combination of SES characteristics: live in public housing, receive public assistance, total household income of $6,720, with less than a high school education. "Average" households live in rental housing, do not receive public assistance, earn $33,000, and have a high school diploma. Affluent households own their homes, do not receive public assistance, earn $100,000, and have at least some college. For Hispanics, the omitted categories for race (nonblack) and national origin (Central/South American) are used.
Source: 1999 HVS and Infoshare, authors' calculations.

whites. Furthermore, because socioeconomic status is *inversely* related to the subarea percentage of one- and two-family homes for whites but *positively* associated for Hispanics, what is a disadvantage for Hispanics at the lowest level of socioeconomic status becomes a very slight advantage at the highest tier. Yet the most advantaged Hispanics still live in neighborhoods with less of a suburban appearance than do the least well-off whites.

An even stronger case for stratification processes is evident in the predicted values for blacks. As was the case for Hispanics, there are large gaps in the neighborhood environments experienced by affluent blacks and poor whites, even for the one neighborhood outcome—the teen fertility rate—that blacks could purchase, in desirable quantities, with fewer dollars and years of education than whites. Perhaps of greater significance, the differences in the neighborhood conditions experienced by blacks and whites at opposite ends of the socioeconomic spectrum are far larger than the comparable Hispanic-white differences, revealing both the far more disadvantaged starting point for blacks (relative to both whites and Hispanics) and the generally lower return they receive for each dollar of income and for each year of education. The starkest example is the percentage that is white in the subarea. Whereas the poorest white household lives in a subarea where just over half of its neighbors are also white, the most affluent black household lives in a subarea where only 17 percent of its neighbors are white. Similarly, the richest black households are exposed to rates of teen fertility and public-assistance use that are almost twice as high as those characterizing the subareas of the least advantaged white households, and they live in subareas where almost 60 percent of students are underperforming in math (compared to less than 40 percent of students in the neighborhoods where poor whites live).

However, as was the case for Hispanics, the negative relationship between socioeconomic status and the percentage of one- and two-family homes for whites enables a black advantage to emerge in the highest socioeconomic stratum. On this measure, affluent blacks live in subareas where more than 36 percent of the housing stock is suburban in appearance, versus just under 30 percent for the most advantaged whites and just under 36 percent for the least advantaged whites. The parity between the blacks with the most resources and the whites with the fewest, as well as the deteriorating quality on this measure for whites as income rises, derives from the unique New York situation, where, again, blacks have long sought ownership opportunities and suburban amenities within the city's boundaries because they were prevented from doing so in the surrounding suburbs. Despite this anomaly, the wealth of the evidence argues quite plainly that blacks are *doubly* disadvantaged by stratification; not only do they begin at a lower level of neighborhood quality than do whites and Hispanics, but they have to spend more in their education and income to gain access to better areas.

Conclusion

Although the assimilation process continues to be a powerful force integrating immigrants into the fabric of American society, it is also clear that the opportunities for integration are not available to the same degree for all groups. Specifically, the pronounced importance of race/ethnicity as a predictor of housing and neighborhood conditions points unmistakably to the presence of a racial hierarchy in New York City's housing market, whereby whites have access to the highest quality housing and the most amenity-rich neighborhoods, followed by Asians, Central/South Americans and other Hispanics, while blacks,' Puerto Ricans,' Dominicans,' and black Hispanics' housing options are disproportionately among the least desirable the housing market has to offer.[29] The presence of such a hierarchy is itself evidence of the continuing strength of stratification processes in the housing market, but the fact that Hispanics and especially blacks in the highest socioeconomic strata live in neighborhoods that are inferior in quality to those in which the poorest whites live on a broad range of outcomes is unmistakable evidence of stratification as the key process channeling Hispanics and especially blacks to less-desirable environments.

The influence of household race/ethnicity indicates that given a white, black, and Hispanic household of equal status, the latter two will be more likely to live in deteriorated and rental housing, in minority neighborhoods, and in areas with high crime, high poverty, underperforming schools, and numerous teens with babies. In short, these households are disproportionately exposed to the health risks associated with inadequate housing, denied the wealth-generating power of owned housing, at risk of being victimized by violent criminals, and involved in networks with far fewer connections to opportunities for social and economic advancement, all as a result of structural barriers in the housing market. Race/ethnicity began to predominate over socioeconomic status as a primary determinant of residential location around the turn of the twentieth century, as tens of thousands of Southern-born and immigrant blacks began streaming into the city, along with large numbers of island-born Puerto Ricans. Given the persistence of housing-market inequalities to this day, the question arises whether these significant and powerful locational disadvantages translate into patterns of downward mobility across generations among the affected groups, as predicted by segmented assimilation theorists. This is the question we turn to in the next chapter.

5

Patterns of Locational Attainment by Race/Ethnicity
Is There Evidence of Segmented Assimilation?

The continuing relevance of assimilation processes for immigrants overall should be sufficient to quell the fears of those who argue that contemporary immigrants either are unable to fully fit into American society or simply refuse to do so. However, what is abundantly clear from our analyses so far is that the prospects for full assimilation—at least as measured by spatial assimilation—hinge on individuals having the *opportunity* to achieve socioeconomically and the *opportunity* to trade in their hard-won socioeconomic gains for residence in better neighborhoods. The persistent power of stratification processes that all but ensure that Latinos and especially African Americans live in inferior environments, regardless of their ability to pay for homes in neighborhoods that are rich with amenities and resources, demonstrates clearly that not every racial/ethnic group is afforded these essential opportunities.

One potential consequence of the persistence of racial/ethnic inequality in access to high-quality housing and neighborhood environments is the possibility that the affected groups, and especially blacks, will not experience the upward trajectory of socioeconomic outcomes across generations, as expected by assimilation theory, but instead will exhibit a deterioration in status at each successive generation. This is a fundamental argument made by segmented assimilation theorists, and it is the question we address in this chapter.

The answer that we offer is an unqualified yes. While each generation of whites and Hispanics typically commands greater socioeconomic resources and enjoys more desirable residential locations than the preceding generation, for blacks the dominant pattern is one of *deteriorating* circumstances, in both socioeconomic resources and housing and neighborhood conditions. The steady worsening of blacks' residential circumstances over the generations is, however, *not* due to the concomitant downward slide in socioeconomic status. Even when we take account of generational differences in those characteristics that underlie tastes and preferences and that enable households to move to their preferred neighborhoods, the native-born generations (the second and third-plus) live in neighborhoods where more teens become parents, more of their neighbors rely on welfare, and more students are failing in school than in neighborhoods of the foreign-born generations (the first and 1.5). This pattern of downward mobility is consistent with our hypothesis that incorporation into American society for black immigrants and their descendants means greater experience with discrimination and thus a progressive restriction of opportunity. The racial stratification system acts to constrain black immigrants' chances for positive incorporation, forcing each successive generation into increasingly dire circumstances. The fact that the structural forces that relegate blacks generally to the bottom rungs of many of society's important institutions also create downward pressure on black immigrants' prospects for incorporation suggests that the future position of the "color line" in American society may shift from the traditional one separating whites from nonwhites to a new one dividing blacks from nonblacks.

Although Hispanics tend to exhibit the kind of generational improvements associated with a positive form of structural integration, they are not immune to the adverse consequences of stratification processes. Instead, the stratification system acts as a brake on their prospects for incorporation, stalling improvements at very low levels, even for the most fortunate households. Thus, although Hispanics tend to experience improving conditions over time and generation, the structural barriers that channel Hispanics in general into neighborhoods that are not simply distant from whites' neighborhoods but also of far lower quality also prevent their full incorporation into the housing market. Because Hispanics' limited access to high-quality place-based resources will also help, on average, to slow their progress toward social and economic success, they may be assigned an intermediate position in the future racial/ethnic hierarchy, not fully accepted by the dominant nonblack group, but not fully consigned to sharing the bottom rungs with blacks.[1]

Our Approach

As in chapter 4, we use a mix of descriptive and multivariate statistical techniques to assess whether generational patterns in housing and neighborhood outcomes for whites, blacks, and Hispanics follow the trajectory suggested by spatial assimilation theory or whether there are differences across the groups, with blacks in particular exhibiting the deteriorating patterns suggested by segmented assimilation theory. The multivariate "locational attainment" regression models we estimate are identical to those we used in the previous chapter, except that here we focus on the models estimated for each group separately. As described earlier, because our data set does not contain a sufficient number of Asian households to estimate the necessary regression models, we limit our attention to comparisons between whites, blacks, and Hispanics. Equally unfortunate is the fact that adequate sample sizes for separate analyses of Puerto Ricans, Dominicans, and black Hispanics—theoretically very important groups—also elude us.

As we did in the previous chapter, when we focus on generational differences we test whether the differences, between the first, 1.5, and the second generations, on the one hand, and the third-plus generation, on the other, are statistically significant. Yet when we focus in on each racial/ethnic group separately, we run into a potentially serious limitation in the data set, namely, the absence of information on ancestry or ethnic identity for whites and blacks (recall that we are able to take account of national-origin differences for Hispanics). Without this information, when we examine generational patterns for these groups, we face the risk of taking as generational effects what are really differences among ethnic groups. This danger is most acute for the analysis concerning blacks. Many of the white immigrant groups currently arriving in the city were represented among the earlier waves of European immigrants (e.g., Russians, Poles, and the Irish). Most blacks in the third-plus generation trace their roots to the waves of Southern-born migrants who began arriving in the city around the turn of the twentieth century, whereas members of the immigrant and second generations are largely of Caribbean origin. Of course, because of the long history of Caribbean migration to New York, there is a segment of the third-plus generation that is of Caribbean origin and identifies as such. The problem is that, with our data, we cannot identify them, and thus they are "lost" among the descendants of Southern-born migrants. As a result, we also perform a set of statistical tests that pits the first and 1.5 generations against the second generation as a way to avoid confounding generation with ethnicity and thus to strengthen the validity of our interpretations.

Generational Patterns: A First Look

Do generational differences in housing and neighborhood conditions for whites, blacks, and Hispanics reflect a pattern of positive incorporation into the housing market, or do patterns vary across the groups? As a first step toward addressing this question, we provide the observed levels of each of the nine outcomes across the generations for each racial/ethnic group in table 5.1. Recall that for some outcomes rising levels denote improvements (e.g., homeownership, subarea percentage white, and percentage of one- and two-family homes), and for others declining levels signal improvements (subarea crime and teen-fertility rates and percentage receiving public assistance and underperforming students).

The table contains a great deal of information, but it relates a fairly simple story. First, the racial/ethnic hierarchy that we found in the previous chapter stands out clearly, with black households typically experiencing the lowest level of housing and neighborhood quality of the three groups. There are two exceptions to this general statement. The first is that for crowding, Hispanics are consistently at the greatest disadvantage, experiencing the highest level of crowding at each generation (table 5.1, panel C). The second exception is a reordering of the hierarchy by generation for five of the nine outcomes. At the first generation, black households are the *most* likely of all to be homeowners and to live in subareas with suburban-like housing stocks (panel B), but by the third-plus generation white households emerge as the most advantaged group (panel A). With respect to subarea teen-fertility rates and the percentage on welfare, first-generation Hispanics live in the least desirable conditions but cede this position to blacks at the third-plus generation. For the percentage of underperforming students, blacks and Hispanics at the first generation live in neighborhoods that are very similar, but by the third-plus generation a gap has emerged that works to the disadvantage of blacks.

The reordering of the hierarchy across the generations stems from the most important feature of the story told by this data, namely, that the

TABLE 5.1

Housing and Neighborhood Characteristics of Households by Generational Status and Race/Ethnicity, New York City, 1999

Race/ethnicity and characteristic	First	1.5	Second	Third-plus
		Generation		
A. *Non-Hispanic whites*				
Owner	32.41**	49.50*	52.42**	41.58
Crowded (> 1 person per room)	9.70**	6.74**	2.78	2.00
Three or more maintenance deficiencies	7.51	7.13	5.42†	6.97
Percentage white[a]	53.22**	50.12**	54.48**	57.96
Crime rate[b] (per 1,000 residents)	6.27†	6.22	5.82†	6.05
Teenage fertility rate[c] (per 1,000 residents)	2.76**	2.81	2.71**	2.95
Percentage of households receiving public assistance[d]	5.26**	5.15**	4.48**	4.12
Percentage of students at or below grade level in math[e]	38.57*	39.37*	38.25	37.57
Percentage of one- and two-family units[f]	31.39	37.48**	35.69**	30.39
(N of cases)	(1,099)	(293)	(1,331)	(2,494)
B. *Non-Hispanic blacks*				
Owner	36.46**	27.41	27.32	26.30
Crowded (> 1 person per room)	15.00**	14.58**	9.48	5.91
Three or more maintenance deficiencies	19.96	19.06	26.93	21.21
Percentage white[a]	16.39**	15.39**	17.99	17.08
Crime rate[b] (per 1,000 residents)	10.45**	10.83**	11.42	11.61
Teenage fertility rate[c] (per 1,000 residents)	4.67**	4.88**	5.22†	5.49
Percentage of households receiving public assistance[d]	10.21**	11.24**	11.60**	13.22
Percentage of students at or below grade level in math[e]	55.80**	56.63*	56.22**	58.49
Percentage of one- and two-family units[f]	37.93**	36.28**	30.19	28.22
(N of cases)	(772)	(226)	(189)	(1,804)
C. *Hispanics*				
Owner	10.96*	15.05	16.24	18.41
Crowded (> 1 person per room)	20.09**	18.65**	10.58	9.52
Three or more maintenance deficiencies	18.59	21.63	21.20	16.94
Percentage white[a]	23.21**	24.93*	26.98	30.17
Crime rate[b] (per 1,000 residents)	9.27	8.97†	9.52	9.85
Teenage fertility rate[c] (per 1,000 residents)	5.08	5.03	5.01	4.81
Percentage of households receiving public assistance[d]	11.57	11.70	12.21	11.11
Percentage of students at or below grade level in math[e]	54.91*	54.90*	54.18	52.15
Percentage of one- and two-family units[f]	21.48*	23.31	25.22	25.91
(N of cases)	(1,399)	(741)	(636)	(156)

** p < .01; * p < .05; † p < .10—indicates significance between third-plus generation and other groups; bolded figures represent significance between second generation and first and 1.5 generations at .01 to .10 levels.

[a] Measured for 2000.

[b] Crime refers specifically to crimes against persons (i.e., murder, rape, robbery, assault); measured for 1999.

[c] Average annual number of births to women aged twelve to seventeen for 1997–1999.

[d] Public-assistance receipt includes individuals on AFDC (which includes those receiving Aid to Dependent Children, ADC unemployed fathers, and pre-determined ADC recipients) and those receiving Home Relief; measured for 1999.

[e] Refers to fourth- through sixth-graders; measured for 1998–1999.

[f] Percentage of all housing units that are either one or two units, with or without businesses.

Source: 1999 HVS and *Infoshare,* authors' calculations.

generational patterns of housing and neighborhood conditions clearly differ by race/ethnicity. Specifically, for a vast majority—seven of nine—outcomes, the pattern for blacks moves in a direction *opposite* to that for whites and Hispanics. While each generation of whites and Hispanics tends to enjoy progressively improved housing and neighborhood conditions (with statistical significance observed for seven and five outcomes, respectively), for blacks each step away from the first generation entails a significant deterioration in quality. (The main exception here is crowding, as households from each of the three racial/ethnic groups become significantly and dramatically less crowded with each increase in generational status.) Moreover, for six of the seven outcomes for which blacks display a pattern of deterioration across the generations (homeownership, undermaintained housing, subarea percentage of one- and two-family homes, crime and teen-fertility rates, percentage receiving public assistance, and percentage of underperforming students), members of the immigrant generations live in significantly better conditions than do members of the second generation, indicating that generational decline is *not* an artifact of ethnic differences between the generations but that this decline occurs largely *within* similar ethnic groups. Thus, whereas whites and Hispanics appear, at least at this initial stage, to experience the process of spatial assimilation, integration into the urban housing market is a far more difficult process for black immigrants. Indeed, it appears that the path black immigrants' descendants are likely to follow is one of worsening conditions and diminishing access to the kinds of place-based resources that can facilitate socioeconomic success.

What underlies these different patterns of integration? A likely culprit is the set of factors theoretically expected to influence where households live, namely, measures of socioeconomic status. And in fact, to a very large degree, the group-specific patterns we see in household income, educational attainment, and receipt of public assistance mirror those we see in housing and neighborhood conditions. For example, there is a general tendency for socioeconomic status to improve as generation rises among whites (table 5.2, panel A), as well as among Hispanics (table 5.2, panel C). However, the starting and end points for Hispanics are far lower than for whites: while first-generation white households earn an average of $30,000 compared to $55,100 for third-plus generation households, among Hispanics the corresponding values are $20,000 and $31,000. That each generational group is in a rela-

TABLE 5.2
Household and Subarea Characteristics by Generational Status and
Race/Ethnicity, New York City, 1999

	Generation			
Race/ethnicity and characteristic	First	1.5	Second	Third-plus
A. Non-Hispanic whites				
Household socioeconomic status				
Householder education				
Less than high school	21.42**	23.75**	14.25**	5.85
High school diploma	27.82**	30.77**	34.28**	21.04
At least some college	50.76**	45.48**	51.47**	73.11
Receipt of public assistance	16.99**	5.45	6.03*	4.32
Median household income/10,000	30.00	39.00	32.54	55.10
Public housing	1.83	0.69	2.47†	1.30
Household composition				
Householder's age (mean)	53.02**	51.67**	60.48**	46.15
Couple headed	55.44**	44.68	39.63	40.28
Presence of children under eighteen	20.54†	17.25	11.75**	17.97
Extended household	27.26	32.16*	20.86**	24.97
Subarea characteristics				
Percentage of recent immigrants	13.22**	13.24**	11.21**	9.89
Percentage of blacks	10.77	11.26	10.50	10.83
(N of cases)	(1,099)	(293)	(1,331)	(2,494)
B. Non-Hispanic blacks				
Household socioeconomic status				
Householder education				
Less than high school	25.49	9.63**	14.41**	25.35
High school diploma	33.73	25.05*	20.24**	31.26
At least some college	40.79	65.32**	65.35**	43.39
Receipt of public assistance	12.80**	15.49**	23.19	27.72
Median household income/10,000	32.00	38.27	30.00	23.54
Public housing	3.94**	4.18**	16.70**	27.15
Household composition				
Householder's age (mean)	48.76	36.08**	47.08	49.34
Couple headed	44.46**	37.03**	26.56	24.18
Presence of children under eighteen	23.30	46.10**	22.54	25.16
Extended household	47.25**	37.59	34.13	32.95
Subarea characteristics				
Percentage of recent immigrants	14.60**	14.51**	13.30**	11.62
Percentage of blacks	51.67**	53.63**	49.89	47.92
(N of cases)	(772)	(226)	(189)	(1,804)
C. Hispanics				
Household socioeconomic status				
Householder education				
Less than high school	52.85**	40.44**	24.26	19.35
High school diploma	22.22	28.42	29.10	27.22
At least some college	24.94**	31.14**	46.63	53.43
Receipt of public assistance	32.22**	29.43**	33.12**	19.99
Median household income/10,000	20.00	24.00	24.60	31.00
Public housing	11.19	12.20	13.95	12.73
Household composition				
Householder's age (mean)	50.60**	41.17*	37.18	38.17
Couple headed	42.27†	37.63	30.58	34.96
Presence of children under eighteen	23.75**	32.70	45.77*	35.07
Extended household	45.13**	43.25**	29.97	28.16

(continued)

TABLE 5.2 *(continued)*

Race/ethnicity and characteristic	First	1.5	Second	Third-plus
		Generation		
Subarea characteristics				
Percentage of recent immigrants	**16.46****	**14.97****	12.65*	11.57
Percentage of blacks	**21.98**	22.30	24.61	24.27
(N of cases)	(1,399)	(741)	(636)	(156)

** p < .01; * p < .05; † p < .10—indicates significance between third-plus generation and other groups; bolded figures represent significance between second generation and first and 1.5 generations at .01 to .10 levels.
Source: 1999 HVS, authors' calculations.

tively more favorable position to afford to live in better locations may explain why each generational group also lives in progressively better housing and neighborhood circumstances.

The generally declining fortunes of black households as generation rises also suggests that the different residential circumstances experienced by the different generational groups may simply reflect corresponding differences in their ability to purchase high-quality locations (table 5.2, panel B). For example, although median household income rises between the first and 1.5 generations, it then falls steadily for third-plus-generation households to a value that is *lower* than that for the first generation. Declining income is matched by rising levels of need: levels of public-assistance receipt rise steadily and significantly from the first through the third-plus generations, until the third-plus generation is more than twice as likely to rely on welfare as is the first generation. From a purely logical standpoint, then, the constrained economic resources of the third-plus generation must be at the root of this group's corresponding disadvantages in housing and neighborhood environments.

However, this logic begins to fall apart when we consider how the generational patterns in socioeconomic status differ for the three racial/ethnic groups. Indeed, blacks and whites actually have quite similar incomes from the first through the second generations; it is only at the third-plus generation that income levels diverge greatly (table 5.2). However, at each generation the housing and neighborhood conditions of blacks and whites are quite disparate, with whites typically enjoying better conditions (table 5.1). Similarly, at each generation apart from the third-plus, black households are *not* the most economically disadvantaged of the groups; instead, at the first, 1.5, and second generations, black household income exceeds that of Hispanics, yet this advantage in income is not mirrored in corresponding advantages in housing and neighborhood circumstances. For example, there are only small differences in housing quality between blacks and Hispanics at the first and 1.5 generations, and black 1.5-generation households live in areas with higher crime rates than do Hispanic 1.5-generation households (table 5.1), despite the fact that blacks' median household income is almost double that of Hispanics in that generation (table 5.2). These comparisons suggest that the main reason why black households in New York City are experiencing downward mobility in residential quality is not that successive generations are less able to afford to live in more desirable places but that something *other* than economic disadvantage is at work. Indeed, if the conditions they experience were purely due to differences in socioeconomic status, then black households would be doing better than Hispanics; however, the data indicate that they are doing worse.

Do Generational Patterns in Housing and Neighborhood Conditions Persist? Evidence of Spatial and Segmented Assimilation

Thus, we are faced with an intriguing question: To what extent is the generational pattern of deteriorating housing and neighborhood conditions for blacks *real* and to what extent does it simply reflect the parallel pattern of increasingly constrained resources? This question goes to the heart of the issues raised by segmented assimilation theory, at least insofar as we have conceptualized them in regard to locational outcomes. That is, should the unique generational patterns in housing and neighborhood outcomes that we observe among blacks *disappear* when we statistically take account of the fact that some generational groups are simply poorer than others, then the kinds of structural constraints in the housing market that differentially constrain blacks' housing choices in general do not differentiate *between* generational groups *among* blacks. However, should the generational patterns prove resistant to statistical controls for socioeconomic status, then the evidence will point more clearly toward the notion that differences in the opportunity structure disproportionately cause members of the native-born generations to live in the least desirable places. Thus, to answer this question we must turn to the results of our multivariate regression models, since these models statistically equalize the resources that households in different generational groups have at their disposal to live in the housing and neighborhoods of their choice.

As we did in the previous chapter, we use the results of our locational attainment models to predict the levels of each of the nine outcomes that correspond to selected values of the theoretically important predictor variables. We begin with the measures of socioeconomic status, which indicate that the spatial assimilation process is at work for each group, generating better locational outcomes for higher-status households (table 5.3; the full results of all models are available in appendix C, tables C.2–C.10). That is, apart from some exceptions (which are largely matters of statistical significance rather than of the direction of the effects), for whites, blacks, and Hispanics, higher levels of education and income and lower levels of public-assistance use translate into better housing and neighborhood conditions.

Because of the numerous results and the complexity of table 5.3, for simplicity's sake we illustrate the general tone of the findings in four graphs. First, we see that there are very large (and statistically significant) differences in the extent of household crowding for households that do and do not receive public assistance, and that these differences hold (although at very disparate levels) for each of the racial/ethnic groups we examine (figure 5.1). Similarly, as household income rises from $25,000 to $100,000, households from all three racial/ethnic groups are increasingly likely (at a significant level) to own their homes (figure 5.2). Furthermore, as householder educational attainment improves from less than a high school diploma to having at least some college, white, black, and Hispanic households all increasingly reside in safer subareas and in subareas with less-widespread welfare use (figures 5.3 and 5.4). These findings confirm the basic tenet of the theory that where you live is (at least partly) determined by the social and economic resources you bring to the market.

A similar conclusion concerning the broad relevance of the spatial assimilation process is found in the tendency for housing conditions to deteriorate and for homeownership opportunities to diminish as the subarea percentage of recent immigrants rises, a pattern we saw generally in the previous chapter but that apparently applies to all three groups (with the sole exception being the significance of the effect on crowding for blacks).[2] The influence of this variable is clearest when we compare, in ratio form, the chance of owning and of living in a badly maintained housing unit for households in the subareas that lie at the two extremes (those with no recent immigrants and those where 35 percent of the population consists of recent immigrants). As shown in figure 5.5 (and table 5.3), white households living in subareas where none of their neighbors have recently arrived in the country are more than three times more likely to be homeowners than white households living in subareas where 35 percent of their neighbors are recent arrivals. The corresponding ratios are even higher for blacks and Hispanics, approaching seven times more likely and exceeding four times more likely, respectively.

Similarly, as the concentration of recent immigrants in the subarea rises, so does the prevalence of deteriorated housing. As shown in figure 5.5 (and table 5.3), when households living in subareas with no recent immigrants are compared to those living in subareas with many recent immigrants, the relative chance of living in a badly maintained housing unit varies from about one-third for whites to about two-thirds for Hispanics. This suggests again that areas where newly arrived immigrants concentrate may be more rundown, perhaps because of the constant turnover of households and the consequent heavy use of the housing infrastructure. Moreover, insofar as these neighborhoods also have high concentrations of the remaining stock of tenements, the relatively shoddy original construction of these buildings, as well as their advanced age, would contribute greatly to the relatively higher prevalence of undermaintained housing in such areas. As a result, in order to improve their housing, households—regardless of their race/ethnicity— would have to move away from the immigrant neighborhood to areas inhabited largely by the native-born, the basic process described in spatial assimilation theory.

The wealth of evidence presented so far strongly indicates that spatial assimilation remains an important process generating the integration of each racial/ethnic group into the housing market. The consistency of the effects of socioeconomic status across the range of outcomes, moreover, suggests that the generational patterns we observed earlier may disappear once we take group differences in socioeconomic status into account, both for whites and Hispanics and for blacks. That is, because rising levels of education and income and decreasing levels of need translate into significantly better conditions for all groups, the residential advantages we observe for white and Hispanic native-born households, and paradoxically for black foreign-born households, may have

TABLE 5.3
Prediction of Housing and Neighborhood Characteristics: Assessing the Effect of Socioeconomic Status and Subarea Percentage of Recent Immigrants, by Race/Ethnicity

Predictor	Housing characteristics			Neighborhood characteristics					
	Own	Crowded	3+ defs.	Percentage white	Crime rate	Teen fertility rate	Percentage using public assistance	Percentage under-performing in math	Percentage one- and two-family homes
A. Non-Hispanic whites									
SOCIOECONOMIC STATUS									
Education									
less than high school	32.64***	1.55***	4.43	55.88***	5.73†	2.79†	4.34***	38.18	34.86***
high school diploma	43.39	1.11***	4.66	56.05***	5.68	2.79**	4.27***	38.27*	35.47***
some college or more	46.51	0.65	5.82	58.90	5.62	2.86	4.03	37.82	27.09
Income									
$25,000	38.11***	0.92**	5.03	57.38***	5.67**	2.83	4.17**	38.09*	30.90***
$50,000	42.51***	0.86**	5.24	57.68***	5.65**	2.83	4.14**	38.01*	30.41***
$100,000	45.14**	0.82**	5.37	57.86***	5.64**	2.84	4.13**	37.96*	30.12***
Receives public assistance									
Yes	16.49***	1.95***	6.63	56.90	5.89***	2.85	4.54**	37.69	30.19
No	46.67	0.78	5.21	57.85	5.63	2.83	4.10	38.01	30.26
Housing market sector									
owned		0.90	2.58	57.23	5.58	2.79	4.04	38.01	33.38
rental (not public)		2.44***	9.01***	58.25**	5.69**	2.86***	4.20**	37.95	27.88***
public housing		0.99	6.15	54.73	5.83	2.88	4.27	39.03	29.78
PERCENTAGE OF RECENT IMMIGRANTS IN SUBAREA									
0	58.89***	0.63†	3.58**						
10	45.40***	0.81†	5.10**						
35	17.60***	1.56†	11.98***						

B. Non-Hispanic blacks

SOCIOECONOMIC STATUS

Education									
less than high school	14.95***	5.30***	20.70*	13.06*	10.98	5.40*	11.43*	58.91**	26.92*
high school diploma	19.27***	3.08	14.76	13.87	10.92	5.25	11.01	58.75**	28.08
some college or more	31.50	2.56	15.64	14.15	10.82	5.24	10.91	58.15	28.68
Income									
$25,000	20.65***	3.22	16.65†	13.78	10.90*	5.29***	11.13***	58.56*	27.96*
$50,000	25.28***	3.23	16.26†	13.83	10.87*	5.26***	11.01***	58.47*	28.19*
$100,000	28.28***	3.23	16.03†	13.86	10.85*	5.25***	10.94***	58.42*	28.32*
Receives public assistance									
Yes	9.46***	4.87***	21.57***	11.91***	11.10**	5.37*	11.63**	59.28***	26.63**
No	29.00	2.85	15.13	14.36	10.83	5.25	10.90	58.29	28.51
Housing market sector									
owned		1.76	6.28	15.61	10.72	4.94	9.65	57.83	34.77
rental (not public)		4.01***	23.54***	12.75***	10.94*	5.41***	11.64***	58.90***	25.14***
public housing		4.57***	22.96***	14.38†	11.05*	5.43***	11.66***	58.33	26.17***
PERCENTAGE OF RECENT IMMIGRANTS IN SUBAREA									
0	41.96***	2.83	12.34**						
10	26.57***	3.13	15.48**						
35	6.03***	4.03	26.12**						

C. Hispanics

SOCIOECONOMIC STATUS

Education									
less than high school	4.93***	9.41***	18.24*	21.15***	9.11***	5.05***	11.00***	56.99***	20.00*
high school diploma	9.19***	7.17†	14.71	22.24**	9.03**	4.99***	10.58**	56.44***	20.75
some college or more	14.79	5.51	14.28	24.27	8.71	4.78	9.81	54.98	21.34
Income									
$25,000	7.81***	7.36	15.91	22.36**	8.97*	4.96***	10.54***	56.24*	20.60
$50,000	9.86***	7.44	16.07	22.66**	8.93*	4.92***	10.41***	56.09*	20.72
$100,000	11.27***	7.49	16.16	22.83**	8.90*	4.91***	10.33***	56.02*	20.79

(continued)

TABLE 5.3 (continued)

Predictor	Housing characteristics			Neighborhood characteristics					
	Own	Crowded	3+ defs.	Percentage white	Crime rate	Teen fertility rate	Percentage using public assistance	Percentage under-performing in math	Percentage one- and two-family homes
Receives public assistance									
Yes	4.70**	10.46***	20.07***	21.05***	9.27***	5.07**	11.01**	56.78*	19.97†
No	10.77	6.29	14.34	23.08	8.82	4.89	10.28	55.93	20.93
Housing market sector									
owned		3.12	3.73	24.82	8.64	4.66	9.23	54.46	23.59
rental (not public)		8.56***	19.92***	21.92***	8.94*	4.98***	10.59***	56.52***	20.25***
public housing		7.49***	17.36***	23.21	9.52**	5.08***	11.52***	56.09*	19.58***
PERCENTAGE OF RECENT IMMIGRANTS IN SUBAREA									
0	15.16***	5.50*	13.25†						
10	10.26***	6.70*	15.01†						
35	3.61**	10.81*	20.25†						

Note: Predicted values are based on group-specific models using generation * year of arrival interactions, and means shown in Appendix Table C.1. For income, significance is shown for all predicted values. For categorical variables, significance is shown only for those categories achieving statistical significance and reference categories are shown in italics.
*** p < 0.001; ** p < 0.01; * p < 0.05; † p < 0.10 for comparisons relative to third-plus generation.
Source: 1999 HVS and Infoshare, authors' calculation.

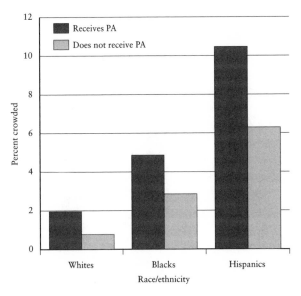

Fig. 5.1. Predicted level of crowding among households receiving and not receiving public assistance, by race/ethnicity

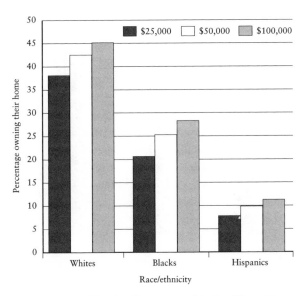

Fig. 5.2. Predicted levels of homeownership for different levels of household income, by race/ethnicity

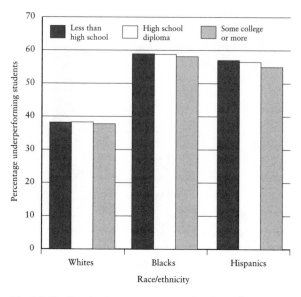

Fig. 5.3. Predicted subarea percentage of underperforming students for different levels of householder education, by race/ethnicity

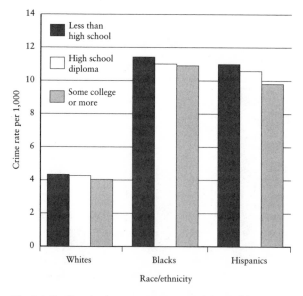

Fig. 5.4. Predicted subarea percentage receiving public assistance for different levels of householder education, by race/ethnicity

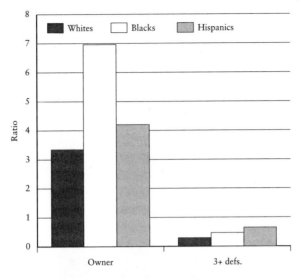

Fig. 5.5. Relative chances of owning and living in an undermaintained housing unit for household living in subareas
with no recent immigrants versus those in subareas where 35
percent of the population consists of recent immigrants

their roots in the socioeconomic advantages these groups have relative to the other generational groups.

To a very significant degree, this logic applies to the experiences of whites (table 5.4, panel A) and Hispanics (table 5.4, panel C). Among whites, generational improvements in homeownership, household crowding, and the subarea crime rate and percentage of welfare users remain statistically significant (with some differences between the immigrant generations and the second generation—in bold type in the table—also attaining significance). Similarly, when we add year of arrival, the differences that emerge indicate that conditions improve the longer that households have lived in the country, another basic concept of spatial assimilation theory. For Hispanics, however, there are very few statistically significant generational differences in housing and neighborhood conditions once we take account of the varying abilities of the generations to pay for housing. The one clear pattern that remains (apart from crowding) is a significant tendency for households in each successive generation to live in subareas that are increasingly "whiter." Households in the second generation live in subareas with relatively larger

TABLE 5.4
Prediction of Housing and Neighborhood Characteristics: Assessing the Effect of Generation

Predictor	Housing characteristics			Percentage white	Neighborhood characteristics				
	Own	Crowded	3+ defs.		Crime rate	Teen fertility rate	Percentage using public assistance	Percentage underperforming in math	Percentage one- and two-family homes
A. Non-Hispanic whites									
GENERATION									
first	34.59***	1.70***	5.51	58.05	5.83***	2.84	4.33***	38.12	29.46
1.5	52.37†	1.51***	6.25	57.11	5.81**	2.82	4.40***	38.16	31.31
second	47.97	1.14***	4.89	57.35	5.63	2.82	4.17**	37.98	31.16†
third-plus	46.07	0.48	5.34	57.93	5.55	2.84	4.00	37.95	29.92
first, arrived 1980 and later	23.79***	1.76***	5.67	58.74	5.83***	2.82	4.35***	37.72	31.27
first, arrived before 1980	50.39	1.53**	5.21	57.21	5.83***	2.88	4.30**	38.60	26.69**
1.5, arrived 1980 and later	28.84†	2.07**	7.55	58.54	5.69	2.78	4.40†	38.13	34.93*
1.5, arrived before 1980	56.87**	1.31**	5.91	56.79	5.83**	2.82	4.40***	38.18*	30.45
second	49.04†	1.14***	4.89	57.33	5.63	2.82	4.17**	37.99	30.95
third-plus	45.48	0.49	5.37	57.92	5.55	2.84	4.00	37.93	30.07
B. Non-Hispanic blacks									
GENERATION									
first	26.78*	5.55***	16.88	13.77	10.76*	5.08***	10.11***	57.42***	30.74***
1.5	27.92†	4.12*	11.67*	13.88	10.86	5.20†	10.59**	57.76**	29.11*
second	21.63	4.11†	21.16	14.36	10.89	5.38	11.32	58.64	27.16
third-plus	21.47	2.39	16.54	13.77	10.94	5.36	11.52	59.07	26.83

first, arrived 1980 and later	19.39	6.02***	16.61	13.45	10.75†	5.06***	10.14***	57.31***	31.53***
first, arrived before 1980	38.65***	4.52*	17.35	14.12	10.79	5.13**	10.03***	57.56***	29.83**
1.5, arrived 1980 and later	19.22	4.05†	11.26	14.03	10.88	5.11**	9.93**	57.26***	30.66*
1.5, arrived before 1980	31.77*	4.44*	11.99	13.71	10.84	5.27	11.04	58.16†	27.98
second	22.03	4.17†	21.10	14.36	10.89	5.38	11.31	58.63	27.21
third-plus	*21.78*	*2.42*	*16.49*	*13.78*	*10.94*	*5.36*	*11.52*	*59.07*	*26.84*
C. Hispanics									
GENERATION									
first	5.70**	8.92	15.69	21.93***	8.97	4.94*	10.44	56.37	20.42
1.5	11.56	7.35	17.64	22.30**	8.92	4.99	10.69	56.25	20.63
second	12.59	5.31	16.62	23.31*	8.96	4.93	10.53	56.05	20.85
third-plus	*12.91*	*5.96*	*16.17*	*25.82*	*9.01*	*4.90*	*9.98*	*55.29*	*21.68*
first, arrived 1980 and later	4.62***	10.97	14.95	21.30***	9.05†	4.94†	10.56	56.70†	20.43
first, arrived before 1980	7.22*	5.13†	15.87	22.74*	8.83	4.95†	10.28	55.81	20.41
1.5, arrived 1980 and later	8.93	9.07	14.86	22.67*	8.99	4.96	10.62	56.66	20.86
1.5, arrived before 1980	12.37	7.43	18.28	21.98**	8.91	5.00	10.74	56.07	20.52
second	12.50	6.03	16.03	23.10*	8.98	4.93	10.55	56.09	20.85
third-plus	*12.71*	*6.77*	*15.58*	*25.58*	*9.04*	*4.89*	*10.01*	*55.34*	*21.68*

Note: Predicted values are based on group-specific means shown in Appendix Table C.1. *** p < 0.001; ** p < 0.01; * p < 0.05; † p < 0.10 for comparisons relative to third-plus generation (which is in italics). Significance (at p < .10) relative to the second generation is indicated in bold.

Source: 1999 HVS and Infoshare, authors' calculations.

white populations than do first-generation households, and the tendency to live among whites also tends to increase with time since arrival. The fact that the generational pattern of improvement in the subarea percentage that is white remains statistically significant suggests that there is something linked to generational status and acculturation more generally that we have not measured—such as English-language fluency—that is an important quality for Hispanics in particular to possess in order to gain access to neighborhoods dominated by whites. In contrast, higher levels of socioeconomic status are sufficient to open doors in neighborhoods that are "better" on the other dimensions we examine.

Yet although the generational patterns exhibited by Hispanics appear to conform to the patterns of improvement predicted by spatial assimilation theory, the highest levels of quality that Hispanic households attain are quite low, when compared to the achievements of white households. These differences suggest that the processes associated with the stratification system that keep Hispanics in far lower quality circumstances than whites (chapter 4) may also operate to retard the improvements that assimilation processes are able to generate for this group. To evaluate this hypothesis we calculated predicted levels of the six neighborhood outcomes for whites and Hispanics belonging to the three socioeconomic composition categories used earlier ("poor," "average," and "affluent") and to the four generational groups.[3] The results of these simulations are shown in table 5.5.

Moving down each column in table 5.5 illustrates the general pattern of improvement that occurs as generation rises for each racial/ethnic group, and moving across each row demonstrates the improvements gained by increases in socioeconomic status for each generational group. As we found in chapter 4, rising levels of socioeconomic resources tend to bring Hispanics greater improvements in neighborhood quality than they do for whites, but the most affluent Hispanics in a given generation remain in neighborhoods of lower quality—and often of far lower quality—than the poorest whites in that same generational group. However, what is of greatest importance here is the fact that the combined forces of rising socioeconomic status and generational change still do not bring Hispanics into the best neighborhoods. Instead, the most fortunate type of Hispanic households—affluent third-plus-generation households—live in neighborhoods that are more diverse, more dangerous, and have more teens with babies and more underperforming students than the neighborhoods in which poor, first-generation whites

TABLE 5.5

Prediction of Neighborhood Conditions for White and Hispanic Households
by Generation and Socioeconomic Status

Neighborhood condition/ Generation	Non-Hispanic white			Hispanic		
	Poor	Average	Affluent	Poor	Average	Affluent
Percentage white						
First	51.62	56.85	59.15	24.27	29.72	32.11
1.5	50.68	55.91	58.21	24.64	30.09	32.48
Second	50.91	56.15	58.44	25.65	31.10	33.48
Third-plus	51.39	56.63	58.92	28.16	33.61	35.99
Crime rate						
First	6.40	5.92	5.71	9.41	7.89	7.50
1.5	6.38	5.90	5.69	9.36	7.84	7.45
Second	6.20	5.72	5.52	9.40	7.88	7.49
Third-plus	6.12	5.64	5.44	9.45	7.94	7.54
Teen fertility rate						
First	2.83	2.81	2.81	4.57	3.83	3.56
1.5	2.81	2.78	2.78	4.62	3.88	3.61
Second	2.81	2.78	2.79	4.56	3.81	3.54
Third-plus	2.84	2.81	2.81	4.53	3.78	3.51
Percentage receiving public assistance						
First	5.16	4.53	4.08	9.55	5.79	4.82
1.5	5.23	4.60	4.15	9.80	6.04	5.07
Second	5.00	4.37	3.92	9.36	5.88	4.91
Third-plus	4.83	4.20	3.75	9.10	5.33	4.36
Percentage of under- performing students						
First	39.15	38.26	37.74	54.42	51.03	49.34
1.5	39.19	38.30	37.78	58.30	50.91	49.22
Second	39.01	38.12	37.60	54.10	50.71	49.03
Third-plus	38.99	38.09	37.58	53.34	49.95	48.27
Percentage of one- and two-family homes						
First	35.45	32.97	29.10	23.06	29.04	29.83
1.5	37.29	34.83	30.95	23.27	29.25	30.03
Second	37.14	34.68	30.80	23.49	29.47	30.26
Third-plus	35.91	33.44	29.56	24.31	30.30	31.08

Note: Predictions are based on model using only generation. All households are headed by a forty-five-year-old, couple headed, with no children under eighteen present and no other adults present. "Afflu-ent" households own their homes, do not receive public assistance, earn $100,000, and have at least some college. "Average" households live in rental housing, do not receive public assistance, earn $33,000, and have a high school diploma. Affluent households own their homes, do not receive public assistance, earn $100,000, and have at least some college. For Hispanics, the omitted categories for race (nonblack) and national origin (Central/South American) are used.
Source: 1999 HVS and Infoshare, authors' calculations.

live.[4] Thus, although Hispanics in each successive generation tend to live in progressively better locations, stratification processes appear to "cap" the improvements available to Hispanics through assimilation, forcing even the most fortunate households into neighborhoods that are lower in quality than the areas in which the poorest whites live.

For blacks, however, the story is very different. Although the generational pattern for crowding is one of improving conditions as generation rises (as it is for all groups), this is the exception to the rule of a persistently significant pattern of generational decline in housing and neighborhood quality (table 5.4, panel B). Indeed, on five of the nine outcomes—homeownership, subarea teen-fertility rate, percentage on public assistance, percentage of underperforming students, and percentage of one- and two-family homes—residential quality steadily (and significantly) deteriorates as generation rises. For four of these five outcomes, all neighborhood conditions, the immigrant generations live in significantly better areas than does the second generation (in bold type print), indicating that these patterns are *not* reflecting differences between the descendants of Southern migrants and immigrants from the Caribbean but are truly capturing a deterioration in the fortunes of black households as they move further from the immigrant generation. When we add year of arrival, for three outcomes (homeownership, subarea percentage on welfare and percentage of one- and two-family, homes) time since arrival translates into improved conditions, as spatial assimilation theory would predict, but for the remaining two outcomes (subarea teen-fertility rate and percentage of underperform-ing students) black immigrant households who have been in the country longer live in *less*-desirable circumstances.

Thus, the weight of the evidence indicates that as the generations pass, blacks experience a far different integration experience than do whites and Hispanics. For the latter groups, moving from the first generation to the third-plus generation entails moving from lower-quality housing and neighborhoods to those of higher quality, both in physical attributes and in the availability of amenities such as resources, role models, and networks linking individuals to opportunities for social and economic success. This is the process described by general assimilation theory and its variant, spatial assimilation theory; these models implicitly argue that becoming "American" means moving up the socioeconomic, and residential, hierarchies. While stratification processes constrain the ability of Hispanics to successfully incorporate into the housing market, for blacks these processes generate a unique and unmistakable downward pattern of in-tegration. For this group, it is members of the immigrant generations who do the best, both in the social and economic resources they have at their disposal and in the kinds of housing and neighborhoods they live in. But, it is clear that for blacks, the generational pattern of deteriorating residential circumstances is independent of the fact that the later generations are simply less well off than the immigrant generations. That pattern is also apparent relative to the second generation, which largely shares the same ethnic origins as do the immigrant generations. Instead, there is clearly something salient about generational status that leads to the patterns of downward mobility that we uncover.

What could this salient feature of generational status be? One factor may be economic resources that are available only to immigrants and that may facilitate their access to better housing and neighborhoods. An example may be the *sou-sou,* or rotating credit association, whereby a group of people, more typically immigrants than native-born, regularly place money into a general pool and take turns receiving the accumulated amount. Access to such money could help to finance a down payment or a move to a better neighborhood. Indeed, as one Brooklyn-based West Indian informant recounted, "Well, I was tired of the neighborhood and decided to purchase a house in Laurelton, Queens. I needed $8,000 for the down payment. I had $7,000. . . . the only way I could have topped off the down payment was with a *box* hand."[5] If participation in *sou-sous* is limited to immigrants and if participants utilize the funds toward housing improvements, this could help to explain why first- and perhaps 1.5-generation blacks do better than their native-born counterparts, even when more regular (and measured) aspects of socioeconomic status like income are statistically taken into account.

A second possible factor suggested by segmented assimilation theorists may be the adoption, by members of successively higher generations, of the "adversarial stance" attributed to the urban underclass. The behaviors subsumed under this rubric include a dismissal of the value of education as a means of upward mobility and a disregard for the value of working at a steady and legitimate job. To the extent that black immigrants are disproportionately exposed to such behaviors in the neighborhoods to which they have access, their children may adopt such behaviors as they learn the realities of racial discrimination in American society from their native-born black peers and thus may lose the optimism of the immigrant generation. However, because we have statistically removed the effect of differences in education (and their presumed roots), the only way that such attitudes and behaviors would translate into worsening locational attainments is if they trigger discriminatory behavior on the part of housing-market actors that is of greater intensity than that aimed at other blacks.

One way this might occur is through the adoption of linguistic patterns that are associated with "ghetto" culture. The use of such linguistic patterns may elicit discriminatory treatment on the part of landlords or realtors who use them as signals to screen out tenants they deem to be undesirable or potential troublemakers, in their behavior or their ability to pay rent. For example, Douglas Massey and Garvey Lundy report that blacks seeking to rent housing in the Philadelphia metropolitan area receive very different treatment by rental agents according to the linguistic patterns used in telephone conversations. Specifically, in a series of test audits conducted over the telephone, home seekers speaking Black Vernacular English, largely associated with lower-class blacks, received far less favorable treatment than did home seekers speaking Black Accented English, a cue of middle-class status.[6] Many West Indian immigrants are proud of their use of "proper" English[7] and believe that speaking properly is essential for accessing key social and economic goods, such as good jobs and desirable housing.[8] However, one of the facets of the "American" identity held by some second-generation youth is the use of Black Vernacular English.[9]

As discussed earlier, another linguistic cue that can vary across the generations is the use of accented English, which may signal higher status (especially if involving a British lilt)[10] but more importantly identifies the speaker as being of foreign birth. Indeed, use of an accent is one of the clearest ways that black immigrants can telegraph their ethnic identities and thus avoid being mistaken as African Americans in a society that will not recognize the possibility of ethnic differences among blacks as easily as it does among whites[11] and that socially stigmatizes black race to such a degree that a black individual's very individuality and personal accomplishments become invisible.[12] By using an accent and other ethnic markers, black immigrants can thus evade the harsher aspects of discrimination and prejudice that are directed at African Americans. The distinction that whites make between African Americans and foreign-born blacks has been amply described. For example, Bogle, a Jamaican informant interviewed by Milton Vickerman, described how, when he moved his family from Flatbush, Brooklyn, to a predominantly white suburban neighborhood, his new neighbors initially were hostile but grew more welcoming upon learning that he and his family were Jamaican. Bogle explained his neighbors' change of heart as reflecting whites' perceptions of West Indians as having more desirable traits—like respecting the law and working steadily—than

African Americans.[13] More harshly, a West Indian informant inter-viewed by Vilna Bashi Bobb and Averil Clarke said when describing American society, "You know, you have blacks on one side and whites on one side and unless you're a foreign-born black they look at you like you're diseased or something."[14] Although accents and other ethnic markers are easily available to the immigrant generations, their children and their children's children must consciously and overtly adopt ways to distinguish themselves as being of Caribbean heritage. While many do, many do not, at least partly because they have come to identify as Americans rather than as members of their parents' (or their parents' parents') ethnic group. But the point here is that since the likelihood of using a foreign accent decreases over the generations, members of the later generations are increasingly vulnerable to the "oppressive aspects of the American racial structure."[15] In other words, as generation rises, the strength of ethnic markers diminishes, causing the descendants of black immigrants to melt into the larger African American population and thus to become increasingly vulnerable to the structural barriers that limits blacks' opportunities in general. This translates directly into the realm of housing: the progressive constriction of opportunity that follows from the dissipating strength of ethnic markers steadily narrows the range of housing options, which is reflected in a steady deterioration in housing quality. In short, the main cause of the patterns of down-ward mobility that emerge among blacks has far less to do with culture than with persistent inequities in the structure of opportunity.[16]

Given these findings, an important question arises: Are the patterns we uncover unique to New York City or would they hold even if we had data for a larger and perhaps more representative geographic area? In other words, do we find evidence of generational decline because members of the second and third-plus generations among blacks dispro-portionately leave the city to seek better housing opportunities else-where? To answer this question, we estimated group-specific models of homeownership—the only outcome possible—using pooled data from the 1997, 1999, and 2001 Current Population Surveys (CPS) for the New York Consolidated Metropolitan Area (NY-CMSA). Doing so enables us to include suburban residents and thus "reclaim" the mem-bers of the native-born generations who might have left the city. In ad-dition, by using a control for central-city residence, we can eliminate one of the key factors that might differentiate the third-plus genera-tion from its foreign-born counterparts. The results of this model reveal generational patterns among blacks that largely mimic those we un-cover for New York City (appendix C, table C.11). The general con-sistency of the generational patterns in the two data sets suggests that our interpretation of generational decline among blacks is fundamen-tally valid.

Conclusions

Blacks, therefore, uniquely experience a downward trajectory in hous-ing and neighborhood conditions. This slide in status suggests very clearly that black immigrants encounter serious obstacles to "making it" in American society and offers unambiguous support for the expec-tations of segmented assimilation theory. Moreover, because our ap-proach enables us to demonstrate that the downward mobility experi-enced uniquely by blacks has its origins in structural sources of inequal-ity, rather than in the adoption of a pathological culture, our analyses advance the theory beyond its emphasis on the undesirable behaviors of a small segment of the inner-city population to refocus attention on the real problem: the persistence of structural forms of inequality in the broader American society. Because the root of the problem lies in the American opportunity structure, it seems unlikely that current patterns of inequality, which have blacks on the lower rungs of many institu-tions in American society, will fade over time. Indeed, the unique situa-tion experienced by blacks, by setting them apart from other racial/ethnic groups, suggests that the "color line" in American society may shift, from separating whites from nonwhites to dividing blacks from nonblacks.

Although there remains little doubt about the continuing power of stratification processes and the salience of race in American society, im-portant questions concerning the status of Hispanics persist. The fact that stratification processes stymie the power of assimilation and socio-economic status to allow Hispanics to enter the best neighborhoods indicates that this group may be relegated to a position perhaps on or just above the color line, not yet fully accepted by the dominant non-black group but not fully forced to share the bottom of the hierarchy with blacks. Other researchers, however, using data for various metropoli-tan areas including New York, have found that affluent His-panics tend to live in neighborhoods that largely resemble those in which affluent whites live, in their residents' economic status, the percentage that is white, and the level of crime.[17] Thus, although we believe that our interpretation concerning Hispanics' future position in the racial/ethnic hierarchy applies to the case of New York (and possibly other cities as well), we hesitate to apply it more broadly to the nation as a whole.

In the end, however, the bottom line is that scholars and policy makers who argue that current waves of immigrants are of lower quality than those that arrived in earlier periods and that they are unable or unwilling to "make it" in American society need to focus their attention on the inequitable distribution of opportunity in American society and not on their perceptions of immigrants' failings. Indeed, policy makers must identify ways to remove, at last, the barriers that prevent Americans of African ancestry from achieving whatever success they desire, including access to desirable housing and resource-rich neighborhoods.

6

Conclusions and Policy Implications

The previous chapters suggest that immigrants' integration into New York City's housing market broadly adheres to the tenets of the spatial assimilation model. For all groups, higher educational attainment and higher income are positively associated with better residential quality, and time since arrival tends to exert the same influence. When comparing immigrant groups' integration into the housing market by race/ethnicity, however, our findings suggest that the integration of immigrants is not the result of the influence of individual or household characteristics operating alone. Instead, there appear to be structural barriers at work within the housing market that impede blacks and, to a lesser extent, Hispanics from achieving the same locational outcomes as do whites who have the same socioeconomic resources. In addition, such structural factors appear to be exerting downward pressure on the ability of blacks to assimilate into the housing market across generations.

Because locational attainment is inextricably linked to households' current and future social and economic well-being, this chapter explores some of the policy implications of these findings. After summarizing the results presented in the previous chapters, we discuss two sets of policies. First, we discuss immigration policies and the debate surrounding the quality of today's immigrants, inherent within such policies. In particular, we argue that those who advocate severe restrictions on immigration because of concerns over the "quality" of immigrants should focus less on the characteristics of immigrants and the skills they bring with them than on the structure of opportunity available in the United States. As our results demonstrate, this structure of opportunity denies many people, particularly those of African ancestry, the same kinds of opportunities for quality housing and neighborhood outcomes as those enjoyed by whites. On the basis of these findings, we then discuss policies that address households' access to high-quality housing and neighborhoods. A combination of "pro-people" and "pro-place" policies seems to be the appropriate remedy in light of the salience of race/ethnicity as a determinant of locational outcomes.

How Generations of Immigrants Fare in New York City's Housing Market

The primary goal of this study was to examine generational patterns in housing and neighborhood characteristics to evaluate whether the generational dynamic implicit in assimilation theory—and its variant, spatial assimilation theory—was present. When we examined all households, regardless of race/ethnicity, we found in descriptive analyses fairly consistent evidence of this generational dynamic, in that housing and neighborhood conditions tended to improve in quality across generations. Most of the differences across generations disappeared once we statistically took account of the fact that some generational groups were simply better off economically than others, a result consistent with the expectations of spatial assimilation theory. The one outcome that exhibited persistent improvement as generation rose was crowding. We believe that this finding reflects the salience of membership in certain generational groups. In particular, the first and 1.5 generations are likely to be embedded in the social networks that drive immigration streams and are thus either obligated or desire to take in friends and family members who follow them to a new life in New York. That the presence of adults other than those in the core household falls steadily from the first to the third-plus generation provides clear, though indirect, support for this perspective. Crowding for immigrants may not be a negative housing condition, but a strategy to maximize the well-being not only of the newcomer but also of the household already in the country; by economizing on rent, immigrants can remit more money back to their origin communities and can better afford the other necessities of life in their new homes. In addition, differences across generations in preferences for co-residence may reflect cultural values that stress the importance of the group over the individual and de-emphasize the importance of privacy for the individual and family. However, as generation rises and time in the United States increases, the strength of these preferences and values apparently wanes; as a result, third-plus-generation households are the least crowded of all households.

Other findings also supported the basic tenets of the spatial assimilation framework. Specifically, we found consistent evidence, detailed in chapter 4, that residence in better housing and neighborhoods appeared to follow from gains in social and economic achievements. However, we also found a consistently large and significant effect of household race/ethnicity on the quality of locational attainments, indicating that the allocation of desirable housing and neighborhood characteristics across race/ethnicity remains unequal. In particular, there is a distinct racial hierarchy in the New York City housing market, whereby whites enjoy the broadest access to high-quality housing and neighborhoods, followed by Asians and then Hispanics. Blacks, however, are at the bottom of this hierarchy; even in the presence of all available controls for socioeconomic status, acculturation, and preferences related to life-cycle stage, blacks occupy the most deteriorated housing located in the most problem-ridden neighborhoods. Race/ethnicity, then, is a far more potent predictor of locational outcomes than are social and economic achievements, a conclusion that is not limited to this study but that holds nationally.[1] Such results are more consistent with the propositions of the place stratification framework than with those articulated by spatial assimilation theory.

That we find support for both models indicates that they are not mutually exclusive explanations of locational attainment. Instead, we have argued consistently that they largely agree on the most basic points, disagreeing most prominently on what they view as underlying observed racial/ethnic disparities in residential quality. Spatial assimilation theory argues that such differences reflect simple differences in the social and economic attributes that determine tastes and preferences and that enable households to afford to live in the neighborhoods of their choice. The persistence of racial/ethnic inequality even in the presence of statistical controls for these differences disproves this argument. In contrast, place stratification theory sees such differences as rooted in the racial/ethnic stratification system, which is maintained by the deliberate actions of those who seek to maintain their privileged positions. As a result, place stratification theory views race/ethnicity as a macrolevel variable, reflecting households' placements in the larger racial/ethnic stratification system.

What causes racial/ethnic inequality in access to desirable housing and neighborhoods? Our analyses tell us that racial/ethnic inequality is not due to group differences in socioeconomic status, but we are unable to accurately identify the factor or factors that give rise to our results. One possible explanation relates to varying preferences for different kinds of neighborhoods, a factor that may contribute to the persistence of high levels of racial segregation.[2] However, there is reason to believe that the preferences argument may not provide a compelling explanation for our results. In our models predicting housing outcomes, we included indicators of the composition of the surrounding subarea; such measures could account for preferences for co-residence among large numbers of blacks and recently arrived immigrants. Although we found that the chance of living in deteriorated housing was sensitive to the presence of many blacks and many recently arrived immigrants, our findings with respect to race/ethnicity remained significant, indicating that preferences alone cannot explain the differences observed by race/ethnicity. Even though we did not include contextual predictors in the models predicting neighborhood outcomes, the effects of race/ethnicity mirrored those in the models predicting housing outcomes; thus, even if we had been able to include measures that tap into household preferences for neighborhood composition, we likely would have found similar results with respect to race/ethnicity (although perhaps weaker in strength and significance).

Furthermore, there is little reason to expect that blacks should be most likely of all groups to prefer living in undermaintained housing and in neighborhoods plagued with social and economic problems.[3] Indeed, evidence from the Multi-City Survey of Urban Inequality indicates that members of all racial/ethnic groups tend to agree on their relative evaluations of different neighborhoods (with some minor exceptions relating to racial composition).[4] This kind of evidence suggests that preferences for neighborhood amenities may not differ greatly across racial/ethnic groups and thus that explanations based on variation in preferences cannot fully account for the patterns of racial/ethnic inequality we uncover.

A more compelling argument focuses on structural forces of inequality—namely, housing-market discrimination—as the factors producing our results. The history of New York City reveals the various individual and institutional acts of discrimination that have, over time, relegated blacks and some Hispanics to the least desirable housing and neighborhoods. Moreover, other evidence, including housing audits, indicates that blacks in the city continue to experience various forms of discrimination in the housing market.[5] These kinds of barriers all but ensure that minorities, and particularly blacks, will occupy areas that are more diverse, less prosperous, and of lower quality than those in which whites reside.[6] Thus, despite our inability to definitively identify discrimination as the dominant cause of the patterns of inequality we uncover, we emphatically believe that it would be foolish to ignore the potential role played by structural barriers in the housing market.

The persistence of structural forces of inequality has been identified by revisionist theorists as responsible for the varying patterns of adaptation to American society emerging among children of immigrants and immigrant youths,[7] including declining levels of educational performance and psychological well-being as generation and time in the United States rises.[8] Indeed, such patterns of worsening, rather than improving, outcomes across generations suggests that, for some contemporary immigrants, the process of "becoming American" is harmful to their well-being. As a result, segmented assimilation theory argues that the immigrant groups most at risk of these negative outcomes across generations are those that share with native-born minorities the experience of discrimination on the basis of race/ethnicity—namely, those of African and Hispanic ancestry.[9] More broadly, however, segmented assimilation theory implies that patterns of downward incorporation extend beyond just two generations and emerge over the longer term, that is, over three or more generations. Thus, a second—and perhaps more important—goal of our project was to examine the generational patterns in housing and neighborhood conditions for individual racial/ethnic groups to evaluate whether there is any evidence of the kinds of downward patterns of adaptation hypothesized by segmented assimilation theorists.

What we found is that for whites and Hispanics, the spatial assimilation theory provides the best explanation for generational patterns in housing and neighborhood conditions. Specifically, for these groups, housing and neighborhood conditions tend to improve across generations, as do indicators of socioeconomic status. Moreover, when we controlled for all available indicators of socioeconomic status and preferences associated with life-cycle stage, most of the generational patterns disappeared.

Although each generation of Hispanics did occupy a better place in the residential hierarchy than the previous generation, it was clear that the combination of socioeconomic mobility and assimilation could not overcome the counterbalancing effects of stratification processes. That is, in New York, stratification processes appear to limit the gains that Hispanic households can make, relegating even the most fortunate Hispanic households to neighborhoods that are more dangerous and more removed from the larger opportunity structure than those in which the least fortunate white households live. As a result, Hispanics in New York City, regardless of their achievements and generational status, are more likely to live in areas where their children attend schools where high achievement is not the norm and to have among their peers teens who enter parenthood at an early age and friends who commit crimes. Such differences in institutional contexts of whites' and Hispanics' neighborhoods will help to carry other forms of inequality far into the future. Thus, despite the apparently positive generational pattern of incorporation, Hispanics—at least in New York City—remain vulnerable to the pernicious effects of stratification processes.

In contrast to the cases of whites and Hispanics, we found very different generational patterns in locational outcomes among blacks, a pronounced and consistent pattern of downward mobility on the majority of our outcomes. The deterioration in housing and neighborhood conditions, however, is not an artifact of differences between descendants of Southern-born migrants and immigrants from the Caribbean; instead, differences in housing and neighborhood outcomes between the immigrant (first and 1.5) generations and the second generation (our best attempt at controlling for ethnicity) are as numerous and statistically significant as the differences separating the early generational groups from the third-plus generation. We also found that socioeconomic status also declines across generations for blacks; yet when we controlled for these factors, we found that the generational declines in housing and neighborhood conditions remain significant, even when the immigrant generations are compared to the coethnic second generation. Thus, our findings provide strong evidence to support the expectations of generational decline in adult-level outcomes as voiced by segmented assimilation theorists.

What lies at the roots of this pattern of generational decline among blacks? Because the diminished quality of the second and third-plus generations' housing and neighborhood conditions cannot be attributed to lower levels of education or economic status, we speculate that the frequency and intensity of discrimination varies across generations.

Specifically, we argue that as markers of their ethnic origins dissipate, descendants of black immigrants melt into the larger African American population, making them more vulnerable to forms of prejudice and discrimination than were their immigrant parents and grandparents. In other words, we argue that as generation rises for blacks, so does the frequency and the strength of discrimination, resulting in a progressive narrowing of housing opportunities. As a result, for black immigrants, "becoming American" is not associated with upward mobility (as implied in assimilation theory) but with a loss of status. Evidence to support such a contention can be found in Massey and Lundy's innovative work using telephone housing audits.[10] Their study demonstrated that home seekers receive very different treatment from landlords and realtors based on their linguistic patterns. Such evidence aligns with the belief held by many Caribbean immigrants that maintaining their accents will distance them from African Americans in the eyes of whites and will thus facilitate their access to important resources such as jobs and housing.[11]

Our findings thus confirm segmented assimilation theory's contention that racially stigmatized immigrant groups stand at risk of downward assimilation. More important, by demonstrating that the roots of this pattern of downward mobility lie not in the assumption of a defective set of cultural values and practices but in the inequitable distribution of opportunity, our findings should help to move the theory away from an overemphasis on the behaviors of a small segment of the inner-city population. Indeed, our findings demand that attention be directed at the real problem, namely, the persistence of structural barriers to opportunity that continue to keep blacks from rising from the bottom rungs of many institutions in American society.

In summary, our results tell a compelling story about the continuing salience of race in American society. Despite the fact that over thirty years have passed since the passage of the Fair Housing Act, housing and neighborhood outcomes remain unevenly allocated across racial/ethnic groups, with the result that blacks disproportionately occupy the least desirable units located in neighborhoods with the fewest resources necessary for social and economic success in American society. Furthermore, the longevity of the structural barriers that create and maintain these inequalities appears to have given rise to patterns of generational decline in socioeconomic status and locational outcomes among blacks. The separation of blacks from the other groups—both in their overall levels of locational outcomes and in their patterns of generational decline—suggests little reason to believe that racial/ethnic inequality in this arena of social life will be eliminated in the near future. Instead, these findings suggest that the nature of the dual housing market, which has traditionally operated separate submarkets for whites and blacks, may be evolving into a dual market offering one set of options to blacks and a different set to those who are not black. Although our findings of Hispanics' limited success in becoming fully assimilated in the housing market suggest that this group may come to occupy an intermediate position between these two extremes, the fact that our findings appear to be limited to the case of New York City prevents us from confidently applying such an interpretation to the nation as a whole. Yet the evidence concerning the prospects of blacks generally, and black immigrants specifically, do appear to be generalizable, suggesting that the predicted shifts in the nature of the dual housing market are just one part of a general shift in society's "color line" from the traditional line separating whites from nonwhites to one dividing blacks from the rest of society.

Immigrants' Integration in the Housing Market as It Reflects on U.S. Immigration Policy

Since the passage of the Immigration and Nationality Amendments Act in 1965, which eliminated country of origin as a qualification for individuals to obtain immigrant visas, there has been concern among many Americans about the "quality" of immigrants coming to the United States. Many of the countries sending immigrants during the past three decades have been much poorer than the countries dominating the immigrant flows in earlier periods. As a result, many scholars, policy makers, and members of the public have argued that the increased flow of immigrants from poorer areas is producing a more needy immigrant population than had heretofore been the case.

The fact that restrictions have been placed on immigrants that limit their access to many social welfare programs reflects the anti-immigrant sentiment of the public in recent years. In 1996, the rights of many noncitizen immigrants to receive government assistance were substantially narrowed when Congress passed and President Bill Clinton signed into law the Personal Responsibility and Work Opportunity Reconciliation

Act of 1996 (PRWORA). Although many states and localities stepped in to fill the gap in social welfare programs and many federal benefits were subsequently restored, at least for some classes of immigrants,[12] it is clear that recent decades have witnessed a resurgence of anti-immigrant feelings.

More recently, another wave of restrictionist sentiment has emerged on the part of the American public. The destruction of the World Trade Center and the devastating airliner crash into the Pentagon on September 11, 2001, both of which were carried out by foreign nationals, have resulted in an increased level of security by the former Immigration and Naturalization Service (INS, now a part of the Department of Homeland Security) in issuing immigrant visas. This legislative change now appears to have been only one of many other changes.

Countering this anti-immigrant sentiment, many researchers, policy makers, and members of the public contend that the majority of today's immigrants come to the United States with economic needs that are no different than those of earlier waves. Evidence is accumulating that counters the fears of overutilization of social welfare benefits among immigrants. For example, a number of studies have found that most immigrants utilize social welfare programs at rates comparable to those of native-born households, controlling for the influence of other relevant factors.[13] According to one study,[14] poor immigrants are actually significantly less likely than poor native-born Americans to use public assistance. Similarly, Friedman, Schill, and Rosenbaum demonstrate that in both New York City and the nation, income-eligible immigrants from non-refugee-sending countries are significantly less likely to use any form of rental assistance than are comparable native-born households.[15] In addition, evidence suggests that immigrants fill many low-skill jobs without displacing native-born workers. Indeed, many important industries, such as the garment industry or service industries related to tourism (e.g., hotels, restaurants), would have a difficult time existing without immigrants.[16]

There are also more-indirect economic benefits of the recent trends in immigration. In many cities, such as New York and Washington, D.C., where there have been substantial losses in population since the 1950s, immigrants have helped to curtail these losses; indeed, other cities that have not benefited from immigration's effect on population growth are now implementing policies designed to attract immigrants.[17] By helping to maintain a solid tax base in such cities, and by investing in small businesses and in the local housing stock,[18] immigrants have helped to revitalize many urban neighborhoods and have prevented further economic decline in these areas.[19] The fact that immigrants' fertility rates exceed those of the native-born population provides another indirect, positive economic benefit to American society. By the time members of the Baby Boom reach retirement, there will be a need for the working-age cohort to provide enough of a tax base to support the Social Security system; the higher fertility of immigrants has helped to ensure that a pool of workers will be available.

Although the debate about the flow of immigration is alive and well in the American public, the research in the previous chapters suggests that perhaps this debate is too focused on the immigrants themselves, as the same patterns of upward mobility attributed to earlier waves of immigrants remain evident in the current context. The society into which immigrants integrate is hardly discussed. Specifically, the structure of opportunities available to immigrants, whether in the labor market or the housing market, is largely ignored in debates over the "quality" of immigrants. As a result, the downward patterns of mobility evidenced by some immigrant groups is attributed to the immigrants themselves and not to the true cause, namely, the external constraints placed on them.

Indeed, what the results in the previous chapters demonstrate is that immigrants' integration into the housing market is influenced by their own economic circumstances but more profoundly shaped by their race/ethnicity. The residential outcomes of blacks and Hispanics, regardless of nativity status, are of significantly poorer quality than those of their white counterparts with the same socioeconomic backgrounds. Because preferences for low-quality housing and neighborhoods are unlikely to vary by race/ethnicity,[20] such results indicate the persistence of structural barriers that limit minorities' housing choices, and particularly those of blacks, to the least desirable housing units and the most resource-poor neighborhoods in the city. Therefore, race/ethnicity plays more of a role in immigrants' locational attainment than does their socioeconomic status, a finding that is not limited to New York City.[21]

The debate over immigration would be much more useful to policy makers if it considered the structural aspects of the labor and housing markets that affect immigrants' integration into American society. Such a focus might unify native- and foreign-born minorities who are often pitted against one another in the current discussions of immigration policy. Moreover, instead of "blaming the victim," a debate on immigration focusing on the structure of opportunity would be more amenable to changes through policy making. The results in this book have clearly shown the need to strengthen policies that combat discrimination present in the housing market.

Policies to Improve Racial/Ethnic Access to High-Quality Housing and Neighborhoods

Nonwhites—native-born and immigrant alike—simply do not enjoy the same opportunities as do whites in New York City's housing market. The differences in these opportunities are not a function of income or time in the United States. Instead, they seem to be rooted in the operation of the housing market itself. These findings suggest a number of policy initiatives targeted at people, in order to broaden their residential choices, as well as at places, in order to improve the residential options of those who are constrained in their choices within the housing market.

People-Based Policies

The different housing outcomes achieved by blacks and Hispanics as compared to whites of similar socioeconomic standing suggests that discrimination remains a salient factor in New York City's current housing market. Moreover, the findings of generational decline in socioeconomic standing and residential circumstances among blacks suggest that one of the pernicious effects of housing-market (and other forms of) discrimination is a progressive deterioration in the status of blacks and perhaps a widening of the distance separating blacks from other groups in American society. In order to improve the structure of opportunity within the housing market so that minorities, and especially blacks, have an equal chance of translating their socioeconomic success into the same residential attainment as whites, it is necessary to step up enforcement of the Fair Housing Act. Although the current fair-housing climate is more amenable to enforcement of the act, the government needs to put more pressure on the violators of the act to reduce the overall incidence of discrimination.

When the Fair Housing Act was passed in 1968, one of the compromises required to get the legislation through was to put in place a weak enforcement mechanism.[22] The Department of Justice (DOJ) was given the power to prosecute, but the Department of Housing and Urban Development (HUD), the government's primary agency that deals with housing, was only allowed to conciliate complaints or refer them to DOJ. With the passage of the Fair Housing Amendments Act in 1988, HUD was given enforcement powers of its own.

However, even with the expansion of enforcement powers designed to combat discrimination, the federal government's role in upholding the Fair Housing Act has been limited. Less than 1 percent of illegal acts of housing discrimination actually become a formal complaint.[23] Moreover, of the race-based complaints filed and investigated by HUD between 1989 and 1997, only 2.3 percent resulted in a finding that reasonable cause existed to believe discrimination had taken place; the other cases were either settled or dismissed.[24] Clearly, stronger enforcement is needed.

One important step would be to increase the use of paired testing so that the incidence of discrimination, including that aimed at immigrants, may be documented. Very little is known about how immigrants, particularly black immigrants, experience discrimination in the housing market. One potential explanation for our results of a generational decline in locational outcomes among blacks is that the intensity and perhaps frequency of discrimination may vary across generations. The work of Massey and Lundy demonstrates how simple auditing procedures can be used to document how home seekers may receive different treatment by realtors and landlords depending on their linguistic styles. This work could be extended to test whether home seekers who speak with different foreign accents receive different treatment in the housing market than do their more linguistically "assimilated" peers, and whether such differences vary by race/ethnicity, as we have hypothesized here. In addition to illuminating possible differences in housing-market discrimination across different immigrant groups, increasing and extending the practice of audits has a simple and practical consequence: research has shown that enforcement agencies tend to receive better settlements when testing is employed.[25]

A second step would be for HUD to initiate more systemic investigations[26] and for DOJ to engage in more pattern and practice lawsuits. Although HUD investigates each individual complaint it receives, it does not always respond to the institutionalized discrimination that may be taking place. Yet it is the institutionalized discrimination that needs to be combated in order to truly make inroads on equalizing the structure of opportunity available to minority and white home seekers. Such unlawful discrimination could be more effectively fought against using HUD-initiated complaints and pattern and practice lawsuits.

In addition to making the structure of opportunity more equal in the housing market, HUD and private housing providers could do more to educate the public, particularly the immigrant portion of the public, about fair-housing rights. Many individuals protected by the law may not realize that HUD is required to investigate all complaints brought to it or that HUD appoints a lawyer to the complainant(s) if the case is charged with a reasonable-cause finding and goes on to be adjudicated. The agency already works in tandem with both public and private agencies on a number of initiatives to promote fair housing, but given that so few complaints are filed relative to the true amount of discrimination that is occurring, it appears that the public is not as educated on these issues as it should be. Given that today's immigrants have largely entered the United States after the civil rights movement, it is important to educate them on their fair-housing rights.

Perhaps these agencies should work more closely with community groups, including faith-based groups, to educate the public. In the black community, churches played a vital role in the civil rights movement and continue today to have a socially progressive agenda. In addition, religious organizations are a central part of many immigrant communities. By working with community-based organizations, HUD can educate the public about its mission and the services it provides in the respective language of the immigrant group and in a setting that is most comfortable to the members of the group.

One example of a community-based organization that has been successful in improving immigrants' housing outcomes is Asian Americans For Equality (AAFE).[27] Located in New York City, AAFE serves some of the city's largest Asian enclaves, neighborhoods that include not only a highly diverse set of Asian groups (speaking numerous languages and dialects) but also a number of Hispanic immigrant groups. The organization's original purpose was to combat discriminatory hiring practices that were taking place in Chinatown during the early 1970s, but it has expanded its mission to include educational programs concerning tenants' rights and the home-buying process, as well as advocacy programs for both renters and home buyers. In addition, AAFE has become involved in housing rehabilitation, as well as the production of new affordable housing in the areas it serves. Since the mid-1970s, AAFE has built or rehabilitated more than forty buildings in Chinatown and the Lower East Side, providing housing for more than five hundred low- to moderate-income households, and has renovated or built a substantial number of homes in Queens.[28]

Another example of a collaborative effort to aid immigrants is the publication, in early 2004, of *The New York Times Guide for Immigrants in New York City* by the Lower East Side Tenement Museum and the *New York Times.* Written in Chinese, Spanish, and English, this publication provides information about several important issues, including getting a job and finding an apartment, understanding the New York City school system, and applying for a green card. It also provides information on the range of advocacy groups and other organizations in the city dedicated to helping immigrants. This publication can serve as a useful example for other efforts to inform immigrants about their rights.

Another "pro-people" policy to improve the housing options available to low-income households is tenant-based housing assistance (i.e., housing vouchers). For example, research has shown that low-income households receiving tenant-based assistance are less likely than their project-based counterparts to live in highly segregated and extremely poor neighborhoods.[29] Because of their generally lower levels of income, on average, minority households would benefit more than white households if enough vouchers were approved to meet the need. However, the supply of vouchers and certificates does not come close to meeting the demand for rental assistance; currently, only about one in three eligible households receive some form of rental assistance.[30] Indeed, the long waiting lists for housing assistance is probably one important reason why immigrants (from non-refugee-sending countries) are significantly less likely to utilize housing assistance than comparably income-eligible native-born households in New York City and in the nation as a whole.[31]

However, the benefits of housing assistance, particularly residence in public housing, to immigrants and minorities appear to be mixed. On the positive side, our results indicate that for Hispanic and black renters, living in public housing (relative to other rental housing) confers some benefits in neighborhood quality. Specifically, Hispanic renters in public housing live in neighborhoods with similar percentages of whites as those in which Hispanic owners live, while other Hispanic renters live in neighborhoods with a significantly smaller white presence.[32] In a similar vein, black renters living in public housing were no different than black owners in the percentage of students in their subareas under-performing in math, while other black renters lived in neighborhoods with far higher percentages of low-performing students.[33] Despite these apparent benefits, we found far more negative aspects of living in public housing, including living in neighborhoods with higher levels of crime, teenage fertility rates, and public-assistance rates.[34] Thus, on the whole, public housing does not greatly improve the residential circumstances of minorities and immigrants.

Although tenant-based assistance can help to improve the housing and neighborhood outcomes of low-income households generally, it cannot overcome the barriers in the housing market that differentially constrain the housing options made available to minority home seekers. That is, evidence indicates that the ability of assisted households to ac-quire improved residential outcomes is affected by their race; among assisted households, blacks are more likely than whites to move to more racially segregated and poorer areas.[35] Evidence from housing-mobility programs, however, indicates that additional services—including hous-ing counseling and landlord outreach—can help nonwhite assisted households hurdle these barriers.[36]

For example, evidence from the Moving to Opportunity Demonstra-tion Program in Chicago demonstrated that despite similar pre-move preferences for mixed-race neighborhoods, "experimental" families (i.e., those that had to move to low-poverty neighborhoods and received housing counseling along with their Section 8 vouchers) were more likely to satisfy these preferences than were "comparison" families (that received Section 8 vouchers but no counseling and no constraints on their destinations).[37] Such a difference is probably attributable in large part to the supplemental services received by the experimental group. Thus, to be truly effective in alleviating some of the inequalities we find in our analysis, the housing-choice voucher program must not only be funded to levels that match the need for rental assistance but should also be supplemented with the kinds of services that maximize the abil-ity of assisted households to gain access to higher-quality housing and the kinds of spatially based resources and opportunities necessary for social and economic success. Although supplemental services add to the cost of housing vouchers, direct federal spending on housing assistance is only a fraction of the amount lost to tax incentives, including the mortgage-interest deduction.[38] The equalization of housing benefits for low-income and more-affluent households is long overdue.

A final "pro-people" policy solution lies in New York City's rent-regulation programs, although the effectiveness of such legislation has been significantly weakened in recent years. Following World War II, New York enacted a rent-control program, which protected residents from significant rent increases. However, because the legislation only applies to units built before 1947, where the residents have lived in their units continuously since the early 1970s, it is not as beneficial to New Yorkers as when it was first enacted. Indeed, in 2002, rent-controlled units only constituted 2.8 percent of the city's rental-housing stock.[39]

In 1969, New York enacted a rent-stabilization policy to apply to buildings with six or more units built after 1947. The policy extended the regulations under the rent-control program to these larger, more recently built units. However, in recent years the state has eroded the benefits available under this policy. Under the Rent Regulation Reform Act of 1997, units with rents at or above $2,000, regardless of the incomes of the newly arrived tenants, are no longer covered by the program. In addition, landlords can increase the rent on a vacated unit by 20 percent; if they make repairs, they can charge one-fortieth of the cost to the tenants' monthly rents. There is worry in the housing community that landlords may undertake repairs in order to increase the monthly rent to close to $2,000.

In 2002, 48.6 percent of New York City's rental units fell under the rent-stabilization program,[40] dropping nearly 3 percentage points, from 51.9 percent, in 1999.[41] It appears that the policy has been most beneficial to Dominicans, as 70 percent lived in such housing in 1999, nearly one and a half times the level of the average renter in New York.[42] Blacks are not nearly as likely to live in such housing; in 1999 only 41 percent of blacks lived in rent-stabilized units, well below the average level. Blacks are more likely to live in locally or federally assisted housing, as compared to other groups. Only 26 percent of blacks lived in unregulated rental housing. The percentage that is black in the neighborhoods in which assisted housing is located is much higher than that where unregulated or rent-stabilized units are located (39 percent versus 21 and 23 percent, respectively). Thus, it appears that, as with housing-assistance programs, rent regulation cannot overcome the barriers in the housing market that differentially constrain the housing options available to blacks as compared to other home seekers.

Place-Based Policies

Our findings clearly reveal the uneven distribution over space of high-quality housing and neighborhood-based resources. This is evident not only in the inequalities by race/ethnicity that emerge so starkly in our analyses but also in the effects that the percentage of blacks and the percentage of recently arrived immigrants in the surrounding subarea have on the chance of living in deteriorated housing units. In each case, as the concentration of the particular group (blacks or recently arrived immigrants) rose, so did the likelihood of living in a seriously under-maintained housing unit. Whether such areal variations in the quality of housing represent "benign" processes of wear and tear on the housing stock or more pernicious consequences of purposeful disinvestment, the fact is that minority households are more likely than white households to be exposed to such potentially harmful environments. Although people-based efforts, such as tenant-based assistance, may help to increase the range of options available to households, they cannot help to improve the quality of housing and neighborhood resources, nor to equalize the distribution of the resources across the various neighborhoods of the city.

One way to work toward the latter goal is to invest private and public funds into specific communities. Such investment can help curb racial disparities in residential location by improving the quality of life for all residents in disadvantaged areas and by increasing the attractiveness of such areas to investors, which has the potential to develop the economic infrastructure of these communities.

On the public side of the investment ledger, the city's ten-year plan demonstrated that significant improvements can be achieved in even the most blighted neighborhoods. Begun in 1986, the ten-year plan has devoted over $5 billion—largely of local funds—to creating some 150,000 new units of affordable housing. Some of these new units derived from new construction, but the majority arose from the rehabilitation of city-owned properties. Still in operation today (though on a far smaller scale), the ten-year plan has created new homeownership opportunities and returned tens of thousands of rental units to the city's housing stock through a variety of programs and partnerships with various local and national organizations, including the Local Initiatives Support Corporation (LISC), the Enterprise Foundation, and the New York City Housing Partnership.[43] Journalistic evidence abounds on the successes of the program,[44] but research to quantify the program's effects has only just begun to take shape. One study has shown that production under the ten-year plan appears to be associated with positive "spillover" effects, such as rising sales prices for housing near ten-year plan projects.[45] Other studies have shown additional positive effects associated with the program, like the declining prevalence of vacant and boarded-up buildings.[46] This kind of improvement may lead to further gains for affected neighborhoods, given the association of vacant and boarded-up buildings with various forms of physical and social disorder and the salience of such structures in the minds of potential investors.[47] Although these are all positive effects of the program, other evidence suggests that the plan has contributed to increasing concentrations of poor, welfare-receiving, and single-parent households in certain areas.[48]

The federal Community Reinvestment Act (CRA), passed in 1977, is a piece of national legislation that could prove to be very useful in equalizing the distribution of some neighborhood resources. The CRA requires federally chartered depository institutions to respond to the credit needs of their service areas, including low- and moderate-income communities. It requires bank regulatory agencies to take such responses into account in its evaluation of a depository institution's application or any other request to make a significant change in its business practices. Moreover, the act allows third parties to challenge lenders' applications. These challenges can pose delays in the approval process and therefore can be costly to the financial institution.

The passage of the CRA in 1977 took place at a time when several key pieces of fair-lending legislation were enacted. The motivation for the CRA was based on concerns that inner-city neighborhoods did not have access to credit. It was suspected that the lack of credit was due to racial and ethnic discrimination, or more specifically redlining, occurring within these communities. According to the National Community Reinvestment Coalition, the CRA has led to more than $1 trillion in new private investment for community development.[49] Since the 1990s, the act has been particularly effective. Many financial institutions' applications for changes in their business practices have been denied. Community groups have also been effective at challenging the applications of financial institutions. Indeed, the potential time lost by financial institutions through the challenges posed by community groups has been enough to give leverage to various groups to develop CRA agreements with these institutions. These agreements call for, at a minimum, increases in home-purchase, home-improvement, and small-business lending in low- and moderate-income areas and to racial minorities throughout metropolitan areas.

Recent research suggests that the effects of the CRA extend beyond the potential upgrading of distressed areas. One consequence of the CRA appears to be a higher chance of minority in-movement to predominantly white neighborhoods.[50] Thus, by potentially being an effective component of larger efforts to reduce levels of residential segregation, the CRA extends its usefulness beyond inequities in the availability of credit and thus emerges as a key strategy to ameliorate many urban problems.

Public and private "place-based" approaches can improve the structure of opportunity available in the housing market for minority immigrant and native-born New Yorkers in two general ways. First, reinvestment in distressed neighborhoods can make them more desirable places to live, which in turn can cause property values to increase. Second, reinvestment has the potential to increase the economic integration of residents, particularly if such communities are near downtown offices and cultural attractions. This could greatly diversify the social networks of residents, particularly poorer and immigrant residents, within these communities, which has positive implications for their future social mobility.

Conclusions

Racial discrimination continues to be a salient feature of New York City's housing market. Although the broad tenets of the spatial assimilation model characterize immigrants' locational attainment, race/ethnicity is still a defining element that shapes the structure of opportunity in the housing market available to today's immigrants. Thus, even if immigrants have the socioeconomic resources needed to achieve improvements in their residential environments, the way that their resources translate into residential outcomes depends, in large part, on their race/ethnicity.

Place- and people-based policies are needed to improve the operation of the housing market in New York City so that, over time, immigrants and native-born minorities alike will be afforded the same opportunities in the housing market as are white home seekers. Both types of policies would be strengthened if the needs and experiences of immigrants were included in their formulation. Minority immigrants achieve better residential outcomes when they know more about their rights and when community groups monitor the wealth being funneled into their communities by depository institutions. By appealing to immigrants, the movement toward fair housing and lending would benefit as a whole. Current debates over immigration tend to polarize immigrants and native-born minorities. However, by including immigrants in the discussion of fair housing and lending, these groups could work together to reduce residential segregation and improve their housing and neighborhood conditions. Such an effort would not only benefit the current generation of immigrants and minorities but would also improve the access that future generations have to wealth and ultimately improve their current and future socioeconomic well-being.

Appendix A
Data and Methodology

Data Sources

The analyses of housing and locational attainment in New York City presented in chapters 4 and 5 are based on two sources of data. The first is the 1999 panel of the New York City Housing and Vacancy Survey (HVS), which provides individual-level data on households within the city. The other source of data is *Infoshare,* which provides neighborhood-level indicators that we append to the individual-level data from the HVS.

The HVS is a multistage probability sample of approximately eighteen thousand housing units located throughout the five boroughs of New York City. The sample is surveyed every two to three years by the U.S. Bureau of the Census under contract to New York City in compliance with city and state laws regarding rent regulation. The main focus of the survey is on housing, but because the survey also asks households to provide many demographic and socioeconomic indicators, the data provide the most current source of information on the city's housing, households, and population. In analyzing these data, we use the sample weights (scaled down to maintain unweighted cell sizes) to correct for potential undercoverage and sampling design effects.

The 1999 panel of the HVS is particularly suitable for an analysis of nativity/generational-status differences in locational attainment. Unlike previous waves of the survey, the 1999 wave asked foreign-born householders to report the year that they entered the United States. The HVS also asks foreign-born households to provide the nativity status of both parents. As mentioned earlier, this is one of two existing data sets, to our knowledge, that collects such information. By combining these two pieces of information, we are able to categorize the householders within the HVS by their nativity/generational status.

Although the recent revisions to the HVS make it an excellent source of data on the foreign-born population of New York City, it is—like most quantitative data sets—hampered by a number of limitations, some of which affect our analysis of locational attainment. First, the HVS does not collect information on foreign-born householders' English proficiency, which is a factor that has an impact on the access that immigrants have to better housing and neighborhood opportunities.[1] Second, the HVS does not provide any measures of households' wealth. Although information on homeownership is available, there are no data on present net financial worth. We expect that our measures of nativity/generational status may overstate the "true" net effect that we would obtain if we could control for English-language proficiency and wealth.

Another limitation of the HVS that bears directly on our analyses is the absence of an indicator of ancestry. As a result, we cannot identify the ethnic identity of white and black members of the third-plus generation. This leaves us vulnerable to confounding generation and ethnicity for these two groups. This limitation is particularly acute in our analyses pertaining to blacks since many of the third-plus generation have their roots among the waves of Southern-born migrants who began arriving in the city at the turn of the twentieth century, whereas those in the first, 1.5, and second generations have their roots largely in the Caribbean. Of course, given the long history of substantial migration from the Caribbean, there is also a segment of the third-plus generation that identifies with Caribbean ancestry. The problem is that we cannot identify them. As a result, and as we discuss elsewhere, in our group-specific models we compare the first and 1.5 generations to the second generation, in addition to our usual comparisons that use the third-plus generation as the reference group. Doing so allows us essentially to control for the ethnic differences that set the third-plus generation apart from the earlier generations and thus helps to strengthen our interpretations of generational differences.

The final limitation of the HVS is that it only collects data on households within New York City. Data from Census 2000 for the New York CMSA show that 23 percent of whites, 58 percent of blacks, and 56 percent of Hispanics lived in New York City itself; the remainder of the CMSA population lives outside New York City. As part of the assimilation process, immigrants may leave New York City and move to the suburbs. Because we cannot examine these households, our results may overstate or understate generational differences in locational attainment depending on the race or ethnic group being studied. For blacks and Hispanics, it is likely that we are underestimating the extent to which they are attaining better housing and neighborhood outcomes. Previous research has shown that minorities' gains in neighborhood outcomes are more pronounced in suburbs than in the central cities in the New York metropolitan area.[2]

A major advantage of using the HVS data is that they identify the sub-borough area or "subarea" in which the sampled housing unit is located. Subareas are aggregations of census tracts that total at least 100,000 population. In total, there are fifty-five subareas within New York City. Although subareas are larger than what researchers typically use as a proxy for "neighborhood," they correspond to politically meaningful boundaries within New York City. Subareas are created from the fifty-nine community districts that serve as the city's main administrative units for service provision and other amenities. Thus, results of any analysis based on subareas can provide meaningful information to the city's policy makers.

Because of the ability to identify the subareas within the HVS data, we are able to append subarea-level data to householders' data, creating a multilevel data set for our analyses. The subarea-level data come from a unique database called *Infoshare* that allows us to aggregate a variety of public and private data to different levels of geography within New York City, including the subarea. Indicators derived from *Infoshare* include rates of diseases, vital events, and crime; test scores for schools; information about public-assistance receipt; the racial composition of neighborhoods; and other measures that characterize the quality of life within the city.

Variable Definitions and Construction

Independent Variables

One of the central variables in our analysis is *generational status*. As described earlier, we examine four specific generational groups, the first, 1.5, second, and third-plus generations. The first generation consists of householders who were born abroad (and whose parents were born abroad) and who arrived in the United States at age eighteen or older. In contrast, the 1.5 generation consists of householders who were born abroad (of foreign-born parents) but who arrived in the United States at an age younger than eighteen. The second generation consists of house-holders who were born in the United States but who have at least one parent born abroad. Finally, the third-plus generation consists of house-holders who were born in the United States of native-born parents. We construct generational groups for Puerto Ricans despite the fact that Puerto Ricans are not strictly immigrants. We do so because previous research has suggested that island-born Puerto Ricans who migrate to the mainland experience an integration process that is similar to that experienced by immigrants, and capturing this process is the goal of our analysis.[3]

Another key independent variable in our analysis is householder race/ethnicity. We examine four mutually exclusive racial/ethnic groups: non-Hispanic whites, non-Hispanic blacks, Hispanics, and Asians/Pacific Islanders. The category Hispanic is heterogeneous, consisting of householders reporting Puerto Rican, Dominican, Cuban, Central/South American, Mexican, as well as "other" Hispanic origin. There is also a residual category of race/ethnicity consisting of householders of "other" race, which includes American Indians, Eskimos, and persons reporting "other" race. However, because there are few foreign-born household-ers within this group, an analysis broken down by generational status could not be sustained, forcing us to eliminate this group from our analysis. In addition, because of extremely small cell sizes, we were un-able to estimate locational attainment models for Asians as a separate group. Finally, in the models for Hispanics, we include a dichotomy that differentiates black from nonblack Hispanics, as well as nation-origin dichotomies that differentiate between Puerto Rican, Dominican, and other Hispanic households, and we compare these groups to the refer-ence category of Central/South Americans.

Other independent variables used in the analysis include measures of the household's life-cycle stage and its socioeconomic status. Life-cycle factors are represented by the householder's age and by a dichotomous variable indicating whether the household is headed by a single person (i.e., a noncouple) versus a couple. We also use a dichotomous variable to indicate whether any adults, other than those in the "nuclear" family, are present in the household. We do not specify the relationsh ɔ of these other adults to the householder. This measure allows us to cɔ ɪʹɭol for the use of a multiple-earner strategy that could enable some hc ʋ seholds, particularly immigrant and native-born minority households, ɔ im-prove their living conditions.[4] Finally, we also utilize a dum ay ɣ ɪɪ iable indicating whether there are any children younger than eighteen in the household.

Socioeconomic status is measured by three variables: the educational attainment of the householder, household income, and a dichotomous variable indicating whether anyone in the household receives public assistance. Householders' educational attainment is measured as two dummy variables differentiating those who have less than a high school diploma from those who have received a high school diploma. The reference category for householders' educational attainment is some college or more. In the multivariate models, household income is logged to eliminate the high degree of skew in this variable.

We also control for the housing-market sector of the housing unit. As described earlier, we utilize this variable to tap into an additional aspect of socioeconomic status in all models except for that predicting home-ownership. This variable is operationalized as two dummy variables to differentiate units in public housing from those that are also in the rental sector but are not part of public housing. The reference for these categories is owned units.

Our final independent variables are measured at the aggregate level. The first controls for the borough in which the housing unit is located. We utilize three dummy variables, one for the Bronx, one for Queens, and one for Brooklyn/Staten Island. Because the population of Staten Island remains fairly homogeneous in its race/ethnicity and immigrant status, it is essential to combine this borough with another. The reference for the borough dummies is Manhattan. Controlling for borough location is important since immigrant and racial/ethnic groups tend to live in different boroughs and because the patterns of development have led to very different housing stocks and thus divergent sets of housing opportunities in the boroughs.

Our other aggregate-level predictors are measures of the composition of the subarea surrounding the sampled unit. Both use 1990 census data for their measurement since at the time of the analysis, detailed data on nativity status and year of arrival was not available for small geographic units, preventing us from using data more current than 1990 for this variable. As a result, we decided for the sake of consistency to use 1990 data for the percentage of blacks as well. The first measures the percentage of blacks in the subarea population. As discussed earlier, controlling for percentage of blacks is essential because high-quality housing and neighborhood conditions are not distributed evenly over space, but are more plentiful in areas with fewer black residents. In addition, controlling for percentage of blacks allows us to account for the fact that many black and nonwhite Hispanic households find that their access to areas with few or no black residents remains limited.

The second aspect of subarea composition that we control for is the percentage of recently arrived immigrants. This variable compared the number of immigrants in the subarea who arrived between 1980 and 1990 to the total number of foreign-born persons in the area. Using this variable allows us to take account of the uneven distribution of housing and neighborhood resources, which, as predicted by spatial assimilation theory, suggests that areas serving as the first stop for newcomers to the country would be the most rundown in the city and would thus offer some of the least desirable housing opportunities to its residents.

Dependent Variables

We examine three aspects of housing conditions and six aspects of neighborhood conditions. The three housing conditions are homeownership, crowding, and housing-unit quality, as indicated by the number of maintenance deficiencies. Crowding is measured as the number of persons per room, and housing units are considered crowded if they contain more than one person per room. The number of maintenance deficiencies in a housing unit relies on the householder's reports of the presence, during the three months preceding the survey (which is conducted in January and February of the survey year), of any of the following deficiencies: toilet breakdowns; heating breakdowns; the need for additional heat; the presence of rats or mice; leaks from the outside; cracks or holes in the walls, floor, or ceiling; and large areas of broken plaster on the walls. We define the presence of three or more maintenance deficiencies as indicating a serious level of undermaintenance; this dichotomous variable serves as our measure of housing-unit quality.

Our six neighborhood conditions are all measured at the subarea level and consist of the percentage that is white, the percentage of students performing at or below grade level in math, the violent-crime rate, the percentage of households receiving public assistance, the teenage fertility rate, and the percentage of housing units that are one- and two-family homes. The percentage of whites relies on 2000 census data for its construction, and is simply the number of non-Hispanic whites in the subarea divided by the total subarea population. The percentage of students underperforming in math is based on data from the New York City Board of Education and refers to students in the fourth through sixth grades. This measure divides the number of students whose performance in math is at or below grade level by all fourth- through sixth-graders for the 1998–1999 school year. We chose math scores instead of reading scores because reading scores in immigrant neighborhoods may be influenced by the immigrant children's limited English proficiency. Math scores may be less sensitive to the immigrant composition of the area. The address of the school is what places underperforming students in a particular subarea. Because school districts are not completely coextensive with subareas, this variable may not always represent the quality of schools in a given householder's district. However, it can be argued that this variable may reflect the prevalence of a negative attitude about school, or about the value of education or doing well in school, among youth in the area. The violent-crime rate is measured as the number of violent crimes (murder, rape, assault, robbery) in 1999 divided by the total population in the subarea. The crime rate is expressed per 1,000 population. The percentage of households receiving public assistance relies on data from the New York City Human Resources Administration. The teen fertility rate divides the number of births to women aged twelve to seventeen by the total number of women in that age group and is expressed per 1,000. And finally, the percentage of housing units that are one- and two-family homes relies on 2000 census data.

Analytical Methods

To examine the impact of nativity/generational status on locational attainment, we employ bivariate and multivariate analyses. In the bivariate analyses, we report nativity/generational status differences in locational attainment for all householders (chapter 4) and then by race/ethnicity (chapter 5) in order to determine how well the spatial assimilation model characterizes the assimilation process across subgroups within the population. Our multivariate analyses are also performed for the overall sample and for each racial/ethnic group separately (apart from Asians). The multivariate analyses allow us to examine the effect of nativity/generational status on locational outcomes after controlling for a range of theoretically relevant independent variables. As mentioned in chapter 4, in the results that are reported, we use third-plus-generation households as the reference group. In chapter 5, where we examine racial/ethnic groups separately, we also report results that compare first- and 1.5-generation households' housing and neighborhood outcomes to those of second-generation households to account for the potential differences in ethnicity between members of the third-plus generation and the immigrant generations. This problem, as discussed earlier, is particularly acute for blacks, since most members of the third-plus generation have their roots among the Southern-born migrants who began arriving in the city during the early decades of the twentieth century. However, because of the long history of fairly substantial migration from the Caribbean, among the third-plus generation are individuals of Caribbean heritage, but we cannot identify them. Thus, comparing the immigrant generations to the second generation is one way of controlling for ethnicity.

To examine the relationship between nativity/generational status and homeownership, household crowding, and housing quality, we specify several logistic regression models that estimate the following logit specification of P_i: the probability that household i owns its home; the probability that it lives in housing units with more than one person per room; and the probability that it lives in a housing unit with three or more maintenance deficiencies, where $0 < P_i < 1$:

$$\log\left(\frac{P_i}{1-P_i}\right) = \alpha + \sum_j \beta_j N_{ji} + \sum_n \beta_n X_{ni}$$

The vector N represents the nativity/generational status of the householder. Two different models are run for each of the three housing dependent variables. In the first of the two models, the vector N comprises three dummy variables indicating whether the householder is part of the first, 1.5, or second generation. The reference group is composed of householders who are part of the third-plus generation. In the second logistic regression model, the vector N comprises nativity/generational-status variables that take into account year of entry for foreign-born householders. Specifically, the vector N consists of five dummy variables indicating whether the householder is part of the first generation and entered in or after 1980, the first generation and entered before 1980, the 1.5 generation and entered in or after 1980, the 1.5 generation and entered before 1980, and the second generation. The dummy variable for second generation is not disaggregated by year of entry because these householders were born in the United States to foreign-born parents. As in the first model, the reference group is composed of householders who are part of the third-plus generation.

In the two logistic regression models run for each of the three housing outcomes, the vector X measures the control variables used in the analysis. Specifically, we introduce controls for the following set of characteristics: households' life-cycle stage (i.e., the number of children under eighteen years of age in the household, household headship, and whether the household includes adults beyond those in the nuclear family); household income; receipt of public assistance; and householder's education, age, and race/ethnicity. We also control for contextual-level characteristics, namely, the borough of residence and the percentage of blacks and recent immigrants located within the subarea. In all models, except for those focused on homeownership, we control for the housing-market sector of the housing unit. In sum, six models are run for the overall sample, and for whites, blacks, and Hispanics, for a total of twenty-four models. We do not run models for Asians as a separate group because there are not enough native-born households to sustain such an analysis.

With respect to neighborhood outcomes, we employ the locational attainment model. This model characterizes how households become located in the hierarchy of neighborhoods that exists in society. Like the status attainment model, it focuses on how individuals or households convert their resources into higher status positions within the stratification system.[5] For example, in the status attainment model, one's education influences the access that he or she will have to a particular occupation because of the educational demands of the occupation and the employer's preferences.

To examine the relationship between nativity/generational status and locational attainment we adopt the following multivariate model that has been used in previous research on this topic:[6]

$$Y_{ij} = \alpha + \Sigma \beta_1 N_{1ij} + \Sigma \beta_2 X_{2ij} + \epsilon_{ij},$$

where Y_{ij} is the subarea measure of the context (i.e., percentage white, crime rate, percentage receiving AFDC, teenage fertility rate, percentage with below-grade-level math, percentage of units that are one- and two-family homes) for context j; N_{1ij} are the nativity/generational-status indicators for household i in community j; and X_{2ij} represents the control variables of household *i* in community *j*. The model is estimated with the household as the unit of analysis and separately for each of our six dependent variables. As with the housing outcomes, two models are estimated for each of the five dependent variables. One model contains three nativity/generational-status dummy variables, and the other contains five variables as specified earlier. The vector *X*, which contains the control variables, is also similar to that included in the housing outcome models. The only difference is that we do not control for contextual-level variables here because our outcome is at the contextual level. In sum, twelve models are run for the overall sample, and for whites, blacks, and Hispanics, for a total of forty-eight models.

Such a model can be interpreted in the same manner as other status attainment models.[7] Each β coefficient establishes the degree of conversion of a householder's or household's characteristics, such as income or education, into a residential context of higher quality or, more generally, into a better position in the stratification system. Thus, the dependent variable is an aggregate-level variable regressed on independent variables at the individual or household level of analysis.

In the past, the estimation of such models has been troublesome primarily because researchers have been limited to one source of data for both the individual- and aggregate-level characteristics. Richard Alba and John Logan have developed a method to overcome the problems in estimating models from such data.[8] However, we do not need to use the technique because our individual- and aggregate-level data are drawn from independent sources.

Because we are using data from independent sources, we are able to combat another methodological problem that has been acknowledged but not addressed: spatial autocorrelation.[9] Spatial autocorrelation can arise in models predicting an aggregate-level outcome as a function of individual-level characteristics because multiple cases share the same value on the dependent variable. This problem has the potential of producing correlated error terms and thus of underestimating the standard errors of regression coefficients. To address this problem, we use feasible generalized least squares to estimate the locational attainment regression models specified above.[10] This technique produces regression coefficients and standard errors that take into account the fact that the error variances across subareas are different.[11]

Specifically, we identified that spatial autocorrelation exists by testing for whether the error variances across the subareas were homogeneous using the Lagrange Multiplier test. Based on our results, we find evidence to reject the null hypothesis of homogeneity of the variances. To correct for spatial autocorrelation, we need to superimpose a structure on the covariance matrix. Traditionally this is done using "time" in time-series-analysis data and "distance" in geographic data. In our case, although we can identify the subarea in which respondents live, we cannot identify how respondents within subareas are geographically related to one another. Therefore, we cannot use this traditional technique.

An alternative would be to specify a random effects model with an individual-specific error and a subarea-specific error. However, in our case, since individuals within the same subarea have identical values for each dependent variable, we cannot specify a within-subarea individual-specific error. To address the potential for autocorrelation, then, we used the best of the limited options available to us, namely, feasible generalized least squares (FGLS). This technique allows us to estimate unique error variances for each of the K subareas. FGLS takes the general form

$$y = X\beta + \epsilon$$

where y is the dependent variable and X is the matrix with explanatory variables. The vector β contains the regression coefficients.

To estimate the vector β, we use the FGLS estimator, denoted as

$$\beta_{fgls} = (X'\Omega^{-1}X)^{-1}\Omega^{-1}y$$

where Ω is a consistent estimate of the variance-covariance matrix W. To get this consistent estimate we first do ordinary least squares (OLS) regression on the pooled data and then use the residuals from the OLS regressions to compute the mean squared residual for each of the K subareas respectively. The consistent estimate of W, then, has the following shape:

$$\begin{pmatrix} \sigma_1^2 I & 0 & .\,. & 0 \\ 0 & \sigma_2^2 I & .\,. & .\,. \\ .\,. & .\,. & .\,. & 0 \\ 0 & .\,. & 0 & \sigma_K^2 I \end{pmatrix}$$

where the σ_i^2 are mean squared residuals for each of the subareas.

Aside from the fact that our study focuses only on households' housing and locational attainment in New York City, another limitation of the analyses presented in chapters 4 and 5 is that we use the two sets of nativity/generational-status variables to assess immigrants' housing and locational attainment over time (i.e., across generations and years). Although this approach is the most sensible due to the data that are available, the results should be interpreted cautiously because we are using data from one point in time to examine a process that occurs over years and generations. A preferable way to approach the issue would be to use a cohort method, along the lines of the double cohort method, to assess immigrants' housing and neighborhood outcomes over time.[12] In that way, households could be grouped by the householder's generation, year of entry, age, and the householder's parents' year of entry. However, because the HVS did not begin asking respondents about their year of entry until the 1999 panel and does not include any information on parents' year of entry, this is not possible. Therefore, we interpret the effects of nativity/generational status with these caveats in mind.

Appendix B

Means of Predictors Used in Pooled Models Predicting Housing and
Neighborhood Outcomes

	Mean
Generation	
First	.3694
1.5	.1862
Second	.1140
Third-plus	.3304
Generation by Year of Arrival	
First, arrived 1980 and later	.1232
First, arrived before 1980	.2071
1.5, arrived 1980 and later	.0366
1.5, arrived before 1980	.0774
Race/ethnicity	
White, non-Hispanic	.4429
Black, non-Hispanic	.2378
Puerto Rican	.1026
Dominican	.0577
South/Central American	.0504
Other Hispanic	.0313
Asian	.0772
Household characteristics	
Age	48.4197
Couple headed	.4079
Single-person headed	.5921
Presence of children under eighteen	.2355
Presence of other adults	.3257
Education	
Less than high school diploma	.2256
High school diploma	.2686
Some college or more	.5058
Household income	$47,654.1398
Receives public assistance	.1679
Housing market sector	
Owned	.3188
Rental, not in public housing	.5879
Public housing	.0933
Borough	
Manhattan	.2315
Bronx	.1521
Queens	.2730
Brooklyn/Staten Island	.3434
Percentage of recently arrived immigrants in subarea	.1275
Percentage of blacks in subarea	.2296

APPENDIX TABLE B.2
Logistic Regression Coefficients of Models Predicting Homeownership

Variables	Generation Specific (1)	Generation by Year of Entry (2)
Nativity (ref. native-born)		
Foreign-born by generational status		
Second generation (householder nb; at least one parent fb)	0.1326*	—
	(0.0673)	
1.5 generation (householder fb and parents fb, and householder immigrated when ≤ 18)	0.2969**	—
	(0.0877)	
First generation (householder fb and parents fb, and householder immigrated when > 18)	−0.2822**	—
	(0.0651)	
Foreign-born by generational status and year of entry		
Second generation	—	0.1831**
		(0.0670)
1.5 generation and entered before 1980	—	0.4518**
		(0.0978)
1.5 generation and entered in or after 1980	—	−0.1927
		(0.1643)
First generation and entered before 1980	—	0.2826**
		(0.0839)
First generation and entered in or after 1980	—	−0.7156**
		(0.0787)
Race/ethnicity (ref. white, non-Hispanic)		
Black, non-Hispanic	−0.2081**	−0.2231**
	(0.0762)	(0.0767)
Puerto Rican	−0.8511**	−1.0155**
	(0.1026)	(0.1042)
Dominican	−1.1957**	−1.2574**
	(0.1746)	(0.1772)
South and Central American	−0.7695**	−0.8539**
	(0.1282)	(0.1317)
Other Hispanic	−0.7410**	−0.7935**
	(0.1653)	(0.1690)
Asian	−0.0524	0.0699
	(0.0931)	(0.0957)
Age	0.0486**	0.0428**
	(0.0017)	(0.0018)
Single-person-headed household	−0.7494**	−0.7695**
	(0.0531)	(0.0534)
Presence of		
Children under eighteen	0.1957**	0.2315**
	(0.0691)	(0.0698)
Others in the household beyond the nuclear family	0.3547**	0.3729**
	(0.0580)	(0.0583)
Education (ref. ≥ college)		
Less than high school	−0.7437**	−0.7764**
	(0.0739)	(0.0750)
High school diploma	−0.3002**	−0.2993**
	(0.0570)	(0.0575)

(continued)

APPENDIX TABLE B.2 (*continued*)

Variables	Generation Specific (1)	Generation by Year of Entry (2)
Total household income (logged)	0.3404**	0.3186**
	(0.0259)	(0.0255)
Receiving public assistance	−1.3732**	−1.3383**
	(0.0960)	(0.0961)
Percentage of		
Recent immigrants (in subarea)	−5.2610**	−5.3265**
	(0.3980)	(0.4020)
Blacks (in subarea)	0.2244†	0.2311†
	(0.1201)	(0.1210)
Borough (ref. Manhattan)		
Bronx	0.6816**	0.7240**
	(0.0898)	(0.0902)
Brooklyn/Staten Island	0.8592**	0.8838**
	(0.0690)	(0.0691)
Queens	1.4488**	1.4802**
	(0.0742)	(0.0745)
Intercept	−6.0703**	−5.5638**
	(0.3326)	(0.3292)
Model Chi-Square	3626.60**	3752.00**
df	22	24
N		12,045

** p < 0.01; * p < 0.05; † p < 0.10

APPENDIX TABLE B.3
Logistic Regression Coefficients of Models Predicting Household Crowding

Variables	Generation Specific (1)	Generation by Year of Entry (2)
Nativity (ref. native-born)		
Foreign-born by generational status		
Second generation (householder nb; at least one parent fb)	0.4939**	—
	(0.1406)	
1.5 generation (householder fb and parents fb, and householder immigrated when ≤ 18)	0.7400**	—
	(0.1319)	
First generation (householder fb and parents fb, and householder immigrated when > 18)	0.9860**	—
	(0.1123)	
Foreign-born by generational status and year of entry		
Second generation	—	0.4936**
		(0.1406)
1.5 generation and entered before 1980	—	0.7083**
		(0.1556)
1.5 generation and entered in or after 1980	—	0.7946**
		(0.1648)
First generation and entered before 1980	—	0.5917**
		(0.1596)

APPENDIX TABLE B.3 *(continued)*

Variables	Generation Specific (1)	Generation by Year of Entry (2)
First generation and entered in or after 1980	—	1.0714**
		(0.1143)
Race/ethnicity (ref. white, non-Hispanic)		
Black, non-Hispanic	0.4131**	0.4376**
	(0.1285)	(0.1289)
Puerto Rican	–0.1982	–0.1304
	(0.1511)	(0.1535)
Dominican	0.1606	0.1945
	(0.1468)	(0.1475)
South and Central American	0.4226**	0.4652**
	(0.1489)	(0.1499)
Other Hispanic	0.8989**	0.9204**
	(0.1703)	(0.1715)
Asian	0.4679**	0.4518**
	(0.1305)	(0.1310)
Housing tenure (ref. owner)		
Renter not in public housing	1.0417**	1.0098**
	(0.1065)	(0.1068)
Renter in public housing	1.0029**	0.9578**
	(0.1771)	(0.1773)
Age	–0.0408**	–0.0362**
	(0.0034)	(0.0036)
Single-person-headed household	–1.5088**	–1.5038**
	(0.0883)	(0.0884)
Presence of		
Children under eighteen	2.1318**	2.1276**
	(0.1651)	(0.1653)
Others in the household beyond the nuclear family	2.8277**	2.8318**
	(0.1613)	(0.1614)
Education (ref. ≥ college)		
Less than high school	0.6366**	0.6363**
	(0.0944)	(0.0947)
High school diploma	0.3093**	0.3023**
	(0.0887)	(0.0888)
Total household income (logged)	–0.0278	–0.0277
	(0.0204)	(0.0205)
Receiving public assistance	0.6514**	0.6598**
	(0.0936)	(0.0937)
Percentage of		
Recent immigrants (in subarea)	1.7730**	1.7481**
	(0.5438)	(0.5458)
Blacks (in subarea)	0.1894	0.1819
	(0.1755)	(0.1757)
Borough (ref. Manhattan)		
Bronx	–0.2730*	–0.3070*
	(0.1220)	(0.1227)
Brooklyn/Staten Island	–0.4149**	–0.4318**
	(0.1090)	(0.1093)
Queens	–0.4211**	–0.4336**
	(0.1157)	(0.1161)

(continued)

APPENDIX TABLE B.3 (*continued*)

Variables	Generation Specific (1)	Generation by Year of Entry (2)
Intercept	−3.5838**	−3.7383**
	(0.3508)	(0.3545)
Model Chi-Square	2160.56**	2173.41**
df	24	26
N		12,045

** p < 0.01; * p < 0.05; † p < 0.10

APPENDIX TABLE B.4
Logistic Regression Coefficients of Models Predicting Three or More Maintenance Deficiencies

Variables	Generation Specific (1)	Generation by Year of Entry (2)
Nativity (ref. native-born)		
Foreign-born by generational status		
Second generation (householder nb; at least one parent fb)	0.0709	—
	(0.0982)	
1.5 generation (householder fb and parents fb, and householder immigrated when ≤ 18)	0.0032	—
	(0.1067)	
First generation (householder fb and parents fb, and householder immigrated when > 18)	−0.0314	—
	(0.0868)	
Foreign-born by generational status and year of entry		
Second generation	—	0.0736
		(0.0983)
1.5 generation and entered before 1980	—	0.0576
		(0.1242)
1.5 generation and entered in or after 1980	—	−0.0878
		(0.1528)
First generation and entered before 1980	—	−0.0526
		(0.1194)
First generation and entered in or after 1980	—	−0.0221
		(0.0936)
Race/ethnicity (ref. white, non-Hispanic)		
Black, non-Hispanic	0.6855**	0.6880**
	(0.1009)	(0.1010)
Puerto Rican	0.4930**	0.4845**
	(0.1150)	(0.1178)
Dominican	0.4910**	0.4979**
	(0.1322)	(0.1325)
South and Central American	0.3664*	0.3713*
	(0.1519)	(0.1522)
Other Hispanic	0.1494	0.1559
	(0.1782)	(0.1783)
Asian	0.2281	0.2285
	(0.1439)	(0.1441)

APPENDIX TABLE B.4 *(continued)*

Variables	Generation Specific (1)	Generation by Year of Entry (2)
Housing tenure (ref. owner)		
Renter not in public housing	1.4539**	1.4541**
	(0.1083)	(0.1085)
Renter in public housing	1.4103**	1.4087**
	(0.1435)	(0.1437)
Age	−0.0072**	−0.0074**
	(0.0022)	(0.0023)
Single-person-headed household	0.1590*	0.1590*
	(0.0722)	(0.0723)
Presence of		
Children under eighteen	0.4506**	0.4489**
	(0.0867)	(0.0867)
Others in the household beyond the nuclear family	0.3752**	0.3728**
	(0.0754)	(0.0754)
Education (ref. ≥ college)		
Less than high school	0.2340**	0.2370**
	(0.0824)	(0.0825)
High school dipolma	−0.0577	−0.0562
	(0.0779)	(0.0780)
Total household income (logged)	0.0043	0.0044
	(0.0161)	(0.0161)
Receiving public assistance	0.3912**	0.3915**
	(0.0749)	(0.0749)
Percentage of		
Recent immigrants (in subarea)	2.3863**	2.3881**
	(0.4889)	(0.4889)
Blacks (in subarea)	0.6916**	0.6929**
	(0.1393)	(0.1393)
Borough (ref. Manhattan)		
Bronx	−0.1479	−0.1454
	(0.0921)	(0.0924)
Brooklyn/Staten Island	−0.2992**	−0.2985**
	(0.0820)	(0.0821)
Queens	−0.8258**	−0.8231**
	(0.1024)	(0.1026)
Intercept	−3.7746**	−3.7706**
	(0.2642)	(0.2659)
Model Chi-Square	1145.93**	1146.77**
df	24	26
N	11,072	

** $p < 0.01$; * $p < 0.05$; † $p < 0.10$

APPENDIX TABLE B.5

Results of Feasible Generalized Least Squares Models Predicting Percentage White in New York City Subareas

Variables	Generation Specific (1)	Generation by Year of Entry (2)
Nativity (ref. native-born)		
Foreign-born by generational status		
Second generation (householder nb; at least one parent fb)	−0.4606	—
	(0.5227)	
1.5 generation (householder fb and parents fb, and householder immigrated when ≤ 18)	−1.9463**	—
	(0.6352)	
First generation (householder fb and parents fb, and householder immigrated when > 18)	−1.2229*	—
	(0.4875)	
Foreign-born by generational status and year of entry		
Second generation	—	−0.3752
		(0.5244)
1.5 generation and entered before 1980	—	−1.2712†
		(0.7297)
1.5 generation and entered in or after 1980	—	−3.4625**
		(0.9988)
First generation and entered before 1980	—	−0.6183
		(0.6420)
First generation and entered in or after 1980	—	−1.6371**
		(0.5479)
Race/ethnicity (ref. white, non-Hispanic)		
Black, non-Hispanic	−32.8157**	−32.8115**
	(0.4683)	(0.4687)
Puerto Rican	−23.8094**	−24.1201**
	(0.6701)	(0.6818)
Dominican	−28.4235**	−28.3795**
	(0.8628)	(0.8648)
South and Central American	−17.8687**	−17.9034**
	(0.8706)	(0.8729)
Other Hispanic	−17.3276**	−17.2695**
	(1.0705)	(1.0721)
Asian	−6.9225**	−6.7733**
	(0.7045)	(0.7079)
Housing tenure (ref. owner)		
Renter not in public housing	−0.3615	−0.2613
	(0.4183)	(0.4209)
Renter in public housing	3.3158**	3.3844**
	(0.8292)	(0.8298)
Age	−0.0382**	−0.0475**
	(0.0123)	(0.0130)
Single-person headed household	−0.8244*	−0.8284*
	(0.3987)	(0.3990)
Presence of		
Children under eighteen	−2.6395**	−2.6274**
	(0.5118)	(0.5126)
Others in the household beyond the nuclear family	−2.7714**	−2.7876**
	(0.4249)	(0.4252)

APPENDIX TABLE B.5 *(continued)*

Variables	Generation Specific (1)	Generation by Year of Entry (2)
Education (ref. ≥ college)		
Less than high school	−5.0889**	−5.0825**
	(0.4993)	(0.4999)
High school diploma	−3.8930**	−3.8728**
	(0.4223)	(0.4228)
Total household income (logged)	0.6544**	0.6487**
	(0.0946)	(0.0947)
Receiving public assistance	−3.7183**	−3.7296**
	(0.5131)	(0.5132)
Intercept	50.4592**	50.9222**
	(1.3926)	(1.4087)
Adjusted R-squared	0.4333	0.4338
N		12,045

** $p < 0.01$; * $p < 0.05$; † $p < 0.10$

APPENDIX TABLE B.6

Results of Feasible Generalized Least Squares Models Predicting Crime Rate in New York City Subareas

Variables	Generation Specific (1)	Generation by Year of Entry (2)
Nativity (ref. native-born)		
Foreign-born by generational status		
Second generation (householder nb; at least one parent fb)	−0.0258	—
	(0.0730)	
1.5 generation (householder fb and parents fb, and householder immigrated when ≤ 18)	0.0934	—
	(0.0853)	
First generation (householder fb and parents fb, and householder immigrated when > 18)	0.1032	—
	(0.0659)	
Foreign-born by generational status and year of entry		
Second generation	—	−0.0322
		(0.0732)
1.5 generation and entered before 1980	—	0.0565
		(0.0991)
1.5 generation and entered in or after 1980	—	0.1652
		(0.1290)
First generation and entered before 1980	—	0.0572
		(0.0883)
First generation and entered in or after 1980	—	0.1292†
		(0.0728)
Race/ethnicity (ref. white, non-Hispanic)		
Black, non-Hispanic	3.6751**	3.6759**
	(0.0636)	(0.0636)
Puerto Rican	2.2529**	2.2728**
	(0.0910)	(0.0929)

(continued)

APPENDIX TABLE B.6 (continued)

Variables	Generation Specific (1)	Generation by Year of Entry (2)
Dominican	2.1688**	2.1679**
	(0.1187)	(0.1191)
South and Central American	1.2804**	1.2819**
	(0.1096)	(0.1099)
Other Hispanic	1.4249**	1.4217**
	(0.1421)	(0.1425)
Asian	0.3918**	0.3859**
	(0.0977)	(0.0979)
Housing tenure (ref. owner)		
Renter not in public housing	0.1996**	0.1944**
	(0.0566)	(0.0569)
Renter in public housing	0.2654*	0.2626*
	(0.1258)	(0.1259)
Age	−0.0014	−0.0008
	(0.0017)	(0.0018)
Single-person-headed household	0.2796**	0.2816**
	(0.0543)	(0.0543)
Presence of		
Children under eighteen	0.1596*	0.1571*
	(0.0703)	(0.0704)
Others in the household beyond the nuclear family	0.2135**	0.2132**
	(0.0586)	(0.0586)
Education (ref. ≥ college)		
Less than high school	0.5192**	0.5169**
	(0.0677)	(0.0679)
High school diploma	0.2561**	0.2532**
	(0.0578)	(0.0578)
Total household income (logged)	−0.0516**	−0.0511**
	(0.0137)	(0.0137)
Receiving public assistance	0.5160**	0.5159**
	(0.0706)	(0.0705)
Intercept	6.1922**	6.1606**
	(0.1987)	(0.2010)
Adjusted R-squared	0.2616	0.2616
N		12,045

** $p < 0.01$; * $p < 0.05$; † $p < 0.10$

APPENDIX TABLE B.7
Results of Feasible Generalized Least Squares Models Predicting Teenage Fertility Rate in New York City Subareas

Variables	Generation Specific (1)	Generation by Year of Entry (2)
Nativity (ref. native-born)		
Foreign-born by generational status		
Second generation (householder nb; at least one parent fb)	–0.0659†	—
	(0.0350)	
1.5 generation (householder fb and parents fb, and householder immigrated when < 18)	–0.0437	—
	(0.0443)	
First generation (householder fb and parents fb, and householder immigrated when > 18)	–0.0827*	—
	(0.0334)	
Foreign-born by generational status and year of entry		
Second generation	—	–0.0648†
		(0.0352)
1.5 generation and entered before 1980	—	–0.0526
		(0.0510)
1.5 generation and entered in or after 1980	—	–0.0257
		(0.0708)
First generation and entered before 1980	—	–0.0558
		(0.0455)
First generation and entered in or after 1980	—	–0.0978**
		(0.0373)
Race/ethnicity (ref. white, non-Hispanic)		
Black, non-Hispanic	1.6903**	1.6896**
	(0.0325)	(0.0325)
Puerto Rican	1.4013**	1.3981**
	(0.0484)	(0.0493)
Dominican	1.7171**	1.7138**
	(0.0643)	(0.0644)
South and Central American	0.7245**	0.7226**
	(0.0598)	(0.0599)
Other Hispanic	0.7621**	0.7593**
	(0.0750)	(0.0752)
Asian	0.1268*	0.1298*
	(0.0513)	(0.0515)
Housing tenure (ref. owner)		
Renter not in public housing	0.1856**	0.1882**
	(0.0282)	(0.0283)
Renter in public housing	0.2198**	0.2229**
	(0.0657)	(0.0658)
Age	–0.0001	–0.0002
	(0.0008)	(0.0009)
Single-person-headed household	0.1536**	0.1534**
	(0.0275)	(0.0275)
Presence of		
Children under eighteen	0.0354	0.0366
	(0.0352)	(0.0353)
Others in the household beyond the nuclear family	0.0307	0.0311
	(0.0295)	(0.0295)

(continued)

APPENDIX TABLE B.7 (*continued*)

Variables	Generation Specific (1)	Generation by Year of Entry (2)
Education (ref. ≥ college)		
Less than high school	0.3433**	0.3409**
	(0.0364)	(0.0365)
High school diploma	0.1472**	0.1471**
	(0.0300)	(0.0301)
Total household income (logged)	−0.0351**	−0.0353**
	(0.0069)	(0.0069)
Receiving public assistance	0.3015**	0.3010**
	(0.0381)	(0.0382)
Intercept	3.0773**	3.0853**
	(0.0992)	(0.1004)
Adjusted R-squared	0.3525	0.3526
N	12,045	

$** p < 0.01; * p < 0.05; \dagger p < 0.10$

APPENDIX TABLE B.8
Results of Feasible Generalized Least Squares Models Predicting Percentage Receiving Public Assistance in New York City Subareas

Variables	Generation Specific (1)	Generation by Year of Entry (2)
Nativity (ref. native-born)		
Foreign-born by generational status		
Second generation (householder nb; at least one parent fb)	−0.0585	—
	(0.1135)	
1.5 generation (householder fb and parents fb, and householder immigrated when ≤ 18)	0.1169	—
	(0.1440)	
First generation (householder fb and parents fb, and householder immigrated when > 18)	−0.1455	—
	(0.1077)	
Foreign-born by generational status and year of entry		
Second generation	—	−0.0599
		(0.1141)
1.5 generation and entered before 1980	—	0.2124
		(0.1650)
1.5 generation and entered in or after 1980	—	−0.0985
		(0.2306)
First generation and entered before 1980	—	−0.2601†
		(0.1467)
First generation and entered in or after 1980	—	−0.0874
		(0.1192)
Race/ethnicity (ref. white, non-Hispanic)		
Black, non-Hispanic	4.5895**	4.6073**
	(0.1100)	(0.1103)
Puerto Rican	3.7846**	3.7973**
	(0.1607)	(0.1636)

APPENDIX TABLE B.8 (*continued*)

Variables	Generation Specific (1)	Generation by Year of Entry (2)
Dominican	4.7605**	4.7910**
	(0.2052)	(0.2062)
South and Central American	1.1455**	1.1731**
	(0.1971)	(0.1981)
Other Hispanic	1.8383**	1.8614**
	(0.2427)	(0.2432)
Asian	−0.1343	−0.1330
	(0.1523)	(0.1528)
Housing tenure (ref. owner)		
Renter not in public housing	0.5845**	0.5748**
	(0.0896)	(0.0903)
Renter in public housing	0.9339**	0.9143**
	(0.2222)	(0.2223)
Age	0.0027	0.0029
	(0.0028)	(0.0029)
Single-person-headed household	0.2418**	0.2451**
	(0.0882)	(0.0884)
Presence of		
Children under eighteen	0.4689**	0.4637**
	(0.1143)	(0.1146)
Others in the household beyond the nuclear family	0.3281**	0.3237**
	(0.0955)	(0.0957)
Education (ref. ≥ college)		
Less than high school	1.1344**	1.1531**
	(0.1140)	(0.1144)
High school diploma	0.6075**	0.6133**
	(0.0938)	(0.0940)
Total household income (logged)	−0.1803**	−0.1802**
	(0.0225)	(0.0226)
Receiving public assistance	1.1687**	1.1693**
	(0.1217)	(0.1221)
Intercept	5.1005**	5.0856**
	(0.3214)	(0.3252)
Adjusted R-squared	0.3740	0.3741
N	12,045	

** p < 0.01; * p < 0.05; † p < 0.10

APPENDIX TABLE B.9
Results of Feasible Generalized Least Squares Models Predicting Percentage
Performing Below Grade in Math in New York City Subareas

Variables	Generation Specific (1)	Generation by Year of Entry (2)
Nativity (ref. native-born)		
Foreign-born by generational status		
Second generation (householder nb; at least one parent fb)	–0.8458**	—
	(0.2726)	
1.5 generation (householder fb and parents fb, and householder immigrated when ≤ 18)	–0.7785*	—
	(0.3246)	
First generation (householder fb and parents fb, and householder immigrated when > 18)	–1.1142**	—
	(0.2488)	
Foreign-born by generational status and year of entry		
Second generation	—	–0.8578**
		(0.2736)
1.5 generation and entered before 1980	—	–0.8396*
		(0.3739)
1.5 generation and entered in or after 1980	—	–0.6392
		(0.5035)
First generation and entered before 1980	—	–1.2276**
		(0.3295)
First generation and entered in or after 1980	—	–1.0381**
		(0.2805)
Race/ethnicity (ref. white, non-Hispanic)		
Black, non-Hispanic	15.0155**	15.0187**
	(0.2354)	(0.2360)
Puerto Rican	12.5399**	12.5878**
	(0.3445)	(0.3510)
Dominican	15.4263**	15.4236**
	(0.4599)	(0.4610)
South and Central American	8.5929**	8.5960**
	(0.4436)	(0.4448)
Other Hispanic	9.1298**	9.1318**
	(0.5582)	(0.5595)
Asian	1.7864**	1.7690**
	(0.3860)	(0.3873)
Housing tenure (ref. owner)		
Renter not in public housing	0.7767**	0.7613**
	(0.2166)	(0.2183)
Renter in public housing	–0.3767	–0.3922
	(0.4346)	(0.4350)
Age	0.0116†	0.0130†
	(0.0065)	(0.0069)
Single-person-headed household	1.0662**	1.0661**
	(0.2076)	(0.2078)
Presence of		
Children under eighteen	0.8722**	0.8699**
	(0.2673)	(0.2678)
Others in the household beyond the nuclear family	0.9916**	0.9919**
	(0.2224)	(0.2227)

APPENDIX TABLE B.9 (*continued*)

Variables	Generation Specific (1)	Generation by Year of Entry (2)
Education (ref. ≥ college)		
Less than high school	2.6520**	2.6565**
	(0.2565)	(0.2572)
High school diploma	1.6586**	1.6584**
	(0.2189)	(0.2192)
Total household income (logged)	–0.3176**	–0.3170**
	(0.0519)	(0.0519)
Receiving public assistance	1.9085**	1.9172**
	(0.2659)	(0.2661)
Intercept	41.1998**	41.1350**
	(0.7529)	(0.7611)
Adjusted R-squared	0.4062	0.4063
N		12,045

** $p < 0.01$; * $p < 0.05$; † $p < 0.10$

APPENDIX TABLE B.10

Results of Feasible Generalized Least Squares Models Predicting Percentage of One- and Two-Family Homes in New York City Subareas

Variables	Generation Specific (1)	Generation by Year of Entry (2)
Foreign-born by generational status		
Second generation (householder nb; at least one parent fb)	2.2540**	—
	(0.4521)	
1.5 generation (householder fb and parents fb, and householder immigrated when ≤ 18)	2.1878**	—
	(0.5293)	
First generation (householder fb and parents fb, and householder immigrated when > 18)	1.5922**	—
	(0.4099)	
Foreign-born by generational status and year of entry		
Second generation	—	2.0871**
		(0.4529)
1.5 generation and entered before 1980	—	1.4401*
		(0.6094)
1.5 generation and entered in or after 1980	—	3.7126**
		(0.8084)
First generation and entered before 1980	—	0.2375
		(0.5392)
First generation and entered in or after 1980	—	2.3891**
		(0.4538)
Race/ethnicity (ref. white, non-Hispanic)		
Black, non-Hispanic	–2.6905**	–2.6678**
	(0.3953)	(0.3954)
Puerto Rican	–5.8108**	–5.3290**
	(0.5267)	(0.5379)

(*continued*)

APPENDIX TABLE B.10 (*continued*)

Variables	Generation Specific (1)	Generation by Year of Entry (2)
Dominican	−10.4752**	−10.4851**
	(0.7248)	(0.7256)
South and Central American	−2.0559**	−1.9946**
	(0.6721)	(0.6732)
Other Hispanic	−4.4178**	−4.4415**
	(0.8630)	(0.8647)
Asian	0.9736	0.7344
	(0.6124)	(0.6123)
Housing tenure (ref. owner)		
Renter not in public housing	−5.7047**	−5.8773**
	(0.3622)	(0.3641)
Renter in public housing	−7.5252**	−7.6641**
	(0.6748)	(0.6752)
Age	0.0284**	0.0446**
	(0.0105)	(0.0111)
Single-person-headed household	−3.4334**	−3.3847**
	(0.3350)	(0.3348)
Presence of		
Children under eighteen	2.1045**	2.0759**
	(0.4272)	(0.4268)
Others in the household beyond the nuclear family	1.7397**	1.7252**
	(0.3587)	(0.3584)
Education (ref. ≥ college)		
Less than high school	0.7031†	0.7078†
	(0.4100)	(0.4100)
High school diploma	2.5981**	2.5563**
	(0.3574)	(0.3569)
Total household income (logged)	−0.0372	−0.0202
	(0.0804)	(0.0804)
Receiving public assistance	−1.4472**	−1.4434**
	(0.4066)	(0.4065)
Intercept	31.9892**	31.1693**
	(1.1838)	(1.1962)
Adjusted R-squared	0.1702	0.1718
N		12,045

** $p < 0.01$; * $p < 0.05$; † $p < 0.10$

Appendix C

Means of Independent Variables Used in Models Predicting Housing and
Neighborhood Outcomes, by Race/Ethnicity

	Whites	Blacks	Hispanics
Generation			
First	.2106	.2580	.4770
1.5	.0562	.0755	.2529
Second	.2552	.0632	.2169
Third-plus	.4780	.6032	.0532
Generation by Year of Arrival			
First, arrived 1980 and later	.0785	.1598	.2653
First, arrived before 1980	.1321	.0982	.2118
1.5, arrived 1980 and later	.0097	.0340	.0787
1.5, arrived before 1980	.0785	.0416	.1742
Household characteristics			
Age	51.5639	48.0469	44.6438
Single-person headed	.5644	.6947	.6183
Presence of children			
under eighteen	.1688	.2609	.3139
Presence of other adults	.2481	.3707	.4046
Education			
Less than high school diploma	.1228	.2351	.4173
High school diploma	.2639	.3073	.2555
Some college or more	.6133	.4577	.3273
Household income	$62,041.9121	$36,331.7526	$30,726.5738
Receives public assistance	.0749	.2266	.3106
Black race			.1832
Housing-market sector			
Owned	.4286	.2907	.1354
Rental, not in public housing	.5620	.5722	.7575
Public housing	.0094	.1371	.1071
Borough			
Manhattan	.2937	.1421	.2145
Bronx	.0613	.2158	.2937
Queens	.2725	.2137	.2431
Brooklyn/Staten Island	.3725	.4284	.2487
Percentage of recently arrived			
immigrants in subarea	.1111	.1272	.1500
Percentage of blacks in subarea	.1076	.4944	.2276

Source: 1999 HVS, authors' calculations.

APPENDIX TABLE C.2
Logistic Regression Coefficients of Homeownership Models by Race/Ethnicity (Weighted)

Variables	Non-Hispanic White		Non-Hispanic Black		Hispanics	
	Generation Specific (1)	Generation by Year of Entry (2)	Generation Specific (3)	Generation by Year of Entry (4)	Generation Specific (5)	Generation by Year of Entry (6)
Nativity (ref. native-born)						
Foreign-born by generational status						
Second generation (householder nb; at least one parent fb)	0.0762 (0.0813)	—	0.0091 (0.2165)	—	-0.0288 (0.2634)	—
1.5 generation (householder fb and parents fb, and householder immigrated when ≤ 18)	0.2521† (0.1423)	—	0.3480† (0.1973)	—	-0.1257 (0.2679)	—
First generation (householder fb and parents fb, and householder immigrated when > 18)	-0.4798** (0.0906)	—	0.2909* (0.1181)	—	-0.8972** (0.2793)	—
Foreign-born by generational status and year of entry						
Second generation	—	0.1428† (0.0813)	—	0.0142 (0.2144)	—	-0.0187 (0.2617)
1.5 generation and entered before 1980	—	0.4578** (0.1547)	—	0.5137* (0.2367)	—	-0.0308 (0.2745)
1.5 generation and entered in or after 1980	—	-0.7219† (0.4009)	—	-0.1575 (0.3252)	—	-0.3947 (0.3879)
First generation and entered before 1980	—	0.1968 (0.1286)	—	0.8162** (0.1602)	—	-0.6265* (0.3038)
First generation and entered in or after 1980	—	-0.9829** (0.1184)	—	-0.1464 (0.1493)	—	-1.1007** (0.2975)
Black (ref. nonblack)	—	—	—	—	-0.1997 (0.1828)	-0.1941 (0.1828)
Hispanic origin (ref. Central/South American)						
Puerto Rican	—	—	—	—	-0.2337 (0.1793)	-0.2682 (0.1805)
Dominican	—	—	—	—	-0.4034† (0.2102)	-0.4038† (0.2114)
Other Hispanic	—	—	—	—	-0.1601 (0.2125)	-0.1436 (0.2139)

Age	0.0429**	0.0385**	0.0618**	0.0558**	0.0616**	0.0553**
	(0.0023)	(0.0024)	(0.0041)	(0.0042)	(0.0052)	(0.0059)
Household headed by noncouple	0.7567**	0.7670**	-0.8534**	0.8802**	-0.7227**	-0.7323**
	(0.0734)	(0.0738)	(0.1134)	(0.1141)	(0.1415)	(0.1415)
Presence of children under eighteen	0.2600**	0.2947**	0.1302	0.1554	0.1914	0.1927
	(0.0987)	(0.1000)	(0.1498)	(0.1507)	(0.1833)	(0.1839)
Presence of others beyond the nuclear family	0.2992**	0.3202**	0.4883**	0.5069**	0.2233	0.2241
	(0.0809)	(0.0815)	(0.1223)	(0.1229)	(0.1557)	(0.1557)
Education (ref. ≥ college)						
Less than high school	-0.4533**	-0.5845**	-1.0249**	-0.9620**	-1.2116**	-1.2065**
	(0.1134)	(0.1160)	(0.1526)	(0.1539)	(0.1763)	(0.1769)
High school diploma	-0.0887	-0.1261	-0.6703**	-0.6558**	-0.5489**	-0.5391**
	(0.0807)	(0.0817)	(0.1195)	(0.1205)	(0.1520)	(0.1523)
Total household income (logged)	0.2785**	0.2639**	0.3996**	0.3782**	0.3829**	0.3683**
	(0.0312)	(0.0310)	(0.0617)	(0.0601)	(0.0873)	(0.0868)
Receiving public assistance	-1.6418**	-1.4889**	-1.3234**	-1.3636**	-0.8766**	-0.8943**
	(0.1624)	(0.1643)	(0.1729)	(0.1738)	(0.2044)	(0.2044)
Percentage of recent immigrants (in subarea)	-5.3546**	-5.4375**	-6.8689**	-6.9204**	-4.4604**	-4.4672**
	(0.6268)	(0.6317)	(0.8116)	(0.8205)	(0.9310)	(0.9395)
Percentage of black (in subarea)	0.5682*	0.5127*	0.7226**	0.7373**	-0.2940	-0.2818
	(0.2363)	(0.2377)	(0.1877)	(0.1894)	(0.3385)	(0.3395)
Borough (ref. Manhattan)						
Bronx	0.4147**	0.4302**	1.7800**	1.7972**	0.2499**	0.2856
	(0.1481)	(0.1487)	(0.2110)	(0.2115)	(0.2148)	(0.2153)
Brooklyn/Staten Island	0.7431**	0.7876**	1.4000**	1.3947**	0.6858**	0.6887**
	(0.0878)	(0.0883)	(0.1996)	(0.1999)	(0.2054)	(0.2050)
Queens	1.1727**	1.1995**	2.5453**	2.5563**	1.1522**	1.1533**
	(0.0996)	(0.1002)	(0.2107)	(0.2111)	(0.2063)	(0.2064)
Intercept	-5.0196**	-4.6560**	-8.3489**	-7.8270**	-6.9391**	-6.5209**
	(0.4094)	(0.4084)	(0.7652)	(0.7526)	(1.0584)	(1.0672)
Model Chi-square	1231.347**	1294.826**	1060.653**	1087.979**	534.969**	540.190**
df	16	18	16	18	20	22
N	5,218		2,991		2,932	

** p < 0.01; * p < 0.05; † p < 0.10; shaded cells indicate significance relative to second-generation householders.
Source: 1999 HVS and *Infoshare*, authors' calculations.

APPENDIX TABLE C.3

Logistic Regression Coefficients of Household Crowding Models by Race/Ethnicity (Weighted)

Variables	Non-Hispanic White		Non-Hispanic Black		Hispanics	
	Generation Specific (1)	Generation by Year of Entry (2)	Generation Specific (3)	Generation by Year of Entry (4)	Generation Specific (5)	Generation by Year of Entry (6)
Nativity (ref. native-born)						
Foreign-born by generational status						
Second generation (householder nb; at least one parent fb)	0.8627** (0.2374)	—	0.5593† (0.2925)	—	-0.1223 (0.3231)	—
1.5 generation (householder fb and parents fb, and householder immigrated when ≤ 18)	1.1506** (0.3040)	—	0.5606* (0.2415)	—	0.2246 (0.3169)	—
First generation (householder fb and parents fb, and householder immigrated when > 18)	1.2726** (0.2014)	—	0.8739** (0.1702)	—	0.4354 (0.3221)	—
Foreign-born by generational status and year of entry						
Second generation	—	0.8539** (0.2376)	—	0.5637† (0.2923)	—	-0.1231 (0.3221)
1.5 generation and entered before 1980	—	0.9925** (0.3631)	—	0.6287* (0.3184)	—	0.1013 (0.3335)
1.5 generation and entered in or after 1980	—	1.4585** (0.4641)	—	0.5317† (0.3126)	—	0.3186 (0.3447)
First generation and entered before 1980	—	1.1463** (0.3536)	—	0.6467* (0.2697)	—	-0.2935 (0.3751)
First generation and entered in or after 1980	—	1.2907** (0.2072)	—	0.9488** (0.1816)	—	0.5294† (0.3216)
Black (ref. nonblack)	—	—	—	—	0.0033 (0.1520)	0.0114 (0.1525)
Hispanic national origin (vs. Central/South American)						
Puerto Rican	—	—	—	—	-0.6224* (0.1909)	-0.5888** (0.1946)
Dominican	—	—	—	—	-0.2564 (0.1667)	-0.2660 (0.1677)
Other Hispanic	—	—	—	—	0.4003* (0.1875)	0.3762* (0.1896)

	(1)	(2)	(3)	(4)	(5)	(6)
Housing tenure (ref. Owner)						
Renter not in public housing	1.0303**	1.0133**	0.8775**	0.8449**	1.0900**	1.0685**
	(0.2035)	(0.2044)	(0.2000)	(0.2021)	(0.2412)	(0.2422)
Renter in public housing	0.1513	0.0925	1.0127**	0.9820**	0.9699**	0.9230**
	(1.1508)	(1.1567)	(0.2806)	(0.2818)	(0.3148)	(0.3156)
Age	-0.0462**	-0.0444**	-0.0313**	-0.0295**	-0.0468**	-0.0348**
	(0.0071)	(0.0074)	(0.0064)	(0.0067)	(0.0057)	(0.0063)
Household headed by noncouple	-2.0777**	-2.0749**	-1.3437**	-1.3391**	-1.2205**	-1.2249**
	(0.2279)	(0.2279)	(0.1641)	(0.1643)	(0.1339)	(0.1347)
Presence of children under eighteen	1.6525**	1.6720**	2.6235**	2.6208**	2.5532**	2.5476**
	(0.2460)	(0.2474)	(0.4178)	(0.4179)	(0.3814)	(0.3815)
Presence of others beyond the nuclear family	2.0865**	2.0989**	3.2539**	3.2572**	3.4133**	3.4267**
	(0.2410)	(0.2417)	(0.4105)	(0.4106)	(0.3762)	(0.3765)
Education (ref. ≥ college)						
Less than high school	0.8582**	0.8740**	0.7757**	0.7531**	0.5713**	0.5780**
	(0.2421)	(0.2449)	(0.1888)	(0.1904)	(0.1470)	(0.1480)
High school diploma	0.5270**	0.5346**	0.1977	0.1895	0.2927†	0.2819†
	(0.1926)	(0.1931)	(0.1683)	(0.1687)	(0.1540)	(0.1546)
Total household income (logged)	-0.1113**	-0.1114**	0.0074	0.0052	0.0179	0.0176
	(0.0350)	(0.0350)	(0.0444)	(0.0444)	(0.0374)	(0.0374)
Receiving public assistance	0.9308**	0.9279**	0.5405**	0.5562**	0.5262**	0.5536**
	(0.2503)	(0.2513)	(0.1737)	(0.1747)	(0.1380)	(0.1392)
Percentage of recent immigrants (in subarea)	2.6233†	2.6346†	1.0165	1.0469	2.1993*	2.0950*
	(1.4353)	(1.4389)	(1.0844)	(1.0868)	(0.8701)	(0.8769)
Percentage of black (in subarea)	0.2070	0.2219	-0.1420	-0.1474	0.6248*	0.6076*
	(0.5877)	(0.5885)	(0.2692)	(0.2696)	(0.3047)	(0.3050)
Borough (ref. Manhattan)						
Bronx	-1.6660**	-1.6824**	0.0462	0.0327	-0.1408	-0.1937
	(0.4996)	(0.4990)	(0.2684)	(0.2688)	(0.1710)	(0.1724)
Brooklyn/Staten Island	-0.9340**	-0.9527**	0.0388	0.0350	-0.3782*	-0.3842*
	(0.2249)	(0.2262)	(0.2461)	(0.2462)	(0.1795)	(0.1801)
Queens	-1.0174**	-1.0295**	-0.0322	-0.0364	-0.3806*	-0.3732*
	(0.2552)	(0.2554)	(0.2799)	(0.2802)	(0.1840)	(0.1850)
Intercept	-1.8243**	-1.8913**	-4.3252**	-4.3494**	-3.6596**	-4.0209**
	(0.6098)	(0.6153)	(0.7817)	(0.7819)	(0.7442)	(0.7549)
Model Chi-square	533.548**	534.399**	389.032**	390.379**	656.218**	671.398**
df	18	20	18	20	22	24
N	5,218		2,991		2,932	

** p < 0.01; * p < 0.05; † p < 0.10; shaded cells indicate significance relative to second-generation householders.

Source: 1999 HVS and *Infoshare*, authors' calculations.

APPENDIX TABLE C.4

Logistic Regression Coefficients of Maintenance Deficiencies Models by Race/Ethnicity (Weighted)

Variables	Non-Hispanic White		Non-Hispanic Black		Hispanics	
	Generation Specific (1)	Generation by Year of Entry (2)	Generation Specific (3)	Generation by Year of Entry (4)	Generation Specific (5)	Generation by Year of Entry (6)
Nativity (ref. native-born)						
Foreign-born by generational status						
Second generation (householder nb; at least one parent fb)	-0.0911 (0.1621)	—	0.3035 (0.1971)	—	0.0330 (0.2628)	—
1.5 generation (householder fb and parents fb, and householder immigrated when ≤ 18)	0.1672 (0.2594)	—	-0.4052* (0.2039)	—	0.1048 (0.2639)	—
First generation (householder fb and parents fb, and householder immigrated when > 18)	0.0341 (0.1608)	—	0.0245 (0.1294)	—	-0.0357 (0.2708)	—
Foreign-born by generational status and year of entry						
Second generation	—	-0.0986 (0.1629)	—	0.3030 (0.1972)	—	0.0338 (0.2629)
1.5 generation and entered before 1980	—	0.1024 (0.2975)	—	-0.3714 (0.2762)	—	0.1919 (0.2760)
1.5 generation and entered in or after 1980	—	0.3645 (0.4900)	—	-0.4422 (0.2728)	—	-0.0563 (0.3066)
First generation and entered before 1980	—	-0.0324 (0.2684)	—	0.0611 (0.2035)	—	0.0215 (0.3027)
First generation and entered in or after 1980	—	0.0570 (0.1789)	—	0.0084 (0.1463)	—	-0.0490 (0.2753)
Black (ref. nonblack)	—	—	—	—	0.3446** (0.1254)	0.3500** (0.1256)
Hispanic national origin (vs. Central/South American)						
Puerto Rican	—	—	—	—	0.0771 (0.1767)	0.0517 (0.1783)
Dominican	—	—	—	—	0.0128 (0.1714)	0.0161 (0.1714)
Other Hispanic	—	—	—	—	-0.2767 (0.2117)	-0.2678 (0.2121)

Housing tenure (ref. owner)

	(1)	(2)	(3)	(4)	(5)	(6)
Renter not in public housing	1.3229**	1.3169**	1.5202**	1.5254**	1.8553**	1.8604**
	(0.1657)	(0.1661)	(0.1826)	(0.1836)	(0.3286)	(0.3287)
Renter in public housing	0.9121	0.9047	1.4871**	1.4929**	1.6891**	1.6915**
	(0.6399)	(0.6401)	(0.2198)	(0.2208)	(0.3583)	(0.3584)
Age	0.0048	0.0054	-0.0168**	-0.0171**	-0.0074†	-0.0095†
	(0.0040)	(0.0041)	(0.0038)	(0.0040)	(0.0045)	(0.0052)
Single-person-headed household	0.3428*	0.3435*	0.0020	0.0009	0.1584	0.1548
	(0.1470)	(0.1471)	(0.1256)	(0.1257)	(0.1255)	(0.1255)
Presence of children under eighteen	0.6412**	0.6411**	0.2755*	0.2760*	0.5943**	0.5855**
	(0.1848)	(0.1848)	(0.1392)	(0.1392)	(0.1647)	(0.1650)
Presence of others beyond the nuclear family	0.4072**	0.4070**	0.2490*	0.2487*	0.6435**	0.6335**
	(0.1435)	(0.1436)	(0.1261)	(0.1261)	(0.1443)	(0.1447)
Education (ref. ≥ college)						
Less than high school	-0.2982	-0.2882	0.3397*	0.3424*	0.2832*	0.2916*
	(0.2168)	(0.2184)	(0.1365)	(0.1369)	(0.1371)	(0.1375)
High school diploma	-0.2396	-0.2358	-0.0706	-0.0684	0.0253	0.0341
	(0.1605)	(0.1606)	(0.1233)	(0.1235)	(0.1462)	(0.1465)
Total household income (logged)	0.0617	0.0622	-0.0416†	-0.0415†	0.0174	0.0173
	(0.0390)	(0.0389)	(0.0243)	(0.0243)	(0.0301)	(0.0300)
Receiving public assistance	0.2652	0.2558	0.4358**	0.4334**	0.4052**	0.4060**
	(0.2071)	(0.2096)	(0.1197)	(0.1200)	(0.1181)	(0.1183)
Percentage of recent immigrants (in subarea)	3.7054**	3.7118**	2.6306**	2.6301**	1.4402†	1.4531†
	(1.1375)	(1.1382)	(0.7882)	(0.7886)	(0.8641)	(0.8651)
Percentage of blacks (in subarea)	0.1287	0.1334	0.5080**	0.5092**	1.0145**	1.0161**
	(0.4469)	(0.4468)	(0.1958)	(0.1958)	(0.2657)	(0.2661)
Borough (ref. Manhattan)						
Bronx	0.2643	0.2561	-0.2744	-0.2735	-0.1719	-0.1597
	(0.2442)	(0.2448)	(0.1670)	(0.1671)	(0.1444)	(0.1452)
Brooklyn/Staten Island	-0.2378	-0.2457	-0.2497†	-0.2497†	-0.3212*	-0.3205*
	(0.1543)	(0.1552)	(0.1483)	(0.1483)	(0.1526)	(0.1527)
Queens	-0.8357**	-0.8411**	-0.6559**	-0.6557**	-0.9276**	-0.9188**
	(0.1983)	(0.1985)	(0.1918)	(0.1918)	(0.1884)	(0.1885)
Intercept	-5.0056**	-5.0268**	-2.0502**	-2.0446**	-4.0614**	-3.9769**
	(0.5670)	(0.5684)	(0.4356)	(0.4363)	(0.6232)	(0.6300)
Model Chi-square	171.043**	171.335**	313.938**	314.027**	261.255**	262.396**
Df	18	20	18	20	22	24
N	4,828		2,738		1,160	

** p < 0.01; * p < 0.05; † p < 0.10; shaded cells indicate significance relative to second-generation householders.
Source: 1999 HVS and *Infoshare*, authors' calculations.

APPENDIX TABLE C.5

Feasible Generalized Least Squares Coefficients of Percentage White Models by Race/Ethnicity (Weighted)

Variables	Non-Hispanic White		Non-Hispanic Black		Hispanics	
	Generation Specific (1)	Generation by Year of Entry (2)	Generation Specific (3)	Generation by Year of Entry (4)	Generation Specific (5)	Generation by Year of Entry (6)
Nativity (ref. native-born)						
Foreign-born by generational status						
Second generation (householder nb; at least one parent fb)	-0.4812 (0.4067)	—	0.5882 (0.6241)	—	-2.5107* (1.2043)	—
1.5 generation (householder fb and parents fb, and householder immigrated when ≤ 18)	-0.7162 (0.7335)	—	0.1111 (0.5669)	—	-3.5140** (1.1965)	—
First generation (householder fb and parents fb, and householder immigrated when > 18)	0.2236 (0.4374)	—	-0.0032 (0.3536)	—	-3.8867** (1.2244)	—
Foreign-born by generational status and year of entry						
Second generation	—	-0.5834 (0.4131)	—	0.5734 (0.6250)	—	-2.3996† (1.4136)
1.5 generation and entered before 1980	—	-1.1244 (0.8030)	—	-0.0740 (0.7140)	—	-3.8550* (1.5672)
1.5 generation and entered in or after 1980	—	0.6195 (1.7553)	—	0.2462 (0.8222)	—	-3.1329 (3.4827)
First generation and entered before 1980	—	-0.7038 (0.6317)	—	0.3379 (0.4655)	—	-4.6335* (1.8562)
First generation and entered in or after 1980	—	0.8182 (0.5264)	—	-0.3290 (0.4585)	—	-4.8767** (1.8792)
Race (1 = black; 0 = nonblack)	NA	NA	NA	NA	-4.1855** (0.6305)	-8.4869** (1.1671)
Hispanic national origin (vs. Central/South American)						
Puerto Rican	—	—	—	—	-3.5624** (0.7381)	—
Dominican	—	—	—	—	-5.8053** (0.7188)	—
Other Hispanic	—	—	—	—	-0.8953 (0.8613)	—

	(1)	(2)	(3)	(4)	(5)	(6)
Housing tenure (ref. owner)						
Renter not in public housing	1.0634**	1.0174**	-2.8965**	-2.8506**	-2.9493**	-2.5982*
	(0.3572)	(0.3610)	(0.3553)	(0.3599)	(0.7023)	(1.0752)
Renter in public housing	-2.4173	-2.5013	-1.2633†	-1.2285†	-1.7408	-1.1293
	(1.5335)	(1.5403)	(0.7244)	(0.7256)	(1.1201)	(1.4174)
Age	-0.0030	0.0021	-0.0187	-0.0209†	0.0201	0.0241
	(0.0111)	(0.0115)	(0.0122)	(0.0125)	(0.0204)	(0.0363)
Single-person-headed household	0.7281*	0.7888*	-1.2135**	-1.2134**	-0.7499	1.4544
	(0.3656)	(0.3690)	(0.3505)	(0.3513)	(0.5516)	(0.9204)
Presence of children under eighteen	-0.9859†	-0.9780†	-0.2287	-0.1847	-0.9443	-1.0013
	(0.5104)	(0.5153)	(0.4637)	(0.4659)	(0.7306)	(1.1616)
Presence of others beyond the nuclear family	-1.9252**	-1.9512**	0.4676	0.4675	-0.9077	0.6645
	(0.3862)	(0.3896)	(0.3754)	(0.3759)	(0.6375)	(1.0076)
Education (ref. ≥ college)						
Less than high school	-3.2144**	-3.0171**	-1.1334*	-1.0845*	-2.9618**	-3.9562**
	(0.5244)	(0.5345)	(0.4438)	(0.4479)	(0.6452)	(1.1039)
High school diploma	-2.8864**	-2.8433**	-0.2603	-0.2733	-1.9233**	-4.2515**
	(0.3961)	(0.3984)	(0.3561)	(0.3582)	(0.6476)	(1.0461)
Total household income (logged)	0.4248**	0.4408**	0.0674	0.0689	0.4196**	0.3492
	(0.0967)	(0.0975)	(0.0843)	(0.0844)	(0.1493)	(0.2335)
Receiving public assistance	-0.7526	-0.9477	-2.4108**	-2.4557**	-2.0011**	-2.7806**
	(0.6397)	(0.6491)	(0.4663)	(0.4688)	(0.5946)	(0.9030)
Intercept	54.1695**	53.7957**	17.4189**	17.4791**	30.2590**	27.9474**
	(1.3431)	(1.3694)	(1.2608)	(1.2648)	(2.3500)	(3.3651)
Adjusted R-squared	0.0372	0.0379	0.0189	0.0188	0.1094	0.1108
N	5,218		2,991		2,932	

** p < 0.01; * p < 0.05; † p < 0.10; shaded cells indicate significance relative to second-generation householders.
Source: 1999 HVS and Infoshare, authors' calculations.

Appendix Table C.6
Feasible Generalized Least Squares Coefficients of Crime Rate Models by Race/Ethnicity (Weighted)

Variables	Non-Hispanic White		Non-Hispanic Black		Hispanics	
	Generation Specific (1)	Generation by Year of Entry (2)	Generation Specific (3)	Generation by Year of Entry (4)	Generation Specific (5)	Generation by Year of Entry (6)
Nativity (ref. native-born)						
Foreign-born by generational status						
Second generation (householder nb; at least one parent fb)	0.0788 (0.0498)	—	-0.0531 (0.1657)	—	-0.0529 (0.2121)	—
1.5 generation (householder fb and parents fb, and householder immigrated when ≤ 18)	0.2550** (0.0804)	—	-0.0857 (0.1364)	—	-0.0879 (0.2229)	—
First generation (householder fb and parents fb, and householder immigrated when > 18)	0.2796** (0.0498)	—	-0.1801* (0.0873)	—	-0.04214 (0.2165)	—
Foreign-born by generational status and year of entry						
Second generation	—	0.0807 (0.0502)	—	-0.0538 (0.1659)	—	-0.0536 (0.2129)
1.5 generation and entered before 1980	—	0.2806** (0.0879)	—	-0.1066 (0.1745)	—	-0.1247 (0.2245)
1.5 generation and entered in or after 1980	—	0.1359 (0.1792)	—	-0.0671 (0.1940)	—	-0.04163 (0.2532)
First generation and entered before 1980	—	0.2768** (0.0728)	—	-0.1518 (0.1274)	—	-0.2055 (0.2433)
First generation and entered in or after 1980	—	0.2815** (0.0593)	—	-0.1965† (0.1023)	—	0.0178 (0.2218)
Race (1 = black; 0 = nonblack)	NA	NA	NA	NA	0.4227** (0.1197)	0.4185** (0.1200)
Hispanic national origin (vs. Central/South American)						
Puerto Rican	—	—	—	—	0.7113** (0.1303)	0.7257** (0.1321)
Dominican	—	—	—	—	0.4561** (0.1309)	0.4572** (0.1311)
Other Hispanic	—	—	—	—	0.2538† (0.1486)	0.2518† (0.1494)

	(1)	(2)	(3)	(4)	(5)	(6)
Housing tenure (ref. owner)						
Renter not in public housing	0.1107**	0.1102**	0.2143*	0.2191*	0.3041*	0.2966*
	(0.0410)	(0.0413)	(0.0920)	(0.0929)	(0.1280)	(0.1287)
Renter in public housing	0.2409	0.2420	0.3276*	0.3323*	0.8847**	0.8765**
	(0.1762)	(0.1762)	(0.1655)	(0.1661)	(0.2135)	(0.2136)
Age	-0.0032*	-0.0033*	0.0024	0.0022	0.0019	0.0050
	(0.0014)	(0.0014)	(0.0028)	(0.0029)	(0.0037)	(0.0044)
Single-person-headed household	0.0166	0.0171	0.1124	0.1114	0.1400	0.1376
	(0.0426)	(0.0425)	(0.0874)	(0.0877)	(0.1006)	(0.1008)
Presence of children under eighteen	-0.1040†	-0.1061†	0.0426	0.0430	0.1962	0.1898
	(0.0609)	(0.0612)	(0.1086)	(0.1088)	(0.1329)	(0.1333)
Presence of others beyond the nuclear family	0.0722	0.0731	0.0483	0.0480	0.0246	0.0197
	(0.0467)	(0.0468)	(0.0917)	(0.0918)	(0.1150)	(0.1157)
Education (ref. ≥ college)						
Less than high school	0.1055†	0.1069†	0.1557	0.1560	0.3995**	0.4009**
	(0.0620)	(0.0630)	(0.1061)	(0.1065)	(0.1126)	(0.1137)
High school diploma	0.0614	0.0604	0.0998	0.1009	0.3159**	0.3140**
	(0.0445)	(0.0446)	(0.0883)	(0.0886)	(0.1148)	(0.1157)
Total household income (logged)	-0.0298**	-0.0299**	-0.0463*	-0.0465*	-0.0676*	-0.0674*
	(0.0115)	(0.0115)	(0.0206)	(0.0206)	(0.0276)	(0.0277)
Receiving public assistance	0.2580**	0.2579**	0.2727**	0.2717**	0.4398**	0.4452**
	(0.0728)	(0.0734)	(0.1008)	(0.1013)	(0.1084)	(0.1085)
Intercept	5.9219**	5.9320**	10.9103**	10.9173**	8.2378**	8.1246**
	(0.1608)	(0.1623)	(0.3027)	(0.3047)	(0.4303)	(0.4417)
Adjusted R-squared	0.0150	0.0150	0.0764	0.0762	0.1210	0.1211
N	5,218		2,991		2,932	

** $p < 0.01$; * $p < 0.05$; † $p < 0.10$; shaded cells indicate significance relative to second generation householders.
Source: 1999 HVS and Infoshare, authors' calculations.

APPENDIX TABLE C.7

Feasible Generalized Least Squares Coefficients of Teenage Fertility Rate Models by Race/Ethnicity (Weighted)

	Non-Hispanic White		Non-Hispanic Black		Hispanics	
Variables	Generation Specific (1)	Generation by Year of Entry (2)	Generation Specific (3)	Generation by Year of Entry (4)	Generation Specific (5)	Generation by Year of Entry (6)
Nativity (ref. native-born)						
Foreign-born by generational status						
Second generation (householder nb; at least one parent fb)	-0.0234 (0.0227)	—	0.0187 (0.0937)	—	0.0319 (0.1098)	—
1.5 generation (householder fb and parents fb, and householder immigrated when ≤ 18)	-0.0274 (0.0409)	—	-0.1549† (0.0835)	—	0.0990 (0.1105)	—
First generation (householder fb and parents fb, and householder immigrated when > 18)	-0.0026 (0.0246)	—	-0.2727** (0.0528)	—	0.0458 (0.1140)	—
Foreign-born by generational status and year of entry						
Second generation	—	-0.0201 (0.0233)	—	0.0192 (0.0937)	—	0.0318 (0.1100)
1.5 generation and entered before 1980	—	-0.0185 (0.0455)	—	-0.0851 (0.1081)	—	0.1107 (0.1165)
1.5 generation and entered in or after 1980	—	-0.0600 (0.0932)	—	-0.2484* (0.1173)	—	0.0708 (0.1333)
First generation and entered before 1980	—	0.0380 (0.0396)	—	-0.2300** (0.0768)	—	0.0528 (0.1286)
First generation and entered in or after 1980	—	-0.0244 (0.0292)	—	-0.2996** (0.0625)	—	0.0445 (0.1165)
Race (1 = black; 0 = nonblack)	NA	NA	NA	NA	0.4781** (0.0608)	0.4782** (0.0610)
Hispanic national origin (vs. Central/South American)						
Puerto Rican	—	—	—	—	0.7299** (0.0729)	0.7255** (0.0740)
Dominican	—	—	—	—	0.9924** (0.0729)	0.9912** (0.0732)
Other Hispanic	—	—	—	—	0.3101** (0.0885)	0.3119** (0.0890)

	(1)	(2)	(3)	(4)	(5)	(6)
Housing tenure (ref. owner)						
Renter not in public housing	0.0647**	0.0700**	0.4607**	0.4713**	0.3254**	0.3263**
	(0.0199)	(0.0203)	(0.0561)	(0.0567)	(0.0749)	(0.0751)
Renter in public housing	0.0808	0.0817	0.4799**	0.4906**	0.4240**	0.4196**
	(0.0964)	(0.0971)	(0.0933)	(0.0936)	(0.1170)	(0.1170)
Age	-0.0005	-0.0007	0.0024	0.0019	0.0018	0.0014
	(0.0006)	(0.0006)	(0.0017)	(0.0017)	(0.0020)	(0.0024)
Single-person-headed household	0.0886**	0.0907**	0.1240*	0.1229*	0.1198*	0.1192*
	(0.0207)	(0.0211)	(0.0532)	(0.0533)	(0.0547)	(0.0548)
Presence of children under eighteen	-0.0612*	-0.0631*	0.0214	0.0243	0.0760	0.0763
	(0.0281)	(0.0286)	(0.0645)	(0.0646)	(0.0711)	(0.0714)
Presence of others beyond the nuclear family	-0.0609**	-0.0623**	-0.0228	-0.0213	0.0920	0.0909
	(0.0222)	(0.0225)	(0.0547)	(0.0547)	(0.0620)	(0.0623)
Education (ref. ≥ college)						
Less than high school	-0.0618†	-0.0671†	0.1541*	0.1602*	0.2645**	0.2682**
	(0.0339)	(0.0345)	(0.0629)	(0.0631)	(0.0625)	(0.0630)
High school diploma	-0.0676**	-0.0699**	0.0061	0.0101	0.2081**	0.2112**
	(0.0231)	(0.0235)	(0.0532)	(0.0533)	(0.0638)	(0.0641)
Total household income (logged)	0.0028	0.0026	-0.0427**	-0.0427**	-0.0538**	-0.0540**
	(0.0054)	(0.0055)	(0.0123)	(0.0123)	(0.0155)	(0.0155)
Receiving public assistance	0.0128	0.0189	0.1278*	0.1219*	0.1795**	0.1789**
	(0.0426)	(0.0433)	(0.0594)	(0.0596)	(0.0579)	(0.0581)
Intercept	2.8001**	2.8113**	5.2123**	5.2286**	4.0516**	4.0686**
	(0.0760)	(0.0779)	(0.1826)	(0.1838)	(0.2355)	(0.2405)
Adjusted R-squared	0.0394	0.0410	0.1494	0.1493	0.1905	0.1903
N	5,218		2,991		2,932	

** p < 0.01; * p < 0.05; † p < 0.10; shaded cells indicate significance relative to second-generation householders.
Source: 1999 HVS and *Infoshare,* authors' calculations.

APPENDIX TABLE C.8

Feasible Generalized Least Squares Coefficients of Public Assistance Models by Race/Ethnicity (Weighted)

Variables	Non-Hispanic White		Non-Hispanic Black		Hispanics	
	Generation Specific (1)	Generation by Year of Entry (2)	Generation Specific (3)	Generation by Year of Entry (4)	Generation Specific (5)	Generation by Year of Entry (6)
Nativity (ref. native-born)						
Foreign-born by generational status						
Second generation (householder nb; at least one parent fb)	0.1684** (0.0598)	—	-0.2033 (0.3549)	—	0.5486 (0.4809)	—
1.5 generation (householder fb and parents fb, and householder immigrated when ≤ 18)	0.3971*** (0.0986)	—	-0.9354** (0.3335)	—	0.7094 (0.4784)	—
First generation (householder fb and parents fb, and householder immigrated when > 18)	0.3273** (0.0619)	—	-1.4109** (0.2114)	—	0.4596 (0.4878)	—
Foreign-born by generational status and year of entry						
Second generation	—	0.1664** (0.0604)	—	-0.2029 (0.3553)	—	0.5407 (0.4828)
1.5 generation and entered before 1980	—	0.3953** (0.1089)	—	-0.4774 (0.4215)	—	0.7260 (0.4960)
1.5 generation and entered in or after 1980	—	0.4029† (0.2157)	—	-1.5816** (0.4896)	—	0.6046 (0.5686)
First generation and entered before 1980	—	0.2969** (0.0941)	—	-1.4855** (0.3142)	—	0.2679 (0.5354)
First generation and entered in or after 1980	—	0.3470** (0.0731)	—	-1.3763** (0.2502)	—	0.5447 (0.5005)
Race (1 = black; 0 = nonblack)	NA	NA	NA	NA	1.1111** (0.2263)	1.1148** (0.2279)
Hispanic national origin (vs. Central/South American)						
Puerto Rican	—	—	—	—	3.4807** (0.2980)	3.4838** (0.3012)
Dominican	—	—	—	—	3.1296** (0.2811)	3.1322** (0.2828)
Other Hispanic	—	—	—	—	1.1156** (0.3464)	1.1145** (0.3486)

	(1)	(2)	(3)	(4)	(5)	(6)
Housing tenure (ref. owner)						
Renter not in public housing	0.1697**	0.1668**	1.9938**	1.9937**	1.3722**	1.3606**
	(0.0514)	(0.0519)	(0.2157)	(0.2167)	(0.2997)	(0.3010)
Renter in public housing	0.2276	0.2277	2.0049**	2.0189**	2.3383**	2.2909**
	(0.2200)	(0.2199)	(0.3371)	(0.3378)	(0.4690)	(0.4697)
Age	-0.0017	-0.0016	0.0073	0.0065	0.0052	0.0072
	(0.0017)	(0.0017)	(0.0063)	(0.0065)	(0.0080)	(0.0093)
Single-person-headed household	-0.0536	-0.0540	0.5985**	0.6098**	0.4745*	0.4706*
	(0.0530)	(0.0532)	(0.2063)	(0.2065)	(0.2141)	(0.2151)
Presence of children under eighteen	0.0747	0.0718	0.0978	0.0961	0.5723*	0.5586†
	(0.0743)	(0.0749)	(0.2463)	(0.2465)	(0.2898)	(0.2912)
Presence of others beyond the nuclear family	0.1270*	0.1271*	-0.1650	-0.1597	0.4022	0.3885
	(0.0566)	(0.0569)	(0.2091)	(0.2092)	(0.2488)	(0.2507)
Education (ref. ≥ college)						
Less than high school	0.2985**	0.3075**	0.5122*	0.5159*	1.1607**	1.1849**
	(0.0762)	(0.0775)	(0.2424)	(0.2429)	(0.2452)	(0.2476)
High school diploma	0.2334**	0.2385**	0.0972	0.1068	0.7559**	0.7694**
	(0.0554)	(0.0557)	(0.2073)	(0.2077)	(0.2505)	(0.2521)
Total household income (logged)	-0.0397**	-0.0398**	-0.1777**	-0.1766**	-0.1893**	-0.1922**
	(0.0142)	(0.0142)	(0.0454)	(0.0455)	(0.0565)	(0.0568)
Receiving public assistance	0.4460**	0.4426**	0.7301**	0.7290**	0.7132**	0.7311**
	(0.0977)	(0.0991)	(0.2269)	(0.2275)	(0.2253)	(0.2264)
Intercept	4.2288**	4.2792**	10.9226**	10.9324**	6.3095**	6.2836**
	(0.1982)	(0.2003)	(0.6777)	(0.6815)	(0.9227)	(0.9432)
Adjusted R-squared	0.0593	0.0595	0.1417	0.1412	0.1838	0.1851
N	5,218		2,991		2,932	

** $p < 0.01$; * $p < 0.05$; † $p < 0.10$; shaded cells indicate significance relative to second-generation householders.

Source: 1999 HVS and *Infoshare*, authors' calculations.

APPENDIX TABLE C.9

Feasible Generalized Least Squares Coefficients of Underperforming Students Models by Race/Ethnicity (Weighted)

Variables	Non-Hispanic White		Non-Hispanic Black		Hispanics	
	Generation Specific (1)	Generation by Year of Entry (2)	Generation Specific (3)	Generation by Year of Entry (4)	Generation Specific (5)	Generation by Year of Entry (6)
Nativity (ref. native-born)						
Foreign-born by generational status						
Second generation (householder nb; at least one parent fb)	0.0243 (0.2037)	—	−0.4327 (0.4064)	—	0.7593 (0.6970)	—
1.5 generation (householder fb and parents fb, and householder immigrated when ≤ 18)	0.2044 (0.3549)	—	−1.3045** (0.3977)	—	0.9567 (0.6929)	—
First generation (householder fb and parents fb, and householder immigrated when > 18)	0.1682 (0.2207)	—	−1.6478** (0.2390)	—	1.0790 (0.7096)	—
Foreign-born by generational status and year of entry						
Second generation	—	0.0663 (0.2055)	—	−0.4329 (0.4064)	—	0.7462 (0.6987)
1.5 generation and entered before 1980	—	0.2527 (0.3813)	—	−0.9027† (0.5216)	—	0.7242 (0.7260)
1.5 generation and entered in or after 1980	—	0.1996 (0.9260)	—	−1.8103** (0.5589)	—	1.3183 (0.8259)
First generation and entered before 1980	—	0.6778* (0.3198)	—	−1.5057** (0.3357)	—	0.4654 (0.7849)
First generation and entered in or after 1980	—	−0.2032 (0.2710)	—	−1.7577** (0.2918)	—	1.3523† (0.7284)
Race (1 = black; 0 = nonblack)	NA	NA	NA	NA	1.5672** (0.3447)	1.5775** (0.3477)
Hispanic national origin (vs. Central/South American)						
Puerto Rican	—	—	—	—	2.7431** (0.4440)	2.8445** (0.4498)
Dominican	—	—	—	—	3.9945** (0.4331)	3.9883** (0.4357)
Other Hispanic	—	—	—	—	0.7975 (0.5248)	0.7695 (0.5280)

Housing tenure (ref. owner)					
Renter not in public housing	-0.1033	-0.0598	1.0342**	1.0755**	2.1138**	2.0631**
	(0.1772)	(0.1791)	(0.2488)	(0.2503)	(0.4477)	(0.4499)
Renter in public housing	1.0248	1.0198	0.4675	0.5070	1.7139**	1.6365*
	(0.7181)	(0.7174)	(0.3807)	(0.3811)	(0.6482)	(0.6516)
Age	-0.0033	-0.0053	0.0021	0.0000	0.0057	0.0182
	(0.0060)	(0.0061)	(0.0074)	(0.0077)	(0.0120)	(0.0140)
Single-person-headed household	0.2933	0.3186†	0.3327	0.3298	0.6441*	0.6543*
	(0.1803)	(0.1812)	(0.2383)	(0.2382)	(0.3271)	(0.3287)
Presence of children under eighteen	-0.2829	-0.2373	0.0284	0.0299	0.9833*	0.9848*
	(0.2592)	(0.2607)	(0.2894)	(0.2894)	(0.4328)	(0.4354)
Presence of others beyond the nuclear family	0.4596*	0.4837*	-0.1643	-0.1616	0.8106*	0.8133*
	(0.2006)	(0.2018)	(0.2402)	(0.2401)	(0.3750)	(0.3788)
Education (ref. ≥ college)						
Less than high school	0.4843†	0.3639	0.7351**	0.7555**	2.0246**	2.0117**
	(0.2651)	(0.2713)	(0.2824)	(0.2828)	(0.3724)	(0.3759)
High school diploma	0.4944*	0.4574*	0.5933*	0.6009*	1.4690**	1.4589**
	(0.1946)	(0.1958)	(0.2402)	(0.2402)	(0.3825)	(0.3851)
Total household income (logged)	-0.1134*	-0.1183*	-0.1310*	-0.1316*	-0.1967*	-0.2000*
	(0.0525)	(0.0528)	(0.0524)	(0.0524)	(0.0846)	(0.0851)
Receiving public assistance	-0.4063	-0.3124	1.0086**	0.9953**	0.8073*	0.8524*
	(0.3213)	(0.3255)	(0.2642)	(0.2646)	(0.3394)	(0.3415)
Intercept	39.0282*	39.1256**	58.9252**	58.9998**	50.2722**	49.7958**
	(0.7205)	(0.7280)	(0.7785)	(0.7835)	(1.3778)	(1.4152)
Adjusted R-squared	0.0158	0.0150	0.0835	0.0831	0.1782	0.1806
N	5,218		2,991		2,932	

** $p < 0.01$; * $p < 0.05$; † $p < 0.10$; shaded cells indicate significance relative to second-generation householders.

Source: 1999 HVS and *Infoshare*, authors' calculations.

APPENDIX TABLE C.10

Feasible Generalized Least Squares Coefficients of One- and Two-Family Homes Models by Race/Ethnicity (Weighted)

Variables	Non-Hispanic White		Non-Hispanic Black		Hispanics	
	Generation Specific (1)	Generation by Year of Entry (2)	Generation Specific (3)	Generation by Year of Entry (4)	Generation Specific (5)	Generation by Year of Entry (6)
Nativity (ref. native-born)						
Foreign-born by generational status						
Second generation (householder nb; at least one parent fb)	1.2370† (0.6548)	—	0.3262 (1.0995)	—	-0.8257 (1.0081)	—
1.5 generation (householder fb and parents fb, and householder immigrated when ≤ 18)	1.3869 (1.0849)	—	2.2787* (1.0797)	—	-1.0470 (1.0108)	—
First generation (householder fb and parents fb, and householder immigrated when > 18)	-0.4611 (0.6675)	—	3.9040** (0.6670)	—	-1.2512 (1.0284)	—
Foreign-born by generational status and year of entry						
Second generation	—	0.8849 (0.6573)	—	0.3681 (1.1012)	—	-0.8327 (1.0086)
1.5 generation and entered before 1980	—	0.3842 (1.1782)	—	1.1372 (1.4329)	—	-1.1599 (1.0559)
1.5 generation and entered in or after 1980	—	4.8621* (2.4846)	—	3.8264* (1.5110)	—	-0.8235 (1.2275)
First generation and entered before 1980	—	-3.3803** (0.9887)	—	2.9941** (0.9859)	—	-1.2713 (1.1361)
First generation and entered in or after 1980	—	1.2088 (0.7765)	—	4.6896** (0.7875)	—	-1.2469 (1.0570)
Race (1 = black; 0 = nonblack)	NA	NA	NA	NA	-2.4959** (0.5567)	-2.5021** (0.5568)
Hispanic national origin (vs. Central/South American)						
Puerto Rican	—	—	—	—	-3.5623** (0.6291)	-3.5212** (0.6392)
Dominican	—	—	—	—	-7.2033** (0.6628)	-7.2049** (0.6630)
Other Hispanic	—	—	—	—	-2.5722** (0.7488)	-2.5710** (0.7485)

	(1)	(2)	(3)	(4)	(5)	(6)
Housing tenure (ref. owner)						
Renter not in public housing	-5.2507**	-5.4977**	-9.5676**	-9.6311**	-3.3239**	-3.3349**
	(0.5507)	(0.5529)	(0.6829)	(0.6902)	(0.7360)	(0.7371)
Renter in public housing	-3.4842	-3.0611	-8.5440**	-8.6083**	-3.9910**	-4.0031**
	(2.6769)	(2.6639)	(0.9434)	(0.9443)	(0.9581)	(0.9592)
Age	0.0690**	0.0860**	-0.0209	-0.0112	-0.0362*	-0.0345†
	(0.1746)	(0.0179)	(0.0199)	(0.0204)	(0.0178)	(0.0208)
Single-person-headed household	-4.4695**	-4.4248**	-2.3526**	-2.4126**	-1.8274**	-1.8246**
	(0.5699)	(0.5675)	(0.6322)	(0.6314)	(0.4962)	(0.4963)
Presence of children under eighteen	5.4186**	5.2469**	0.7250	0.7613	-0.5517	-0.5413
	(0.7866)	(0.7844)	(0.7512)	(0.7517)	(0.6413)	(0.6420)
Presence of others beyond the nuclear family	4.1061**	3.9789**	0.1901	0.2236	0.1552	0.1660
	(0.6247)	(0.6224)	(0.6447)	(0.6441)	(0.5472)	(0.5485)
Education (ref. ≥ college)						
Less than high school	7.2558**	7.7769**	-1.6491*	-1.7565**	-1.3304*	-1.3394*
	(0.8182)	(0.8282)	(0.7606)	(0.7601)	(0.5503)	(0.5520)
High school diploma	8.2979**	8.3834**	-0.5911	-0.6031	-0.5833	-0.5922
	(0.6039)	(0.6018)	(0.6404)	(0.6381)	(0.5677)	(0.5692)
Total household income (logged)	-0.7501**	-0.7142**	0.3317*	0.3325*	0.1779	0.1781
	(0.1447)	(0.1444)	(0.1410)	(0.1410)	(0.1212)	(0.1212)
Receiving public assistance	0.5481	-0.0670	-1.9549**	-1.8820**	-0.9458†	-0.9645†
	(0.8924)	(0.9019)	(0.7004)	(0.7025)	(0.4997)	(0.5004)
Intercept	35.0896**	34.1026**	33.3863**	32.9953**	30.6632**	30.5764**
	(2.0271)	(2.0271)	(2.0935)	(2.1033)	(2.0122)	(2.0650)
Adjusted R-squared	0.2037	0.2046	0.1964	0.1963	0.1540	0.1541
N	5,218		2,991		2,932	

** p < 0.01; * p < 0.05; † p < 0.10; shaded cells indicate significance relative to second-generation householders.

Source: 1999 HVS and *Infoshare*, authors' calculations.

APPENDIX TABLE C.11

Logistic Regression Coefficients of Homeownership Models among Blacks, 1997, 1999, 2001 Current Population Surveys for New York Consolidated Metropolitan Statistical Area (Weighted)

Variables	Non-Hispanic Black	
	Generation Specific (1)	Generation by Year of Entry (2)
Nativity (ref. native-born)		
Foreign-born by generational status		
Second generation (householder nb; at least one parent fb)	0.5886†	—
	(0.3473)	
1.5 generation (householder fb and parents fb, and householder immigrated when ≤ 18)	0.7470**	—
	(0.2812)	
First generation (householder fb and parents fb, and householder immigrated when > 18)	0.0310	—
	(0.1699)	
Foreign-born by generational status and year of entry		
Second generation	—	0.5860†
		(0.3454)
1.5 generation and entered before 1980	—	1.2095**
		(0.3169)
1.5 generation and entered in or after 1980	—	−1.0999
		(0.7899)
First generation and entered before 1980	—	0.3518
		(0.2362)
First generation and entered in or after 1980	—	−0.2147
		(0.2126)
Black (ref. nonblack)	—	—
Age	0.0574**	0.0534**
	(0.0058)	(0.0059)
Couple-headed household	0.9835**	1.0273**
	(0.1619)	(0.1638)
Presence of children under eighteen	0.5057**	0.5030**
	(0.1606)	(0.1620)
Presence of others beyond the nuclear family	0.4597**	0.4483**
	(0.1564)	(0.1576)
Education (ref. ≥ college)		
Less than high school	−0.8810**	−0.8536**
	(0.2219)	(0.2225)
High school diploma	−0.1826	−0.1448
	(0.1651)	(0.1666)
Total household income (logged)	0.8192**	0.7902**
	(0.1047)	(0.1052)
Receiving public assistance	−1.3468**	−1.3521**
	(0.4953)	(0.4938)
Residential location (1 = suburbs; 0 = central cities)	0.9508**	0.9478**
	(0.1561)	(0.1572)
Intercept	−13.0824**	−12.6005**
	(1.2161)	(1.2221)
Model Chi-square	500.491**	515.618**
df	12	14
N	1,509	

** $p < 0.01$; * $p < 0.05$; † $p < 0.10$; shaded cells indicate significance relative to second-generation householders.

Notes

NOTES TO THE INTRODUCTION

1. Farley 1996a; Waldinger 1997.

2. A number of historical events in the decade and a half leading up to 1930 helped to severely curtail the number of immigrants arriving in the United States. For example, immigration virtually ceased during World War I. Perhaps more significant were the restrictive laws passed by Congress during the 1920s that essentially eliminated any further immigration from Southern and Eastern Europe. The dramatic reduction in immigrant flows led to the continued decline in the percent foreign-born among New York's population through 1970.

3. These figures originate from the Immigration and Naturalization Service's (INS) annual immigrant data files. The INS data define "immigrants" as green-card holders or those individuals who changed their status in the particular year (New York City Department of City Planning 1999).

4. Estimates suggest that about another quarter of the city's population (in 2000) is made up of the sons and daughters of foreign-born parents (Kasinitz, Mollenkopf, and Waters 2002), while 40 percent of the 1900 population consisted of native-born persons with at least one foreign-born parent (Rosenwaike 1972). Thus, when we consider the entire "foreign stock," it is clear that a majority of the city's population at both dates has direct familial ties to the immigrant experience.

5. Mollenkopf 1999.

6. Muller 1993; Sanjek 1998; Smith 1995; Winnick 1990.

7. Salvo and Lobo 1997.

8. Schmitt 2001.

9. Smith 1995: 82; see also Sanjek 1998 and Jones-Correa 1998.

10. Kilgannon 2004.

11. Sanjek 1998.

12. Casimir 2000.

13. Bean and Stevens 2003; Salins 2004.

14. Lazaroff 2003.

15. Farley 1996a; Foner 2000; Johnson, Farrell, and Guinn 1999; Sanchez 1999.

16. Gerstle 1999.

17. This perspective on housing as a marker of and a factor underlying social mobility and assimilation has deep roots in urban sociology, dating to the work of the Chicago School and its intellectual descendants.

18. Massey 1985.

19. Alba and Nee 2003.

20. Rosenbaum and Argeros 2005.

21. Logan and Molotch 1987.

22. DeWind and Kasinitz 1997.

23. Aaronson 2000; Alba and Logan 1992a; Boehm and Schlottmann 1999; Charles 2001; Conley 1999, 2001; Green and White 1997; Levy and Michel 1991; Millennial Housing Commission 2002; Oliver and Shapiro 1995; Rohe, Van Zandt, and McCarthy 2002; Shapiro 2004; Yinger 2001.

24. Brooks-Gunn, Duncan, and Aber 1997; Ellen and Turner 1998; Leventhal and Brooks-Gunn 2000.

25. Massey and Denton 1993.

26. Massey, Condran, and Denton 1987.

27. Portes 1995; Portes and Zhou 1993; Zhou 1997a.

28. Waters 1999.

29. Bashi 1998; Bashi and McDaniel 1997; Bashi Bobb and Clarke 2001; Gans 2004; Massey 2004a.

30. Waters 1999.

31. Portes 2004.

32. Gans 2004: 34. As Waters (1999) explains, class background can influence the identities that second-generation Caribbean youths adopt (see also Stepick et al.). In general, youths who adopted an ethnic identity tended to be of middle-class origins, with parents who could afford to send them to private schools outside their neighborhoods. These youths, correspondingly, were also doing well in school. In contrast, youths who reported an identification with African Americans tended to be from the working class and attended local public high schools. In general, these youths were also less academically successful.

33. DeWind and Kasinitz 1997.

34. Bean and Stevens 2003; Hirschman 1996.

35. Massey 2004a; Waters 1999.

36. It is important to note that, increasingly, suburban residence is immediate for some new immigrant groups, notably some Asian groups. This "deviation" from the standard expectations of the spatial assimilation framework is related to the high level of socioeconomic status of many immigrants in these groups, as well as the increasing suburbanization of earlier-arriving immigrants. These earlier arrivals have established enclaves in some suburban areas that serve the same kinds of functions that urban ethnic enclaves have traditionally served, allowing later immigrants to settle there immediately upon arrival.

Perhaps equally important, recent work by Fong and Shibuya (2000) suggests that the link between suburban residence and assimilation is not necessarily straightforward. That is, these authors have found that high levels of acculturation and socioeconomic resources increases the odds of owning in the central city versus renting in the suburbs, suggesting that it is ownership per se rather than simple residence in suburban neighborhoods that may be the emerging hallmark of assimilation.

37. For examples, see Alba and Logan 1991; Alba, Logan, and Bellair 1994; Friedman and Rosenbaum 2006; Logan, Alba, McNulty, and Fisher 1996; South and Crowder 1997a, 1997b, 1998 a, b.

38. This value, which is based on data at the census-tract level of analysis, pertains to the New York Primary Metropolitan Statistical Area (PMSA) and is available, along with values of D for other metropolitan areas, from the Census Bureau's website (http://www.census.gov/hhes/www/housing/housing_patterns/data_excel_text.html).

39. This value was calculated by Greg Argeros at Fordham University and is based on census-tract-level data.

40. The values for Miami and Washington, D.C., pertain to PMSAs and were taken from the Census Bureau's website (http://www.census.gov/hhes/www/housing/housing_patterns/data_excel_text.html).

41. Friedman and Rosenbaum 2004, 2006.

NOTES TO CHAPTER 1

1. Alba and Nee 2003.
2. Foner 2000.
3. Massey 2004a.
4. Alba and Nee 2003.
5. Gerstle 1999; Ignatiev 1995; Jacobson 1998.
6. Massey and Denton 1993.
7. Zhou 2004.
8. Charles 2003.
9. Kasinitz 2001; Rosenbaum and Friedman 2001a.
10. Portes and Zhou 1993; Zhou 1997a, 1997b.
11. Waters 1999.
12. Bashi Bobb and Clarke 2001; Vickerman 1999; Waters 1999.
13. Foley 1980; Shlay 1995.
14. Clark 2003; Shlay 1995.
15. Adams 1987; Foley 1980.
16. Clark 2003.
17. The locational attainment model posits a hierarchical ordering of neighborhoods and evaluates how individual household characteristics translate into

location in a particular area (or placement in the hierarchy of place). Thus, the locational attainment model is conceptually similar to the more general status attainment model (Blau and Duncan 1967), in that both models reveal how individual- or household-level attributes are converted into access to larger social groups, such as occupations or communities, that form the stratification system within society.

18. Aaronson 2000; Boehm and Schlottmann 1999; Charles 2001; Conley 1999, 2001; Green and White 1997; Levy and Michel 1991; Millennial Housing Commission 2002; Oliver and Shapiro 1995; Rohe, Van Zandt, and McCarthy 2002; Shapiro 2004; Yinger 2001.

19. Dunn 2002; Dunn and Hayes 2000; Evans, Wells, and Moch 2003; Rosenbaum 2004.

20. Docs4Kids Project of Boston Medical Center 1998.

21. Rosenbaum 2004.

22. Green and White 1997; Haurin, Parcel, and Haurin 1998; Rohe, McCarthy, and Van Zandt 2000.

23. Harkness and Newman 2003.

24. Brooks-Gunn, Duncan, and Aber 1997; Ellen and Turner 1998, 2003; Jencks and Meyer 1991; Leventhal and Brooks-Gunn 2000; Lopez Turley 2003; Sampson, Morenoff, Cannon-Rowey 2002; South and Baumer 2000.

25. Ellen, Mijanovich, and Dillman 2001; Rosenbaum 2004.

26. Massey 2004b.

27. Charles 2003; Massey 2001, 2004b; Yinger 2001.

28. Massey, Condran, and Denton 1987; Yinger 2001.

29. Massey and Denton 1993.

30. Charles 2003; Farley 1996b; Farley and Frey 1994; Frey and Farley 1996; Iceland 2004; Iceland, Weinberg, and Steinmetz 2002; Logan, Stults, and Farley 2004; Massey 2001; Massey and Denton 1993.

31. The values are based on data at the census-tract level of analysis, pertain to the New York PMSA, and are available, along with values of D for other metropolitan areas, from the Census Bureau's website (http://www.census.gov/hhes/www/housing/housing_patterns/data_excel_text.html).

32. In New York City, the level of black-white segregation (based on census tracts) rose from 82.8 in 1980 to 83.9 in 2000 (calculated by Greg Argeros at Fordham University).

33. Lewis Mumford Center 2001.

34. Charles 2003; Farley 1996b; Farley, Fielding, and Krysan 1998; Massey 2001; Massey and Denton 1993; Rosenbaum 1996a; Zubrinsky and Bobo 1997.

35. Clark 1986.

36. Denton and Massey 1988; Massey and Fischer 1999.

37. Alba et al. 2000a; see also Adelman 2004.

38. Patterson 1997; Thernstrom and Thernstrom 1997.

39. Charles 2001, 2003; Farley 1996b; Farley, Schuman, et al. 1978; Farley, Steeh, et al. 1993; Krysan 2002b; Krysan and Farley 2002; Zubrinsky and Bobo 1997.

Some (e.g., Ellen 2000; D. Harris 1999) have argued that part of whites' antipathy to black neighbors reflects the importance of nonracial factors, such as preferences for neighbors who are well educated and affluent and for neighborhoods where housing values will rise (see also Charles 2001; Farley, Fielding, and Krysan 1998). If measures of such nonracial factors were used in predicting whites' preferences, they may account for some of whites' stated intolerance for sharing neighborhoods with blacks.

40. In contrast, while almost 45 percent of whites indicated a preference for "all white" or "mostly white" neighborhoods, only 4.5 percent of black respondents preferred such neighborhoods (*New York Times* 1990).

41. Charles 2001, 2003.

42. Farley, et al. 1994; Massey and Denton 1993; Yinger 1995.

43. K. Jackson 1985; Massey and Denton 1993; Yinger 1995.

44. Massey 2001; Turner 1993; Yinger 1995, 2001.

45. Patillo-McCoy 1998, 1999, 2000; see also Adelman 2004; Anderson 1990.

46. These values and those for 1980 and 1990 are all based on tract-level data, pertain to the New York Primary Metropolitan Statistical Area (PMSA), and are available (along with values for other metropolitan areas) from the Census Bureau's website (http://www.census.gov/hhes/www/housing/housing_patterns/data_excel_text.html). In New York City, levels of Hispanic-white segregation (based on census tracts) rose between 1980 and 2000, moving from 64.1 to 67.1. In contrast, levels of Asian-white segregation remained virtually stable, rising almost imperceptibly from 49.4 in 1980 to 49.6 in 2000 (calculated by Greg Argeros of Fordham University).

47. Denton and Massey 1988; Massey and Fischer 1999.

48. Alba and Nee 2003.

49. Charles 2001, 2003; Zubrinsky and Bobo 1997.

50. Charles 2003.

51. Denton and Massey 1989; Freeman 1999; Massey and Bitterman 1985; Rosenbaum 1996a.

52. Denton and Massey 1989; Rosenbaum 1996a.

53. Waters 1999.

54. Alba, Logan, and Stults 2000b; Alba and Logan 1993.

55. In addition, studies have also shown that Latinos who are phenotypically black or whose appearance resembles that of their Indian ancestors experience more discrimination in the workplace than do Latinos who are more European in appearance (Espino and Franz 2002).

56. Deane 1990; Rossi 1955; Speare 1974.
57. South and Deane 1993.
58. McLanahan and Booth 1989.
59. This is conceptualized within a cross-sectional framework. A change in income—either an increase or a decrease—could motivate a move. Rising income could motivate a move to a better location, and a decrease in income could motivate a move to a more affordable location, as often occurs in the aftermath of a divorce.
60. Lee, Oropesa, and Kanan 1994; Long 1987.
61. Lee, Oropesa and Kanan 1994; South and Deane 1993; South and Crowder 1998 a, b.
62. Crowder 2000; South and Crowder 1998a; South and Deane 1993.
63. Lee 1978.
64. Logan and Molotch 1987.
65. Fitchen 1980, 1994.
66. Duncan and Newman 1975; Newman and Duncan 1979.
67. Crowder 2001.
68. South and Crowder 1997a, 1997b, 1998a, 1998b.
69. Massey, Gross, and Shibuya 1994.
70. Massey and Denton 1993; Turner et al. 2002; Yinger 1995.
71. Krysan 2002b.
72. Buell 1982.
73. DeSena 1990; Reider 1985; Susser 1982.
74. Turner et al. 2002. These are gross measures. The net measures (e.g., the percent of white testers treated more favorably minus the percent of minority testers treated more favorably) are lower.
75. Turner et al. 2002.
76. Turner, Struyk, and Yinger 1991.
77. Charles 2003.
78. Hevesi 1995. While housing market discrimination can clearly influence the type and amount of information households receive, minorities' expectation of discriminatory treatment by landlords, home sellers, and others may also influence their housing searches. That is, should minorities perceive certain neighborhoods as being hostile to them, they may avoid searching for housing in those neighborhoods, concentrating their searches in minority areas where they expect a more welcoming atmosphere (Charles 2003). Such effects on housing searches would have the same kinds of consequences for segregation patterns as would direct experiences with discrimination.
79. Clearly, racial/ethnic variations in preferences for certain racial/ethnic compositions will also result in differences in the destinations chosen by relocating households of different race/ethnicity.
80. Crowder 2001.

81. Long and Spain 1978; Marullo 1985; Rosenbaum 1992; Spain 1980; Spain, Reid, and Long 1980.

82. Rosenbaum 1992, 1994; Rosenbaum and Argeros 2005; Rosenbaum and Friedman 2001b; Rosenbaum and Schill 1999.

83. Rosenbaum 1992, 1994; Rosenbaum and Argeros 2005; Rosenbaum and Friedman 2001b; Rosenbaum and Schill 1999.

84. Alba and Nee 1997, 2003.

85. Hochschild 1995.

86. Hochschild 1995.

87. Alba and Nee 1997, 2003.

88. Zhou 1999.

89. Alba and Nee 2003; Bean and Stevens 2003; Zhou 1999. Although the idea that assimilation followed a straight line is simplistic and does not genuinely reflect reality for all groups, to a large degree the strength of immigrants' cultures and institutions have eroded over the course of generations, as the straight-line trajectory implies (Gans 2004).

90. Waters 2001: 202.

91. Alba, Logan, Zhang, and Stults 1999.

92. Massey 1985.

93. Alba and Nee 1997.

94. Massey 1985.

95. Alba and Logan 1991; Logan and Alba 1993.

96. Charles 2003.

97. Alba and Nee 1997, 2003.

98. Denton and Massey 1988; Massey and Fischer 1999.

99. Alba and Logan 1991, 1993; Logan and Alba 1993, 1995; Logan, Alba, McNulty, and Fisher, 1996; Rosenbaum 1996b; Rosenbaum and Friedman 2001a; Rosenbaum, Friedman, Schill, and Buddelmeyer 1999; Schill, Friedman, and Rosenbaum 1998.

100. Bashi and McDaniel 1997.

101. Alba and Logan 1993.

102. Logan and Molotch 1987.

103. K. Jackson 1985; Leahy 1985; Massey and Denton 1993; Munnell, et al. 1992; Schill and Wachter 1995; Shlay and Rossi 1981; Squires 1994; Yinger 1995.

104. Galster et al. 1999; Massey 2001; Turner 1993; Yinger 1995, 2001.

105. Jackson 1985.

106. Bashi and McDaniel 1997.

107. Turner et al. 2002.

108. Alba and Nee 1997; Massey 1995.

109. See, for example, Perlmann and Waldinger 1999.

110. Gans 1992.

111. Alba and Nee 2003.
112. Lopez and Stanton-Salazar 2001.
113. Perlmann and Waldinger 1999.
114. Portes and Rumbaut 1996; Waters 1994, 1999.
115. Bankston and Zhou 1997; Portes and Rumbaut 2001; Zhou 1997b.
116. One of these paths involves remaining within the ethnic enclave. As illustrated by Bankston and Zhou's (1997) work on Vietnamese youth, children and adolescents residing within the ethnic enclave can benefit from the shared values of the community and other forms of interfamilial social capital. Thus, the potential upward mobility of the second generation can also be counted among the possible benefits of voluntary segregation.
117. Bankston and Zhou 1997; Portes and Rumbaut 2001; Zhou 1997b.
118. Hirschman 1996; Stepick, et al. 2003; Waters 1999.
119. Bashi 1998; Bashi and McDaniel 1997; Bashi Bobb and Clarke 2001.
120. Portes 2004; Waters 2001.
121. Alba and Nee 2003; Waters 2001.
122. Portes and Rumbaut 1996; Zhou 1997a, 1997b.
123. Gans 1992; Waters 1994.
124. See, for example, Alba and Nee 2003; Neckerman, Carter, and Lee 1999.
125. Neckerman, Carter, and Lee 1999: 946.
126. For example, Foner 2002; Kasinitz, Mollenkopf, and Waters 2002; Waters 1999.
127. Kasinitz 2001.
128. Landale, Oropesa, and Gorman 1999, 2000.
129. Landale, Oropesa, and Gorman 2000.
130. Oropesa and Landale 1997.
131. Hirschman 2001.
132. Kasinitz, Mollenkopf, and Waters 2002.
133. Portes and Rumbaut 2001.
134. Waters 1999; Stepick et al. 2003.
135. Zhou 1999: 300.
136. Zhou 1999.
137. Kasinitz, Mollenkopf, and Waters 2002.
138. Farley and Alba 2002. The Current Population Survey (CPS), the data source used by Farley and Alba (2002) can identify the generational status of respondents but does not link individual members of the second generation to their immigrant parents. Thus, the best way to approximate parent-child (and thus generational) differences in economic status is to mimic parents' attainments with those reported by first-generation individuals who are of the same age as the second generation's parents themselves may be.

139. Bean et al. 1994; Bean and Stevens 2003; Farley and Alba 2002; Livingston and Kahn 2002; Zhou 1999.

140. Bean and Stevens 2003; Livingston and Kahn 2002; Lopez and Stanton-Salazar 2001.

141. Kao and Tienda 1995.

142. Livingston and Kahn 2002.

143. For example, Kasinitz, Mollenkopf, and Waters 2002; Portes and Rumbaut 2001.

144. For example, Glick and White 2003; Harker 2001; K. Harris 1999; Kao 1999.

145. Zhou 1999.

146. For example, Farley and Alba 2002; Landale, Oropesa, and Gorman 1999, 2000.

147. Bean and Stevens 2003.

148. Rosenbaum and Friedman 2004. An alternative, and arguably preferred, method would be one that is cohort based, along the lines of the double-cohort method (cf. Myers and Lee 1996). With this method, households could be grouped by the householder's generation, year of entry, age, and the householder's parents' year of entry. However, because the HVS did not begin asking respondents about their year of entry until the 1999 panel and does not include any information on parents' year of entry, this kind of analysis is not possible.

149. Although studies that have demonstrated patterns of generational decline in health behaviors and outcomes and in psychological well-being certainly raise important questions concerning the adaptation of new immigrants (Rumbaut 1997, 1999), such outcomes do not truly lie at the core of segmented assimilation theory. Moreover, some scholars have argued that by examining such outcomes among adolescents, a stage of the life cycle where rebellious or risky behavior is not unusual, analysts run the risk of confusing what are the byproducts of adolescent development with structural obstacles to opportunity (Bean and Stevens 2003).

150. Waters 1999.

151. Bashi 1998; Bashi and McDaniel 1997; Bashi Bobb and Clarke 2001.

152. Waters 1999.

153. Bashi Bobb and Clarke 2001; Portes 2004; Vickerman 1999.

154. Portes 2004; Vickerman 2001a; Waters 1999.

155. Alba and Nee 2003.

156. Vickerman 1999.

157. Waters 2001.

158. Bashi and McDaniel 1997; Bashi Bobb and Clarke 2001.

159. Waters 1999; see also Bashi Bobb and Clarke 2001; Portes 2004.

Notes to Chapter 2

1. Logan and Molotch 1987.
2. Harris 2003; Rosenwaike 1972.
3. Burrows and Wallace 1995.
4. Burrows and Wallace 1995.
5. Burrows and Wallace 1995.
6. L. Harris 2003; Osofsky 1971.
7. Rosenwaike 1972; Groneman and Reimers 1995.
8. Because the Irish originated from the British Isles, they clearly contributed to the majority status of the group identified as of English origin. Similarly, persons of both Scottish and Welsh descent were also present in sizable numbers (Binder and Reimers 1995; Groneman and Reimers 1995).
9. Binder and Reimers 1995; Burrows and Wallace 1995.
10. Rosenwaike 1972.
11. Shammas 2000.
12. During the yellow fever outbreaks of 1803 and 1805, upwards of one-third of New Yorkers evacuated the crowded lower wards during the summer and early fall (Shammas 2000).
13. Blackmar 1989; Stansell 1987.
14. Blackmar 1989; Ernst [1949] 1994.
15. Blackmar 1989: 51.
16. Binder and Reimers 1995; Rosenwaike 1972.
17. Rosenwaike 1972: 39.
18. Logan and Molotch 1987.
19. Ernst [1949] 1994; Rosenwaike 1972.
20. Regular steam-ferry service connecting Manhattan to Brooklyn began in 1814, making Brooklyn the nation's first commuter suburb. On the island of Manhattan itself, the omnibus was introduced in 1829, and steam-powered railroads were introduced in 1832. After only five years, the New York and Harlem Railroad was offering regular service to 125th Street, propelling the development of Harlem as a middle-class enclave. Additions to this line led into lower Westchester County by 1844, enabling development around newly opened stations in Fordham, Morrisania, and Tremont in the Bronx. By 1855, horsecars were replacing omnibuses on major routes in Manhattan, with their tracks connecting newly emerging middle-class and genteel areas with the business district downtown. By 1856, the horsecar lines on Second and Third Avenues extended as far north as 60th Street (K. Jackson 1985).
21. Binder and Reimers 1995: 36.
22. Land values in Manhattan rose about 750 percent between the Revolutionary War and the War of 1812, and another 300 percent between 1826 and 1836 (Burrows and Wallace 1995).

23. See also L. Harris 2003.

24. During the first half of the nineteenth century the home and the family were increasingly accorded sacred status in middle-class culture. As middle-class men increasingly worked outside the home, their wives took responsibility for all that involved the residence and family life. The home became a sanctuary where the working man could renew himself not only for work but spiritually as well. The single-family dwelling became an important symbol of middle-class status and respectability (Cromley 1990).

25. Massey and Denton 1993.

26. The widespread acceptance of this connection between place and health is revealed in the frequent mention of the healthfulness of the location in advertisements of middle-class and affluent homes (Blackmar 1995).

27. Blackmar 1989; Spann 1981.

28. Binder and Reimers 1995; Blackmar 1989; Ernst [1949] 1994.

29. Anbinder 2001: 73–74.

30. Blackmar 1989; Ernst [1949] 1994.

31. L. Harris 2003.

32. Osofsky 1971.

33. Anbinder 2001: 12.

34. Stott 1990.

35. Rosenwaike 1972.

36. Connelly 1977.

37. L. Harris 2003.

38. Ernst [1949] 1994: 1.

39. Ernst [1949] 1994.

40. Ernst [1949] 1994.

41. Stott 1990.

42. However, a substantial number of Irish women also immigrated to the United States, and in many years women even outnumbered men. In fact, Binder and Reimers (1995) point out that the number of Irish women counted in New York City in the 1860 census exceeded the number of Irish men. Stott's (1990) analysis focuses on immigrants from the British Isles as a whole.

43. Stott 1990, Nadel 1990.

44. L. Harris 2003.

45. Ernst [1949] 1994.

46. Nadel 1990.

47. Nadel 1990.

48. The shortage of housing was exacerbated by the depression of 1837–43, which virtually halted all housing construction. Blackmar (1989) argues that prior to 1840, housing speculators could realize a competitive rate of profit only from the construction of housing for middle-class or affluent households, and they therefore ignored the working-class market. Instead of creating new units

through new construction, additional units were created through subdivision and by carving up cellars and attics. Following the depression of 1837–43, the building industry shifted from being composed largely of small projects conducted by individuals to larger projects undertaken by partnerships of housing speculators. The larger capital accumulation afforded by these partnerships and the lower acquisition costs for land and buildings in the lower wards that resulted from the economic crisis allowed builders to "rationalize" new construction of working-class housing, building it on a new scale but retaining its characteristics of crowding and absent amenities.

49. The preexisting absence of amenities from working-class housing was interpreted as indicating that light, air, connection to sewers, and fresh water were simply not necessities for working-class households. This interpretation further justified their omission from new tenements (Blackmar 1989).

50. Ernst [1949] 1994: 48–49

51. Ernst [1949] 1994.

52. Rosner 1995.

53. Condran 1995.

54. Blackmar 1995.

55. Blackmar 1995: 94.

56. Lubove 1974: 3.

57. Lubove 1974: 8.

58. Plunz and Abu-Lughod 1994.

59. It was not unusual for profits deriving from tenements to fall in the 10–30 percent range (Day 1999).

60. Many authors have noted that by defining tenements as structures with a minimum of three resident families, the legislation would not apply to some of the worst working-class housing, which consisted of buildings with fewer than three families (Blackmar 1989; Lubove 1974).

61. The figures from the Council of Hygiene's report are reported in Lubove (1974: 257). The total population of the city in 1860 was 813,669.

62. Lubove 1974: 26.

63. J. Schwartz 1995a.

64. Rischin 1962: 11.

65. Binder and Reimers 1995; Kantrowitz 1995.

66. Binder and Reimers 1995.

67. Binder and Reimers 1995.

68. Binder and Reimers 1995.

69. Kasinitz 1992.

70. Osofsky 1971.

71. Rosenwaike 1972.

72. Kasinitz 1992; Watkins-Owens 1996.

73. The 1860 value is taken from Massey and Denton 1993:21, table 2.1. The original source is Berlin 1974.

74. The 2000 level was calculated by Greg Argeros of Fordham University, using tracts as the unit of analysis. Because it relies on tracts, it is not directly comparable to a measure calculated over wards. Wards are far larger than tracts; the larger the geographic unit in calculating the index of dissimilarity, the lower the value. Massey and Denton (1993) suggest that the difference in using wards versus tracts amount to about ten points. If we accept this, then the 1860 level of segregation remains in the moderate range and about 30 points lower than the 1990 level.

75. Binder and Reimers 1995; Fitzpatrick 1971; Rodriguez 1989; Sanchez-Korrol 1983.

76. Binder and Reimers 1995; Rodriguez 1989; Sanchez-Korrol 1983.

77. Chin 1995; Wang 2001; Yu 1995.

78. Kwong 1987; Wang 2001; Zhou 1991.

79. Kwong 1987; Zhou 1991.

80. Reimers 1998.

81. The earlier quota-based laws used different censuses and different base populations, but each system had the effect of severely curtailing immigration from the nations of Southern and Eastern Europe in favor of immigration from Western and Northern Europe (Reimers 1998).

82. Binder and Reimers 1995.

83. Hammack 1987.

84. Logan 1997.

85. Logan 1997.

86. Gurock 1995.

87. Rischin 1962.

88. Laidlaw 1932.

89. Kantrowitz 1995.

90. Kessner 1977.

91. Hammack 1987.

92. Orsi 1985.

93. Orsi 1985: 35–36.

94. Logan 1997.

95. Joseph 1914.

96. Joseph 1914.

97. Rischin 1962.

98. Lubove 1974.

99. Howe 1976.

100. Kessner 1977: 132.

101. Pritchett 2002.

102. Moore 1992; Pritchett 2002.
103. Howe 1976; Moore 1992.
104. Moore 1992.
105. Logan 1997.
106. Gurock 1995; Moore 1992.
107. J. Schwartz 1995a.
108. J. Schwartz 1995a.
109. Rischin 1962.
110. Rischin 1962; J. Schwartz 1995b.
111. Connelly 1977; L. Harris 2003.
112. L. Harris 2003.
113. Osofsky 1971: 92.
114. Osofsky 1971: 93.
115. Osofsky 1971.
116. Osofsky 1971: 129.
117. Massey and Denton 1993.
118. Osofsky 1971.
119. Laidlaw 1932.
120. Indeed, Kenneth Jackson (1985) notes that more residential development occurred during the 1920s in city neighborhoods accessible only by car than in those accessible by public transportation. In particular he uses as an example the neighborhood of Flatlands in eastern Brooklyn, which even today lacks a subway connection.
121. Plunz 1990.
122. Rosenwaike 1972.
123. Osofsky 1971: 135.
124. Osofsky 1971: 140.
125. Osofsky 1971: 130.
126. Sanchez-Korrol 1983.
127. Rosenwaike 1972.
128. Rosenwaike 1972.
129. Denton and Massey 1989; Logan 1997; Massey and Bitterman 1985; Rosenbaum 1996b; Rosenberg and Lake 1976. More-direct evidence of discrimination against Puerto Ricans exists: 9 percent of the 791 housing discrimination complaints filed between April 1958 and December 1960 were initiated by Puerto Ricans (Benjamin 1974).
130. Logan 1997.
131. Massey and Denton 1993.
132. Connelly 1977; Wilder 2000.
133. Massey and Denton 1993.
134. Kasinitz 1992.
135. Because legislative changes allowed Chinese women to join their hus-

bands in the United States, for the first time women made up a significant proportion of Chinese immigrants, approximately one-half (Zhou 2001).

136. Binder and Reimers 1995.
137. New York City Department of City Planning 1992.
138. Binder and Reimers 1995; Tolnay, Crowder, and Adelman 2002.
139. Figures are from Rosenwaike 1972:134, table 65.
140. Waldinger 1996.
141. Waldinger 1996.
142. Binder and Reimers 1995.
143. Massey and Denton 1993; Duncan and Duncan 1957; Taveber and Tauber 1965.
144. Mayor Fiorello La Guardia had the Tenement House Department embark on a determined campaign to enforce the provisions of the 1929 Multiple Dwelling Law. Tenement landlords were required to bring their buildings up to code or vacate them in preparation for demolition. The losses in low-cost housing during the period thus stem from the increased rents charged for upgraded units (which forced most low-income tenants to move) and from tremendous losses from demolition and abandonment. This policy affected neighborhood conditions as older tenement neighborhoods, such as the Lower East Side, became pockmarked by vacant lots and boarded-up buildings, reinforcing their images as slums (Kessner 1989; Wasserman 1994).
145. Rent regulation in New York City was initially managed by the federal government (1943–50), afterward becoming the responsibility first of New York State (1950–62) and then of the city (1962–84), and is currently administered by the New York State Division of Housing and Community Renewal (DHCR). The evolution of federal, state, and city legislation has resulted in a mix of housing units that fall within the two categories of regulation: rent control and stabilization. The main characteristics distinguishing controlled from stabilized units are the size and age of the building and the length of continuous occupancy of the unit. Rent-controlled units are currently found in buildings with three or more dwelling units that were built prior to 1947 and that have been continuously occupied by the same tenant and/or his or her immediate family since before July 1971. Although there is an unknown amount of illegal movement in and out of controlled units, current legislation dictates that controlled units either become decontrolled (and no longer subject to rent regulation) or stabilized upon vacancy. The deciding factor is building size: units in buildings with five or fewer units become decontrolled. In addition to formerly controlled units in buildings with six or more dwelling units, stabilized units are found in buildings built before 1974 and those whose owners voluntarily participated in the city's tax-abatement programs that helped finance rehabilitation or construction.
146. New York City Department of City Planning 1982.
147. New York City Department of City Planning 1982; Rodriguez 1989.

148. Wilder 2000: 184.
149. By 1930 the "demographic distribution of blacks pointed toward the possible evolution of central Brooklyn into the primary place of residence for the borough's black population" (Connelly 1977: 54).
150. Wilder 2000: 185.
151. Biondi 2003; Massey and Denton 1993.
152. Radford 2000.
153. K. Jackson 1985; Massey and Denton 1993.
154. Wilder 2000: 193.
155. Wilder 2000: 193.
156. K. Jackson 1985.
157. Massey and Denton 1993: 55.
158. Figures are taken from Massey and Denton 1993:48, table 2.4. In addition, the tract-level index of dissimilarity between blacks and native whites of native parentage rose from 72 in 1920 to 84 in 1960 (Logan 1997).
159. K. Jackson 1985.
160. Farley, Schuman, et al. 1978; Farley, Steeh, et al. 1993.
161. K. Jackson 1985; Von Hoffman 2000.
162. Plunz 1990: 207.
163. K. Jackson 1985.
164. Plunz 1990.
165. Kessner 1989.
166. Genevro 1986.
167. As a consequence of the PWA's increasing insistence on direct federal involvement in slum clearance, a federal judge in Louisville, Kentucky, ruled that the federal government could not acquire land by eminent domain for the purpose of building public housing. Consequently, the PWA would have to purchase sites at market rates; the higher cost of land reduced the number of projects the PWA would be able to initiate and forced rents to a level that would have precluded tenancy by the working poor. In the process of NYCHA's attempt to assemble parcels for the First Houses project, a New York State judge ruled in a suit brought by a property owner against NYCHA that local municipalities could use eminent domain for the purpose of constructing public housing. The joint effects of these rulings made local implementation of eminent domain the only feasible way to proceed with the public housing program and ultimately settled the controversy that had held up the transfer of the $25 million promised to New York City (K. Jackson 1985; Kessner 1989).
168. Genevro 1986; Marcuse 1986; Wasserman 1994.
169. Greenberg 1991; Marcuse 1986.
170. Marcuse 1986: 369.
171. Marcuse 1986.
172. Plunz 1990.

173. K. Jackson 1985: 224.

174. The 1937 act also stipulated that no single state should receive more than one-tenth of the total federal outlay for public housing. Given that the level of need for low-cost and adequate housing was so dire in New York City, the city council determined that the city must view housing as it did other city services; to help finance the construction of housing, La Guardia proposed a plan whereby the city could issue its own bonds. Also in 1938 a public referendum passed that allowed New York State to begin building public housing. Despite the fact that Congress would not authorize any new public-housing units between 1938 and 1949, during the twenty years beginning in 1937, NYCHA built almost 88,000 low-rent housing units under the various federal, state, and city housing programs (A. Jackson 1976; Plunz 1990; Von Hoffman 2000).

175. K. Jackson 1985; Massey and Denton 1993; Pritchett 2002.

176. Von Hoffman 2000.

177. Massey and Denton 1993: 55.

178. Biondi 2003; Caro 1974; K. Jackson 1985; Massey and Denton 1993; Pritchett 2002; Von Hoffman 2000.

179. Von Hoffman 2000: 317.

180. Caro 1974; J. Schwartz 1993.

181. Caro 1974.

182. To evaluate the uneven distribution of public-housing units across the neighborhoods of New York, we used microdata on housing units from the 1999 panel of the New York Housing and Vacancy Survey to calculate the dissimilarity index for public versus all other housing units in the fifty-five subareas. The calculated value is 52, indicating that if it were possible to move housing units, more than half of public-housing units in the city would have to be relocated across subareas to achieve an even distribution. If we had used data on public-housing units in census tracts, the dissimilarity index would have been even higher, partly because using a smaller geographic unit always inflates the value but also because many public-housing projects are located in "super blocks" which themselves constitute individual census tracts. Thus, even larger proportions of public housing would have been concentrated in just a handful of tracts, greatly inflating the value of the dissimilarity index. However, to place the spatial segregation of public housing at the subarea level into perspective, it should be noted that public-housing units make up only about 6 percent of all housing units in the city. What is a very small segment of the housing stock is disproportionately concentrated in a small number of subareas.

183. Pritchett 2002: 99.

184. Parkchester was also a whites-only development (Capeci 1978; J. Schwartz 1993).

185. Binder and Reimers 1995; Biondi 2003; J. Schwartz 1995b. In 1958 the city passed the Sharkey-Brown-Isaacs bill, which prohibited discrimination

in privately owned, unsubsidized housing. This was the nation's first fair-housing law (Schill 1996).

186. Binder and Reimers 1985. Municipal government became almost an employment niche for blacks. However, it could not function as successfully as other niches had for white immigrant groups, by expanding employment opportunities to those with less education or few skills. The level of skills and education necessary for jobs in the public sector made the least advantaged of the community ineligible for employment and its consequent opportunities for upward mobility. The movement of blacks into public-sector employment may thus have contributed to the growing socioeconomic bifurcation of the community (Waldinger 1996).

187. Biondi 2003.

NOTES TO CHAPTER 3

1. Lobo and Salvo 1999.

2. Data taken from New York City Department of City Planning, *Demographic Profiles,* www.nyc.gov/html/dcp/html/census/popdiv.html (accessed on June 14, 2002). The figures for non-Hispanic whites, blacks, and Asians are for non-Hispanic persons reporting a single race. New York first became a "majority minority" city in 1990.

3. Salvo, Banks, and Mann 1990; Salvo, Ortiz, and Lobo 1994.

4. Schmitt 2001.

5. Sanjek 1998.

6. Sanjek 1998.

7. Waldinger 1987–88.

8. Kraly and Miyares 2001; New York City Department of City Planning 1992.

9. For detailed discussion of the preferences system, see Kraly and Miyares 2001; New York City Department of City Planning 1992; and Reimers 1992.

10. Kraly and Miyares 2001; New York City Department of City Planning 1992.

11. New York City Department of City Planning 1999.

12. New York City Department of City Planning 1996, 1999.

13. New York City Department of City Planning 1999.

14. New York City Department of City Planning 1992, 1996, 1999.

15. Pessar and Graham 2001.

16. New York City Department of City Planning 1996.

17. New York City Department of City Planning 1999.

18. Pessar and Graham 2001.

19. Figures are calculated using microdata on households and persons available in the 1999 panel of the New York City Housing and Vacancy Survey

(HVS). Total household income represents the sum of all reported income from all sources for all members of the household. Differences in household income (reported in 1999 for calendar year 1998) are more extreme when the mean is used. Using this measure, the average household income in the city was $48,966, and that for Dominicans was $26,252.

20. New York City Department of City Planning 1988.

21. New York City Department of City Planning 1992, 1999.

22. Figures are calculated from the 1999 HVS.

23. New York City Department of City Planning 1992, 1996, 1999.

24. Pessar and Graham 2001.

25. Figures are calculated from the 1999 HVS.

26. Rosenbaum, Friedman, Schill, and Buddelmeyer 1999; Schill, Friedman, and Rosenbaum 1998.

27. Freeman 1999.

28. New York City Department of City Planning 1996, 1999.

29. Orleck 2001.

30. New York City Department of City Planning 1999.

31. Dobkowski and Share 1995; Lieber 1995.

32. Orleck 2001.

33. Reider 1985.

34. New York City Department of City Planning 1999.

35. Yu 1995; Zhou 1991.

36. New York City Department of City Planning 1996, 1999.

37. The source for the 1970 figure is Rosenwaike 1972:141, table 69. The source for the 2000 figure is New York City Department of City Planning, *Demographic Profiles,* www.nyc.gov/html/dcp/html/census/popdiv.html (accessed on June 14, 2002).

38. Zhou 1991.

39. However, over time, the Chinese population in Flushing is becoming more diverse, with representatives from mainland China becoming more numerous (Zhou 2001).

40. Zhou 1991, 2001.

41. Zhou 2001.

42. New York City Department of City Planning 1999.

43. Kasinitz 1987–88.

44. Kasinitz 1987–88, 1992; New York City Department of City Planning 1988, 1996.

45. New York City Department of City Planning 1996, 1999.

46. Kasinitz 1992.

47. Denton and Massey 1991.

48. Farley, Fielding, and Krysan 1998; Farley, Schuman, et al. 1978; Farley, Steeh, et al. 1993; Zubrinsky and Bobo 1997.

49. Ellen 2000; Lee and Wood 1991; Wood and Lee 1991.
50. Sanjek 1998.
51. Bowles 1992; Gambardello 1991.
52. Scott 2001: A1.
53. Scott 2001.
54. New York City Department of City Planning 1999.
55. Lobo and Salvo 1999; Rosenbaum and Friedman 2001b.
56. Crowder and Tedrow 2001; Lobo and Salvo 1999.
57. Crowder and Tedrow 2001.
58. Crowder and Tedrow 2001; Rosenbaum and Friedman 2001a.
59. For example, Kasinitz 1992; Marshall [1959] 1981.
60. Scott 2001: A1.
61. Kasinitz 1987–88.
62. Rosenbaum, Friedman, Schill, and Buddelmeyer 1999; Schill, Friedman, and Rosenbaum 1998.
63. Rosenbaum, Friedman, Schill, and Buddelmeyer 1999; Schill, Friedman, and Rosenbaum 1998.
64. Braconi 1999.
65. Rodriguez 1989.
66. A. Schwartz 1999. The city stopped foreclosing on tax-delinquent properties in 1993 but did not announce this action until 1995 (Braconi 1999).
67. A. Schwartz 1999; van Ryzin and Genn 1999; Wylde 1999.
68. Rosenbaum 1989.
69. Bernstein 1994; Finder 1995; Purdy 1994.
70. Yardley 1997.
71. Ellen, Schill, Susin, and Schwartz 2001.
72. A. Schwartz 1999; van Ryzin and Genn 1999.
73. Skogan 1990.
74. van Ryzin and Genn 1999.
75. Finder 1995.

NOTES TO CHAPTER 4

1. Rosenbaum 2004; Yinger 2001.
2. For each outcome we estimate two separate models. The first is the basic locational attainment model, which predicts the specific housing or neighborhood outcome of interest as a function of a set of household characteristics. In general, the models we estimate for all outcomes contain an identical set of predictors, with two exceptions. The first exception is the use of variables to reflect the housing-market sector to which the housing unit belongs. That is, we utilize a pair of dummy variables to differentiate units in public housing and other rental units from owned units in all models except for that predicting home

ownership. Utilizing these controls is necessary because, in general, housing and neighborhood conditions tend to be better for owned than for rental units. In addition, given the history of public-housing site location, it is also likely that the housing and especially the neighborhood conditions associated with public-housing units may differ from those of owned units as well as those in the rest of the rental sector.

The second exception to the general approach involves the use of contextual variables in the models predicting housing characteristics. Two sets of contextual variables are used. The first is borough location. Controlling for borough location is important because different immigrant and racial/ethnic groups tend to live in different boroughs and because different patterns of borough development have led to very different housing stocks and thus divergent sets of housing opportunities. The second set of contextual variables used in the models predicting housing characteristics includes measures of the composition of the subarea surrounding the sampled unit—specifically, the percentage of recent immigrants and the percentage of blacks (both measured with 1990 census data).

The second model we estimate for all outcomes differs from the first in the way we treat generational status. In the first model, we enter three dummy variables that differentiate the first, 1.5, and second generations from each other and from the third-plus generation (which serves as the reference group). In the second model, we add controls for the year of arrival for the first and 1.5 generations—i.e., the foreign-born generations. (Because Puerto Ricans are citizens of the United States, most Puerto Rican householders in the HVS did not answer the question regarding the year they arrived in the United States but did respond to a similar question that asked the year they arrived in New York. Thus, to gauge their year of entry, we used this latter variable. Because the majority of island-born Puerto Ricans who migrated to the United States historically came to New York City, this question is a fairly good measure of their time on the mainland. The main limitation of this measure is that it cannot account for circular flows of migration that occur among some island-born Puerto Ricans.) These controls take the form of interactions between dummy variables differentiating householders who arrived in 1980 and later from those who arrived prior to 1980, with the dummy variables identifying the first and the 1.5 generations. These interactions provide an additional view to the spatial assimilation process—namely, that pertaining to the passage of time versus passage of generation.

3. Blau and Duncan 1967.

4. Logan and Alba 1993.

5. The definition and construction of all variables are described in detail in appendix A, which also contains an in-depth description of the statistical techniques we utilized in our multivariate models.

6. Controlling for age not only satisfies the theoretical needs of the two

models but also accounts for the likelihood that the four generational groups have different age distributions.

7. As discussed in note 2, we include these subarea characteristics only in the models predicting housing conditions.

8. Alba, Logan, Stults, Marzan, and Zhang 1999; Massey 1985; Massey and Denton 1987, 1988; but see Fong and Shibuya 2000 and Friedman and Rosenbaum 2004, 2006 on the current limitations of the view.

9. Hevesi 1995; Lueck 1991; Rosenbaum 1992, 1994, 1996a; Schill 1996.

10. To predict the values of each outcome for each generational group, the means for all variables (apart from generation) are used; thus, the only values allowed to vary are those for each generational group. The variable means are presented in appendix B, table B.1, and the coefficients are shown in appendix B, tables B.2–B.10.

11. Clark 2003.

12. Vickerman 1999, 2001b.

13. Zhou 2001.

14. The length of waiting lists for public housing and other forms of housing assistance, such as housing certificates/vouchers, means that immigrants are less likely than the native-born to utilize any kind of housing subsidies (Friedman, Schill, and Rosenbaum 1999).

15. As was the case in table 4.3, each predicted value is calculated using the means on all the variables in the model, apart from the variable under evaluation. The exception to this statement is household income, which is entered as a continuous variable (logged) in the model. As a result, the predicted value for each outcome is computed for three values of household income: $25,000, $50,000, and $100,000. The predicted values in this and subsequent tables in this chapter utilize the model containing the interaction between generation and time since arrival.

16. As described in note2, home ownership is used as a predictor of all neighborhood conditions and in the crowding and maintenance-deficiencies models.

17. As indicated in note 2, in the models predicting the three housing conditions we include two contextual indicators, the percentage of blacks and the percentage of recent immigrants in the subarea. No contextual indicators are used in the models predicting subarea conditions due to the detrimental effects of the resulting correlations.

18. Lobo and Salvo 1999; Scott 2001.

19. The Hispanic-specific model is identical to the pooled model except for the use of a dichotomous variable for race, as well as three dichotomies differentiating Puerto Ricans, Dominicans, and other Hispanics from Central/South Americans (who constitute the reference category for national origin).

20. All households in table 4.7, regardless of race, also have the following

characteristics: householder aged forty-five, headship by a couple, no children under eighteen present, no other adults present, and Central/South American origin.

21. Logan and Alba 1993.

22. As indicated in note 10, the group-specific models are identical to the pooled models, with the exceptions noted for the Hispanic-specific models. The group-specific models form the basis of our analyses in chapter 5, and their full results are shown in appendix C, tables C.2–C.10.

23. Logan and Alba 1993.

24. Logan and Alba 1993.

25. Alba and Logan 1991; Alba, Logan, and Bellair 1994; Logan and Alba 1993; Villemez 1980.

26. Gross and Massey 1991; Massey and Denton 1985.

27. Alba and Logan 1991; Alba, Logan, and Bellair 1994; Logan and Alba 1993.

28. All the variables apart from household income, receipt of public assistance, education, and market sector in the group-specific regression models were evaluated at their reference categories when calculating the predicted values. The only exception here is age, which was set at forty-five for each group. Although differing coefficients for age will contribute to the differences in predicted values shown in table 4.8, the contribution of age is not great enough to affect the substance of our interpretations.

29. For evidence of the same racial hierarchy in Los Angeles, see Zubrinsky and Bobo 1997.

NOTES TO CHAPTER 5

1. Alba and Nee 2003; Gans 1999.

2. As discussed in chapter 4 and appendix A, we include the subarea percentage of recent immigrants in the models predicting housing outcomes only.

3. As indicated in chapter 4, to calculate these predictions, all households are assumed to be aged forty-five, and headed by a couple, with no children under eighteen or other adults present. "Affluent" households are defined as those who own their homes, do not receive public assistance, earn $100,000, and have at least some college. "Average" households live in rental housing, do not receive public assistance, earn $33,000, and have a high school diploma. "Poor" households live in public housing, receive public assistance, earn $6,720, and have less than a high school diploma. For Hispanics, the omitted categories for race (nonblack) and national origin (Central/South American) are used in the predictions.

4. In contrast, all affluent Hispanic households live in neighborhoods with slightly less-widespread welfare use than do all poor white households in the

same generation, and affluent third-plus-generation Hispanics live in neighbor-hoods with more one- and two-family homes than do comparable white house-holds, largely because of the perverse negative effect of socioeconomic status on this outcome for whites.

5. Bonnett 1981: 352. A "box hand" refers to the amount of money a member of a rotating or credit association can withdraw from the general fund.

6. Massey and Lundy 2001.

7. Waters 1999.

8. Vickerman 1999.

9. Waters 1999, 2001.

10. Waters 1999.

11. In a similar way, many middle-class blacks go to great lengths to tele-graph their class status, particularly in public, so as to avoid being mistaken for a "ghetto" black and to avoid discrimination (Anderson 1990; Feagin and Sikes 1994).

12. Loury 2005.

13. Vickerman 1999.

14. Bashi Bobb and Clarke 2001: 226.

15. Bashi Bobb and Clarke 2001: 233.

16. Waters 1999.

17. For example, Alba and Logan 1991; Alba, Logan, and Bellair 1994; Logan and Alba 1993.

Notes to Chapter 6

1. For example, Friedman and Rosenbaum 2004, 2006.

2. Charles 2001, 2003; Farley, Fielding, and Krysan 1998; Farley, Schuman, et al. 1978; Farley, Steeh, et al. 1993; Zubrinsky and Bobo 1997.

3. Darden 1987.

4. Zubrinsky and Bobo 1997.

5. Hevesi 1995; Lueck 1991; Schill 1996.

6. Turner 1993; Yinger 1995.

7. Portes 1995; Portes and Zhou 1993; Zhou 1997a.

8. For example, see Harker 2001; K. Harris 1999; Kao 1999.

9. Gans 1992; Waters 1994.

10. Massey and Lundy 2001.

11. Waters 1999.

12. Aleinikoff 2001; Firestone 1997; Tumlin and Zimmerman 2003.

13. Bean et al. 1997; Fix et al. 1996.

14. Fix et al. 1996.

15. Friedman, Schill, and Rosenbaum 1999.

16. Waldinger and Lichter 2003.

17. Schmitt 2001.
18. Winnick 1990.
19. Sanjek 1998.
20. Darden 1987.
21. Friedman and Rosenbaum 2004, 2006.
22. Massey and Denton 1993.
23. Fix, Galster, and Struyk 1992.
24. Schill and Friedman 1999.
25. Fix and Turner 1999.
26. Squires, Friedman, and Saidat 2002.
27. Listokin and Listokin 2001.
28. Hevesi 2003.
29. Newman and Schnare 1997; see also Goering, Stebbins, and Siewert 1995; Varady and Walker 2000.
30. Millennial Housing Commission 2002.
31. Friedman, Schill, and Rosenbaum 1999.
32. See appendix C, table C.5.
33. See appendix C, table C.9.
34. See appendix C, tables C.6, C.7, and C.8, respectively.
35. Goering, Stebbins, and Siewert 1995; Turner 1998.
36. Goering, Stebbins, and Siewert 1995; Turner 1998.
37. Rosenbaum, Harris, and Denton 2003.
38. Millennial Housing Commission 2002.
39. Bhalla, et al. 2004.
40. Bhalla et al. 2004.
41. Wallin, Schill, and Daniels 2002.
42. This figure and subsequent figures in this paragraph come from the authors' tabulations of the 1999 New York City Housing and Vacancy Survey data.
43. A. Schwartz 1999; van Ryzin and Genn 1999; Wylde 1999.
44. See, for example, Bernstein 1994; Finder 1995; Purdy 1994.
45. Ellen, Schill, Susin, and Schwartz 2001.
46. A. Schwartz 1999; van Ryzin and Genn 1999.
47. Skogan 1990.
48. van Ryzin and Genn 1999.
49. Silver 1999.
50. Friedman and Squires 2005.

Notes to Appendix A

1. Alba and Logan 1992b; Alba, Logan, and Stults 2000b; Krivo 1995.
2. Alba, Logan, and Stults 2000b.

3. Rosenbaum, Friedman, Schill, and Buddelmeyer 1999; Schill, Friedman, and Rosenbaum 1998.

4. Jensen 1991; Rosenbaum 1996a.

5. Blau and Duncan 1967.

6. Alba and Logan 1991, 1993; Alba, Logan, Stults, Marzan, and Zhang 1999; Logan and Alba 1993; Logan, Alba, McNulty and Fisher 1996; Rosenbaum and Friedman 2001.

7. Blau and Duncan 1967.

8. Alba and Logan 1992b.

9. Logan and Alba 1993.

10. Greene 1997.

11. Greene 1997.

12. See, for example, Myers and Lee 1996.

References

Aaronson, Daniel. 2000. "A Note on the Benefits of Homeownership." *Journal of Urban Economics* 47: 356–69.

Adams, John. 1987. *Housing America in the 1980s*. New York: Russell Sage Foundation.

Adelman, Robert. 2004. "Neighborhood Opportunities, Race, and Class: The Black Middle Class and Residential Segregation." *City and Community* 3: 43–64.

Alba, Richard, and John Logan. 1991. "Variations on Two Themes: Racial and Ethnic Patterns in the Attainment of Suburban Residence." *Demography* 28: 431–53.

———. 1992a. "Assimilation and Stratification in Home Ownership Patterns of Racial and Ethnic Group." *International Migration Review* 26: 1314–41.

———. 1992b. "Analyzing Locational Attainments: Constructing Individual-Level Regression Models Using Aggregate-Level Data." *Sociological Methods and Research* 20: 367–97.

———. 1993. "Minority Proximity to Whites in Suburbs: An Individual-Level Analysis of Segregation." *American Journal of Sociology* 98: 1388–1427.

Alba, Richard, John Logan, and Paul Bellair. 1994. "Living with Crime: The Implications of Racial/Ethnic Differences in Suburban Location." *Social Forces* 73: 395–434.

Alba, Richard, John Logan, and Brian Stults. 2000a. "How Segregated Are Middle-Class African Americans?" *Social Problems* 47: 543–58.

———. 2000b. "The Changing Neighborhood Contexts of the Immigrant Metropolis." *Social Forces* 79: 587–621.

Alba, Richard, John Logan, Brian Stults, Gilbert Marzan, and Wenquan Zhang. 1999. "Immigrant Groups in Suburbs: A Reexamination of Suburbanization and Spatial Assimilation," *American Sociological Review* 64: 446–60.

Alba, Richard, John Logan, Wenquan Zhang, and Brian Stults. 1999. "Strangers Next Door: Immigrants and Suburbs in Los Angeles and New York." In *A Nation Divided: Diversity, Inequality, and Community in American Society*, edited by Phyllis Moen, Donna Dempster-McClain, and Henry Walker. Ithaca, N. Y.: Cornell University Press.

Alba, Richard, and Victor Nee. 1997. "Rethinking Assimilation Theory for a New Era of Immigration." *International Migration Review* 31: 826–74.
———. 2003. *Remaking the American Mainstream: Assimilation and Contemporary Immigration.* Cambridge, Mass.: Harvard University Press.
Aleinikoff, T. Alexander. 2001. "Policing Boundaries: Migration, Citizenship, and the State." In *E Pluribus Unum: Contemporary and Historical Perspectives on Immigrant Political Incorporation,* edited by Gary Gerstle and John Mollenkopf. New York: Russell Sage Foundation.
Anbinder, Tyler. 2001. *Five Points: The Nineteenth-Century New York City Neighborhood That Invented Tap Dance, Stole Elections, and Became the World's Most Notorious Slum.* New York: Free Press.
Anderson, Elijah. 1990. *Streetwise: Race, Class, and Change in an Urban Community.* Chicago: University of Chicago Press.
Bankston, Carl, and Min Zhou. 1997. "The Social Adjustment of Vietnamese-American Adolescents: Evidence for a Segmented Assimilation Approach." *Social Science Quarterly* 78: 508–23.
Bashi, Vilna. 1998. "Racial Categories Matter Because Racial Hierarchies Matter: A Commentary." *Racial and Ethnic Studies* 21: 959–68.
Bashi, Vilna, and Antonio McDaniel. 1997. "A Theory of Immigration and Racial Stratification." *Journal of Black Studies* 27: 668–82.
Bashi Bobb, Vilna, and Averil Clarke. 2001. "Experiencing Success: Structuring the Perception of Opportunities for West Indians." In *Islands in the City: West Indian Migration to New York,* edited by Nancy Foner. Berkeley: University of California Press.
Bean, Frank, Jorge Chapa, Ruth Berg, and Kathryn Sowards. 1994. "Educational and Sociodemographic Incorporation among Hispanic Immigrants to the United States." In *Immigration and Ethnicity: The Integration of America's Newest Arrivals,* edited by Barry Edmonston and Jeffrey Passel. Washington, D.C.: Urban Institute Press.
Bean, Frank D., Jennifer V. W. Van Hook and Jennifer E. Glick. 1997. "Country of Origin, Type of Public Assistance, and Patterns of Welfare Recipiency among U.S. Immigrants and Natives." *Social Science Quarterly* 78 (2): 432–51.
Bean, Frank, and Gillian Stevens. 2003. *America's Newcomers and the Dynamics of Diversity.* New York: Russell Sage Foundation.
Benjamin, Gerald. 1974. *Race Relations and the New York City Commission on Human Rights.* Ithaca, N.Y.: Cornell University Press.
Berlin, Ira. 1974. *Slaves without Masters: The Free Negro in the Antebellum South.* New York: Pantheon.
Bernstein, Emily. 1994. "A New Bradhurst: Harlem Trades Symbols of Decay for Symbols of Renewal." *New York Times,* January 6.

Bhalla, Caroline K., Ioan Voicu, Rachel Meltzer, Ingrid Gould Ellen, and Vicki Been. 2004. *State of New York City's Housing and Neighborhoods, 2004.* New York: New York University School of Law; Furman Center for Real Estate and Urban Policy.

Binder, Thomas, and David Reimers. 1995. *All the Nations under Heaven: An Ethnic and Racial History of New York City.* New York: Columbia University Press.

Biondi, Martha. 2003. *To Stand and Deliver: The Struggle for Civil Rights in Post-War New York City.* Cambridge, Mass.: Harvard University Press.

Blackmar, Elizabeth. 1989. *Manhattan for Rent, 1785–1850.* Ithaca, N.Y.: Cornell University Press.

———. 1995. "Accountability for Public Health: Regulating the Housing Market in Nineteenth-Century New York City." In *Hives of Sickness,* edited by David Rosner. New Brunswick, N.J.: Rutgers University Press.

Blau, Peter, and Otis Dudley Duncan. 1967. *The American Occupational Structure.* New York: Free Press.

Boehm, Thomas P., and Alan M. Schlottmann. 1999. "Does Homeownership by Parents Have an Economic Impact on Their Children?" *Journal of Housing Economics* 8: 217–32.

Bonnett, Aubrey. 1981. "Structured Adaptation of Black Migrants from the Caribbean: An Examination of an Indigenous Banking System in Brooklyn." *Phylon* 42: 346–55.

Bowles, Pete. 1992. "Guilty in Firebombing: Fueled Brooklyn Racial Clashes." *New York Newsday,* April 21. p.8.

Braconi, Frank. 1999. "In Re *In Rem:* Innovation and Expediency in New York's Housing Policy." In *Housing and Community Development in New York City: Facing the Future,* edited by Michael Schill. Albany: SUNY Press.

Brooks-Gunn, Jeanne, Greg Duncan, and J. Lawrence Aber. 1997. *Neighborhood Poverty, Vol. 1: Context and Consequences for Children.* New York: Russell Sage Foundation.

Buell, Emmet. 1982. *School Desegregation and Defended Neighborhoods.* Lexington, Mass.: Lexington Books.

Burrows, Edwin, and Mike Wallace. 1995. *Gotham: A History of New York City to 1898.* New York: Oxford University Press.

Capeci, Dominic, Jr. 1978. "Fiorello H. La Guardia and the Stuyvesant Town Controversy 1943." *New-York Historical Society Quarterly* 62: 289–310.

Caro, Robert. 1974. *The Power Broker: Robert Moses and the Fall of New York.* New York: Vintage Books.

Casimir, Leslie. 2000. "Ad Rips Growing American City: Group Encourages a No-Immigrant Policy." *Daily News,* October 12. p.2.

Charles, Camille. 2001. "Processes of Racial Residential Segregation." In *Urban*

Inequality: Evidence from Four Cities, edited by Alice O'Connor, Chris Tilly, and Lawrence Bobo. New York: Russell Sage Foundation.

Charles, Camille. 2003. "The Dynamics of Racial Residential Segregation." *Annual Review of Sociology* 29: 167–207.

Chin, Charlie. 1995. "Chinatown." In *Encyclopedia of New York City,* edited by Kenneth T. Jackson. New Haven, Conn.: Yale University Press.

Clark, William A. V. 1986. "Residential Segregation in American Cities: A Review and Reinterpretation." *Population Research and Policy Review* 8: 193–97.

———. 2003. *Immigrants and the American Dream.* New York: Guilford Press.

Condran, Gretchen. 1995. "Changing Patterns of Epidemic Disease in New York City." In *Hives of Sickness,* edited by David Rosner. New Brunswick, N.J.: Rutgers University Press.

Conley, Dalton. 1999. *Being Black, Living in the Red: Race, Wealth, and Social Policy in America.* Berkeley: University of California Press.

———. 2001. "A Room with a View or a Room of One's Own? Housing and Social Stratification." *Sociological Forum* 16: 263–80.

Connelly, Harold X. 1977. *A Ghetto Grows in Brooklyn.* New York: New York University Press.

Cromley, Elizabeth. 1990. *Alone Together: A History of New York's Earliest Apartments.* Ithaca, N.Y.: Cornell University Press.

Crowder, Kyle. 2000. "The Racial Context of White Mobility: An Individual-Level Assessment of the White Flight Hypothesis." *Social Science Research* 29: 223–57

Crowder, Kyle. 2001. "Racial Stratification in the Actuation of Mobility Expectations: Microlevel Impacts of Racially Restrictive Housing Markets." *Social Forces* 79: 1377–96.

Crowder, Kyle, and Lucky Tedrow. 2001. "West Indians and the Residential Landscape of New York." In *Islands in the City: West Indian Migration to New York,* edited by Nancy Foner. Berkeley: University of California Press.

Darden, Joe. 1987. "Choosing Neighbors and Neighborhoods: The Role of Race in Housing Preferences." In *Divided Neighborhoods: Changing Patterns of Racial Segregation,* edited by Gary Tobin. Beverly Hills, Calif.: Sage.

Day, Jared. 1999. *Urban Castles: Tenement Housing and Landlord Activism in New York City, 1890–1943.* New York: Columbia University Press.

Deane, Glenn. 1990. "Mobility and Adjustments: Paths to the Resolution of Residential Stress." *Demography* 27: 65–79.

Denton, Nancy, and Douglas Massey. 1988. "Residential Segregation of Blacks, Hispanics, and Asians by Socioeconomic Status and Generation." *Social Science Quarterly* 69: 797–817.

———. 1989. "Racial Identity among Caribbean Hispanics: The Effect of Double Minority Status on Residential Segregation." *American Sociological Review* 54: 790–808.

———. 1991. "Patterns of Neighborhood Transition in a Multiethnic World: U.S. Metropolitan Areas, 1970–1980." *Demography* 28: 41–63.

DeSena, Judith. 1990. *Protecting One's Turf: Social Strategies for Maintaining Urban Neighborhoods.* Lanham, Md.: University Press of America.

DeWind, Josh, and Philip Kasinitz. 1997. "Everything Old Is New Again? Processes and Theories of Immigrant Incorporation." *International Migration Review* 31: 1096–1111.

Dobkowski, Michael, and Allen Share. 1995. "Hebrew Immigrant Aid Society." In *Encyclopedia of New York City,* edited by Kenneth T. Jackson. New Haven, Conn.: Yale University Press.

Docs4Kids Project of Boston Medical Center, Children's Hospital. 1998. *Not Safe at Home: How America's Housing Crisis Threatens the Health of Children.* Boston: The Project.

Duncan, Greg, and Sandra Newman. 1975. "People as Planners: The Fulfillment of Residential Mobility Expectations." In *Five Thousand American Families: Patterns of Economic Progress, vol. 3,* edited by Greg Duncan and J. N. Morgan. Ann Arbor, Mich.: Institute for Social Research.

Duncan, Otis, and Beverly Duncan. 1957. *The Negro Population of Chicago: A Study of Residential Succession.* Chicago: University of Chicago Press.

Dunn, James. 2002. "Housing and Inequalities in Health: A Study of Socioeconomic Dimensions of Housing and Self-Reported Health from a Survey of Vancouver Residents." *Journal of Epidemiology and Community Health* 56: 671–81.

Dunn, James, and Michael Hayes. 2000. "Social Inequality, Population Health, and Housing: A Study of Two Vancouver Neighborhoods." *Social Science and Medicine* 51: 563–87.

Ellen, Ingrid Gould. 2000. *Sharing America's Neighborhoods: The Prospects for Stable Racial Integration.* Cambridge, Mass.: Harvard University Press.

Ellen, Ingrid Gould, Tod Mijanovich, and Keri-Nicole Dillman. 2001. "Neighborhood Effects on Health: Exploring the Links and Assessing the Evidence." *Journal of Urban Affairs* 23: 391–408.

Ellen, Ingrid Gould, Michael Schill, Scott Susin, and Amy Ellen Schwartz. 2001. "Building Homes, Reviving Neighborhoods: Spillovers from Subsidized Construction of Owner-Occupied Housing in New York City." *Journal of Housing Research* 12: 185–216.

Ellen, Ingrid Gould, and Margery Austin Turner. 1998. "Does Neighborhood Matter? Assessing Recent Evidence." *Housing Policy Debate* 8: 833–66.

———. 2003. "Do Neighborhoods Matter and Why?" In *Choosing a Better Life? Evaluating the Moving to Opportunity Social Experiment,* edited by John Goering and Judith Feins. Washington, D.C.: Urban Institute Press.

Ernst, Robert. [1949] 1994. *Immigrant Life in New York City, 1825–1863.* Syracuse, N.Y.: Syracuse University Press.

Espino, Rodolfo, and Michael Franz. 2002. "Latino Phenotypic Discrimination Revisited: The Impact of Skin Color on Occupational Status." *Social Science Quarterly* 83: 612–23.

Evans, Gary, Nancy Wells, and Annie Moch. 2003. "Housing and Mental Health: A Review of the Evidence and a Methodological and Conceptual Critique." *Journal of Social Issues* 59: 475–500.

Farley, Reynolds. 1996a. *The New American Reality: Who We Are, How We Got Here, Where We Are Going.* New York: Russell Sage Foundation.

———. 1996b. "Black-White Segregation: The Views of Myrdal in the 1940s and Trends of the 1980s." In *An American Dilemma Revisited: Race Relations in a Changing World,* edited by Obie Clayton. New York: Russell Sage Foundation.

Farley, Reynolds, and Richard Alba. 2002. "The New Second Generation in the United States." *International Migration Review* 36: 669–701.

Farley, Reynolds, Elaine Fielding, and Maria Krysan. 1998. "The Residential Preferences of Blacks and Whites: A Four Metropolis Analysis." *Housing Policy Debate* 8: 763–800.

Farley, Reynolds, and William Frey. 1994. "Changes in the Segregation of Whites from Blacks during the 1980s: Small Steps toward a More Racially Integrated Society." *American Sociological Review* 59: 23–45.

Farley, Reynold, Tara Jackson, Keith Reeves, Charlotte Steeh, and Maria Krysan. 1994. "Stereotypes and Segregation: Neighborhoods in the Detroit Area." *American Journal of Sociology* 100: 750–80.

Farley, Reynolds, Howard Schuman, Suzanne Bianchi, Diane Colasanto, and Shirley Hatchett. 1978. " 'Chocolate City, Vanilla Suburbs': Will the Trend toward Racially Separate Communities Continue?" *Social Science Research* 7: 319–44.

Farley, Reynolds, Charlotte Steeh, Tara Jackson, Maria Krysan, and Keith Reeves. 1993. "Continued Racial Residential Segregation in Detroit: 'Chocolate City, Vanilla Suburbs' Revisited." *Journal of Housing Research* 4: 1–38.

Feagin, Joe, and Melvin Sikes. 1994. *Living with Racism: The Black Middle-Class Experience.* Boston: Beacon Press.

Finder, Alan. 1995. "New York Pledge to House Poor Works a Rare, Quiet Revolution." *New York Times,* April 30. Section 1, p.1.

Firestone, David. 1997. "Rise in Hunger Prompts City to Approve $2 Million for Food." *New York Times,* November 27. Section B, p.1.

Fitchen, Janet M. 1980. *Poverty in Rural America: A Case Study.* Boulder, Colo.: Westview Press.

———. 1994. "Residential Mobility among the Rural Poor." *Rural Sociology* 59: 416–36.

Fitzpatrick, Joseph. 1971. *Puerto Rican Americans: The Meaning of Migration to the Mainland.* Englewood Cliffs, N.J.: Prentice-Hall.

Fix, Michael, George C. Coalster, and Raymond J. Struyk. 1992. An overview of auditing for discrimination. In *Clear and Convincing Evidence: Measurement of Discrimination in America,* edited by Michael Fix and Raymond J. Struyk, p. 1–67. Washington, D.C.: Urban Institute Press.

Fix, Michael, Jeffrey S. Passel, and Wendy Zimmerman. 1996. The Use of SSI and other Welfare Programs by Immigrants. Testimony before the House Representatives Ways and Means Committee. Washington, D.C.: The Urban Institute Press.

Fix, Michael, and Margery A. Turner. 1999. *A National Report Card on Discrimination in America: the Role of Testing.* Washington, D.C.: The Urban Institute Press.

Foley, Donald. 1980. "The Sociology of Housing." *Annual Review of Sociology* 6: 457–78.

Foner, Nancy. 2000. *From Ellis Island to JFK: New York's Two Great Waves of Immigration.* New Haven, Conn.: Yale University Press.

———. 2002. "Response." *Journal of American Ethnic History* 20: 102–19.

Fong, Eric, and Kimiko Shibuya. 2000. "Suburbanization and Home Ownership: The Spatial Assimilation Process in U.S. Metropolitan Areas." *Sociological Perspectives* 43: 137–57.

Freeman, Lance. 1999. "A Note on the Influence of African Heritage on Segregation: The Case of Dominicans." *Urban Affairs Review* 35: 137–46.

Frey, William, and Reynolds Farley. 1996. "Latino, Asian, and Black Segregation in U.S. Metropolitan Areas: Are Multiethnic Metros Different?" *Demography* 33: 35–50.

Friedman, Samantha, and Emily Rosenbaum. 2004. "Nativity-Status Differences in Access to Quality Housing: Does Home Ownership Bring Greater Parity?" *Housing Policy Debate* 15: 865–902.

———. 2006. "Does Suburban Residence Mean Better Neighborhood Conditions for All Households?" *Social Science Research* (in press).

Friedman, Samantha, Michael Schill, and Emily Rosenbaum. 1999. "The Utilization of Housing Assistance by Immigrants in the United States and New York City." *Housing Policy Debate* 10: 443–75.

Friedman, Samantha, and Gregory Squires. 2005. "Does the Community Reinvestment Act Help Minorities Access Traditionally Inaccessible Neighborhoods?" *Social Problems* 52: 209–31.

Galster, George, Kurt Metzger, and Ruth Waite. 1999. "Neighborhood Opportunity Structures of Immigrant Populations, 1980 and 1990." *Housing Policy Debate* 10: 395–442.

Gambardello, Joseph. 1991. "Realty Office Bombed Again." *New York Newsday,* September 25. p.22.

Gans, Herbert. 1992. "Second-Generation Decline: Scenarios for the Economic and Ethnic Futures of the Post-1965 American Immigrants." *Ethnic and Racial Studies* 15: 173–92.

———. 1999. "The Possibility of a New Racial Hierarchy in the Twenty-first-Century United States." In *The Cultural Territories of Race: Black and White Boundaries,* edited by Michele Lamont. Chicago: University of Chicago Press.

———. 2004. "The American Kaleidoscope, Then and Now." In *Reinventing the Melting Pot: The New Immigrants and What It Means to Be American,* edited by Tamar Jacoby. New York: Basic Books.

Genevro, Rosalie. 1986. "Site Selection and the New York City Housing Authority, 1934–1939." *Journal of Urban History* 12: 334–52.

Gerstle, Gary. 1999. "Liberty, Coercion, and the Making of Americans." In *The Handbook of International Migration: The American Experience,* edited by Charles Hirschman, Philip Kasinitz, and Josh DeWind. New York: Russell Sage Foundation.

Glick, Jennifer, and Michael White. 2003. "The Academic Trajectories of Immigrant Youths: Analysis within and across Cohorts." *Demography* 40: 759–83.

Goering, John, Helene Stebbins, and Michael Siewert. 1995. "Promoting Choice in HUD's Rental Assistance Programs." Washington, D.C.: U.S. Department of Housing and Urban Development.

Gordon, Milton. 1964. *Assimilation in American Life.* New York: Oxford University Press.

Green, Richard, and Michelle White. 1997. "Measuring the Benefits of Home-owning: Effects on Children." *Journal of Urban Economics* 41: 441–61

Greenberg, Cheryl. 1991. *Or Does It Explode? Black Harlem in the Great Depression.* New York: Oxford University Press.

Greene, William. 1997. *Econometric Analysis,* 3rd ed. Upper Saddle River, N.J.: Prentice Hall.

Groneman, Carol, and David Reimers. 1995. "Immigration." In *Encyclopedia of New York City,* edited by Kenneth T. Jackson. New Haven, Conn.: Yale University Press.

Gross, Andrew, and Douglas Massey. 1991. "Spatial Assimilation Models: A Micro-Macro Comparison." *Social Science Quarterly* 72: 347–60.

Gurock, Jeffrey. 1979. *When Harlem Was Jewish, 1870–1930.* New York: Columbia University Press.

———. 1995. "Jews." In *Encyclopedia of New York City,* edited by Kenneth T. Jackson. New Haven, Conn.: Yale University Press. .

Hammack, David. 1987. *Power and Society: Greater New York at the Turn of the Century.* New York: Columbia University Press.

Harker, Kathryn. 2001. "Immigrant Generation, Assimilation, and Adolescent Psychological Well-Being." *Social Forces* 79: 969–1004.

Harkness, Joseph, and Sandra Newman. 2003. "Differential Effects of Home-ownership on Children from Higher- and Lower-Income Families." *Journal of Housing Research* 14: 1–19.

Harris, David. 1999. " 'Property Values Drop When Blacks Move In, Because . . .': Racial and Socioeconomic Determinants of Neighborhood Desirability." *American Sociological Review* 64: 461–79.

Harris, Kathleen Mullan. 1999. "The Health Status and Risk Behaviors of Adolescents in Immigrant Families." In *Children of Immigrants: Health, Adjustment, and Public Assistance,* edited by Donald Hernandez. Washington, D.C.: National Academy Press.

Harris, Leslie. 2003. *In the Shadow of Slavery: African Americans in New York City, 1629–1863.* Chicago: University of Chicago Press.

Haurin, Donald, Toby Parcel, and R. Jean Haurin. 1998. "The Impact of Homeownership on Child Outcomes." Unpublished paper.

Hevesi, Dennis. 1995. "Four in Brooklyn Are Fined $40,000 for Prejudice in Renting to Minorities." *New York Times,* May 10. Section B, p.3.

———. 2003. "Chinatown Journey: From Protesters to Developers." *New York Times,* January 12. Section 11, p.1.

Hirschman, Charles. 1996. "Studying Immigrant Adaptation from the 1990 Population Census: From Generational Comparisons to the Process of 'Becoming American.' " In *The New Second Generation,* edited by Alejandro Portes. New York: Russell Sage Foundation.

———. 2001. "The Educational Enrollment of Immigrant Youth: A Test of the Segmented Assimilation Hypothesis." *Demography* 38: 317–36.

Hochschild, Jennifer. 1995. *Facing Up to the American Dream: Race, Class, and the Soul of the Nation.* Princeton, N.J.: Princeton University Press.

Howe, Irving. 1976. *World of Our Fathers.* New York: Harcourt Brace Jovanovich.

Iceland, John. 2004. "Beyond Black and White: Metropolitan Residential Segregation in Multi-ethnic America." *Social Science Research* 33: 248–71.

Iceland, John, Daniel Weinberg, and Erika Steinmetz. 2002. *Racial and Ethnic Segregation in the United States: 1980–2000.* Washington, D.C: U.S. Census Bureau.

Ignatiev, Noel. 1995. *How the Irish Became White.* New York: Routledge.

Jackson, Anthony. 1976. *A Place Called Home: A History of Low-Cost Housing in Manhattan.* Cambridge, Mass.: MIT Press.

Jackson, Kenneth. 1985. *Crabgrass Frontier: The Suburbanization of the United States.* New York: Oxford University Press.

Jacobson, Matthew Frye. 1998. *Whiteness of a Different Color: European Immigrants and the Alchemy of Race.* Cambridge, Mass.: Harvard University Press.

Jencks, Christopher, and Susan Meyer. 1991. "The Social Consequences of

Growing Up in a Poor Neighborhood." In *Inner-City Poverty in the United States,* edited by Lawrence Lynn and Michael McGeary. Washington, D.C.: National Academy Press.

Jensen, Leif. 1991. "Secondary Earner Strategies and Family Poverty: Immigrant-Native Differentials, 1960–1980." *International Migration Review* 25: 113–39.

Johnson, James, Walter Farrell, and Chandra Guinn. 1999. "Immigration Reform and the Browning of America: Tensions, Conflicts, and Community Instability in Metropolitan Los Angeles." In *Handbook of International Migration: The American Experience,* edited by Charles Hirschman, Philip Kasinitz, and Josh DeWind. New York: Russell Sage Foundation.

Jones-Correa, Michael. 1998. *Between Two Nations: The Political Predicament of Latinos in New York City.* Ithaca, N.Y.: Cornell University Press.

Joseph, Samuel. 1914. *Jewish Immigration to the United States from 1881 to 1910.* New York: Columbia University Press.

Kantrowitz, Nathan 1995. "Population." In *Encyclopedia of New York City,* edited by Kenneth T. Jackson. New Haven, Conn.: Yale University Press.

Kao, Grace. 1999. "Psychological Well-Being and Educational Achievement among Immigrant Youth." In *Children of Immigrants: Health, Adjustment, and Public Assistance,* edited by Donald Hernandez. Washington, D.C.: National Academy Press.

Kao, Grace, and Marta Tienda. 1995. "Optimism and Achievement: The Educational Performance of Immigrant Youth." *Social Science Quarterly* 76: 1–19.

Kasinitz, Philip. 1987–88. "The Minority Within: The New Black Immigrants." *New York Affairs* 10: 44–58.

———. 1992. *Caribbean New York: Black Immigrants and the Politics of Race.* Ithaca, N.Y.: Cornell University Press.

———. 2001. "Invisible No More? West Indian Americans in the Social Scientific Imagination." In *Islands in the City: West Indian Migration to New York,* edited by Nancy Foner. Berkeley: University of California Press.

Kasinitz, Philie, John Mollenkopf, and Mary Waters. 2002. "Becoming American/Becoming New Yorkers: Immigrant Incorporation in a Majority Minority City." *International Migration Review* 36: 1020–36.

Kessner, Thomas. 1977. *The Golden Door: Italian and Jewish Immigrant Mobility in New York City, 1880–1915.* New York: Oxford University Press.

———. 1989. *Fiorello H. La Guardia and the Making of Modern New York.* New York: Penguin.

Kilgannon, Corey. 2004. "Ethnic Friction over Signs That Lack Translation." *New York Times,* January 10. Section B, p.5.

Kraly, Ellen, and Ines Miyares. 2001. "Immigration to New York: Policy, Population, and Patterns." In *New Immigrants in New York,* edited by Nancy Foner. New York: Columbia University Press.

Krivo, Lauren. 1995. "Immigrant Characteristics and Hispanic-Anglo Housing Inequality." *Demography* 32: 599–616.

Krysan, Maria. 2002a. "Whites Who Say They'd Flee: Who Are They, and Why Would They Leave?" *Demography* 39: 675–96.

———. 2002b. "Community Undesirability in Black and White: Examining Racial Residential references through Community Preferences." *Social Problems* 49: 521–43.

Krysan, Maria, and Reynolds Farley. 2002. "The Residential Preferences of Blacks: Do They Explain Persistent Segregation?" *Social Forces* 80: 937–80.

Kwong, Peter. 1987. *The New Chinatown.* New York: Hill and Wang.

Laidlaw, Walter. 1932. *Population of the City of New York, 1890–1930.* New York: Cities Census Committee.

Landale, Nancy, R. Salvatore Oropesa, and Bridget Gorman. 1999. "Immigration and Infant Health: Birth Outcomes of Immigrant and Native-Born Women." In *Children of Immigrants: Health, Adjustment, and Public Assistance,* edited by Donald Hernandez. Washington, D.C.: National Academy Press.

———. 2000. "Migration and Infant Death: Assimilation or Selective Migration among Puerto Ricans?" *American Sociological Review* 65: 888–909.

Lazaroff Leon. 2003. "One Town's Struggle to Accept Immigrants: An Influx of Immigrants has Brought Tension and Violence to a Long Island Community." *Christian Science Monitor.* July 23. p.3.

Leahy, Peter. 1985. "Are Racial Factors Important for the Allocation of Mortgage Money?" *American Journal of Economics and Sociology* 44: 185–96

Lee, Barrett. 1978. "Residential Mobility on Skid Row: Disaffiliation, Powerlessness, and Decision Making." *Demography* 15: 285–300.

Lee, Barrett, R. Salvatore Oropesa, and James Kanan. 1994. "Neighborhood Context and Residential Mobility." *Demography* 31: 249–69.

Lee, Barrett, and Peter Wood. 1991. "Is Neighborhood Succession Place-Specific?" *Demography* 28: 21–40.

Leventhal, Tama, and Jeanne Brooks-Gunn. 2000. "The Neighborhoods They Live In: The Effects of Neighborhood Residence on Child and Adolescent Outcomes." *Psychological Bulletin* 126: 309–37.

Levy, Frank, and Richard Michel. 1991. *The Economic Future of America's Families.* Washington, D.C.: Urban Institute Press.

Lewis Mumford Center. 2006. "Ethnic Diversity Grows, Neighborhood Integration Lags Behind." December 18. Available at www.albany.edu/mumford/census.

Lieber, Joseph. 1995. "New York Association for New Americans." In *Encyclopedia of New York City,* edited by Kenneth T. Jackson. New Haven, Conn.: Yale University Press.

Listokin, David and Barbara Listokin. 2001. "Asian Americans for Equality: A

Case Study of Strategies for Expanding Immigrant Homeownership." *Housing Policy Debate* 12(1): 47–75.

Livingston, Gretchen, and Joan Kahn. 2002. "An American Dream Unfulfilled: The Limited Mobility of Mexican Americans." *Social Science Quarterly* 83: 1003–12.

Lobo, Arun Peter, and Joseph Salvo. 1999. "The Role of Nativity and Ethnicity in the Residential Settlement Patterns of Blacks in New York City: 1970–1990." In *Immigration: Pastoral and Research Challenges,* edited by Mary Powers and Lydio Tomasi. Staten Island, N.Y.: Center for Immigration Studies.

Logan, John. 1997. "The Ethnic Neighborhood, 1920–1970." Working Paper #113. New York: Russell Sage Foundation.

Logan, John, and Richard Alba. 1993. "Locational Returns to Human Capital: Minority Access to Suburban Community Resources." *Demography* 30: 243–68.

———. 1995. "Who Lives in Affluent Suburbs? Racial Differences in Eleven Metropolitan Regions." *Sociological Focus* 28: 353–64.

Logan, John, Richard Alba, Tom McNulty, and Brian Fisher. 1996. "Making a Place in the Metropolis: Locational Attainment in Cities and Suburbs." *Demography* 33: 443–53.

Logan, John, and Harvey Molotch. 1987. *Urban Fortunes: The Political Economy of Place.* Berkeley: University of California Press.

Logan, John, Brian Stults, and Reynolds Farley. 2004. "Segregation of Minorities in the Metropolis: Two Decades of Change." *Demography* 41: 1–22.

Long, Larry. 1987. *Household and Residential Mobility in the United States.* New York: Russell Sage Foundation.

Long, Larry, and Daphne Spain. 1978. "Racial Succession in Individual Housing Units." *Current Population Reports,* Series P-23, No. 71. Washington, D.C.: Government Printing Office.

Lopez, David, and Ricardo Stanton-Salazar. 2001. "Mexican Americans: A Generation at Risk." In *Ethnicities: Children of Immigrants in America,* edited by Ruben Rumbaut and Alejandro Portes. New York: Russell Sage Foundation.

Lopez Turley, Ruth. 2003. "When Do Neighborhoods Matter? The Role of Race and Neighborhood Peers." *Social Science Research* 32: 61–79.

Loury, Glenn. 2005. "Racial Stigma and Its Consequences." *Focus* 24: 1–6.

Lubove, Roy. 1974. *The Progressives and the Slums: Tenement Reform in New York City, 1890–1917.* Westport, Conn.: Greenwood Press.

Lueck, Thomas. 1991. "New York Ranks High in Housing Bias." *New York Times,* November. 3. Section A, p.10.

Marcuse, Peter. 1986. "The Beginnings of Public Housing in New York." *Journal of Urban History* 12: 353–90.

Marshall, Paule. [1959] 1981. *Brown Girl, Brownstones*. New York: Feminist Press.

Marullo, Samuel. 1985. "Targets for Racial Invasion and Reinvasion: Housing Units Where Racial Turnovers Occurred, 1974 and 1977." *Social Forces* 63: 748–75.

Massey, Douglas. 1985. "Ethnic Residential Segregation: A Theoretical Synthesis and Empirical Review." *Sociology and Social Research* 69: 315–50.

———. 1995. "The New Immigration and Ethnicity in the United States." *Population and Development Review* 21: 631–52.

———. 2001. "Residential Segregation and Neighborhood Conditions in U.S. Metropolitan Areas." In *America Becoming: Racial Trends and Their Consequences*, vol. 1, edited by Neil Smelser, William Julius Wilson, and Faith Mitchell. Washington, D.C.: National Research Council.

———. 2004a. "The American Side of the Bargain." In *Reinventing the Melting Pot: The New Immigrants and What It Means to Be American*, edited by Tamar Jacoby. New York: Basic Books.

———. 2004b. "Segregation and Stratification: A Biosocial Approach." *Du Bois Review* 1: 7–25.

Massey, Douglas, and Brooks Bitterman. 1985. "Explaining the Paradox of Puerto Rican Segregation." *Social Forces* 64: 306–31.

Massey, Douglas, Gretchen Condran, and Nancy Denton. 1987. "The Effect of Residential Segregation on Black Social and Economic Well-being." *Social Forces* 66: 29–56.

Massey, Douglas, and Nancy Denton. 1985. "Spatial Assimilation as a Socioeconomic Outcome." *American Sociological Review* 50: 94–106.

———. 1987. "Trends in the Residential Segregation of Blacks, Hispanics, and Asians: 1970–1980." *American Sociological Review* 52: 802–25.

———. 1988. "Suburbanization and Segregation in U.S. Metropolitan Areas." *American Journal of Sociology* 94: 592–626.

———. 1993. *American Apartheid: Segregation and the Making of the Underclass*. Cambridge, Mass.: Harvard University Press.

Massey, Douglas, and Mary Fischer. 1999. "Does Rising Income Bring Integration? New Results for Blacks, Hispanics, and Asians in 1990." *Social Science Research* 28: 316–26.

Massey, Douglas, Andrew Gross, and Kumiko Shibuya. 1994. "Migration, Segregation, and the Concentration of Poverty." *American Sociological Review* 59: 425–45.

Massey, Douglas, and Garvey Lundy. 2001. "Use of Black English and Racial Discrimination in Urban Housing Markets: New Methods and Findings." *Urban Affairs Review* 36: 452–69.

McLanahan, Sara, and Karen Booth. 1989. "Mother-Only Families: Problems, Prospects, and Politics." *Journal of Marriage and the Family* 51: 557–80.

Millennial Housing Commission. 2002. *Meeting Our Nation's Housing Challenges.* Washington, D.C.: The Commission.

Mollenkopf, John. 1999. "Urban Political Conflicts and Alliances: New York and Los Angeles Compared." In *Handbook of International Migration: The American Experience,* edited by Charles Hirschman, Philip Kasinitz, and Josh DeWind. New York: Russell Sage Foundation.

Moore, Deborah Dash. 1992. "On the Fringes of the City: Jewish Neighborhoods in Three Boroughs." In *Landscape of Modernity: Essays on New York City, 1900–1940* , edited by David Ward and Oliver Zunz. New York: Russell Sage Foundation.

Muller, Thomas. 1993. *Immigrants and the American City.* New York: New York University Press.

Munnell, Alicia, Lynn Browne, James McEneaney, and Geoffrey Tootell. 1992. *Mortgage Lending in Boston: Interpreting HMDA Data,* Working Paper No. 92-7. Boston: Federal Reserve Bank of Boston.

Myers, Dowell, and Seong Woo Lee. 1996. "Immigration Cohorts and Residential Overcrowding in Southern California." *Demography* 33: 51–65.

Nadel, Stanley. 1990. *Little Germany: Ethnicity, Religion, and Class in New York City, 1845–80.* Urbana: University of Illinois Press.

Neckerman, Kathryn, Prudence Carter, and Jennifer Lee. 1999. "Segmented Assimilation and Minority Cultures of Mobility." *Racial and Ethnic Studies* 22: 945–65.

New York City Department of City Planning. 1982. *The Puerto Rican New Yorkers: A Recent History of their Distribution and Population and Household Characteristics.* New York: The Department.

———. 1988. *Caribbean Immigrants in New York City: A Demographic Summary.* New York: The Department.

———. 1992. *The Newest New Yorkers: An Analysis of Immigration into New York City during the 1980s.* New York: The Department.

———. 1996. *The Newest New Yorkers, 1990–1994: An Analysis of Immigration to NYC in the Early '90s.* New York: The Department.

———. 1999. *The Newest New Yorkers 1995–1996: An Update of Immigration to NYC in the Mid-'90s.* New York: The Department.

New York Times. 1990. "New York Times Race Relations Survey, March 1987: New York City." Computer file. New York: New York Times (producer); Ann Arbor, MI: Inter-university Consortium for Political and Social Research (distributor).

Newman, Sandra, and Greg Duncan. 1979. "Residential Problems, Dissatisfaction, and Mobility." *Journal of the American Planning Association* 45: 154–66.

Newman, Sandra, and Ann Schnare. 1997. " '. . . And a Suitable Living Environment': The Failure of Housing Programs to Deliver on Neighborhood Quality." *Housing Policy Debate* 8: 703–41.

Oliver, Melvin, and Thomas Shapiro. 1995. *Black Wealth/White Wealth: A New Perspective on Racial Inequality.* New York: Routledge.

Orleck, Annelise. 2001. "Soviet Jews: The City's Newest Immigrants Transform New York Jewish Life." In *New Immigrants in New York,* edited by Nancy Foner. New York: Columbia University Press.

Oropesa, R. Salvatore, and Nancy Landale. 1997. "Immigrant Legacies: Ethnicity, Generation, and Children's Familial and Economic Lives." *Social Science Quarterly* 78: 399–416.

Orsi, Robert. 1985. *The Madonna of 115th Street: Faith and Community in Italian Harlem, 1880–1950.* New Haven, Conn.: Yale University Press.

Osofsky, Gilbert. 1971. *Harlem: The Making of a Ghetto, Negro New York, 1890–1930.* New York: Harper Torchbooks.

Patillo-McCoy, Mary. 1998. "Sweet Mothers and Gangbangers: Managing Crime in a Black Middle-Class Neighborhood." *Social Forces* 76: 747–77.

———. 1999. *Black Picket Fences: Privilege and Peril among the Black Middle Class.* Chicago: University of Chicago Press.

———. 2000. "The Limits of Out-Migration for the Black Middle Class." *Journal of Urban Affairs* 22: 225–41.

Patterson, Orlando. 1997. *The Ordeal of Integration: Progress and Resentment in America's "Racial" Crisis.* Washington, D.C.: Civitas/Counterpoint.

Perlmann, Joel, and Roger Waldinger. 1999. "Immigrants, Past and Present: A Reconsideration." In *The Handbook of International Migration: The American Experience,* edited by Charles Hirschman, Philip Kasinitz, and Josh DeWind. New York: Russell Sage Foundation.

Pessar, Patricia, and Pamela Graham. 2001. "Dominicans: Transnational Identities and Local Politics." In *New Immigrants in New York,* edited by Nancy Foner. New York: Columbia University Press.

Plunz, Richard. 1990. *A History of Housing in New York City.* New York: Columbia University Press.

Plunz, Richard, and Janet Abu-Lughod. 1994. "The Tenement as a Built Form." In *From Urban Village to East Village: The Battle for New York's Lower East Side,* edited by Janet Abu-Lughod. Oxford, U.K.: Blackwell, 1994.

Portes, Alejandro. 1995. "Children of Immigrants: Segmented Assimilation and Its Determinants." In *The Economic Sociology of Immigration,* edited by Alejandro Portes. New York: Russell Sage Foundation.

———. 2004. "For the Second Generation, One Step at a Time." In *Reinventing the Melting Pot: The New Immigrants and What It Means to Be American,* edited by Tamar Jacoby. New York: Basic Books.

Portes, Alejandro, and Ruben Rumbaut. 1996. *Immigrant America: A Portrait.* Berkeley: University of California Press.

———. 2001. *Legacies: The Story of the Immigrant Second Generation.* Berkeley: University of California Press.

Portes, Alejandro, and Min Zhou. 1993. "The New Second Generation: Segmented Assimilation and Its Variants." *Annals of the American Academy of Political and Social Science.* 530: 74–96.

Pritchett, Wendell. 2002. *Brownsville, Brooklyn: Blacks, Jews, and the Changing Face of the Ghetto.* Chicago: University of Chicago Press.

Purdy, Matthew. 1994. "Left to Die, the South Bronx Rises from Decades of Decay." *New York Times,* November 3. Section 1, p.1.

Radford, Gail. 2000. "The Federal Government and Housing During the Great Depression." In *From Tenements to the Taylor Homes: In Search of an Urban Housing Policy in Twentieth-Century America,* edited by John Bauman, Roger Biles, and Kristin Szylvian. University Park.: Pennsylvania State University Press.

Reider, Jonathan. 1985. *Canarsie: The Jews and Italians of Brooklyn against Liberalism.* Cambridge, Mass.: Harvard University Press.

Reimers, David. 1992. *Still the Golden Door: The Third World Comes to America.* New York: Columbia University Press.

———. 1998. *Unwelcome Strangers: American Identity and the Turn against Immigration.* New York: Columbia University Press.

Rischin, Moses. 1962. *The Promised City: New York's Jews 1870–1914.* Cambridge, Mass.: Harvard University Press.

Rodriguez, Clara. 1989. *Puerto Ricans: Born in the U.S.A.* Boulder, Colo.: Westview.

Rohe, William, George McCarthy, and Shannon Van Zandt. 2000. *The Social Benefits and Costs of Homeownership.* Working Paper No. 00-01. Washington, D.C.: Research Institute for Housing America.

Rohe, William M., Shannon Van Zandt, and George McCarthy. 2002. "Home Ownership and Access to Opportunity." *Housing Studies* 17: 51–61.

Rosenbaum, Emily. 1989. "New Affordable Housing for New Yorkers." New York: New York City Department of Housing Preservation and Development.

———. 1992. "Race and Ethnicity in Housing: Turnover in New York City, 1978–1987." *Demography* 29: 467–86.

———. 1994. "The Structural Constraints on Minority Housing Choices." *Social Forces* 72: 725–47.

———. 1996a. "Racial/Ethnic Differences in Home Ownership and Housing Quality, 1991." *Social Problems* 43: 403–26.

———. 1996b. "The Influence of Race on Hispanic Housing Choices: New York City, 1978–1987." *Urban Affairs Review* 32: 217–43.

———. 2004. "Racial/Ethnic Differences in Asthma Prevalence: The Role of Housing and Neighborhood Environments." Paper presented at the 2004 meeting of the Population Association of America, Boston, Massachusetts.

Rosenbaum, Emily, and Grigoris Argeros. 2005. "Holding the Line: Housing Turnover and the Persistence of Racial/Ethnic Segregation in New York City, 1991–1999." *Journal of Urban Affairs* 27: 261–81.

Rosenbaum, Emily, and Samantha Friedman. 2001a. "Differences in the Locational Attainment of Immigrant and Native-Born Households with Children in New York City." *Demography* 38: 337–48.

———. 2001b. "Mobility Incidence and Turnover as Components of Neighborhood Change in New York City, 1991–1996." *Journal of Housing Research* 12: 27–53.

———. 2004. "Generational Patterns of Home Ownership and Housing Quality in New York City." *International Migration Review* 38: 1492–1533.

Rosenbaum, Emily, Samantha Friedman, Michael Schill, and Hielke Buddelmeyer. 1999. "Nativity Difference in Neighborhood Quality among New York City Households." *Housing Policy Debate* 10: 625–58.

Rosenbaum, Emily, Laura Harris, and Nancy Denton. 2003. "Findings from the Chicago Site." In *Choosing a Better Life?* edited by John Goering and Judith Feins. Washington, D.C.: Urban Institute Press.

Rosenbaum, Emily, and Michael Schill. 1999. "Housing and Neighborhood Turnover among Immigrant and Native-Born Households in New York City, 1991–1996." *Journal of Housing Research* 10: 209–34.

Rosenberg, Terry, and Robert Lake. 1976. "Toward a Revised Model of Residential Segregation and Succession: Puerto Ricans in New York, 1960–1970." *American Journal of Sociology* 81: 1142–50.

Rosenwaike, Ira. 1972. *Population History of New York City.* Syracuse, N.Y.: Syracuse University Press.

Rosner, David. 1995. "Introduction: 'Hives of Sickness and Vice.'" In *Hives of Sickness,* edited by David Rosner. New Brunswick, N.J.: Rutgers University Press.

Rossi, Peter. 1955. *Why Families Move: A Study in the Social Psychology of Urban Residential Mobility.* Glencoe, Ill.: Free Press.

Rumbaut, Ruben. 1997. "Assimilation and Its Discontents: Between Rhetoric and Reality." *International Migration Review* 31: 923–60.

———. 1999. "Assimilation and Its Discontents: Ironies and Paradoxes." In *The Handbook of International Migration: The American Experience,* edited by Charles Hirschman, Philip Kasinitz, and Josh DeWind. New York: Russell Sage Foundation.

Salins, Peter. 2004. "The Assimilation Contract—Endangered but Still Holding." In *Reinventing the Melting Pot: The New Immigrants and What It Means to Be American,* edited by Tamar Jacoby. New York: Basic Books.

Salvo, Joseph, Laurie Banks, and Evelyn Mann. 1990. "Reconceptualizing Migration as a Household Phenomenon: Outmigration from New York City by Race and Hispanic Origin." *International Migration Review* 28: 311–26.

Salvo, Joseph, and Arun Peter Lobo. 1997. "Immigration and the Changing Profile of New York." In *The City and the World,* edited by Margaret Crahan and Alberto Vourvoulias-Bush. New York: Council on Foreign Relations.

Salvo, Joseph, Ronald Ortiz, and Arun Peter Lobo. 1994. *Puerto Rican New Yorkers in 1990.* New York: New York City Department of City Planning.

Sampson, Robert, Jeffrey Morenoff, and Thomas Gannon-Rowley. 2002. "Assessing 'Neighborhood Effects': Social Processes and New Directions in Research." *Annual Review of Sociology* 28: 443–78.

Sanchez, George. 1999. "Face the Nation: Race, Immigration, and the Rise of Nativism in Late Twentieth-Century America." In *The Handbook of International Migration: The American Experience,* edited by Charles Hirschman, Philip Kasinitz, and Josh DeWind. New York: Russell Sage Foundation.

Sanchez-Korrol, Virginia. 1983. *From Colonia to Community: The History of Puerto Ricans in New York City.* Berkeley: University of California Press.

Sanjek, Roger. 1998. *The Future of Us All: Race and Neighborhood Politics in New York City.* Ithaca: Cornell University Press.

Schill, Michael. 1996. "Local Enforcement of Laws Prohibiting Discrimination in Housing: The New York City Human Rights Commission." *Fordham Urban Law Journal* 23: 991–1030.

Schill, Michael H. and Samntha Friedman. 1999. "The Fair Housing Amendments Act of 1988: The First Decade." *Cityscape: A Journal of Policy Development and Research* 4(5): 57–78.

Schill, Michael, Samantha Friedman, and Emily Rosenbaum. 1998. "The Housing Conditions of Immigrants in New York City." *Journal of Housing Research* 9: 201–35.

Schill, Michael, and Susan Wachter. 1995. "The Spatial Bias of Federal Housing Law and Policy: Concentrated Poverty in Urban America." *University of Pennsylvania Law Review* 143: 1285–1342.

Schmitt, Eric. 2001. "To Fill the Gaps, Cities Seek Wave of Immigrants." *New York Times,* May 30. Section A, p.1.

Schwartz, Alex. 1999. "New York City and Subsidized Housing: Impacts and Lessons of the City's $5 Billion Capital Budget Housing Plan." *Housing Policy Debate* 10: 839–77.

Schwartz, Joel. 1993. *The New York Approach: Robert Moses, Urban Liberals, and the Redevelopment of the Inner City.* Columbus: Ohio State University Press.

———. 1995a. "Tenements." In *Encyclopedia of New York City,* edited by Kenneth T. Jackson. New Haven, Conn.: Yale University Press.

———. 1995b. "Housing." In *Encyclopedia of New York City,* edited by Kenneth T. Jackson. New Haven, Conn.: Yale University Press.

Scott, Janny. 2001. "A Region of Enclaves: Amid a Sea of Faces, Islands of Segregation." *New York Times,* June 18. Section A, p.1.

Shammas, Carole. 2000. "The Space Problem in Early United States Cities." *William and Mary Quarterly* 57: 505–42.

Shapiro, Thomas. 2004. *The Hidden Cost of Being African American: How Wealth Perpetuates Inequality.* New York: Oxford University Press.

Shlay, Anne. 1995. "Housing in the Broader Context in the United States." *Housing Policy Debate* 6: 695–720.

Shlay, Anne, and Peter Rossi. 1981. "Keeping Up the Neighborhood: Estimating Net Effects of Zoning." *American Sociological Review* 46: 703–19.

Silver, Joshua. 1999. Email message to membership of the National Community Reinvestment Coalition. 26 January.

Skogan, Wesley. 1990. *Disorder and Decline: Crime and the Spiral of Decay in American Neighborhoods.* New York: Free Press.

Smith, Christopher. 1995. "Asian New York: The Geography and Politics of Diversity." *International Migration Review* 29: 59–84.

South, Scott, and Eric Baumer. 2000. "Deciphering Community and Race Effects on Adolescent Childbearing." *Social Forces* 78: 309–37.

South, Scott, and Kyle Crowder. 1997a. "Residential Mobility between Cities and Suburbs: Race, Suburbanization, and Back-to-the City Moves." *Demography* 34: 525–38.

———. 1997b. "Escaping Distressed Neighborhoods: Individual, Community and Metropolitan Influences." *American Journal of Sociology* 4: 1040–84.

———. 1998a. "Leaving the 'Hood: Residential Mobility between Black, White, and Integrated Neighborhoods." *American Sociological Review* 63: 17–26.

———. 1998b. "Housing Discrimination and Residential Mobility: Impacts for Blacks and Whites." *Population Research and Policy Review* 17: 369–87.

South, Scott, and Glenn Deane. 1993. "Race and Residential Mobility: Individual Determinants and Structural Constraints." *Social Forces* 72: 147–67.

Spain, Daphne. 1980. "Black-to-White Successions in Central-City Housing." *Urban Affairs Quarterly* 15: 381–96.

Spain, Daphne, John Reid, and Larry Long. 1980. "Housing Successions among Blacks and Whites in Cities and Suburbs." *Current Population Reports,* Series P-23, No. 101. Washington, D.C.: Government Printing Office.

Spann, Edward. 1981. *The New Metropolis: New York City, 1840–1857.* New York: Columbia University Press.

Speare, Alden. 1974. "Residential Satisfaction as an Intervening Variable in Residential Mobility." *Demography* 11: 173–88.

Squires, Gregory. 1994. *Capital and Communities in Black and White*. Albany: SUNY Press.

Squires, Gregory D., Samantha Friedman, and Catherine E. Saidat. 2002. "Experiencing Residential Segregation: A Contemporary Study of Washington, DC." *Urban Affairs Review* 38: 155–83.

Stansell, Christine. 1987. *City of Women: Sex and Class in New York, 1789–1860*. Urbana: University of Illinois Press.

Stepick, Alex, Guillermo Grenier, Max Castro, and Marvin Dunn. 2003. *This Land Is Our Land: Immigrants and Power in Miami*. Berkeley: University of California Press.

Stott, Richard. 1990. *Workers in the Metropolis: Class, Ethnicity, and Youth in Antebellum New York City*. Ithaca, N.Y.: Cornell University Press.

Susser, Ida. 1982. *Norman Street: Poverty and Politics in an Urban Neighborhood*. New York: Oxford University Press.

Taueber, Karl, and Alma Taeuber. 1965. *Negroes in Cities: Residential Segregation and Neighborhood Change*. Chicago: Aldine.

Thernstrom, Stephan, and Abigail Thernstrom. 1997. *America in Black and White: One Nation, Indivisible*. New York: Simon and Schuster.

Tolnay, Stewart, Kyle Crowder, and Robert Adelman. 2002. "Race, Regional Origin, and Residence in Northern Cities at the Beginning of the Great Migration." *American Sociological Review* 67: 456–75.

Tumlin, Karen, and Wendy Zimmerman. 2003. "Immigrants and TANF: A Look at Immigrant Welfare Recipients in Three Cities." Urban Institute Occasional Paper Number 69 (October). Washington, D.C.: Urban Institute.

Turner, Margery Austin. 1993. "Limits on Neighborhood Choice: Evidence of Racial and Ethnic Steering in Urban Housing Markets." In *Clear and Convincing Evidence: Measurement of Discrimination in America*, edited by Michael Fix and Raymond Struyk. Washington, D.C.: Urban Institute Press.

———. 1998. "Moving out of Poverty: Expanding Mobility and Choice through Tenant-Based Assistance." *Housing Policy Debate* 9: 373–94.

Turner, Margery Austin, Stephen Ross, George Galster, and John Yinger. 2002. *Discrimination in Metropolitan Housing Markets: National Results from Phase I HDS 2000*. Washington, D.C.: U.S. Department of Housing and Urban Development.

Turner, Margery Austin, Raymond Struyk, and John Yinger. 1991. *Housing Discrimination Study: Synthesis*. Washington, D.C.: U.S. Department of Housing and Urban Development.

van Ryzin, Gregg, and Andrew Genn. 1999. "Neighborhood Change and the City of New York's Ten-Year Housing Plan." *Housing Policy Debate* 10: 799–838.

Varady, David, and Carole Walker. 2000. "Vouchering Out Distressed Subsidized Developments: Does Moving Lead to Improvements in Housing and Neighborhood Conditions?" *Housing Policy Debate* 11: 115–62.

Vickerman, Milton. 1999. *Crosscurrent: West Indian Immigrants and Race.* New York: Oxford University Press.

———. 2001a. "Tweaking a Monolith: The West Indian Immigrant Encounter with 'Blackness.'" In *Islands in the City: West Indian Migration to New York,* edited by Nancy Foner. Berkeley: University of California Press.

———. 2001b. "Jamaicans: Balancing Race and Ethnicity." In *New Immigrants in New York,* edited by Nancy Foner. New York: Columbia University Press.

Villemez, Wayne. 1980. "Race, Class, and Neighborhood: Differences in the Residential Return on Individual Resources." *Social Forces* 59: 414–30.

Von Hoffman, Alexander. 2000. "A Study in Contradictions: The Origins and Legacy of the Housing Act of 1949." *Housing Policy Debate* 11: 299–326.

Waldinger, Roger. 1987–88. "Beyond Nostalgia: The Old Neighborhood Revisited." *New York Affairs* 10: 1–12.

———. 1996. *Still the Promised City? African-Americans and New Immigrants in Postindustrial New York.* Cambridge, Mass.: Harvard University Press.

———. 1997. "From Ellis Island to LAX: Immigrant Prospects in the American City." *International Migration Review* 30: 1078–86.

Waldinger, Roger and Michael Lichter 2003. *How the Other Half Works: Immigration and the Soicla Organization of Labor.* Berkeley: University of California Press.

Wallin, Denise, Michael H. Schill, and Glynis Daniels. 2002. *State of New York City's Housing and Neighborhoods, 2002.* New York: New York University School of Law, Furman Center for Real Estate and Urban Policy.

Wang, Xinyang. 2001. *Surviving the City: The Chinese Immigrant Experience in New York City, 1890–1970.* New York: Rowan and Littlefield.

Wasserman, Suzanne. 1994. "Deja Vu: Replanning the Lower East Side in the 1930s." In *From Urban Village to East Village: The Battle for New York's Lower East Side,* edited by Janet Abu-Lughod. Oxford, U.K.: Blackwell.

Waters, Mary. 1994. "Ethnic and Racial Identities of Second-Generation Black Immigrants in New York City." In *The New Second Generation,* edited by Alejandro Portes. New York: Russell Sage Foundation.

———. 1999. *Black Identities: West Indian Immigrant Dreams and American Realities.* New York: Russell Sage Foundation.

———. 2001. "Growing Up West Indian and African American: Gender and Class Differences in the Second Generation." In *Islands in the City: West Indian Migration to New York,* edited by Nancy Foner. Berkeley: University of California Press.

Watkins-Owens, Irma. 1996. *Blood Relations: Caribbean Immigrants and the Harlem Community, 1900–1930.* Bloomington: University of Indiana Press.

Wilder, Craig Steven. 2000. *A Covenant with Color.* New York: Columbia University Press.

Winnick, Louis. 1990. *New People in Old Neighborhoods.* New York: Russell Sage Foundation.

Wood, Peter, and Barrett Lee. 1991. "Is Neighborhood Succession Inevitable? Forty Years of Evidence." *Urban Affairs Quarterly* 26: 610–20.

Wylde, Kathryn. 1999. "The Contribution of Public-Private Partnerships to New York's Assisted Housing Industry." In *Housing and Community Development: Facing the Future,* edited by Michael Schill. Albany: SUNY Press.

Yardley, Jim. 1997. "Clinton Praises Bronx Renewal as U.S. Model." *New York Times,* December 11.

Yinger, John. 1995. *Closed Doors, Opportunities Lost: The Continuing Costs of Housing Discrimination.* New York: Russell Sage Foundation.

———. 2001. "Housing Discrimination and Residential Segregation as Causes of Poverty." In *Understanding Poverty,* edited by Sheldon Danziger and Robert Haveman. New York: Russell Sage Foundation.

Yu, Renqiu. 1995. "Chinese." In *Encyclopedia of New York City,* edited by Kenneth T. Jackson. New Haven, Conn.: Yale University Press.

Zhou, Min. 1991. *Chinatown: The Socioeconomic Potential of an Urban Enclave.* Philadelphia: Temple University Press.

———. 1997a. "Growing Up American: The Challenge Confronting Immigrant Children and Children of Immigrants." *Annual Review of Sociology* 23: 63–95.

———. 1997b. "Segmented Assimilation: Issues, Controversies, and Recent Research on the New Second Generation." *International Migration Review* 31: 975–1008.

———. 1999. "Progress, Decline, Stagnation? The New Second Generation Comes of Age." In *Strangers at the Gates: New Immigrants in Urban America,* edited by Roger Waldinger. Berkeley: University of California Press.

———. 2001. "Chinese: Divergent Destinies in Immigrant New York." In *New Immigrants in New York,* edited by Nancy Foner. New York: Columbia University Press.

———. 2004. "Assimilation, the Asian Way." In *Reinventing the Melting Pot: The New Immigrants and What It Means to Be American,* edited by Tamar Jacoby. New York: Basic Books.

Zubrinsky, Camille, and Lawrence Bobo. 1997. "Prismatic Metropolis: Race and Residential Segregation in the City of Angels." *Social Science Research* 24: 335–74.

Index

affordable housing, 124, 195, 198
African Americans (*see also* blacks): historical settlement of, 57–58; housing conditions, 121, 155, 181; neighborhood conditions, 121, 155, 181; stratification and, 155, 181
African immigrants, 111
Afro-American Realty Company, 86
Afro-Caribbean immigrants, 72; segmented assimilation theory and, 7; treatment by whites, 44–45
Alba, Richard, 211, 256n138, 272n17
American Indians, 205
Arbitrage, 85–86, 90
Asian Americans for Equality (AAFE), 194
Asian immigrants, 111, 113, 122
Asian Indian immigrants, 117
Asians, 148, 157, 194, 205; assimilation and, 128; housing conditions, 128, 144–147, 154, 184; neighborhood conditions, 128, 146, 154, 184; population and changes in, 107, 108, 266n2
assimilation, 127, 128, 155, 176, 180, 183, 208; criticisms of,

39–41; residential 128; theory 33–34, 127; straight-line 255n89
Association for the Improvement of the Condition of the Poor (AICP), 67–68
Astoria, 62, 75
Austrian immigrants, 71

Baby Boom, 191
Bankston, Carl, 256n116
Basie, Count, 106
Bay Ridge, 96, 115, 118
Bean, Frank, 257n149
Bedford Stuyvesant, 94, 97
Bellair, Paul, 272n17
Bensonhurst, 115
Berlin, Ira, 261n73
Bernstein, Emily, 273n44
Binder, Thomas, 259n42
black immigrants, 72, 154, 188; housing conditions, 127; housing discrimination and, 156, 188–189, 193; neighborhood conditions, 127; settlement patterns, 72
Blackmar, Elizabeth, 259–260n48, 260n60
blacks (*see also* African Americans), 124, 197, 205; African ancestry 114, 126, 181, 182

About the Authors

EMILY ROSENBAUM is Professor of Sociology at Fordham University. She has written numerous articles on racial/ethnic and immigrant-status disparities in housing, educational attainment, and health.

SAMANTHA FRIEDMAN is Assistant Professor of Sociology at Northeastern University. Her research focuses on the residential inequality faced by minorities and immigrants and on policies to combat such inequality.